AF559982

THE WAHHABI MOVEMENT IN INDIA

The Wahhabi Movement in India

(SECOND REVISED EDITION)

QEYAMUDDIN AHMAD

MANOHAR
2026

First published 1966
2nd revised edition 1994
Reprinted 2021, 2022, 2023, 2024, 2025, 2026

ISBN 978-81-7304-042-9

Published by
Ajay Kumar Jain *for*
Manohar Publishers & Distributors
4753/23 Ansari Road, Daryaganj
New Delhi 110 002

Printed at
Replika Press Pvt. Ltd.

Dedicated
to my mother
to whose love and care I owe my education

Contents

Appendices

Preface to the First Edition

Soon after my appointment as Research Fellow, K.P. Jayaswal Research Institute, Patna, in 1952, I was deputed by the Government of Bihar to assist Dr. K.K. Datta, then Joint Honorary Director of the Institute, in the preparation of the Biography of Kunwar Singh and Amar Singh. During the course of that work I delved into the relevant records of practically all the District and Divisional Record Rooms in Bihar as well as those of Central Records Office, Patna, Calcutta, Allahabad and National Archives, Delhi. The main subject of my enquiry then was the Movment of 1857-59 in Bihar, but many records I came across related also to the Wahabis and their activities during those fateful years. The piecemeal information that I got about the Wahabis aroused my interest in the subject.

The work of reconstructing the full history of the Wahabi Movement was arduous and painstaking. Scattered but important pieces of information had to be collected from different Government archives and neglected collections of private papers, old books and manuscripts had to be searched and studied. Besides, some rare, out of print and proscribed Wahabi pamphlets had to be 're-discovered' before the full picture of the Movement emerged.

Although the word Wahabi is a misnomer, its adoption in the title became unavoidable on account of its wide prevalence. To have described the followers of Sayyid Ahmad Barelvi as Ahl-i-Hadis or Puritans or Reformists and used the word Wahabi in brackets all along would have been cumbrous, to say the least. The insistence of the English as also some Indian writers on the use of this appellation seems to be deliberate and actuated by ulterior motives. Some of the early and rather over-zealous acts of the Arabian Wahabis to do away with what they regarded as 'un-Islamic' practices had given them a bad name among the general body of the Muslims in India and elsewhere. In the eyes of the British Government the word Wahabi was synonymous with 'traitor' and 'rebel'. Thus, by describing the followers of Sayyid Ahmad as Wahabis, the contemporary Government officers aimed at killing two birds with one stone–branding them as rebels in the eyes of the higher circles of the government and as 'extremists' and 'desecrators of shrines' in the eyes of the general Muslims. The epithet became a term of religio-political abuse. The prevalent title of Wahabis had been retained in the book without, however, subscribing in the least to the unwarranted implications involved in it.

The book is based, substantially on the thesis for the degree of Ph. D., which I submitted to the Patna University in 1961. It has since been revised, re-arranged and expanded with the help of some fresh materials obtained from outside the country. This explains, partly, the rather long delay in its publication.

It is difficult to express adequately my feelings of gratitude to my two respected teachers, Dr. K.K.Datta, Vice-Chancellor, Patna University, and Professor S.H. Askari. Without Dr. Datta's scholarly guidance and gentle persuasion and interest in the thesis the present work would, perhaps, not have been completed. With his extensive studies on the subject, the advice and help of Professor Askari was invaluable. It was readily available and facilitated my work. Dr. R. S. Sharma, another respected teacher of mine, went through the typescript and gave several valuable general suggestions The late Fasihuddin Balkhi Saheb, of the Persian Manuscripts Section of the Patna University Library, was also a valuable source of help. Dr. J.S. Jha, Research Fellow, K.P. Jayaswal Research Institute, helped me by drawing my attention to some records on the subject.

I am grateful to the authorities of the National Archives, Central Records Office, Patna, Calcutta, Allahabad, and Divisional Commissioner's Office, Patna. Mr. J.C.Goswami of the Calcutta Records Office, in particular, was an unfailing source of help. I am also obliged to the authorities of the National Library, Calcutta, the Bihar Research Society and the Patna College Libraries for the various facilities I obtained during the period of research.

My brother, Hesam, helped me in preparing and correcting the typescript. I am particularly thankful to my wife for her constant and unobtrusive help and interest through the long and, at times, difficult period of the preparation of the book. I would also like to record my appreciation of the care and patience with which Mr. K.L. Mukhopadhyay saw the book through the press.

The map showing the British campaigns against the Wahabis on the Frontier has been reproduced from Paget & Mason's book, and the sketch showing the ground plan of the Sadiqpur premises from an exhibit in the Ahmadullah Trial papers.

The Indian names have been arranged in the Index in the usual and traditional form—Sayyid Ahmad Barelvi, Wilayat Ali, Muhammad Jafar—but the European names are arranged according to surnames.

An irritatingly large number of printing errors have occurred due mainly to my faulty proof-reading. The attention of the readers is particularly drawn to the mistake about place-names on pages 61,62,110,112,128 and 131.

9th September 1966 Q. Ahmad
Khwaja Kalan, Patna City

Preface to the Second Edition

The book was extensively reviewed in many standard journals in and outside the country when it was first published in 1966. The writer felt much benefited by the reviewers' comments and has kept them in mind while preparing the present edition.

Chapters I, II, III, and IX have been extensively revised and rearranged, and some fresh materials have been included. In Chapter X, a new section, Source Materials and Historiography of the Wahhabi Movement has been added. Finally there is a new chapter on the Wahhabi Missionary Literature.

It was clarified in the Preface to the first edition that the word Wahhabi was a misnomer but its adoption in the title of the book became unavoidable on account of its wide prevalence. This was, perhaps missed by some of the reviewers who commented on this point and suggested the use of the word *Mujahidin*, instead. Some of the readers also wrote letters to the same effect. The term *Mujahidin* is, however, generic; it has been used for different groups of persons working at different times and places. Further, *Jihad*, from which *Mujahidin* is derived, does not explain all the aspects and phases of the Movement, which was basically aimed at bringing in social change in the Indo-Muslim society. The adoption of the words *Muhammadi*, or *Muwahhidin*, would have required the addition of 'the so-called Wahhabis' all along. This would have made the text cumbrous, to say the least.

The work owes much to many people and institutions. My work at the Arabic and Persian Research Institute, Tonk (Rajasthan) was very useful and my stay there along with Sayeeda, my wife, was rendered very enjoyable by the warm hospitality of the Director of the Institute, Dr. Shaukat Ali Khan and his wife. Maulawi Imran Sahib of the same Institute, who unfortunately is no more with us, also gave me much oral information. My friend Ram Lakhan Shukla, Professor of History, University of Delhi, read some of the chapters and gave useful suggestions. Imtiaz Ahmad, my son, now a Reader in History, Patna University, also gave much help in the preparation of this edition. A former pupil, Muhammad Anwarul Haque, now Head, Department of History, Oriental College,

Patna City, assisted me much by delving into the collections of old published books and journals, and checking references.

It is a matter of satisfaction to me that since the first publication of this book the subject of the Wahhabi Movement has received greater attention in a number of works, and there is a better appreciation of its significance as a vigorous reform movement in the Indo-Muslim society and as a well-organised and sustained struggle against foreign rule in the country.

Abbreviations

A.P.R.I	Arabic and Persian Research Institute, Government of Rajasthan, Tonk.
B.K.S.	*Biography of Kunwar Singh and Amar Singh*
B.P.P.	*Bengal: Past and Present*
Commr.	Commissioner
C.R.	*The Calcutta Review*
D.M.	*Durr-i-Maqāl*
D.I.G.	Deputy Inspector General (of Police)
For.Dept.Pol.Cons.	Foreign Department Political Consultation
For.Dept.Sec.Cons.	Foreign Department Secret Consultation
H.G.	*District Gazetteer of Hazara*
I.G.	Inspector General (of Police)
I.H.R.	*Indian Historical Review, New Delhi*
I.M.	*The Indian Musalmans*
J.B.R.S.	*Journal of the Bihar Research Society*
J.I.H.	*Journal of Indian History*
Judl.Dept.Progs.	Judicial Department Proceedings
K.B.O.P.L.	Khuda Bakhsh Oriental Public Library, Patna
L.P.	Lower Province
Magt.	Magistrate
N.I.	Native Infantry
O.C.	Original Consultation
H.I.T.	*Hindustan Ki Pahli Islami Tahrik*
Progs. *I.H.C.*	Proceedings Volumes, *Indian History Congress*
Progs. *I.H.R.C.*	Proceedings Volumes, *Indian Historical Records Commission*
P.U.Ms.	Patna University Library Ms. Copy of *Sayyid Ahmad's Letters*
Sawanih	*Sawanih Ahmadi, also called Tawarikh-i'Ajiba.*
Secy.	Secretary
Selections	*Selections from the Bengal Government Records,* Vol. XLII
Sirat.	*Sirat-i Sayyid Ahmad Shahid*

S.M.	*Ṣirāṭ-i Mustaqīm*
S.M.R.	*The Sepoy Mutiny and Revolt of 1857*
T.A.	*Tawarikhi-i 'Ajib, also called Kala Pani*
T.S.	*Tadhkira-i Sādqa*

Transliteration

a, ا ; b, ب ; p, پ ; t, ت ; ṭ, ٹ

th, ث ; j, ج ; ch, چ ; ḥ, ح ; kh, خ

d, د ; dh, ذ ; r; ر ; z, ز ; s, س

sh, ش ; ṣ, ص ; ḍ, ض ; ṭ, ط ; ẓ, ظ

'a ع ; if it occurs in the beginning, or simply '

in the middle or end('Adl, عدل ; jāmi', جامع);

gh, غ ; f, ف ; q, ق

k, ک ; g, گ ; l, ل ; m, م ; n, ن

v or w, و ; h, ھ ; i ی

Short vowels	a, i, u.
Long vowels	ā, ī, ū

Chapter I

Genesis of the Wahhabi Movement in India

1. Political and Socio-Economic Conditions in India in the late 18th and early 19th Centuries : An Outline

The central fact in the political history of India during the period under review is the decline of the Mughal empire and the erosion of Mughal imperial authority. The final extinction was yet to come but the light which had been burning bright and steady for more than two centuries had started flickering and casting ominous shadows. The long, dismal reign of Shah Alam II (1759-1806) illustrates the process effectively. Seeking safety from the violent happenings in the imperial capital, where his father Alamgir II had been deposed and assassinated (November 1759), Prince Ali Gauhar,[1] the future Shah Alam II, had moved on to the eastern provinces. There, between 1759 and 1761, he made three attempts to wrest Bihar from its *Nā'ib Nāẓim,* Raja Ram Narain (1759-63) who administered it on behalf of Nawab Mir Jafar. The attempts failed largely due to the intervention of the East India Company authorities on behalf of the nominal Nawab they had set up at Murshidabad after the battle of Plassey (1757). The Prince, who had meanwhile been crowned as Shah Alam II, made another determined attempt in 1764, this time in alliance with the new Nawab of Bengal, Mir Qasim (1760-64) who had replaced Mir Jafar following the Bengal 'revolution' of 1760 and the *Nawāb-Wazir*[2] Shujaud Dawlah (1754-74), of Awadh. The allies were defeated in the crucial battle of Buxar (1765) which made the East India Company the virtual master of Bihar and Bengal. Shah Alam II was given shelter in the Allahabad Fort by Robert Clive with a promise of being escorted at an opportune time to Delhi, on which Shah Alam's heart was still set. Having waited in vain for the promised escort the throneless Emperor turned towards the Marathas who too, like the East India Company, were not averse to the prospects of utilising the halo of Mughal sovereignty. The arrival of Shah Alam II at Delhi, however, meant only a change of place without an increase of actual power. He passed on from the control of one *farzand*[3] to another. The new master was the great Maratha chief Mahadji Sindhia (d. 1794) who was then making a serious bid to restore the Maratha political domination in northern India. Shah Alam II was brought back to Delhi with the Marathas' help. The grateful Emperor appointed the Peshwa, nominal head of the Maratha Confederacy and chief of Sindhia, as the *Nā'ib*[4] of the Empire, of whose 'withering tree' the trunk had been sought to be struck down by a former Peshwa, the greatest among them all.[5] As the deputy of the Peshwa, Sindhia, came to have full powers at Delhi, but for Shah Alam II, in spite of some respite, the position remained more or less the same. In fact, worse humiliations, even outright torture were in store for him. Some of the Delhi nobles were not reconciled to Sindhia's domination and, taking advantage of his withdrawal to Gwalior following an unsuccessful trial of strength with the Rajput forces, Ghulam Qadir Khan, son of Zabita Khan, pressed for his father's claims and got himself appointed Amīru'l Umarā. He later seized the capital town and the palace, got the helpless Emperor deposed and blinded and put the imperial family to unprecedented indignities (1788). The old and blind Emperor was shortly thereater relieved from virtual inprisonment but remained powerless as before. He spent the rest of his life writing letters and sending emissaries to the British monarch George III (1760-1820) at London and to the Governors General, Cornwallis and Shore at Calcutta, seeking financial help and the restoration of some semblance of power.

From the British monarch he did not get any direct response. The accession of George III had taken place just after that of Shah Alam II, and he had tried at his mother's urging to 'be a King' in the beginning of his reign, but the attempt had failed. He now seemed to be indifferent to the entreaties of another King in distress. As for the Governors General, Cornwallis felt that he was not called upon "either by motives of honour or interest, or even humanity" to intercede on behalf of the Mughal ruler. He thought it was unauthorised under the "present orders of the Court of Directors and the existing Acts of Parliament."[6] Actually, this plea of non-interference in Indian affairs under Pitt's India Act (1784) was hollow, for the Act did not prevent him from forming a defensive and offensive alliance against Tipu Sultan, nor did it prevent his successor Shore from interfering in the affairs of the Awadh kingdom after the death of Nawab Āṣafu'd Dawlah (1797). The fiction of Mughal sovereignty was, however, still maintained even though unwillingly and with much reservation. Lord Wellesley (1798-1805) had quite different ideas on the point but even then it was considered advisable that Lord Lake, when he called upon Shah Alam II after defeating Sindhia's forces (1803), should receive a *Khil'at* (dress of honour) and a title from him.

The position of Shah Alam II's successor, who bore the great name of Akbar, Akbar II (1806-37), was more pitiable. He continued his predecessor's policy of letters and entreaties to the British authorities. He even took the unusual step of sending a special envoy, Rammohun Roy, who was given the title of Raja on this occasion—to the Court of St. James in London, much against the wishes of the East India Company authorities in India. Like his predecessor, he failed to receive any response from the British monarch. Further, the 'reign' of Akbar II coincided with the administration of men who, while sharing the views of Wellesley, were more determined to put to an end the mock-drama of Mughal sovereignty. Lord Hastings (1813-23) declined to meet Akbar II in accordance with the old protocol implying the subordination of the Company to the Mughal emperor. Akbar II had finally to yield, and when he did at last meet the next Governor General, Lord Amherst (1823-28) in 1827 the protocol was so altered as to give them both equal status. Both entered the *Diwān-i-Khās* simultaneously from two sides and took their seats at the same time. A few years later another long-maintained fiction, that of issuing coins, since 1778, in the name of Shah Alam II in the 19th *julus* (regnal year), was also ended.

Thus, both Shah Alam II and Akbar II remained non-entities during the long period of their reigns covering over three-quarters of a century. Effective power had passed on to the 'successor states' of the Deccan, Awadh and Bengal, to the Marathas in central and western India and to the Sikhs in northern India. The tally of the emerging Indian states is completed by Mysore under Haidar Ali (1761-1782) and Tipu Sultan (1782-99). On the other hand, there were the European trading companies whose professed object was trade but to whom the opportunities inherent in the prevalent situation were increasingly becoming evident and attractive. The two more resourceful and serious contenders among these were the

French and English (East India) Companies. The latter by the victories in the South (the Carnatic wars, 1740s & 1750s) and in Bengal (battle of Plassey, 1757 and Buxar, 1764) had virtually assured its success against the European rivals. It had, however, yet to establish its ascendancy over the Indian contenders.

Asaf Jah Niẓāmul Mulk (1724-48) was the first to break away from the main course of Delhi politics and carve out a principality in the Deccan. The leader of the Turani group, and an old disciplinarian of Aurangzeb's time, the *Niẓām* had tried first to bring some order into the affairs of the empire after the revolution of 1719, but he was foiled by the opposition of rival groups as well as the vacillations of a young, inexperienced emperor, Muhammad Shah (1719-48). The beginnings of the Deccan principality may well be marked from 1725 when he was appointed *ṣūbahdār* of that province for a second time; it became a reality from 1740 when he finally moved down to the south.

The affairs of the Carnatic—where a subordinate functionary of the *Niẓām* was, in turn, trying to make his post hereditary—were further complicated by the death of Niẓāmul Mulk. The ensuing succession disputes, enabled Joseph Dupleix, Governor of the French settlement in India to initiate his policy of interfering in the disputes of Indian powers. It was, however, given to his rival, Robert Clive, to reap the fruits of the new policy. The basic element of the new policy, whereby the Indian States were made to pay supposedly, on their behalf but in fact promoting the Company's interests in the process, was further developed in the form of what was called Subsidiary Alliance by Wellesley. A number of Indian States were enmeshed in its ties; and its more immediate results were evident in the south where the *Niẓām* was rendered innocuous and Tipu Sultan, one of the more intrepid adversaries of the East Indian Company was exterminated (1799). Tipu Sultan's resistance was spirited but short-lived. It was concentrated in a smaller area and hence more manageable for the British particularly due to the short-sighted attitude of some of the other India States. The resistance offered by the Marathas, equally if not more spirited, took longer to suppress because it was spread over a larger area and backed by greater resources.

The long reign of Raja Sahu[7] (1708-49) had brought some stability to the affairs of the Maratha kingdom. He had overcome the opposition led by Tara Bāi, the widow of Rajaram (1689-1700) who supported the cause of her son, Shivaji II. More importantly, it was during her reign that the dominance of the Peshwa commenced and reached its climax. The first two Peshwas, Balaji Vishwanath (1713-20) and Baji Rao (1720-40) had lent lustre to the office and greatly extended Maratha domination in the north.[8] Both of them were men of great ability and initiative but Sahu also commanded great respect and exercised a gentle supervision over all the chiefs. The equation between the king and his chief ministers, the Peshwas, worked satisfactorily. But after 1749 the position of both suffered a setback. While the king was completely relegated to the background, the Peshwa too became a titular head and power passed on to some of the Maratha hereditary military commanders, such as the Sindhias, Holkars, Pawars, etc. The former two, particularly, achieved great military successes and carried the Maratha banner to Rajputana (1754) and the Punjab (1758). The Marathas tried to become the power behind the Mughal throne, but they met with a serious reverse at Panipat[9] where Ahmad Shah Abdali inflicted a major defeat on them (1761). The result of the defeat did not prove to be lasting, and during the next two decades Mahadji Sindhia and Malhar Rao Holkar, once again made the Maratha power felt in the north.

The Maratha recovery during the post-Panipat period was, however, more apparent than real, as has been pointed out by the great historian, Jadunath Sarkar.[10] Substantial changes in the political situation had occurred during the period, notably the withdrawal of the Durranis from direct involvement in India, the emergence of the Sikhs in the Punjab and, more importantly, the changed position of the East India Company. The Company's hold over Bengal and Bihar was well-established, and it had gained substantial advantages in Awadh. Its attention was now turned to the Deccan where the Marathas were its main adversary.

The perceptive contemporary historian Ghulam Husain Khan thus describes the affairs of the Maratha confederacy after Raghunath Rao had sought help from the Bombay Council of the East India Company (Treaty of Surat, 1775).[11] He writes:

> Nor is this a novel event. It is in consequence of such and the like divisions that most of the strongholds, nay, almost the whole of Hindustan, have come into the possession of the English. For instance, two princes contend for the same country and one of them applies to the English and informs them of the ways and method of becoming masters of it. By his insinu-

> ations and by their assistance, he draws to himself some of the leading men of the country, who being his friends, are already fast attached to his person; and meanwhile the English having concluded to their own mind some treaty and agreement with him, they for sometime abide by those terms, until they have obtained a good insight into the government and customs of the country, as well as a thorough acquaintance with the several parties in it; and then they discipline an army, and getting themselves supported by one party, they overcome the other, and little by little introduce themselves into the country, and make a conquest of it. And although their introductor should prove too shrewd for them, and should give them the slip, still they never dispute with him; but being a set of men always wise and always in temper, they patiently wait until by his death some unworthy son comes to succeed him; at which time they under his name and without opening any dispute, or creating any ill-renown to themselves, complete the conquest, and have the art to finish their business in such a sly manner that no reproach can be made to them. By which means the downfall of the people of those parts, especially of the great and powerful ones, is soon obtained by the hands of one another; and all this is brought about so artfully that the idiots set up by them, unaware of the above management, do of their own accord and motion work for the ruin of their equals; and meanwhile the English who seem quite passive, as if suffering themselves to be led, are in fact giving motion to the machine and turning those sots into so many objects of raillery both in Hindustan and Europe.... These glorious rulers after burning their own feathers now become sensible of their losses, turn repentant, but it is only at a time when repetance cannot turn their circumstance.[12]

A more succinct description of the situation leading to the first Anglo-Maratha war is difficult to find in all the copious official correspondence and the private papers of the period, and it is very surprising that this passage from a work, otherwise frequently referred to, should have remained virtually unnoticed. The author, as we know, was a distant observer and one not unfavourably disposed towards the English, yet he describes the main elements of the situation dispassionately. He is writing about a specific situation but the passage in fact provides an explanation for the successes of the East India Company. In it we find a rough sketch of the system more methodically worked out by Wellesley through the Subsidiary Alliances which enmeshed many of the Indian states and paved the way for their extinction.

As we know, two Anglo-Maratha wars followed suit and the Maratha challenge was contained and overcome by the British in gradual stages marked by the Treaties of Surji Arjungaon (December, 1808), Gwalior (November, 1817) and Mandasore (January, 1818).

Two specific events during this period of the twilight of Maratha power may be briefly recalled. Small and isolated in themselves, they nevertheless have a bearing on our main subject. Firstly, the emergence of Amir Khan as the Nawab of Tonk, one of the many small states which proliferated during the period. An erstwhile lieutenant of the Holkar and the leader of the Pathan group in the faction-ridden Indore Darbar, Amir Khan had become the Regent of Malhar Rao who had been brought to the *gaddī* by Tulsi Bāi, the mistress of Jaswant Rao Holkar. The British intervened, apparently to restore order, and imposed the Treaty of Mandasore on Holkar who under one of its terms recognised the independent status of his former lieutenant Amir Khan. Later, as the Nawab of Tonk, Amir Khan became an important supporter of Sayyid Ahmad and his Court became one of the chief centres of financial support and asylum to the Wahhabis.[13] Secondly, the meeting between Sayyid Ahmad and Daulat Rao Sindhia, the nephew and successor of Mahadji Sindhia at Gwalior. The Wahhabi sources refer to the meeting during Sayyid Ahmad's stay at Gwalior on his way to the North-Western Frontier and to the lavish hospitality extended to the visitor. Sindhia was ill and his brother-in-law, Hindu Rao, was very influential in the *Darbār*. He held Sayyid Ahmad in high regard. The letter written to him by Sayyid Ahmad from the North-Western Frontier throws fresh light on the nature and objectives of the movement.[14]

Ahmad Shah Abdali (1747-73),[15] like his former master Nadir Shah (1736-47) had inflicted a grievous blow on the Mughal empire and had also gained a major victory against the Marathas at Panipat. But, again like Nadir Shah, he made no serious effort to follow up the victories. Not only was Delhi, then without an actual occupant of the throne, but even Punjab which had been put under the governorship of Timur Shah was allowed to be gradually lost. Within twelve years of the great victory at Panipat eastern and central Punjab had been recovered by the Sikhs. The area was held by a number of Sikh *misls* which had gained strength during the decline of Mughal authority in the area and had harassed the withdrawing Durranis. The *misls* were also engaged in constant mutual strife. By the end of the 18th century they were brought under a strong centralised administration by Maharaja Ranjit Singh ((1799-1839). This was a period during which a Russian advance towards the North-Western Frontier of India was a strong possibility. The British authorities in India considered a stable government in the Punjab under Ranjit Singh to be a safe barrier against that advance. Ranjit Singh too realised the danger to his own position in case of a Russian advance and was aware that he could not face it alone.[16] The relations between the Sikh ruler and the British were governed by considerations of mutual advantage. By the Treaty of Amritsar, 1809, Ranjit Singh agreed to maintain peace and amity with the British, not to keep more troops on the left bank of the Indus and not interfere in the affairs of the 'protected' Cis-Sutlej Sikh chiefs. In return, he was given a free field of expansion in the trans-Sutlej area,[17] and in the course of time, he had conquered Kashmir and Peshawar. Yar Muhammad Khan Barakzai, who held Peshawar, was allowed to continue as a tributary. The area was parcelled out among a number of Pathan chiefs, one of the more important among whom were the Barakzais. It was in a state of anarchy after the death of Ahmad Shah Abdali.[18] The successive reigns of his son Timur Shah (1773-93) and grandson Zaman Shah (1793-1800) were characterised by rebellions and the break-up of the empire. The murder of Painda Khan Barakzai by Zaman Shah had antagonised the powerful Barakzai tribe. Fatah Khan, the eldest son of the murdered chief, joined Mahmud Shah (1800-03; 1809-18), a brother of Zaman Shah, at Kabul and helped him in defeating Zaman Shah. Shah Shuja (1803-09; 1809-18), another brother of Zaman Shah, continued the fight against Mahmud but later took shelter with the British. He was later joined by Zaman Shah too, both of whom were given asylum by the British with a view to using them in extending their influence to Afghanistan. The Afghan tribal factions continued, and Fatah Khan who had helped Mahmud, and thereby increased his own influence in the Court, incurred the jealousy of Mahmud's son, Kamran, who had him murdered. The Barakzais were thus again alienated. Among them were Yar Muhammad Khan, Sultan Muhammad Khan, the Pir Muhammad Khan. The first two held the Peshawar area and paid tribute to Ranjit Singh, as noted above. As we shall see, Sayyid Ahmad before his migration to the North-Western Frontier was in correspondence with some of these chiefs and had received promises of help and cooperation from them.

A closer look is required at the affairs of Awadh where Sayyid Ahmad lived and worked before migrating out of British India, and at the situation in Bengal which was subsequently to become the principal base of support to the movement. Shujaud Dawlah the *Nawāb-Wazīr* of Awadh[19] had fought on Shah Alam II's side in the battle of Buxar and had paid the price for being defeated. He had to cede the territory of Allahabad and Kara where Shah Alam II was put in with a promise to be escorted to Delhi. The rest of his dominion was restored on payment of rupees 50 lakhs. Later, when Shah Alam waiting in vain to be escorted to Delhi moved out on his own, Allahabad and Kara were restored to the Nawab, who had to pay another 50 lakhs for the return of what had earlier been taken from him.[20]

To the west and north-west of the Awadh territory were the two Pathan principalities of the Bangash Nawabs of Farrukhabad [21] and the Rohillas of Rohilkhand.[22] The latter rose to eminence under Ali Muhammad Khan Ruhela who extended his control to the Kumaon region and the Bareli, Moradabad, Bijnore and Pilibhit areas. He further benefited from the resurgence of Pathan influence in the wake of Ahmad Shah Abdali's invasions. The Nawabs of Awadh felt apprehensive of their western neighbours, the Rohillas, and the East India Company reaped political and financial advantages out of their enmity and hostilities. Nawab Āsafud Dawlah (1774-97) agreed to buy British military help in suppressing the Rohillas and thereby opened the gates of perpetual demands from the Company for arrears of the amounts of subsidy due.[23] His death afforded another opportunity to the Company to intervene and benefit further. Wazīr Ali's claim for succession was first accepted and then revoked in favour of Saadat Ali Khan (1797-1818) who had to sign a fresh treaty in January 1798. Awadh's payment to the Company was raised to 76 lakhs of rupees and it was virtually brought under the Company's control. In November 1801, yet another treaty was forced upon Saadat Ali Khan by the new Governor General, Lord Wellesley, under which he 'ceded' to the Company 'in perpetual sovereignty' a large chunk of his territories in repayment of the arrears and the cost of maintaining troops. The financial predicament of Awadh was, undoubtedly, due in the first instance to gross maladministration, particularly of the land-revenue, but it was rendered more difficult by the subsidies demanded by the Company for arbitrarily increased number of troops to be maintained on account of the possibility of foreign invasions, including that of Zaman Shah, which was considered imminent by the Company's authorities.

The 'Ceded Territories', comprising the bulk of the North-Western Provinces constituted under a Lieutenant-Governor in 1836, included the large Rohilkhand area too. It was put under a Board of Commissioners for the Ceded Provinces with headquarters at Bareilly.[24] There was much discontent against the newly imposed British administration and the northern *parganas* of the area were subjected to the raids of Amir Khan's troops. During the war against the Gurkhas (1813-16) Major Hearsey had raised a levy of Pathans at Bareilly but the expedition undertaken in 1815 had proved to be abortive; the Pathans had deserted and Hearsey had been taken prisoner. More importantly, the setback suffered by the British arms had added to the general discontent and engendered 'contempt' for the administration.[25] The imposition of a house tax under Regulation XVI of 1814 had aroused fresh discontent. Those who had at first assented to the new tax were compelled 'by popular clamour' to decline; very few came forward for the work of collecting the tax, and finally on 16th April, 1816, 'mobs of both Musalmans and Hindus assembled in the streets.' The leader of the 'movement' was *Muftī* Muhammad Iwaz, an old man held in great veneration throughout Rohilkhand.[26] When the Magistrate went to the city with some men of the provincial battalion, the mob, after first falling back to the Muftī 's house, attacked the troopers, many of whom were wounded and killed. Help was sought from neighbouring stations, and a regiment of irregular cavalry and a battalion of the 13th Native Infantry from Moradabad were called in. The rising was suppressed, and the Mufti and some of the ringleaders left the Company's territory and retired to Tonk, the new centre of Amir Khan. This rising in Rohilkhand, not generally noticed, had been mentioned here because it is indicative of the political conditions in the area which was being toured by Sayyid Ahmad at about the same time, and established the link between the people of the area and the Court of Nawab Amir Khan of Tonk.

Bengal under the able and long rule of Nawab 'Alivardi Khan Mahābat Jang (1740-56) enjoyed comparative political stability and economic viability. Though virtually independent, Alivardi maintained the appearances, and regularly despatched substantial amounts of revenue to Delhi. In fact, this constituted one of the very few solid sources of revenue to the tottering Imperial Government. Unlike the western inland *sūbahs*, however, the coastal Bengal *sūbah* was faced with a new kind of problem—the presence of the East India Company officials and the incessant disputes between them and the provincial government over the terms of their trade. Since the establishment of a factory at Surat (1612) the East India Company had been trying to enter the rich Bengal market overland through northern India. The attempt had not proved very successful, and subsequently they reached Bengal by the sea route from their base at Masulipatam on the eastern coast and set up an agency at Hugli (1651). The Company had received a *farmān*, as early as the reign of Aurangzeb, permitting it to carry on trade in Bengal without the payment of the usual customs in lieu of a lump sum payment. But the implementation of the imperial order had led to frequent disputes between the Nawab's government and the Company's officials. The problem is frequently referred to in the Company's records, but it is to be noted that we have only the Company's version of the disputes, and we do not know on what grounds the local officers raised the objections. We also have some references indicating that the local officers deliberately sought sanction for higher amounts of 'bribe money' for the Nawab's officers so that they could have some share of it for themselves.[27]

The problem of *dastaks* which gained notoriety during the times of Sirajuddawlah (1756-57) and Mir Qasim (1760-64) has in fact a much earlier beginning. As early as the 1730s, we find the Calcutta Council frequently writing[28] to the Court of Directors about the abuse of *dastaks* by private traders and about the action being taken against them. The Court of Directors too regarded the misuse of *dastaks* as detrimental to the interests of the Company and wanted it to be curbed. Yet, when the Nawabs of Bengal later pressed for the suppression of the abuse of *dastaks* by private unauthorised traders, the Council reacted quite differently, and the crucial battle of Plassey (1757) followed. The battle has rightly been regarded as a landmark in the history of the country. It marks the beginnings of the Company's rule in eastern India. The new Nawab, Mir Jafar (1757-60, 1764) set up by Clive was a puppet in the hands of the Company. All kinds of exorbitant monetary demands were made by the Company's officials on the hapless Nawab; a veritable loot set in and the exchequer was drained dry. When it was felt that the Nawab could not be made to yield further benefits, a new Nawab was brought to the *Masnad* by the 'revolution' of 1760. The new Nawab, Mir Qasim, however, turned out to be of a different mettle and was not as amenable to the wishes of his English patrons as his father-in-law had been. What is more, he took steps, including the strengthening of his army and artillery, to stand up to the East India Company's unreasonable and unjustified demands. There ensued a series of intrigues, diplomatic negotiations and wars culminating with the battle of Buxar (1764) and the grant of the *Diwānī* of Bengal, Bihar and Orissa to the East India Company by Shah Alam II (1765). During the years immediately following, the Company devised, what is commonly called, the 'Dual Government' system. The abuse of the system, namely, the infamous transfer of effective powers to the Company while outwardly retaining the Nawab's administration, was not lost upon some of the more observant contemporaries .

Karam Ali, the author of *Muẓaffar Nāmah* has movingly described the ruinous effects of this system in a passage of his work which has remained unnoticed. He writes:

> The state of affairs is this, that on account of the resumption of the cultivable lands not much scope for profit is left (to the people), because the lands have been confiscated by the government, and the *a'immadārs* (assignment-holders) have stopped cultivating these. They do not undertake cultivation because of the severities and tortures (inflicted for the recovery) of the *māl* (revenue). Those lands are lying barren, and the *a'immadārs* and cultivators are helpless and bewildered. In the year one thousand one hundred eighty-four (A.H.1184 or A.D.1770-71) during the time of the famine, of which more later, many of them lost their lives. On account of the fear of severities—*since there was not the rule of one ruler,* these *riāyā* do not dare to make a detailed submission about their plight before the Exalted Nawab, so that the oppressors and sinners may be punished duly. *Even if it were to reach the Exalted Ears (of the Nawab), of what use would it be, for he has not the power to rectify or render relief. Hence, the smoke from the sighs of the oppressed has gone up to the high skies.*[29]

The post-Dīwānī decade in Bengal was characterised politically by the exercise of power without responsibility, socially, by stagnation and decay, and economically, by extortions and 'the drain' of wealth from the once prosperous *sūbah.*

Generalisations about the social conditions in the country are apt to be misleading because the situation varied in different regions, or within the different parts of broad areas. Certain common tendencies were, however, discernible everywhere—proliferation and greater rigidity of the caste system among the Hindus and the *Ashrāf-Ajlāf* consciousness among the Muslims, a greater show of religiosity reflected in increasing ties of *Pīrī-Murīdī* (preceptor-disciple) relationship and ostentatious celebrations of the *'urs* (saints' death anniversary celebrations), a narrowing of intellectual interests, reflected in the writing of commentaries rather than independent works, common norms of social behaviour in the higher echelons of the society irrespective of religious affiliations, an impoverishment of the aristocracy and a life-style characterised by indulgence and extravagance. The apparent contradiction in the last-mentioned situation is not altogether inexplicable. The pervasive political unrest and financial distress had created two different kinds of reactions, one of seeking solace in religiosity and the other in extravagant living. There are numerous references to extravagance in the ranks of both the higher and middle strata of the society. Major-General Sleeman, who toured the Awadh kingdom just a few years before its annexation (1856), makes this significant observation about the state of affairs in the capital city of Lucknow.

> In this overgrown city there is a perpetual turmoil of processions, illuminations and festivities. The Sovereign spends all that he can get in them, and he has not the slightest wish to perpetuate his name by the construction of any useful or ornamental work beyond the suburbs. All the members of his family and of the city aristocracy follow his example .... Indifferent to the feelings and opinions of the aristocracy and people of the country, with whom they have no sympathy, they spend all that they can spare for the public in gratifying the vitiated tastes of the overgrown metropolis.[30]

Such extravagance did not go unnoticed by the common people and, as Sleeman observed further, "The more sober-minded among the Mahommedans of Lucknow and elsewhere are scandalised at the habit which has grown up among them, in the cities of India, of commemorating every event, whether of sadness or of joy, by brilliant illuminations and splendid processions, to amuse the idle population of such cities. It is, they say, a reprehensible departure from the spirit of their creed, and from the simple tastes of the early Mahommedans, who laid out the superfluities in the construction of great and durable works of ornament and utility. Certainly no event can be more sorrowful among the Mahommedans than that which is commemorated in the mohurrum by illuminations and processions with the Tazeeas; and yet no illuminations are more brilliant, and no processions more noisy, costly and splendid.[31]

It is worthy of remark, that Hindoo princess in Central and Southern India, even of the Brahman caste, commemorate this event in the same way; and in no part of India are these illuminations and processions more brilliant and costly. Their object is solely to amuse the population of their capitals, and to gratify the Mahommedan women whom they have under their protection, and their children, who must all be Mahommedans."[32]

The contrast between the affluence of the few and the miseries of the masses is also not altogether missed. Another European observer, Tennant, writing about the same city of Lucknow just after the death of Nawab Āṣafu'd Dawlah, the builder of its great *Imām Bāṛah*, writes: "I yesterday, went to view the capital, which is said to contain half a million of souls. Happening to enter the town at the west end which contains the poor mechanics and labourers of every sort, I never witnessed so many varied forms of wretchedness, filth and vice. The street which leads to the palace is upwards of five miles long, more than one-half of which you wade through mire and filth.... The show of rich shops and merchandise is remarkably small, though it supplies the luxuries of the court, or rather the palace ; for here there is little affluence beyond the narrow circle of the prince's family."[33] What Tennant writes about Lucknow is true of almost all the other Indian States' capitals and the big towns.

As regards some other sections of the society, we have the testimony of another contemporary of quite a different background. The *Ṣirāṭu'l Mustaqīm* [34] gives an idea of how Sayyid Ahmad himself viewed certain aspects of the social conditions. It states :

> "Among the *bid'āt* of the 'sufistic polytheists' *(mushrikīn-Ṣūfishi'ar)* which are greatly in vogue among the Muslim gentry

and commoners is the performance of *nadhar* and *niyāz* (offering of prayers and eatables in the name of the dead ones). This involves the committing of a sort of polytheism.... Although in principle this is valid and its performance is in accordance with the *Shara'* the general people had introduced their own imaginations and superstitions into it and posterity had not only followed these but exceeded the limits (by) adding new things to what had previously existed; the salutary original principles had fallen into the background and the evil offshoots, assiduously produced by fabrications, had prevailed.[35]

Or again :

The obnoxious ceremonies on the occasions of marriages and mournings, prevalent among the people in India, are so deeprooted that their discontinuance is felt to be extremely difficult due to the fear or taunts and reproaches. The ignorant people consider this more important than the performance of obligatory rites and their discontinuance harder than that of the things prohibited by the *Sharia't*.... For example, the pompous arrangements observed on the occasion of the circumcision ceremony require so much money that the circumcision is often delayed and the boys grow fairly old (by) the time it actually takes place. This is shameful and indecent. Similar delays take place at the time of marriages. Prolonged waiting (for marriage) makes the young people susceptible to commission of sinful acts. Similarly, although (the arrangements for) mournings (ceremonies) cannot be delayed, the arrangements for the customary practices regarding the funeral and digging of graves cause disturbance and delays in (the performance of) other necessary works. While thus shirking from the observance of the *Sunnah*, (such) people indulge in extravagance on the occasions of the ceremonies held on the third and fourth days after the death of a person for fear of incurring social ridicule.... This often drives people to the extreme of selling their properties for the performance of such ceremonies.... It is apparent that one is not so much reproached for absence from performing the prayers as for neglect in arranging the death anniversary celebration of saints (*'urs*) or singing and dancing on the occasions of marriages.[36]

Some of the rulers of the Indian States had sought apparent security by entering into the Subsidiary Alliances with the East India Company. The hope proved to be illusory. The rulers found themselves burdened with heavy financial obligations and faced with discontent among their subjects. They had to meet the ever-increasing demands for the cost of maintaining the Company's troops for their supposed defence. They had to disband, or largely reduce, their own armies, rendering thousands of persons jobless. The disbanded soldiers did not have much scope for falling back upon the land either. The changes in the land revenue administration, particularly the heavy increase in the rates, had rendered cultivation an unattractive, if not a hazardous occupation. Nor could the rulers continue their patronage of the scholars and the skilled artisans, thus creating distress in another section of their subjects. There was a sharp decrease in the grants of *jāgīrs,* the standard method of financing education and patronising scholars and craftsmen. Many old *jāgīrs* had to be cancelled rendering many families destitute. Such things had happened earlier too in the wake of disturbances at Delhi, but then there was the alternative course of migrating to the eastern dominions of Awadh and Bengal. Now, there was no such alternative, and the large number of affected families faced, as it were, a blind alley. There was widespread social distress and discontent.

The right of collecting land-revenue, the Grant of Dīwānī of Bengal, Bihar and Orissa (1765) as it was called, was the first important economic and administrative power obtained by the East India Company outside its normal trading function. It turned out to be a great boon, for it enabled the Company to finance its purchases and investments, and the Company naturally wanted to increase this income as much as possible. It was a new work, however, and between 1765 and 1793 many experiments were made about the settlement and collection of land-revenue. Behind all these experiments the one common persistent attempt was to maximise the collection, mainly by increasing the rates of revenue. The amount collected jumped from Rs. 8,180,000 in 1764, just before the Grant of *Dīwānī,* to Rs. 23,400,000 in 1771.

The same story is repeated more or less in the case of Awadh. The contrast there is more glaring because, unlike any other Indian State, we find there the strange spectacle of the old Indian and the new British administrations often functioning side by side. A glimpse into this rather unnoticed situation is provided by Sleeman's notes quoted above. He writes that under the Treaty of 1801 the country had been divided according to the then rent-roll, "each half was estimated at one crore and thirty-three lacs." Since then the ceded area was yielding more, and in 1849-50 the land revenue along with the stamp duty and tax on spirits yielded "two crores and twelve lacs a year,"[37] while the income from the area under Awadh rule had been reduced to around one crore. This substantial increase of revenue in the company administered area had been accompanied with, it is important to note, a sharp decline in the position of the landed aristocracy. Sleeman refers to the 'rapid decay of landed aristocracy in our territories' and candidly admits that, "A less and less proportion of the annual produce is left to them in our periodical settlements of the land revenue, while family pride makes them spend the same sums in the marriages of their children, in religious and other festivals, personal servants and hereditary retainers. They... incur heavy debts, and estate after estate is put up to auction...."[38] He adds that it was believed that "four times more of these families have gone to decay in the half of the territories made over to us in 1801 than in the half preserved by the Oude sovereign; and this is, I fear, true...."[39] It is evident that the British presence, along with the old *Nawābi* administration, was more directly felt in Awadh, and that their conditions there were such as to generate resentment among the cultivators as well as the landed aristocracy against the expanding grip of British rule.

It also appears, rather strangely, that in spite of the "good management" in the ceded territories, to quote Sleeman once again, "the people generally, or a great part of them" preferred to "reside in Oude," and one of the reasons for this was the "uncertainties of our law, the multiplicity and formality of our Courts and the corruption and insolence" of the Court staff.[40]

As regards the areas more directly under the East India Company's control, we find that monopolising the different commodities of trade in favour of the Company, and the English traders in general, was another notable feature of the economic conditions. Much has been written about the question of trade, its modalities, and the frictions caused by it between the Company and the provincial government, but not adequate attention has been paid to the basic question of the changed attitude towards trade itself as between the Mughal government and the East India Company. Once again we find a contemporary Indian historian putting his finger on the heart of the matter. Contrasting the policy of the earlier Indian rulers with that of the British administrators, Ghulam Husain Khan writes, that the former had "left open to the subjects various ways of revenue and livelihood amounting to many crores a year, as a provision to *the bulk of the inhabitants*... from merchandising and from the exercise of arts and trade, *all these were left open for all the world,* and although they (earlier rulers) were made to see various branches of revenue in those articles, they never turned their eyes that way." The Company's servants, however, had brought in a new attitude — "of the *various branches of trade, heretofore open to all, none is left free. They are all engrossed by the Company* themselves or by the English in general; *as these, whether they enjoy the Company's service,* and of course have power and influence, or *chance to be otherwise circumstanced, very seldom are without concern in trade.* Under the circumstances, how could the poor subjects pretend to derive a subsistence from merchandise? *Would they dare?*"[41]

Another contemporary historian, Karam Ali, referred to above, mentions the changed attitude towards trade and points out more specifically the privations caused by the new policy to the Indian traders, both Muslims and Hindus. He writes, "In all the territories, on account of the Englishmen's trade, which brings in each year large quantities of commodities and unlimited cash amounts, the avenues of profit to the other traders, Hindus and Muslims, have been closed, rather the others have been prohibited from purchasing of goods and other transactions, and from obtaining of interests and other profits. On account of the abolition of the government and zamindar's *chowkies* from the roads, thieves and robbers have created disturbances. Further, the uniform rate of *mahsūl-i sā'ir* (market dues) have also affected the traders, as the (prices of) commodities have been rendered the same from Calcutta to Azimabad."[42]

The Company's administration also struck at another important source of livelihood of a large number of persons—the *madad-i ma'āsh* lands (rent-free landholdings). Such grants had been made over a long period by the kings, princes and local officials, and when the Company took over the *Dīwānī* it was found, according to one estimate, that one-fourth of the land-revenue of the province had been transferred from the State to a large number and variety of rent-free holders of land. Many of these grants had been fraudulently obtained, and undoubtedly, much confusion prevailed. The Company started the Land Resumption Proceedings to check all such grants, and a great majority of these were confiscated. This had been done a little too sweepingly and harshly. A perusal of some of the case-records[43] under the Land Resumption Regulations shows that in a great majority of the cases the resumption proceedings were aimed at the expropriation of the owners under a thinly veiled pretence of legality. Hunter feels constrained to admit that "we demanded an amount of proof in support of rent-free tenures, which, in *the then uncertain state of real property law,* they (the grantees) could not have produced in support of their acknowledged private estates," and adds that "climate and white-ants had been making havoc of their *sanads* and title-deeds."[44] He goes on to remark that "the panic and hatred which ensued (as a result of the land-resumption proceedings) have stamped themselves for ever on the rural records,"[45] and quotes James O'Kinealy, who later worked as an officer incharge of the prosecutions launched against the Wahhabi[46] as citing this to be the second important cause of the decline of, and dissatisfaction among, the Muslims.

It has been argued in some recent works[47] that Hunter's work was an 'ordered' performance, and that he deliberately highlighted the plight of the Bengal Muslims and their sense of resentment. It has been pointed out that these observations of Hunter are applicable only to the Muslims of the Bengal Presidency and not that of the whole of British India. Attention has been drawn to the unevenness of the geographical distribution of the Muslim population in British India, to the social, sectarian, ethnic divisions within the community and to the regional economic disparities among its members. Some figures have also been quoted about the number of Muslims receiving western education, holding middle-range posts in the judicial and revenue services and owning proprietary and intermediary rights in lands in the then North-Western Provinces and Awadh. It has, therefore, been maintained that the Muslims of upper India were in a better position than those of Bengal, and that the social and economic disabilities of the latter could not have created a discontent shared by all British Indian Muslims.

These facts, though true by themselves, do not quite present the whole situation in a proper perspective. For one thing, as mentioned above, there is direct evidence to show that there had been a more rapid decline of the landed aristocracy, as well as the peasantry, in Awadh, particularly in the portions ceded to the British. More importantly, the demographic aspect may also be taken into account. The Muslims in the Bengal Presidency constituted nearly half the total Muslim population of British India.[48] Their condition can be taken as more truly representative of the community as a whole than that of the Muslims of the North-Western Provinces. To show, as these writers have attempted, that the position of the Muslims in other provinces was better, does not explain away their plight in Bengal. No direct evidence has been brought to light to show that the sort of statistical data which *now* help us in determining more exactly the position of the Indian Muslims as a whole was then available to the Bengal Muslims. Assuming that it was, would it not have only sharpened their sense of resentment?

The question of the Indian Muslims' self-image is important in this context.

Happily, some such information is available. A look at the collection of *fatāwa* issued by Shah Abdul Aziz, for example, would show that the consolidation of British rule had brought about a situation about which the Muslims felt concerned. Had British India become a *Dāru'l Ḥarb,* to begin with? Should they migrate from there, or, accept service under the Company's government ? Could they pay interest on loans taken in the *Dāru'l Ḥarb*?

Hardy, writing elsewhere,[49] takes note of this category of source-material, but does not attach much importance to it. He observes that a survey of the *fatāwa* literature shows that "it was Islamic issues rather than the British presence which engrossed the attention of the 'ulama." But this is not quite unexpected. *Fatāwa* were generally sought on specific issues of religious interest. The surprising thing is not that there are so few questions about the British presence but that they are there at all.

Nor is it very relevant, as some may argue, that the opinion of the *'ulama* on these points was not unanimous, or clear-cut. What matters is not what the *'ulama* thought of these, but that the common people raised there problems.

Additionally, we find the *Ṣirāt-i Mustaqīm* and the *Collection of Letters* of Sayyid Ahmad reflecting a strong resentment about what were looked upon as deviations from the fundamentals of Islam, the *Bid'āt,* and a concern about the rising fortunes of the 'foreigners'. It indicates that some of the Indian Muslims felt exercised about certain aspects of the socio-religious conditions, and about certain problems created in the wake of the rise of British power. These anxieties and discontent were not confined to the Muslims belonging to any one particular social group or an area.

II. Islam in India in the 18th Century : An Overview

By the turn of the 18th century, around one thousand years had passed since the advent of the Muslims to India. As a result of proselytisation and other factors their number had increased considerably during this long span of time and they had spread out unevenly in different parts of the country. The process of Islamisation as well as indigenization had been at work and had produced varied patterns of social gradation and behaviour.

It is often remarked, albeit without adequate evidence, that the Delhi Sultanate was a theocracy and that the coercive power of the State played an important role in the expansion of Islam in India. Though some of the Sultans took care to style themselves *al-Mujāhid fī Sabīlu 'llāh* (warrior in the Path of God), *Nāsiru 'l Millat wa 'l Muslimīn* (Helper of the Community and the Muslims), *Muhyyu's Sunnat* (Reviver of the *Sunnat*), etc. on their coins and inscriptions, not much should be read into the use of these grandiloquent titles which did not actually mean much. The state policy was guided mostly by political and military considerations. The Sufis, on the other hand, had played a more positive role in the evolution of the Indian Muslim society. They generally did not do so consciously; in fact those belonging to the more popular *Chishti* Order deliberately kept themselves away from the State and state offices. Yet they exercised a very great moral influence. Their exemplary way of life, their integrity and humanitarianism, their charitable works of medical relief, etc., touched the hearts and won the allegiance of a large number of the local people. Their memories, preserved in the copious *Malfūẓāt* literature which was widely produced and read during the period, came to exercise an abiding influence on the norms of social and religious life.

Sufism emphasises the mystic and inner aspect of religion. It seeks to obtain knowledge of the Reality and a feeling of 'union' with God through a long hard process of absolute devotion to God and recitation of His names and qualities. For this an individual, who is like a traveller *(Sālik)*, has to be led by a spiritual guide *(Murshid)* on the way *(Tariqat)* of Divine knowledge. The *Tariqat* has several stages *(Muqāmāt)*, and one can successfully move on only with the help of a right guide and God's grace. In the course of time the theory of *Waḥdatu'l Wujūd*[50] became widely prevalent and in the eyes of many the *Tariqat* came to acquire a greater prominence than the *Shari'at.*

The taking of *Bai'at*[51] also occupies a crucial importance in the working of the *Sūfi* Orders. It signifies the initiation of a novice in a particular Order and establishes a tie of guidance and discipleship *(pīri-murīdī)* in which the former enjoys the unquestioned obedience of the latter.

The formative period of sufi activities in India covered the 13th and 14th centuries when a considerable number of such devoted and zealous individuals travelled all over the country and a number of *Khānqāhs* came to be established. *Madad-i Ma'āsh* grants (rent-free assignments of land), the standard form of State patronage to religious and cultural institutions, were continuously received by many of the heads of these *Khānqāhs*. Additionally, there were charitable donations from innumerable sources and quite naturally many of these centres became affluent and lost something of the earlier spirit of service. They however continued to play an influential role and during the period under review their popular hold and appeal had increased phenomenally. In fact, the excessive hold of these institutions over the minds and lives of the common people is a significant fact of the contemporary socio-religious conditions.

In Islam, as in other monotheistic religions with a divinely revealed Scripture, attempts have been made at different times and under different social conditions to assert the primacy of the fundamental beliefs and practices. This has assumed various forms, such as the controversy about the *Mujūdiyya* and *Shahūdiyya*[52] schools of thought, or that about the *Sharia't* and the *Tariqat*, etc. In India too there were strong expressions of dissatisfaction with, and opposition to, the existing state of religious affairs. Such feelings had been expressed even during the heyday of political power and dominance, and the first person to raise the banner of reforms and renovation was the famours 16th century *Sūfi*, Shaikh Ahmad Sarhindi (1563-1624), better known as *Mujaddid-i Alif-i Thānī* (Renovator of the First Millennium).[53] He stressed the fact that God was self-existent and self-evident, that everything else was created by Him, that salvation could better be achieved by strict adherence to the *Shari'at* than through mystic attempts to achieve 'union' with Him. He was also of the view that much of the prevalent deviation from the *Shari'at* and moral laxity was due to the weaknesses of the *'Ulamā* who did not have the courage of their convictions and who often connived at the non-observance of the *Shari'at* by the ruling elite in matters affecting their personal comfort and convenience. This had been rendered possible by giving new meanings to the words of the Qurān and the Traditions of the Prophet, and by the growth of the *Bid'at-i Ḥasna* (innovations not so strictly forbidden) which were not quite sinful and hence permissible).

Shaikh Ahmad Sarhindi's method of work was naturally conditioned by the time in which he lived. His was mainly a one-man campaign, and he concentrated his efforts on writing treatises and corresponding with many of his eminent political contemporaries. For obvious reasons he could not establish wider contacts with different sections of the society or organise a popular movement for the implementation of his ideas. Nonetheless, his effort is quite significant. He drew pointed attention to the urgent need for reforms in Islam and tried to counter what he considered to be deviations from the basic beliefs and ideas. A more comprehensive and, as it turned out to be, fruitful attempt in this direction was made by Shah Waliullah, the most towering personality of Islam in India in the 18th century.

Shah Waliullah (1703-62)[54] belonged to a family whose origin can be traced back to the 13th century. Some of its members had first settled at Rohtak and later moved on to Agra and Delhi. They had served with distinction in the army but later took to a life of religious studies and meditation. The change-over is symbolised in the life of Shah Waliullah's grandfather, Shaikh Wajihud Din who having given up his job in the army had devoted himself to mysticism. A modern biographer of Shah Waliullah draws attention to this and remarks that this "combination of the ideal of *futuwwa* (chivalry) with spirituality was a novelty in the general stream of Iranian Sufism, although the *futuwwa* spirit was not unknown among the sufis of the subcontinent."[55] One of the ancestors of Shah Waliullah on the maternal side was Shaikh Tahir of Multan who had lived and studied for some time in Bihar and married the daughter of a local *Qāḍī*. He had later gone to Jaunpur and died there. One of his sons Shaikh Hasan was a contemporary of Sultan Sikandar Lodi (1489-1517).

Shah Waliullah was the son of Shah Abdul Rahim (1646-1719) and was born at Phulit (Muzaffarnagar district, U.P.) on the 4th *Shawwāl*, A.H. 1114 (21 February, 1703). He was a precocious child and had received his early education from his father, who also initiated him in the *Naqshbandīyya* order as well as the *Qadirīyya* and *Chishtīyya* Orders. He married at the age of 14, and after his father's death two years later continued the latter's work of teaching. He performed the *Hajj* ceremony in 1731 and on his return settled permanently at Delhi devoting himself to a life of meditation, studies, teaching and writing. He soon earned a very high reputation as a *Sūfi* and *'Ālim* (scholar) and his *madrasa* situated near the *Jām'Masjid,* Delhi, became a great centre of Islamic learning. It continued to enjoy this reputation till much later under the lineal and spiritual successors of Shah Waliullah.

Shah Waliullah was a prolific writer and his writings[56] encompass almost all the branches of Islamic learning—the *Qur'ān, Tafsīr, Ḥadīth, Fiqh, Kalām, Tasawwuf,* etc. He was also a poet and a biographer and wrote under the pen- name, *Amir.* A significant feature of Shah Waliullah's extensive writings is the attempt to establish a concordance *(tatbīq)* between conflicting schools of thought and to present an integrated view of the different branches of Islamic learning, traditional and rational. On the old and persistent controversy regarding *Waḥdatu'l Wujūd* (Unity of Being) and *Waḥdatu'l Shahūd* (Unity of Perception), for example, he tried to show that the differences were verbal rather than real. Belonging to a family of saintly renown and himself a *Sūfi* of great reputation, he was not oblivious of the decay which had set in the system. He wrote about the different *Sūfi* Orders and criticised some of their ideas and practices.[57] He showed awareness of the existence of a number of what may be called pseudo-Sufis, and categorically advised the Muslims not to take *Bai'at* from such persons—'the *Masha'ikh* of those times who indulged in many kinds of *Bid'āt.*[58] He stressed the significance of the *Bai'at* ceremony and showed a liberal attitude in this matter too. While taking *Bai'at* he invoked the blessings of eminent Sufis belonging to other *silsilahs* also. He stressed the importance of *Wa'z* (Sermon) as a method of educating the people and deprecated the tendency towards hair-splitting controversies over inessential matters.

Examining the question of *Ijtihād*[59] and *Taqlīd,*[60] Shah Waliullah wrote that the Muslims could be divided into two groups of the *'Āmmī* (common, uneducated men) and the *Mujtahidīn.*[61] He fixed gradations for the latter and laid down proper qualifications for them.[62] While an *'Āmmī* was not capable of exercising *Ijtihād,* this did not mean that the doors of *Ijtihād* were closed for ever. Similarly, while

Taqlīd was necessary for an *'Ammī*, it was not so for a *mujtahid* and an *'Ālim*. In fact, if such a person who had recourse to *Taqlīd*, followed the opinions of *faqīhs* and *muffis* even in such matters where they were not in consonance with specific *Aḥādīth* he would be committing a *taqlīd-i harām* (impermissible *taqlīd*). He also drew attention to the two different aspects of the *Dīn* (religion), the external and internal, concerned, respectively, with the maintenance of public good and the purification of heart. In an ideal society attention had to be paid to both these vital aspects.

Shah Waliullah's concern was not confined to what may be called the strictly religious matters but extended also to the political and social conditions. His observations on these aspects, which have not received adequate attention in English writings until very recently, constitute a significant portion of his writings. He writes of two different kinds of *Khilāfat* (Viceregency), the *Khilāfat-i Khāssa* (Special Viceregency) and the *Khilāfat 'Āmma* (Common Viceregency). The former is conceived as a spiritual super-authority regulating the affairs of the latter, which may be equated with temporal rulers and chiefs. His letter to Ahmad Shah Durrani seeking intervention against the rising power of the Marathas is often taken as indicative of a narrow communal outlook, but we know that such an apprehension of the Marathas was shared by many other contemporary Indian powers, including the Rajputs and Jats, and that some among the former had also written to the Durrani ruler for such an intervention.

We have also to note here Shah Waliullah's views on the composition of society. He thinks of the constituent units in inclusive, functional terms not exclusive, religious terms. Among these units he mentions the soldiers, artisans, traders and agriculturists as well as the *'Ulamā,' 'Sūfiā'* and members of the aristocracy. In an ideal society each one of these groups functioned in an equilibrium *(Tawāzun)* and performed its assigned role. If there was any imbalanace there would be social unrest and disturbances. If, for example, in a town a large number of its inhabitants were to be engaged in the production of luxury goods to cater to the unending demands for such goods by the members of a pleasure-loving aristocracy other activities like agriculture and trade and commerce would suffer and the equilibrium would the disturbed. Too much attention to the production of luxury goods or the cultivation of such arts as music and singing had an adverse effect upon the moral character of the members of the community. His deep awareness of the different sections of the society is also evident from the fact that he addressed members of each one of these groups separately and gave counsel to them in a language and in a manner suitable to the concerned group.[63]

Shah Waliullah was of the view that the monarchical form of government as opposed to the early elective tradition of Islam and the cessation of *Ijtihād* had much to do with the prevailing state of affairs. These two factors had affected originality of thinking and initiative among the Muslims. Instead of being a revolutionary movement for the emancipation of mankind from various inequities, Islam had become circumscribed to a set of dogmas and ceremonies. The edifice of Islam had been built on the character of its followers which in turn, was based on spiritual and moral values taught by the *Qur'ān*. Since the character of the individuals—the cells—had been affected, the whole body was afflicted. Political disintegration and social decay were inevitable under the circumstances. The emphasis, it is to be noted, was not so much on the reform of individuals at the top but on that of the community as a whole and hence the need for a widely based movement. The failure of the political struggle led by the Mughal ruling class in the second half of the 18th century[64] also turned the attention of the people to other sections and to other methods.

As we will see in the following chapter, the ideas of Shah Waliullah had a deep impact on Sayyid Ahmad in terms of ideology as well as methodology. On all the important points, such as the prevalence of *Bid'āt,*[65] the question of *Ijtihād,*[66] the procedure of taking *Bai'at,*[67] the two aspects of the *Shari'at,*[68] the nature and functions of the State,[69] etc. Sayyid Ahmad's views are quite similar to Shah Waliullah's. In the later writings of Sayyid Ahmad's followers too, such as the missionary tracts[70] or the polemical literature, one can clearly see a reiteration of some of Shah Waliullah's views.

This, then, sets the background to the beginnings of the movement led by Sayyid Ahmad. On the one hand, there was the general political situation in the country characterised by the disintegration of Mughal imperial authority and the increasing dominance of the British. On the other hand, there was the ideological tradition left behind by Shah Waliullah which had a great re-generative effect upon the Indo-Muslim society. On Sayyid Ahmad, particularly, his impact was very deep. Before presenting, however, an account of Sayyid Ahmad's life and activities and examining the formative phase of the movement, we may briefly notice another similar earlier reform movement in Arabia in the second half of the 18th century. It was started by Muhammad bin Abdul Wahhab whose name came to be associated, commonly but incorrectly, not only with the Arabian movement but also with that in India.

III. The Reform Movement in Arabia started by Muhammad bin Abdul Wahhab: A summing-up

The classical period of the history of Islam came to an end after the sack of Baghdad by the Mongol ruler Halaku in 1258. The last Abbasid Caliph, al-Musta'ṣim (1242-58) was assassinated, but the institution of Caliphate survived. It passed on to Egypt through a surviving member of the Abbasid family who was installed there by the Mamluk ruler Baybārs (1260-77). Later, in 1517, when the great Ottoman Sultan, Salim (1512-20), conquered Egypt, the Caliphate passed on to the Ottomans, and the Arabian peninsula too came under their control. On account of its distant position and inhospitable terrain, however, Arabia was not under effective Turkish control. Local chiefs held sway in its different, geographically well-defined zones such as the Hijaz and Najd areas and the southern coastal areas. Of these, Hijaz, as containing the two holy cities of Makkah and Madina, and as the place of the annual pilgrimage, the *Ḥajj*, was the cynosure of Muslims' eyes all over the world. Here the *Sharifs* (claiming direct descent from the family of the Prophet Muhammad) enjoyed social and political dominance. Though their rival factions often clashed among themselves, they were united in opposing the central government's policy of appointing only the Turks to high posts. At the other end of the peninsula, there were a number of small shaikhdoms on the Persian Gulf coast. The East India Company, ever watchful of its commercial interests in the Gulf region, had established diplomatic contacts with them, and as in India, had enmeshed them in treaty relationships heavily weighted in their own favour. The central desert areas of Najd and Hasa were as yet free from European contact, but similarly parcelled out among small chieftains, including the house of Sa'ud with its capital at Dar'iya.

As stated above, in the course of the long history of Islam, some its adherents had come to feel at different times that some of their co-religionists had deviated from what they considered to be the basic tenets of the faith. The 18th century Arabia was one such area. It was strongly felt that strict monotheism, the bedrock of pristine Islam, had become diluted and had got overlaid by accretions. Philby, the well-known historian of Saudi Arabia basing himself on an authoritative Arab historian of the Wahhabi Movement, writes that, "Forgetting the pure Islamic doctrine of the Oneness of a jealous God, they had gone a-whoring after minor prophets and saints, living and dead. The process had, of course, been gradual and spread over many centuries, with the result that the Arabs of the early eighteenth century had come traditionally to regard their backsliding as the true faith."[71] The more manifest example of all this at the popular level was the practice of seeking the holy men's intercession for God's favours and the visiting of the tombs of religiously eminent personages or the dead saints. Among such places were the tombs of Zaid ibn al Khattab at Wadi Hanifa, that of some of the Companions of the Prophet at Dar'iya and that of Dhamar ibn al Azwar in Wadi Ghubaria. There were even some trees and caves with supposedly miraculous powers.[72]

At a higher level it was felt that after the crystallization of the four *madhāhib* (schools) of Islamic jurisprudence the doors of *ijtihād* had been virtually closed. The Muslims had fallen into a kind of torpor, and they were awakened from it only after the penetration of western influence through political expansion and Christian missionary efforts.[73] The reform movement led by Muhammad bin Abdul Wahhab has to be viewed against this background.

Muhammad bin Abdul Wahhab (1703-92) was born at 'Ayaina[74] in Wadi Hanifa in southern Najd in 1703 and belonged to the well-known Arab tribe of Banū Tamīm. He belonged to a family of prominent theologians, his grandfather having served as *Shaikhu'l Islām* of Najd and his father as a judge at 'Ayaina. Muhammad bin Abdul Wahhab himself seems to have been a precocious child, and had become a *Ḥāfiz* at the age of 10 years. He had performed the *Ḥajj*, and had travelled to, and studied at, important centres of Islamic learning, such as Makkah, Basra, Damascus and Baghdad. Like the people of Najd in general, he followed the *Hanbalī* school of juris prudence, and had studied the writings of the famous Ibn-i Tammiyya (d.1328). Muhammad bin Abdul Wahhab had started preaching at Basra and continued it on returning to Ayaina. He laid great stress on *Tauḥīd* (Unity of God) and denounced *Shirk* (polytheism) in any form, as evidenced by his chief work, *Kitāb al-Tauḥīd.*

In the beginning, Muhammad bin Abdul Wahhab enjoyed the support of the local governor, but his reforming zeal incurred the hostility of the *Amīr* of Hasa to whom the local governor was subordinate. Following an order by the *Amīr* for his arrest and execution, Muhammad bin Abdul Wahhab took refuge in the court of the neighbouring chief, Muhammad bin Saud at Dara'iya. Thus began in 1744 an exemplary companionship between the two which brought about a great moral awakening and aroused "something of a national sense."[75] After the death of Muhammad bin Saud in 1764 the same situation continued under his son and successor, Abdul Āziz bin Saud (1764-1803), whose reign witnessed the extension of Saudi rule not only over the whole of Nejd but even beyond.[76] These developments within the heart of Arabia, which had until then remained unnoticed outside'[77] drew the attention of the Turkish government. The *Sharīf* of Makkah, the nominal deputy of the Turkish government, who was nearer the scene felt more concerned. An attempt was made to establish some sort of a dialogue with the followers of Muhammad bin Abdul Wahhab, and discussions took place between the theologians on the two sides but no real understanding could be worked out. On the contrary, an embargo was put on the free access of the latter's followers to Makkah during the *Ḥajj*.[78] It was later removed and an agreement negotiated under which a kind of demarcation of spheres of influence was made and the safety of the *Ḥajj* pilgrims ensured. The arrangement was soon after upset when a pilgrimage party was robbed by 'Iraqi tribes' who had been instructed from 'the headquarters' in a bid to disturb the above-mentioned arrangement. Abdul Aziz bin Saud, in retaliation, attacked the 'Euphrates districts', and in April 1801 the city of Karbala. On the Hijaz side, Muhammad Saud, the son of Abdul Aziz, carried on similar action, and in April 1803 the holy city of Makkah itself was occupied. Further advance was temporarily stopped by the assassination of Abdul Aziz bin Saud in a mosque at Dar'iya by a Persian Shīa'h as an act of personal vengeance for the happenings at Karbala. The Sa'ūdī force withdrew but Makkah was again occupied in February 1806. "The tenets and practices of Wahhabism were rigorously enforced in the Hijaz both on people and pilgrims; visitations to tombs and other historic sites forbidden; wine, women and song were suppressed ... the Wahhabi system was everywhere dominant, and other systems only maintained themselves silently on sufferance."[79]

The Turkish government sought the help of Muhammad Ali Pasha (1806-1879), another of its nominal deputies. It was a double-edged move, for, it was expected that the power of the Egyptian Pasha would be weakened in the process. The expedition to Hijaz was under the command of Ibrahim Pasha, the son of Muhammad Ali, who started from Suez in 1816. The Saudi force was defeated (1818) and Abdullah, who had succeeded Muhammad bin Saud in 1816, was captured and taken to Constantinople where he was tortured and executed. The Saudi capital was "soon delivered over to pillage and arson."[80] The political power of the Wahhabis had been broken, but the social and religious awakening brought about by the movement could not be suppressed.

Of particular significance is the point, very often overlooked, that the British authorities in India felt alarmed at the extension of the Wahhabi influence and power in the Persian Gulf side. As early as 1809, the government of Bombay had sent a fleet under Captain Wainwright and Colonel Smith to cooperate with the forces of the Imam of Muscat against those who were officially described as Arab pirates but who were mostly Wahhabi, or had 'at least made common cause with them.'[81] Now, in 1818 too, a special messenger was sent by the Government of India to congratulate Ibrahim Pasha on his victory over the Wahhabis.[82] The jubilation of the British Government of India, however, was not without some concern at the substitution of the Ottomans' influence in the area for that of the Wahhabis. "A British officer, Captain G.P. Sadlier, was immediately deputed to visit Ibrahim at Dar'iya and discuss the intentions of the new rulers of Arabia, with the object of discouraging any tendency on their part to establish themselves on the shores of the Persian Gulf, which was already envisaged as a British lake ...."[83]

It is quite understandable that when shortly afterwards a somewhat similar movement started in India the British officers there began to see it as a direct result of the Arabian movement. This official attitude had the additional advantage that the adverse reaction of the orthodox Muslim circles over certain actions of the Wahhabis in Hijaz could be passed on to the followers of the movement in India too.

As we will see in the following chapter, there are some similarities in the movement led by Muhammad bin Abdul Wahhab in Arabia and that by Sayyid Ahmad in India some three-quarters of a century later. This was due mainly to the fact that both the movements were inspired by the common sources of the *Qur'ān* and the *Ḥadīth*. At the same time, it is also to be noted that there were marked differences between the two. The increasing threat of a foreign political domination which lent a strong political undercurrent to the movement in India was not present in Arabia. Secondly, one may refer to 'the tasawwuf-ridden base'[84] of the movement in India. Even a cursory glance at the *Sirātul Mustaqīm* will show that Sayyid Ahmad was strongly influenced by the Sufi ideas and practices. This, again, is something which is not to be found in the Arabian movement.

The apparent similarity between the two movements, perhaps, led Hunter, and some other writers too, to see a causal connection between the two. Hunter writes, "While at Mecca, Sayyid Ahmad attracted the notice of the authorities by the similarity of his teachings to that of the Bedouin Sectaries from whom the holy city of Mecca had suffered so much. The priest publicly degraded him and expelled him from the town. As a natural result of this persecution, he returned to India no longer a religious visionary, and a reformer of idolatrous abuses *but a fanatical disciple of Abdul Wahab.*"[85] Another authoritative writer, Philby, remarks, ... it was at this time that one Saiyid Ahmad of Bareli took back with him from the Meccan pilgrimage to India the seeds from which, after his death in a *Jihad* against the enemies in 1831, grew the Wahhabi reaction of the Black Mountain and its reverbations elsewhere." [86] Actually, there is no evidence, nor does Hunter indicate any, of Sayyid Ahmad being expelled from Makkah or of his becoming a disciple of Abdul Wahab. Philby too, although he had many Arabic sources available to him, does not indicate any basis for his remark. By the time Sayyid Ahmad performed the *Ḥajj* (1822-23), Makkah and Madina had been recovered from the Wahhabis and the Najdis' presence was hardly tolerated there. On the contrary, it appears that Sayyid Ahmad enjoyed the regard and good opinion of some of the learned men of Hijaz. At the request of some of the local *'Ulamā*, Abdul Hayy, a leading companion of Sayyid Ahmad had translated the *Sirāt-i Mustaqīm* into Arabic.[87]

In an article[88] published recently, while commenting on an Indian 'Wahhabi' tract, *Al-Balāgh al-Mubīn*, some remarks have also been made on the question of the influence of the earlier movement in Arabia upon that in India. The writer does not quite agree with the view that the Arabian and Indian movements developed independently, and finds Hunter's and other older British writers' views more acceptable. At least he does not find the question clearly answered. On the one hand, there was 'clearly no continuation with the Waliullahi school,' on the other while drawing attention to the common link of the Hanbali school, and the impact of pilgrims' reports from Arabia and through literature, the writer admits that a direct connection with the Arabian Wahhabis was 'difficult to prove." There was also the added Sufi dimension in the case of Sayyid Ahmad.

Another difference, which has not been mentioned, was the existence of British political ascendancy in India, and the clear awareness of it shown by Sayyid Ahmad. The important evidence of Sayyid Ahmad's letters on this point has not been mentioned, and in a brief reference to Sayyid Ahmad's career his campaigns on the north-western frontier have been viewed as directed against the Sikhs.

This, as it has been shown below,[89] is one of the misconceptions about the nature of the Wahhabi Movement, and it should not be regarded as a characteristic feature of the movement.

Further, it is difficult to agree with the view that there was no continuation with the Waliullahi school. On the contrary, the ideas of Shah Waliullah had a deep impact on Sayyid Ahmad.[90]

Some of the earlier works in English tend to create the impression that Wahhabism represented some sort of a heterodox sect, if not altogether a new revelation. Hunter often refers to Sayyid Ahmad as the prophet and the *Sirāt-i Mustaqīm* as the Kuran of the sect.' O'Kinealy too calls the *Sirāt-i Mustaqīm* as 'the *Qurān* of the Wahhabis of India.'[91] Carsten Niebuhr insinuates that Muhammad bin Abdul Wahhab was a prophet. But neither the Arabian reformer nor his followers even stated this, or even called themselves Wahhabis. That term came to be applied to them later by their opponents in derision. As Philby himself writes, "Muhammad bin Abdul Wahhab died after nearly fifty years of unremitting toil in a cause which he himself initiated and which still perpetuates his memory in the sobriquet first applied to it in derision by its opponents and subsequently acquiesced in by its votaries, though to this day they do not apply it to themselves. The creed he taught never professed to be a new revelation or even a new interpretation of Islam; and the teacher never claimed a prophetic status.'[92] The same thing happened in the case of the reform movement in India, to whose origin and growth we may now turn.

NOTES

1. Named Mirza Abdullah, the Prince is better known by his titles Ali Gauhar (conferred in 1754) and Shah Alam (1756), which latter title he retained as emperor. He was then aged 30 and had incurred the hostility of the domineering *Wazir, 'Imādu'l Mulk* who got Alamgir II assassinated and then set up his own nominee, Shah Jahan II, at Delhi. Ali Gauhar, ignoring this, announced his coronation (December 1759) on hearing of his father's assassination. It took him 12 years to instal himself at Delhi.
2. The Nawabs of Awadh, virtual masters of their territory since 1723, bore this title from the time when Safdar Jung (whose name is borne by the former civil airport of Delhi, near which Safdar Jung's mausoleum stands) was appointed *Wazīr* of the empire (1748). They took regal titles in 1823.
3. Literal meaning, 'son'; the word was used in the Mughal official documents and seals in relation to some favoured Indian chiefs—and often the East India Company, too.
4. Just two days after this, Shah Alam II appointed Sindhia as the *Wakīl-i Mutlaq*.
5. Peshwa Baji Rao I, while expounding the plan of extending the Maratha power northwards, had said to Raja Sahu, "Let us strike at the trunk of the withering tree; the branches will fall of themselves. Thus should the Maratha flag fly from the Krishna to the Indus." To which Raju Sahu had replied, "you shall plant it upon the Himalayas." (Irvine, W., Later Mughals vol. II, Calcutta, 1922, p. 165.
6. Letter from Cornwallis to William Palmer quoted in K.K. Datta, *Shah Alam II and the East India Company*, 1965, p. 101.
7. A grandson of Shivaji (1674-80), Sahu had fallen captive to the Mughals at the young age of seven and had remained under Mughal tutelage for 18 years. Aurangzeb had conferred upon him a *manṣab* of 7000 and got him married to two Maratha girls of high lineage. After Aurangzeb's death, when his son A'zam proceeded to the north in a bid for the throne he took Sahu along. Later, Sahu was released with the idea of fomenting dissensions between his supporters and those of Tarabai. The expectation was not quite fulfilled.
8. The Maratha push to the north was propelled by various factors, political, military and financial. At one stage, a religious colour was also sought to be imparted to it (call for a *Hindu Pad Padshāhī*). The move to the north received an initial, unintended, help from Husain Ali Khan the younger of the Syed brothers, who sought to

use the Marathas' help in consolidating his own position, and under the Treaty of 1718 obtained a legal recognition for the Marathas' claim for *chauth* and *sardeshmukhi* in the *ṣūbahs* of the Deccan. In 1741 Muhammad Shah appointed the Peshwa as *Nāīb Ṣūbahdār* of Malwa in return for which the latter agreed to join the Emperor during a campaign, if asked. The acquisition of Malwa facilitated the progress towards the north.

9. The Maratha army comprising the contingents of their leading chiefs, Jankoji Sindhia, Malhar Rao Holkar and others, and the forces of their Muslim allies such as Ibrahim Khan Gardi, was under the nominal command of Vishwas Rao, the Peshwa's young son. He was, however, put under the guardianship of the experienced Sadashiva Rao, who had gained victories in the south but was comparatively unfamiliar with the conditions in the north.
10. Jadunath Sarkar, *Downfall of the Mughal Empire*, vol.II.
11. As we know, the British were to help Raghunath Rao with a force whose cost was to be borne by the latter. Further, Raghunath Rao was not to side with the Company's enemies.
12. Ghulam Husain Khan, *Siyaru'l Mutakhkhirīn* Eng.tr. Raymond, Calcutta, 1902, vol. III, pp. 93-95. Emphasis added.
13. *Vide infra,* p.61.
14. *Vide infra,* Appendix II.
15. He belonged to the Sadozai clan of the Pathans which enjoyed high popular esteem. One of his ancestors was a disciple of a Chishti saint, Abū Ahmad Abdāl, who on being pleased with the disciple called him *Abdal*—a term which has a spiritual connotation. Ahmed Shah Abdali too was blessed by another saint, Shah Sabir, who foretold his coronation, strewing some barely-shoots on his head as pearls, and called him *Durrānī Pādshāh* (Pearl among the Kings). Hence he came to be knwon as Durrani. Ahmad Shah had served under Nadir Shah who thought highly of his capabilities.
16. M'Gregor, *History of the Sikhs*, vol. I, London, 1846, pp. 203-04.
17. Ibid., p.163; Cunningham, J.D., *History of the Sikhs*, Calcutta, 1904, App. IX, pp. 503-04.
18. The series of political dispatches by Captain Alexander Burnes during the course of his mission to Kabul give us first hand information about the political conditions. See *For. Dept. Pol. Cons.* nos. 69-76, dated the 20th October, 1837; also Cunningham, op. cit.
19. The principality of Awadh was founded by Saadat Ali Khan *Burhānu'l Mulk*, formerly an officer of the *Balāshāhi* troops (personal retrainers of the Emperor), in 1723.
20. It could have been retained by the East India Company, but Clive rightly pointed out that it would arouse the jealousy of the other

powers, and its administration would have been difficult as it was separated from the Company's territories.

21. It is named after Farrukh Siyar (1712-19) the patron of Nawab Muhammad (d. 1743) the founder of the dynasty.
22. This was the old Katehar area of the Delhi Sultanat period. A large area, some 12,000 square miles, with a population of some 6,000,000, the Rohillas, who gave their name to it, had occupied it during the early 18th century.
23. In the process of fulfilling these never-ending demands Asafud Dawlah was persuaded, or forced, not to spare even the Begums of Awadh, the widows of the previous Nawab, Shajaud Dawlah, whose estates and jewellery, worth some 2,000,000 pounds, were also sequestered. The tretment meted out to the Begums of Awadh was one of the charges against Warren Hastings in the impeachment proceedings against him.
24. H.R. Nevill, *District Gazetteer, Bareilly,* vol. XIII, Allahabad, 1911, pp.166-68.
    The place was also called Bans Bareilly to distinguish it from the other, older, Rai Barelī in Awadh which was the birth place of Sayyid Ahmad.
25. Ibid.
26. Ibid.
27. See my article, "Commercial-cum-Political Activities of the Patna Factory of the East India Company, 1707-39", *JBRS*, 1976, 42 (1-4), 168-83.
28. Ibid., Letters from the Calcutta Council to the Court of Directors, dated 24 January, 1735, 31 December, 1737 and 24 December, 1739.
29. Karam Ali, *Muzaffar Nāmah*, K.B.O.P.L. *ms.* copy, f.220. The passage has been rendered into English and emphasis added.
30. W.H. Sleeman, *Journey Through the Kingdom of Oude in 1849-50,* London, 1858, vol.I, pp. 274-76.
31. Incidentally, this shows that the observations made on these practices in the Wahhabi *risālas* do not represent just their own sectarian views but that their sentiments were shared by a wider cross-section of the Indian Muslims.
32. Sleeman, op. cit., p. 276.
33. Tennant's *Indian Recreations*, vol. II, p. 404, quoted in H.R. Neville, *Lucknow: A Gazetteer,* Allahabad, 1904, pp.149-50.
34. Based on Sayyid Ahmad's observations, the work was compiled in Persian by two of his chief disciples Shah Isma 'il and Abdul Hayy around 1817-18. Probably the earliest published edition is the one prepared by Abdur Rahim Safipuri and Muhammad Ali Rampuri at Maṭba' -i -Shaikh Hidayatullah, Calcutta, A.H. 1238 (1822-23).

The extracts, in English translation, presented here and elsewhere are from this edition unless otherwise stated. See also Bibliography.

35. S.M., p. 132.
36. Ibid., pp. 162-63.
37. Sleeman, op. cit., p. 321.
38. Ibid., p.169.
39. Ibid.
40. Much earlier than Sleeman, Ghulam Husain Khan, the 18th century historian, had also commented on this aspect of the early British administration and the Indians' response to the early British rule; see my article 'An Eighteenth Century Indian Historian on Early British Administration.' *J. of Indian History,* Golden Jubilee Volume, 1973, pp. 893-908.
41. Ghulam Husain Khan Tabataba'i, *Siyaru'l Muta'akhkhirin,* English translation, F. Raymond, Calcutta, 1902, vol.III, pp. 202-04. Emphasis mine.
42. Karam Ali, *Muzaffar Nāmah,* K.B.O.P.L. ms. copy, ff. 220b.
43. Voluminous series of such cases are available, and have been examined by me, in the record room of the Divisional Commissioner, Patna, as also in some other District record rooms of Bihar. For a detailed study of the Land Resumption Proceedings and their impact, see also Dr. Kabindra Prasad Singh, *Land Revenue Administration in Bihar, 1793-1858,* Calcutta, 1987.
44. Hunter, W.W., *The Indian Musalmans: Are they Bound in conscience to Rebel against the Queen?* London, 1871, p.183.
45. Ibid, p. 182.
46. He later wrote a series of three very informative articles on the Wahhabis entitled 'A sketch of the Wahhabis in India', in the *Calcutta Review,* vol. L-II (nos. C-CII), 1870, pp.73-104, 177-92 and 381-99. The articles represent the first available detailed account in English of their activities, writing, etc.
47. Anil Seal. *The Emergence of Indian Nationalism,* Cambridge, 1968, pp. 298-308; Peter Hardy, *The Muslims in British India,* (paperback) Cambridge, 1972, pp. 31-60. B.B. Majumdar and B.P.Majumdar, Congress and Congressmen?
48. Seal (op. cit., p.26, Table 4) himself quotes some of the figures from the 1881 *Census India,* and they show that the All-India Muslim population including that of the 'Native' States was 50,121,585, while that of Bengal was 21,704,724, and that the Muslims in Bengal constituted 31.2 per cent of the population as against 19.7 per cent of the total Muslim population of British India as a whole.

49. Pater Hardy, "The Ulama in British India" *JIH,* Golden Jubilee Volume, 1973, pp. 821-45.
50. There are two broad categories among the sufis believing in the *Wujūdiyya* and *Shahūdiyya* schools of thought. The former presents a pantheistic conception of God and is popularly summed up in the formula *Hama Ūst* (Everything is Him). The other maintains a clear distinction between the Creator and the Created and is similarly summed up in a formula *Hama* Az *Ūst* (Everything is from Him).
51. It is done by putting one's hands into those of the *Murshid.* It is a sort of an oath of fealty and signifies the acceptance of one's spiritual guide.
52. See note 50 above.
53. See B.A. Faruqi, *The Mujaddid's Conception of Tawhid,* Lahore, 1940. It is believed that at the end of each millennium of the Islamic era a reformer and a renovator would appear who would cleanse the faith from its accretions. Ahmad Sarhindi's life span (A.H. 935-1035) marks the completion of the first 1000 years of the Islamic era, hence this title.
54. For a comprehensive account of his life, works and ideas, see Saiyid Athar Abbas Rizvi, *Shah Wali-Allah and his Times. A study of Eighteenth century Islam, politics and society in India,* Canberra, 1980.
55. Ibid. p., 205.
    For such a tradition of 'warrior-saints' in the Deccan, see Eaton,. C., *The Sufis in Bijapur.*
56. Rizvi, op. cit., pp. 221-27 for a detailed list showing the approximate time-sequence of his works.
    We know of about 70 works written by him, including some very short treatises. The *Hujjatu'llah al-Bāligha* and *Tafhīmāt-i Ilāhīyya* are two of his most important works. The former examines the basic reasons for the rules of the *Sharia't* and relates to the disciplines of *Hadīth, Fiqh* and *Kalām.* The latter which contains several short treatises on different religious topics also presents some very perceptive comments on matters of social and economic interest.
57. See *al-Qawlu'l Jamīl fi Sawa'u's Sabīl'* Delhi, n.d. (Urdu tr. *Shifā'u'l Alīl* by Kharam Ali, Delhi).
58. See the *Wasiyat Nāmah.*
59. Literally, 'exertion'. The process of personal reasoning based on logical deductions in matters of law and theology. The person qualified to do so is called a *mujtahid.*
60. Conformity to the opinions of any one of the four *Imāms* or founders of the four schools (Madhāhib) of law among the Sunni Muslims.

61. Plural of *Mujtahid* or one qualified to exercise *Ijtihād*, vide note 59 above.
62. See, *'Iqdu'l jid fi Bayān Ahkām al-ijtihād wa'l Taqlid*. Matba'-i Faruqi, Delhi, A.H. 1290 (1873-74). Arabic text with inter-linear translation into urdu.
63. Rizvi, op. cit., pp. 313-14.
64. On this, see infra, p.411.
65. *Vide infra*,pp. 51-53.
66. *Vide Infra*, p.54.
67. *Vide infra*, pp. 50-54.
68. *Vide infra*, p. 54.
69. *Vide infra*, p. 90.
70. The portion of the *Risāla-i-Da'wat* addressed to members of different social groups may be noted in this connection, *vide infra*, pp. 381 ff.
71. He has referred to the work of Shaikh Husain ibn Ghannam al-Najdi which he characterises as the standard authority on Wahhabi history. Philby, J.B., *Arabia*, London, 1930. pp.4-5.
72. Philby, op. cit. p. 5.
73. D. Van Der Meulen, *The Wells of Ibn Sa'ud*, New York, 1957, p.31. Meulen was the Dutch Consul at Jidda in 1926 looking after, among other things, the welfare of the pilgrims from the Dutch East Indies (Java and Sumatra). A close observer of the developments leading to the revival of Wahhabi power in Arabia under Abdul Azia ibn Saud (1925-1953), and having personal contacts with the king, Meulen stresses the moral and religious basis of the Wahhabis' rise to power. He also comments on the erosion of that base by the rising prosperity in the wake of the oil-wealth. Having a colonial service background, but not being British, his comments on the activities of the English men, Philby and Lawrence and the watchful eyes the British kept on the expansion of Wahhabis' power towards the Persian Gulf coast are very valuable.
74. According to another writer he was born in 1703 at Hureimala, north of Riyadh.
75. Philby, op. cit., p. 53.
76. Ibid., pp. 88 ff; Meulen, op. cit., pp. 30-36.
77. Carsten Niebuhr, who led a Danish scientific mission to Jedda and Yemen in 1762-63, and on his return published his *Description de l' Arabie*, was the first to convey to Europe the news of the rise of the Wahhabis.
78. Philby, op. cit., p. 38.
79. Ibid., p. 88.
80. Ibid., p. 103.

81. Selections, p. 124; see also Philby, op. cit., pp. 90-92.
82. P.I.T.
83. Philby, op. cit., p. 103; see also Ahmad Anasi; *Gulf Relations with the West: An Historicai Survey* (Part-II) i.c. 1987, 61 (1): 39-55.
84. See S.A.A. Rizvi's article, 'Ideological Background of the Wahhabi movement in India in the XVIII and XIV centuries, in Bisheshwar Prasad (ed) *Ideas in History*, Delhi, 1968, pp. 93-109.
85. I.M. pp. 60-61.
86. Philby, op. cit., p.110.
87. Vide infra, p.58.
88. Marc Gaborieau, "A Nineteenth Century Indian 'Wahhabi' Tract Against the Cult of Muslim Saints: Al-Balagh al-Mubin", Christian W. Troll *(ed). Muslim Shrines in India: Their Character, History and Significance*, Delhi, 1989,198-239.
89. *Vide infra*, pp. 401-03.
90. *Vide infra*, pp. 37, 50-54, 90.
91. *Vide infra*, pp. 16-67; also infra, p.58.
92. C.R., 1870 (No.C.) p. 81.

Chapter II

Sayyid Ahmad and the Early Phase of the Movement

1. The Life, Ideas and Activities of Sayyid Ahmad

Sayyid Ahmad, popularly remembered as a *shahīd* (martyr), belonged to a family of saintly renown which had migrated to India in the early 13th century and had first settled in the Kara (Allahabad) region. Much later, some of its members had moved on to Rai Bareli.[1] Sayyid Ahmad, the son of Sayyid Muhammad Irfan, was born there in the month of *Safar,* A.H. 1201 (November, 1786).[2] He had his early education at home but did not make much progress at the time. He seems to have continued his self-education later on, and acquired some proficiency in Arabic and Persian.[3]

Some time affter the death of his father (1799-1800), Sayyid Ahmad went to Lucknow in search of employment,[4] and then moved on to Delhi where he met the famous theologian and scholar, Shah Abdul Aziz (1746-1824), spiritual successor of Shah Waliullah. He took *Bai'at* at the hands of Shah Abdul Aziz some time in 1807-08[5] and then returned to Rai Bareli where he stayed for some years. While there, he married a cousin, *Bībī* Zahra, and a daughter named Sarah was born out of this marriage.

We have a detailed description of Sayyid Ahmad's appearance when he was 36 years old and touring the Lower Provinces. It notes that his figure, a little above middle height, was commanding and its effect was further increased by a flowing beard. He was dressed in a cotton *kurta* opening down the middle, a white trouser of the same material reaching to the ankles, and a white turban. It adds that 'his (Sayyid Ahmad's) demeanour was grave, quiet and kind.'[6] A later writer, who was also an important follower of the movement, describes Sayyid Ahmad as "a tall, fair and strongly-built man with a broad forehead, thick eyebrows, moustache and beard, and a pleasing countenance."[7]

Sayyid Ahmad seems to have realised from an early age the urgency of religious reforms and the need for building up an organisation and collecting a band of dedicated followers who could bear arms too, if necessary.[8] His joining the army of Amir Khan of Tonk[9] in A.H. 1227 (1812),[10] also indicates this. It was not an isolated action nor was it motivated by mercenary considerations, as has been suggested by some modern writers. As stated above, Amir Khan's incursions extended up to the Rohilkhand area and some sort of a link existed between him and the anti-British elements on the western border of the Awadh kingdom.[11] Sayyid Ahmad's elder brother, Sayyid Ibrahim, had served in Amir Khan's army, and this probably facilitated the former's entry. Sayyid Ahmad's contemporary biographer narrates various incidents about this period of his life which show the influence he exercised over the lives and conduct of Amir Khan's soldiers.[12] Sayyid Ahmad had his baptism of fire during this service and participated in several military engagements.

Sayyid Ahmad had already been deliberating over his mission and he might have seen some hopeful possibilities in joining the Tonk army. If the soldiers could be reoriented to his line of thinking it would have been so much better than starting from scratch and building up an armed organisation on his own. This is indicated by the fact that Sayyid Ahmad opposed Amir Khan's projected alliance with the British, and when Amir Khan finally agreed to such an alliance Sayyid Ahmad left his service. The English sources do not shed much light on the reasons why Sayyid Ahmad left the Tonk army, but the incident has been noted in some detail in the *Waqāi'*. It records that when the alliance was under contemplation Sayyid Ahmad urged Amir Khan not to worry about lack of resources, to have faith in God, and continue fighting. Amir Khan argued that there was disunity in his camp and that it was advisable to take some money from the British and resume fighting at an opportune moment later as the Maratha chief, Holkar, had done. Sayyid Ahmad pointed out that once Amir Khan entered into an alliance with the British he would be in their clutches and become helpless. He met Amir Khan once again and pointed out that the British were *daghābāz* (treacherous), that they would assign him some *jāgīr* somewhere and render him innocuous. He would never get an opportunity again. Amir Khan reiterated that he was not in a position to fight and a compromise was the only advisable course. Sayyid Ahmad told him that he was free to act as he liked and took leave of him.[13] This account shows that Sayyid Ahmad had some awareness of the British policy of winning over the Indian chiefs and rendering them harmless through treaties drafted with a view to weakening their military power. Amir Khan as a protege of the British was of no use to him. Had Sayyid Ahmad's motives been purely mercenary he would not have left Amir Khan's service at this stage.

Leaving Tonk, Sayyid Ahmad returned to Delhi, around 1818. He gained spiritual eminence there and many distinguished persons took *Bai'at* at his hands. Among them the two most notable were Shah Ismail and Shah Abdul Hayy, the nephew and son-in-law, respectively, of Shah Abdul Aziz. Both were erudite scholars and their adherence came to exercise a deep influence upon the subsequent history of the movement. It marked the beginning of their life-long comradeship with Sayyid Ahmad.[14] Shah Ismail was a prolific writer and his treatises and letters contain some of the most lucid and forceful expositions of the aims and objects of the movement. He was proficient both with his pen and the sword in the defence of the movement. In his religious views he was inclined to be an extremist and a *Ghair Muqallid,* while Abdul Hayy was more moderate. In fact, the two provide an interesting comparative study.

After a short stay at Delhi, Sayyid Ahmad sought the permission of his preceptor to set out on a journey in response to the requests of the people from outside Delhi who wanted to offer *Bai'at.* His itinerary covered the *Dōāb* region between the Ganges and the Jamuna, and included Saharanpur, Shahjahanpur, Phulit, Rampur, Mukteshwar and many other places. It was like a triumphal procession with an ever increasing number of persons taking *Bai'at* at Sayyid Ahmad's hands. It demonstrated a wide popular response to his message. Sayyid Ahmad followed a rather novel procedure of taking *Bai'at*: first in the well-known four *Sūfi* Orders, the Chishtīyya, Surawardīyya, the Qadirīyya and the Naqshbandīyya, and then in the Muhammadī Order, which he claimed to have developed himself.

On completing the tour, he returned to his hometown from where he had been absent for some six or seven years and stayed there for a couple of years. The stay was not quite uninterrupted and some more missionary tours[15] were undertaken during the time. This was a period of quiet organisational and missionary work. The select band of followers were being given ideological as well as military training for the coming struggle. Sayyid Ahmad's basic ideas had developed by this time and were put forth in the *Sirātul Mustaqīm* which was compiled in Persian by Shah Isma'il and Ābdul Hayy around 1817-18 on the basis of Sayyid Ahmad's observations and which may be regarded as a manifesto of the movement, particularly its social and religious objectives. The more notable among Sayyid Ahmad's ideas at this stage are a strong affirmation of *tawḥīd* (monotheism), rejection of *Bid'āt*, and an advocacy of *Ijtihād*. A long portion of the *Sirātul Mustaqīm* is devoted to a discussion of the wide prevalence of *Bid'at*, their various forms, etc. Sayyid Ahmad never ceased strongly criticising the *Bid'at*, and he was also rather harsh on some of the Sufis whom he considered responsible for the state of affairs. The following extracts illustrate the point :

1. "Among the *bid'āt* of the 'heretics in Sufistic garb' *(mulāhidah-i sūfi Shi'ār)* which have gained prevalence among the people of this age, and are true of some of the chosen ones too, is the use of blasphemous language in relation to God and the dictates enjoined upon by him. Seekers after Truth must refrain from hearing such utterances and must never utter such words themselves. Disrespect can never bring forth any good result."[16]

2. "Among the *bid'āt* of the *'Wujūdia* heretics' *(mulāhidah-i Wujūdia)* which have gained prevalence among the masses as well as the elite, and which are supposed to be in consonance with the sayings of the eminent personages of the Sūfi Orders, is the 'heretical' talk about the pantheistic conception of God *(guftugūhā-i tawḥīd Wujūdī ilhādī)*. Such persons imagine themselves to be in union with God and derive sensuous pleasure from this sense of co-mingling. They, due to Satanic delusions and perverse self-deception, imagine themselves to have an insight into the knowledge of divine truth. They waste their precious time in obnoxious talks."[17]

3. "Among the *bid'āt* of the 'heretics in Sufistic garb' which has gained prevalence among the Muslims in general is the indulgence in the controversy, and discussions, on the question of Fate. Belief in predestination is one of the fundamental doctrines of the faith of Islam and is obligatory by the canons of the *Sharīa't*. Therefore, controversy over this question is very objectionable. The *Sharīa't* has forbidden any deliberation on this intricate and deep subject. It is, therefore, incumbent on all Muslims to be content with the complete acceptance of this (position), and to refrain from plunging into the surging sea of high waves which the scrutiny of this question implies."[18]

4. "Among the *bid'āt* of the 'polytheists in Sufistic garb' *(mushrikīn-i Sūfi shi'ār)* which are in vogue in our time, particularly in India, and which is true of the chosen ones too, is the excessive respect shown to the spiritual guide (murshid), even to the extent of regarding him as a deity or a prophet. The moderate limits (in this matter) must be understood. The spiritual guide is undoubtedly a means to reach the faith of God. .. and it is hardly possible to find the Path without a guide. Therefore, one should take someone as a guide who does not act contrary to the *Shara'* and treads firmly on the Straight Path *(Rāh-i Mustaqīm)* which means implicit faith in the *Qur'ān* and the *Ḥadīth*.[19]

5. "Among the *bid'āt* of the 'polythesists in Sufistic garb' which appear to be virtuous in the eyes of the people of this region one is the performance of disgusting rites over the graves of the pious ... in the same category comes the imploring from the dead for help and support ... By such supplications the people pave the way towards polytheism ... God has ordained that the process of teaching and guidance should continue and benefits should be derived from those who are alive. If by chance someone does not find a living person helpful for the purpose, he should not perform a journey to such tombs from distant lands but should follow the *Qur'ān* and the *Ḥadīth* which are the key to all intricate problems."[20]

6. "Among the *bid'āt* of the 'polytheists in Sufistic garb' which are extremely in vogue among all classes of the Muslims, commoners as well as the gentry, are *nadhar* and *niyāz* (offering of prayers and eatables in the names of dead ones). This involves the committing of a sort of polytheism. Although in principle this is valid and its performance is in accordance with the *Shara'*, the people had commonly introduced their own imagination and superstitions into it, and posterity not only followed these but also exceeded the limits (by) adding new things to what had previously existed; the virtuous principles had fallen into the background and the evil offshoots, assiduously produced by fabrications, had prevalied."[21]

Additional light is thrown on Sayyid Ahmad's religious ideas from the text of a unique document, the *Sanad of Khilāfat*[22] given by him to Shah Muhammad Husain of Patna. It is explained therein that the *Shari'at* had two aspects, the internal and external. The former related to the discipline of one's self for the attainment of spiritual bliss and this was attended to by the general Sūfi Orders. The other was concerned with the observance of an ethical code of conduct in one's day-to-day life, and this was attended to by the *Muhammadī*

Order.[23] The taking of *Bai'at* in this manner encompassed both the inner and external life of an individual.

Another possible explanation of this method might have been the consideration that the Sūfi Orders, though devoid of the earlier spirit, were deeply rooted in the common people's minds and a total rejection of these might not have been considered advisable.[24]

On *Ijtihād* and *Taqlīd*, Sayyid Ahmad observed that although in one's actions conformity to the four *madhāhib* current among the Muslims was good, one should not think that the knowledge (of the life and ideas) of Prophet Muhammad was confined to any one from among the *Mujtahids*. In all such matters where there was a explicit *Ḥadīth* one should not follow a *Mujtahid's* opinion.[25] It is also important to note that Sayyid Ahmad is quite explicit even in this pre-*Hijrat* (migration) phase of his life that many portions of India had become a *Dāru 'lḤarb* in A.H. 1233 (1817-18).[26]

The five essentials of Islam, *Kalima* (profession of faith), *Namāz* (prayers), Roza (fasting), *Ḥajj* (pilgrimage to Ka'ba) and *Zakāt* (alms) were, of course to be scrupulously observed.[27] Along with these, other moral virtues such as humility, contentment and perseverance were to be acquired while greed jealousy and pride were to be eschewed. The idea that certain persons with saintly eminence could intercede on one's behalf for the grant of God's forgiveness and favours was strongly denounced. God was nearer to a man than his 'jugular vein', and man should always pray to God directly. Passive belief was not enough, one shoud also have the courage for one's actions.

II. The Journey for Hajj (1821-24)

During the course of his missionary tours, Sayyid Ahmad had seen for himself the extent of the prevalence of *Bid'āt* among the common Muslims, including the reluctance, particularly among the gentry, for the re-marriage of widows,[28] and the tendency to avoid the performance of *Ḥajj* on the ground of danger and insecurity on the way.[29] Seeking to set some personal examples, Sayyid Ahmad married *Bībī* Walia, the widow of his elder brother, and decided to set out on a journey for *Ḥajj*. The decision was rather unexpected for he had already made considerable preparations for another journey, of *Hijrat* (migration) from the British territory. He wanted to perform the *Ḥajj* before migrating to the North-Western Frontier's independent tribal area and starting a more active phase of his career, the outcome of which was not quite certain.[30] The journey for *Ḥajj*, an important and spectacular event in the life of Sayyid Ahmad, is also significant as indicative of his ability to organise and lead a large body of men over a long and arduous journey.

Sayyid Ahmad invited volunteers from all over the country to join the *Ḥajj* party.[31] They were to assemble at Rai Bareli from where they were to proceed down the Ganges to Calcutta. The whole party consisting of several hundred persons was divided into smaller units. The journey commenced on the last day of the month of *Shawwāl* A.H. 1236,[32] (30th July, 1821) and the party proceeded leisurely down the Ganges halting at some of the important cities situated along on its bank. At all these places a large number of persons flocked to offer *Bai'at*[33] and many intending pilgrims joined in.

The arrival of the large party at Calcutta created a stir.[34] Some of its members moved about in the town openly carrying arms, and some local Muslims submitted a *Maḥḍar Nāmah* (petition) bearing 150 signatures and seals to the police stating that Sayyid Ahmad's objective was to fight against the *Firgangis* (the Christians, but denoting here the British). A contemporary versified account[35] of Sayyid Ahmad's life also records that the arrival of the *Ḥajj* party at Calcutta created a fear in the hearts of the *Naṣrānīs* (Christians) and they instructed their servants (local officers?) not to obstruct Sayyid Ahmad's men who were armed and fearless.

Before setting sail the pilgrims were divided into 10 units, each under a chief. The different units boarded different ships, which had other passengers too. The *Waqāi'* provides painstaking details[36] about the total number of the Ḥajj pilgrims, the amount of fare and freight paid, the foodgrains and utensils purchased for the journey, etc. Starting from Calcutta early in 1822, the ships sailed down the east coast. Passing by the side of Ceylon they turned north after rounding off the *Qāf Qamrī* (Cape of Comorin) and halted for some time at Calicut. Then, passing through the Laccadive Islands and Scotra, they halted at Aden and Babel Mandap, and moving up the Red Sea coast halted at Mocha, Hodeida and, finally Jedda. The pilgrims reached Makkah on the 29th *Sha'bān*, 1237 (May, 1822). During their stay in Arabia, Sayyid Ahmad came into contact and held discussions with several leading theologians and scholars, and many persons took *Bai'at* at his hands. Shah Ismail and Abdul Hayy delivered lectures which were well-attended. The *Sirātul Mustaqīm* was translated into Arabic by Shah Abdul Hayy for the benefit of those who could read it only in that language. Having performed the *Ḥajj*, and after a stay of about 8 months in Arabia, the party returned to Bombay. It sailed from there to Calcutta and after a stay there of two months proceeded up the Ganges as on the outward journey. It reached Rae Bareli in *Sha'bān* 1239 (April, 1824).

Further details about the outward and return journey, including events which took place at some of the important places of halt such as Allahabad, Benares, Ghazipur, Danapur,[37] Patna, Barh, Monghyr,[38] Bhagalpur,[39] and Rajmahal, are available in the two primary sources, the *Makhzan* and the *Waqāi'*, and these have been extensively utilised by the two modern writers[40] in Urdu on the career and mission of Sayyid Ahmad. These need not be restated, but certain events which took place at Patna deserve closer notice because they had a bearing on the subsequent history of the movement and because we have additional sources of information about these. It was at Patna that the foundation of a permanent organisation for collecting men and money for the impending struggle was laid. It was also at Patna that the initiation took place of the members of the Sadiqpore family, whose efforts went a long way in sustaining the movement after Sayyid Ahmad's death took place.

Sayyid Ahmad halted at Patna both on the outward and return journeys. On the former occasion Wilayat Ali had written to his relatives to meet Sayyid Ahmad and take *Bai'at*, but for some reason this could not be done. On the second occasion,[41] Wilayat Ali received Sayyid Ahmad at Monghyr, brought him to Patna and introduced other family members to him. Some of them such as *Maulawī* Elahi Baksh,[42] Fath Ali[43] and Shah Muhammad Husain[44] invited Sayyid Ahmad to their home and the last two also took Bai'at. Several others accompanied Sayyid Ahmad to Rai Bareli and later to the North-Western Frontier.[45] Shah Muhammad Husain was appointed a *Khalīfa*[46] and authorised to initiate new members. A beginning was thus made for the establishment of organisational-cum-missionary centres all over the country.

The significance of Sayyid Ahmad's work at Patna was not lost upon some of the early English writers on the Wahhabi Movement. One such observant writer remarked, "on his return from Hajj Syed Ahmad visited Patna where he was met by Syed Muhammad Hussain of Patna with a large body of Crescentaders. A general meeting of his Caliphs was held and *a permanent arrangement was made to forward supplies of men and money to support the enterprise long contemplated.*[47] Another writer remarks, "Having thus *established a central organisation at Patna* he (Sayyid Ahmad) continued his journey along the banks of the Ganges to Calcutta."[48] It thus appears that Patna was chosen as the first organised centre by Sayyid Ahmad himself, and its subsequent active role justified the choice. In fact, the period preceding the journey for Ḥajj, and that immediately affter the return, witnessed the commencement of the movement.

III. The Hijrat (Migration) from British India and the Frontier Campaigns

For some two years after his return to Rai Bareli, Sayyid Ahmad was engaged in the preparation for the next most crucial step in his life —the migration from British India into the independent tribal territories on the North-Western Frontier. He himself and some of his chief followers were constantly addressing meetings and writing letters to their followers and supporters. They were also organising volunteer units and collecting arms, including matchlocks and guns.[49]

The fateful journey began in January 1826. The party was divided into three groups, of which two were sent ahead to Tonk, which was selected as the rendezvous.[50] Sayyid Ahmad himself started later, and travelling through Dalmau and Fatahpur, reached Gwalior, where he had a meeting with Mahārājā Daulat Rao Sindhia. It was probably arranged through the initiative of the Mahārājā's brother-in-law, Hindu Rao, who then wielded much influence in the *darbār* and who seems to have developed some admiration and respect for Sayyid Ahmad.[51] The party then proceeded to Tonk where Nawāb Amir Khan and his son Waziru'd Dawlah (1834-64) extended hospitality and financial help. It may be noted here that Tonk served as a very important source of financial support to the movement and a safe place of refuge for its members. It was to Tonk that the family members of Sayyid Ahmad were brought for a safe stay after the disaster at Balakote. The Nawābs treated them with great respect and arranged for their housing and maintenance. Other parties of Wahhabis, commonly called *Sādaāt-i Qāfila,* continued to pass through Tonk and they were settled in a large, open area close to the palace which came to be known as *Bazār-i Qāfila.*[52] Sayyid Ahmad maintained contact with the Nawābs subsequently too. Some of his letters written to them, including an important one regarding transfer of money through one Muhammad Ishaq of Delhi, are extant. Proceeding from Tonk, and marching through the deserts of Rajputana and Sind, the party reached Peshawar in 1826.

The campaigns of Sayyid Ahmad were fought mostly in the areas comprising the old Hazara and Peshawar districts and the adjacent tribal areas of Swat and Buner. These can be broadly divided into those directed (i) against the Sikh government and (ii) the local Pathan chiefs who had turned hostile. For the sake of convenience these have been examined briefly in the chronological order.

From Peshawar Sayyid Ahmad moved on to the neighbouring Yusuffzai[53] country and stayed at Hashtnagar[54] and Nowshera. His arrival generated a great political fervour and enthusiasm, which put the Sikh *darbār* on its guard and a Sikh army of 10,000[55] under General Budh Singh, a cousin of Maharaja Ranjit Singh and one of the best Sikhs generals, was sent to watch the situation. In the ensuing encounter, which took place at Akora [56] on 20th December 1826 the Sikhs lost 500 men,[57] but in spite of the initial success of the Wahhabis, the Sikh rallied again and the former suffered a setback.

Shortly after, Khade Khan, the chief of Hund[58] joined Sayyid Ahmad, took *Bai'at,* and invited Sayyid Ahmad to stay at Hund which became the first organised centre of the Wahhabis. Khande Khan suggested attacking Hazru,[59] a commercial centre of the Sikhs at night. He was motivated by the prospect of plunder, but Sayyid Ahmad's aims were quite different and he dissociated himself from the move. The tribesmen, however, organised a typical tribal raid and were chased out by the Sikhs. The retreat would have turned into a disaster but for the timely support given by the Wahhabis who covered the withdrawal and saved the tribesmen from much loss of life. The divergence of attitude, shown on this occasion, worked as a great handicap to Sayyid Ahmad's plan of action and upset his military calculations again and again. He felt that it was necessary to assume effective control of the movement. It involved a rather technical religio-political decision— the declaration of *Imāmat.*

The *Imām* had to possess certain qualifications, the details of which do not concern us here. The conditions on the Frontier necessitated the election of a leader with full, plenary powers. Sayyid Ahmad was accordingly elected *Imām* (1827). Explaining the position, he wrote, in a letter[60] addressed to his followers in British India, "The strangest part of the situation is that on both the occasions (the battles of Akora and Hazru) the *mujāhidīn* acted like a leaderless band and in matters of marching and campaigning also acted in a disorganised manner. It was accordingly decided by all those present at the time, faithful followers, Sayyids, learned doctors of law, nobles and generality of Muslims that the successful establishment of *jihād* and the dispelling of disbelief and disorder could not be achieved without the election of an *Imām*." The declaration of *Imāmat* was followed by the *Bai'at* of several important chiefs and several thousands of tribesmen. Yar Muhammad and Pir Muhammad in charge of the Peshawar area also took *Bai'at* by correspondence. The sincerity of these two was doubted by some but Sayyid Ahmad took them at their word. He felt that these chiefs, after years of internal dissensions and defeat at the hands of the Sikhs, were suffering from a sense of uncertainty and frustration. Being united for a common objective would instil confidence among them and stabilise their wavering allegiance. Soon after the Wahhabis moved towards Nowshera where Budh Singh was still encamped. In the ensuing battle of Shaidu, situated to the south of Akora, the Peshawar chiefs were won over by Budh Singh and they deserted the Wahhabis. There followed a period of great privation and suffering, owing to the short supply of men and materials from India. The Wahhabis abandoned the centre at Hund and moved for some time from one place to another until they finally settled at Panjtar.[61]

Sayyid Ahmad sent letters to the rulers of Chitral, Kashmir and Bukhara. Meanwhile, he received overtures of cooperation from the chiefs of the Hazara area which was seething with discontent against the oppressive rule of Hari Singh Nalwa, the Sikh general and the governor of Hazara. If the area could be brought under control the road to Kashmir would be open. Kashmir occupied an important place in Sayyid Ahmad's plan of action. Its occupation would have given him control of an extensive area with ample resources, a large majority of Muslim population and a strong line of natural defence, secure against Sikh incursions. It would have provided him with a stable base for further operations. In a letter written earlier to Shah Sulaiman of Kashghar he had referred to his intention of proceeding to Kashmir after tackling the Peshawar chiefs, and also to the promise of aid from the ruler of Chitral. Shah Ismail was deputed to the Pakhli area,[62] and he led some raids on the Sikh military outposts, of which the one at Shinkiari, [63] where he dispersed a large Sikh force with a small famished party, is the most notable. Soon after, Sayyid Ahmad moved to Khahar,[64] where Abdul Hayy, ailing since some time, died on the 24th February, 1828.

In dealing with the Durrani chiefs Sayyid Ahmad was faced with a rather ironical situation. He loathed the idea of fighting against the very people whose cooperation he had sought and whose lot he wanted to improve. But their continued hostility forced his hands, and there followed the battle of Usmanzai (1828). During the battle, a party of Wahhabis captured some cannons from the Durranis and used them effectively against the latter. The *Waqāi*[65] records the interesting case of a Rajput named Raja Ram, resident of Baiswara, who fought in the Wahhabi force on this occasion. At one stage, when the Wahhabis had been ordered to withdraw from one sector under the cover of darkness, he was left alone with the cannons. He kept on firing them throughout the night so that the enemies might think that the Wahhabis were still there. The next morning he abandoned the cannons, which were recaptured by the Durranis, and joined the Wahhabis.

Although the Durrani chiefs were defeated in the battle of Usmanzai, the advance on Peshawar had to be abandoned due, once again, to the defection of the tribesmen who were expected to help. In order to obtain a more firm support from the tribesmen and their chiefs a big gathering was organised at Panjtar (1829). A fresh undertaking was obtained from all those present that they would administer their principalities according to the laws of the *Shariat*' and would give up the 'customary' practices, such as family feuds, usury, polygamy, distribution of a deceased man's wife and children among his brothers, etc. The extent of success in this regard was, however, rather limited.

Panjtar now became the chief centre of the Wahhabis. This was resented by Khade Khan of Hund, who started harassing the bands of volunteers coming from India who had to pass through his principality. He also entered into negotiation with General Ventura, who had been sent to the Frontier by the Sikh *Darbār* for the usual collection of revenues, for an attack on Panjtar. Eventually, he was defeated and killed in the battle of Hund (August, 1829) and the Wahhabis occupied the strong strategic fort of Hund. Their position however, was not secure, as they were expecting a retaliatory attack by the Durranis whose help was sought by the relatives of the deceased chief.

The *Waqāi*[66] notes a significant conversation on this occasion between Sayyid Ahmad and one Sayyid Ahmad Ali regarding the advantages of the cannon. The latter remarked that he had been suggesting that some cannons should be cast, or a few purchased locally. Had there been some cannons, they could have set them upon the fort and face the Durranis on equal terms—cannon for cannon and gun for gun. Sayyid Ahmad replied that his faith was in God, not cannons and guns.[67]

The attack led by the relatives of Khade Khan and Yar Muhammad took place a little later, but their joint force was defeated in the battle of Zeda[68] (September, 1829) and Yar Muhammad was killed. A possible advance on Peshawar by the Wahhabis was averted due to the presence of General Ventura, who had gone there for the collection of tribute.

After the battle Sayyid Ahmad moved out of Panjtar, and stayed for some time at Khabal,[69] where he came into contact with the Sayyid chiefs of Sittana.[70] He was invited to Sittana where Sayyid Akbar Shah and members of his family took *Bai'at.* Meanwhile, Painda Khan Tanaoli,[71] the chief of Amb,[72] also sent messages to Sayyid Ahmad expressing a desire to meet him. His had been an eventful career. His succession had synchronised with the advance of Sikh power in that area, and he had been holding his own against them. He was valiant, but years of unequal struggle against a wily opponent had dimmed the finer traits of his character. Sayyid Ahmad was interested in obtaining his cooperation because his principality occupied a strategic position on the way to Kashmir. A detachment was sent under Shah Isma'il to move towards Kashmir through Amb, but its request for passage was refused strangely enough on the plea that it would antagonise the Sikhs. Sayyid Ahmad decided to force his way and Painda Khan was compelled to let the Wahhabis pass through Amb. The prospects for an advance on Kashmir were further improved by the offer of help from Zamin Shah of Kawai in the Kaghan valley,[73] adjacent to Kashmir. A detachment was sent under the command of Sayyid Ahmad Ali, nephew of Sayyid Ahmad, to Phulera[74] but it was taken by surpirse by the Sikh army and suffered heavy losses, including the leader of the unit.

The activities of Sayyid Ahmad were by now causing some concern to the Sikh *darbār* and Mahārājā Ranjit Singh sent a force under Sher Singh, Allard and Ventura.[75] At the same time he sent a diplomatic mission, consisting of his close and trusted adviser *Ḥakīm* 'Azizu'din and his relative, Wazir Singh, to Sayyid Ahmad. They offered an area on 'this' side of the Indus river, yielding a revenue of Rs. 9 lakhs, as also the *na'lbandī* (horse-shoer's free, a special impost collected by the Sikhs) of the area on the other side, where Sayyid Ahmad was then staying.[76] This was not what Sayyid Ahmad had been striving for, and nothing came of the negotiations. It may be recalled here that earlier too General Ventura and Budh Singh had written or sent word to Sayyid Ahmad enquiring as to why he had moved into the Frontier area and whether he wanted to carve out a principality for himself. They had pointed out to him the hopelessness of his position, but Sayyid Ahmad had replied that territorial acquisition was an idea farthest from his mind, that he had gone to the Frontier area with a mission, and that in the pursuit of the mission it did not matter to him whether he lacked resources or whether his adversary was more powerful.[77]

The *Waqai'*[78] records that a party of 50 Dogras, headed by a *jama'dār* had joined the Wahhabi army after leaving the Mahārājā's service due to some personal grievance. When the diplomatic mission from the Lahore *Darbār*, mentioned above, called upon Sayyid Ahmad it also brought letters for the Dogras, offering them re-employment on increased salary. They returned to the Mahārājā ater obtaining Sayyid Ahmad's permision.

At this stage Sayyid Ahmad's position was comparatively stable though not very secure. Friendly contacts had been established with many tribal chiefs but the enforcement of certain socio-religious measures by the Wahhabis was resented by some of the chiefs and other vested interests. The promised amount of *'Ushr*[79] had not been sent by some chiefs and an attempt to collect it by force fomented further trouble. The chief of Hoti Mardan, who was chastised in this connection, joined Sultan Muhammad, the brother of Yar Muhammad, and instigated him against the Wahhabis. In the ensuing battle of Mayar (1830) Sultan Muhammad was defeated and Peshawar finally came under the control of the Wahhabis. A cross-section of the local people, *'ulamā* and gentry, *Seths* and *Sāhūkārs* (Hindu businessmen and money-lenders) made their submission. They were all consoled and assured of protection, including the *'ulamā* who had issued a *fatwa* declaring Sayyid Ahmad a *kāfir*. Not wanting to get too entangled in local politics, Sayyid Ahmad restored the government of Peshawar to Sultan Muhammad, after ignoring the requests of local *Khāns*, *Seths* and *Sāhūkārs* not to do so. Some persons were, however, appointed with supervisory powers for the implementation of the injuctions of the *Sharī'at*. *Muḥassils* were appointed in different *mauḍā'* and *parganas* for collection of *'ushr* and the *Khāns* began to pay it regularly. *Qāḍīs* were also appointed, Mazhar Ali being appointed *Qāḍī* of Peshawar. [80] By and large, the autonomy of the local chief remained unaffected. The decision was in accordance with Sayyid Ahmad's long-term objectives. Any other course would have resulted in prolonged conflict with Sultan Muhammad and would have retarted the achievement of the real mission. But the gesture was neither appreciated nor reciprocated. Sultan Muhammad and some other chiefs began to organise secretly a general uprising. Certain religious charges were fabricated against the Wahhabis, and some of the measures enforced by them were utilised for inciting the people. The conspirators' task was rendered easier because the Wahhabis, owing to the extended area of their influence, were scattered at several places. Uprisings occurred at all the places where the Wahhabis were stationed. A beginning was made with Peshawar where Mazhar Ali [81] and his associates were killed. Other parties were similarly set upon and murdered. Only a few managed to escape to Panjtar to tell the sad story. Sayyid Ahmad had suffered a military as well as an emotional setback, and at one stage he even thought of moving out from the Frontier area to Sind where his family members were staying but was persuaded to stay on.

Towards the end of 1830 Sayyid Ahmad left Panjtar and moved out north, to the Kaghan valley. Next January he arrived at Rajduari, a strategic place commanding the passes into the Pakhli plains. The nearby pass of Bhogarmarg,[82] a military outpost of the Sikhs, was occupied. An attempt was also made to capture Muzaffarabad but it failed, once again, due to the defection of the local ally, Zabardast Khan. The detachment was recalled to Balakote,[83] where Sayyid Ahmad had arrived in April 1831. Sher Singh, having heard of the attack on Muzaffarabad, had immediately returned from Peshawar, but on finding that the Wahhabis had left it and assembled at Balakote, he also moved there. He perhaps intended to have a final showdown with the full Wahhabi force assembled there.

IV. The Battle of Balakote and the Death of Sayyid Ahmad: A Re-appraisal

A detailed discussion of the battle of Balakote (May, 1831) has been presented by Mehr and A.H. Nadvi[84] on the basis of the accounts given in the *Waqāi*[85] and the *Manzūra.*[86] These accounts, though detailed and reliable, are lacking in some respects, particularly in regard to the events of the last few hours of the battle, the manner of the death of Sayyid Ahmad, his burial, etc. This is understandable, for almost all of Sayyid Ahmad's associates, who were fighting with him, died in that battle. Those who survived, and were called upon to recall and record their reminiscences, died not much later. It may also be pointed out by some that these sources present the Wahhabis version of the events.

Fortunately, it is possible to check this account with some other equally reliable sources. We have, first, the completely unnoticed account prepared by Mahtab Singh,[87] who was posted at Hazara as a revenue officer from 1824 to 1854, and wrote a histroy of the Hazara district at the instance of James Abbott, the first British Deputy Commissioner, in 1854, in which he gives a long account of the battle. Then, there are the news reports of the Lahore *darbār* about the battle, extracts from which were forwarded to the Government of India by their Political Assistant at Ludhiana, C.R. Wade.[88] These were written immediately after the event, and present the other, Sikh, version of the event. Finally, there is the graphic eye-witness account, completely unnoticed so far, of Gardner, a European soldier of fortune who happened to arrive as the battle was raging and saw Sayyid Ahmad falling down fighting.

Each one of these sources has its own merit. The *Waqāi*'and the *Manzūra* are very rich in detail. To the Wahhabis the battle represented their finest hour, and they wanted to recapitulate and record it in full. To Mahtab Singh, the battle represented an important event in the history of the area where he had lived and worked, and of which he was preparing an historical account at the instance of his English employer, James Abbott. Writing under the aegis of the British, he could well afford to take a dispassionate view of the struggle between the two erstwhile opponents of his master. To the Sikh newswriter, the battle marked the removal of a danger, initially perhaps an irritant but assuming a more alarming dimension. The relief and happiness felt by the Lahore *darbār* is evident from the fact that the city of Amritsar was illuminated 'in honour of the event.' The news reports are also important in point of immediacy and nearness of time, as they were drafted soon after the events. A comparative study of these sources is very revealing. While enabling us to hold on to the bedrock of the details provided by the *Waqāi'* and the *Manzūra*, it brings to light additional information, gives us a glimpse of things from the other side, and clarifies many obscure points, particularly those about the manner of Sayyid Ahmad's death. The following pages therefore summarise Mehr's account first, and then, a fuller summary is given of Mahtab Singh, Wade and Gardner's accounts. This is followed by our comments on these different versions.

The account given by Mehr is as follows:

The village of Balakote was situated on an elevation on the western bank of the river Kunhar. The forces of Sher Singh and Sayyid Ahmad faced each other across the river. Sher Singh's camp was located a short distance to the south of Balakote, and he could attack it either by moving up the river and crossing it opposite Balakote, or by ascending the hills from the Pakhli side and rushing down upon the village. He at first chose the former course, but later modified the plan of attack. A part of the army crossed over to the western bank and moved up the Matikot hillock, while another part remained on the other side, as before. The Matikot hillock, situated to the west of Balakote, slopes gradually towards the south until on reaching village Pooriyan it almost levels off. The village Matikot is situated in the northern portion of the hillock and commands the approach to Balakote.

Between Matikot hillock and the inhabited part of Balakote there was a low-lying area which had been watered and made slushy by the Wahhabis with a view to hampering the advance of the Sikhs, should they come that way. A guard had also been placed to protect the secret path leading up the hillock, but the Sikhs were told about it by some local people and they overwhelmed the party guarding it before any reinforcement could be sent, and occupied the hillock. It was a tactical blow to the Wahhabis' plan, and it exposed Balakote to an attack from a new side. As the day of the battle dawned (28 *Dhīqa'd*, 1246 or 6 May, 1831) Sayyid Ahmad ordered his followers to let the Sikhs come up the high ground on which the houses stood. It was as good a plan as could be chalked out under the circumstances. When the Sikhs started coming down the hills, the Wahhabis stood their ground as planned. Then, suddenly, Sayyid Ahmad himself took the lead and dashed out with some followers towards the foothills. The battle was joined. The small band of Wahhabis split up in even smaller groups and lost contact with each other. The battle was a pitched one and fought at close quarters. Sayyid Ahmad fell down fighting bravely at the foot of the hills. No one actually saw him fall, all those fighting around him having died along with him.

Following the battle, Sher Singh searched for the dead body of his adversary. A headless body was brought before him which, it was said, was that of Sayyid Ahmad. He tried to get it identified. Later, the head was also found and he got the body buried by the side of the river. The next day he crossed the river on his way back. On the following day some of the Nihangs,[89] who had stayed behind, disentombed the body and threw it in the river. The head and the body were later discovered at two different places, down the river, and were buried at Garhi Habibullah and Telhatta, respectively.[90]

The account given in the *Tawārīkh-i-Hazāra* is as follows :

After the treacherous massacre (of the Wahhabis stationed at different places) Sayyid Ahmad left Panjtar and was brought to Rajduari by Habibullah Khan *Garhiwala*, who was disaffected against the Sikhs. Later Sayyid Ahmad moved into the Kaghan valley. He let it be known that he intended to advance to Kashmir and started giving *jāgīrs* in Kashmir to Habibullah Khan and some other chiefs. On hearing about Sayyid Ahmad's advance towards Kashmir Mahārājā Ranjit Singh felt disturbed and deputed Sher Singh with 8000 men and some guns to tackle the situation. Among the other chiefs, who were in Sher Singh's army, were Sardar Atar Singh Kalianwala, Sardar Shyam Singh Nahang, Sardar Pratap Singh Atariwala, Sardar Ratan Singh Garjakia, Sadhu Singh Kanhal, Ratan Singh Kunglu, Wazir Singh Rangharikalia, Gurmukh Singh Lahna and Lakhmir Singh, the uncle of Jwala Singh Bhidanu.[91] This army was engaged in settling the affairs of Yusufzai area. Having collected the revenues and the horses, Sher Singh, passing through Hazara, encamped at Shinkiari in Pakhli. Sayyid Ahmad was then at Bhogarmang some 16-20 miles rom Shinkiari. It was resolved by the Sikh chiefs that their assignment was to prevent the Wahhabis from creating disturbances in the area belonging to the *darbār*. Sayyid Ahmad was then in Bhogarmang which belonged to the *jāgīrs* of Sardar Hari Singh who, it was argued, should take care of him, while they should proceed to Muzaffarbad. Sardar Mahan Singh[92] objected to the plan and pointed out that it would be a mistake to proceed to Muzaffarabad without tackling Sayyid Ahmad first, but he was overruled. Sher Singh proceeded to Muzaffarabad and the beseiged fortress was relieved.

Meanwhile, Sayyid Ahmad moved on to Balakote and the local people offered allegiance to him. Mahan Singh (who had been left behind with a small force) wrote to Sher Singh that Sayyid Ahmad's men were collecting the revenues and the local people were joining them. How then could he support his troops? Sher Singh ordered Mahan Singh to withdraw with his troops and those of Wazir Singh Rangharikalia and Sadhu Singh Kanhal and Ratan Singh Kunglu to the *Garhi* (Garhi Habibullah). All these men numbered about 800. On reaching the *Garhi* (a few miles south of Balakote) Mahan Singh started repairing the fortress known as Fatahgarh. While the repairs were going on a rumour reached them that their opponents intended makig a surprise raid after crossing the river. Worried, the Sikhs dug up trenches, surrounded them with thorny bushes, and made a great din and bustle by firing their guns and by blowing conches and running to and fro. At the same time they sent a messenger to convey news of their plight, seeking reinforcements that very night. Sher Singh immediately ordered his troops to proceed to *Garhi* Habibullah. The hard-pressed Sikhs who had passed the night in great consternation were relieved to see the reinforcement columns next morning. The fortress was fully repaired during the next sixteen days. After that the Sikhs moved their camp to Phallakot, situated six miles from Balakote on the eastern side of the river. The commanders of the two armies kept a steady watch on each other from their respective encampments between which ran the river. Sher Singh often rode up with his officers to a point opposite Balakote and inspected the enemy's camp by binoculars.

One day Sayyid Ahmad got some grain scattered near his dwelling as a result of which a large number of birds flocked near the place. At the same time he sent some 500 men across the river to lay in hiding in the forests near the Sikh encampment. When Sher Singh, during the course of his daily watch on the enemy's camp, saw a large number of birds hovering on the other side he thought that the Wahhabis had withdrawn. He sent a reconnaissance party to the other side to report. The party was ambushed by the Wahhabis. Only two men somehow swam across the river and escaped.

Sher Singh once again took counsel on how to attack the enemy. It was resolved that part of the army should remain where it was to guard the camp. The rest crossed the river at a convenient spot and, passing through Basiyan, got a foothold on the Matikot hillock. The

Hazara and Shinkiari contingents also reached atop the hillock by another route through Tamri.(?) The small party of the Wahhabis who were deputed to guard the secret path leading to the top were overwhelmed. Three or four of them were killed while the rest fled. A relief column sent by Sayyid Ahmad arrived too late to be of any help to the small guard and returned. The Sikh spent the night on the top of the hillock. On reaching the top the Sikh faced great dificulties. There was no water to be had anywhere. But luck came their way. There was thunderstorm and a shower of hailstorms fell on their camps.

Next morning (27 *Baisākh,* 1887 *Samvat,* corresponding to 7 May, 1831)[93] the attack commenced. Originally it was decided that the hill-top should be guarded by a small force. So Mohan Singh with the Hazara army and Lakhmir Singh, uncle of Jwala Singh Phindana, were sent to attack the Wahhabis while the rest were to remain on the top and send reinforcements as the situation developed. Shyam Singh Atariwala, however, pointed out that it would not look nice at the time of reporting victory (if they won) that only those two Sardars had fought nor would it look better in the case of defeat. Moreover, if they were defeated the rest could not hope to return to Lahore acros the enemy-held territories. So it was decided that they should attack together.

At the foot of the Matikot hillock there was a low ground beyond which stood, on an elevation, the village of Balakote where Sayyid Ahmad and his followers were waiting, ready with their bows and arrows and matchlocks *(zambooraks).* An exchange of fire commenced between the two sides. The Sikhs had brought a cannon from Kashmir. They set it down and started firing shells. The standard-bearers of both Mahan Singh's and Jwala Singh's troops were shot down by the Wahhabis and as the standard fell other Sikhs rallied to hold them aloft. On seeing the standard falling all the Wahhabis, who were inside, came out. Sayyid Ahmad himself and Maulvi Ismail led the attack and dashed towards the low lands which lay between the two armies. They called out that the enemy was falling back, and now was the time to attack. Other parties of Wahhabis too started towards the hillock where the troops of Sardar Attar Singh Kalianwala and Gurmukh Singh Lahna stood. Those of Mahan Singh and Kunwar Sher Singh also arrived there and the battle was joined.

At first the Sikhs started falling back. Sher Singh drew out his sword and wanted to go to the battleground himself. Mahan Singh and others asked him not to go along but he did not listen to them and started rallying the Sikhs. He abused and threw stones at the retreating Sikhs and thrust them back in the battle field. He sent a messenger to Shyam Singh and Pratap Singh ordering them to start firing their guns and sent another person to Atter Singh for the same purpose. They started firing. As many as 187 Wahhabis along with the *Khalīfa* fell to the ground. The *Khalīfa's* dead body bore marks of gun-shot bullet injuries on the right hand and on the chest below the left nipple. Another 400 Hindustanis who adored Sayyid Ahmad also fell.

The remaining Wahhabis, numbering some eighty-odd persons, made three attempts to take away the body of their leader but they failed due to heavy firing. At last one Wahhabi cut off his head and ran with it.[94] That man was shot and finding it impossible to go further with the head he hid it in a heap of harvested mustard plants.

The Sikhs entered the village and looted and burnt the house of Sayyid Ahmad and others. Eight guns *(zambooraks)*, one elephant, ten horses and ten mules were captured.

Sher Singh on inspecting the battlefield saw the dead body of Sayyid Ahmad and thinking it to be of some chief he took it to his camp and asked his men to arrange for its identification.[95] Nawab Khan Tanaoli, who had been with Sayyid Ahmad for some years, was brought before Sher Singh. He said it was difficult to identify without the head but pointed out that Sayyid Ahmad's body bore some marks of personal identification—the nails of his toes were 'deformed' *(nāqis)*. On lifting the shroud it was seen that the nails of the toes were deformed. Some doubt, however, still remained. In the meantime a servant of Alam Khan Tanaoli came forward to say that he could disclose the whereabouts of the *Khalīfa's* head if he were given a reward of twenty-five rupees. Sher Singh at once gave him Rs. 25/- and deputed 25 *Sawārs* and 50 foot soldiers to go with him. The servant pointed out the hidden head. The head was put along with the body and Nawab Khan Tanaoli was again called and he duly identified it. The body was handed over to some Muslims who were among the camp-followers of the Sikh army. The recited the *Qurān* for the whole night and on the next day having obtained orders from Sher Singh buried the body in a grave by the side of the river Kunhar. Sher Singh departed on the next day. Sardar Mahan Singh and Lakhmir Singh were ordered to supervise the withdrawal of troops to

Garhi Habibullah and to follow after all the troops had crossed the river. During Sher Singh's absence the two *Sardārs* conspired among themselves. Sayyid Ahmad has caused them enough trouble in his lifetime and if his dead body was allowed to remain in a grave, the Muslims would make it a 'centre-of worship.' It would, therefore, be better if it was disentombed and thrown in the river. There were 7 or 8 Nahang Sikh standing by, and the two *Sardārs* gave them rupees twenty-five and told them that they would be performing a good deed if they disentombed the *Khalīfa's* body and threw it in the river. They did so immediately and having cut up the body in several pieces threw them into the river. Having done the deed the two *Sardārs* marched to Nowshera and thereafter they along with Sher Singh entered Lahore.

Wade, forwarding extracts from the reports of the *darbār* news writers, reported to the Government of India as follows: "Despatches (have) arrived from Kuer Sher Singha and Bheman Singh (Mahan Singh ?) Governor of Cashmere, stating that having obtained information of Sayed Ahmad being at Doobh... they left their position and engaged him. As the troops of the State were ignorant of the strongholds and passes of these hills they were defeated with the loss of nearly 300 men and about the same number wounded. At length finding it impossible to maintain contact they retreated seven and eight *kos* and encamped. They added that it was their intention to resume the offensive immediately but the grain was dear in their camps, five small seers of wheat for the rupee. On hearing the intelligence the Mahārājā sent for his astrologers, Sankernath and Madosoden and after explaining the affairs desired them to ascertain by astrology whether Kuer Singh would be victorious or not in his intended attack. They replied that they would enquire and let him know."[96]

Wade added that since the foregoing information was sent, letters had been received in the *darbār* announcing the "entire defeat" of the fanatics. "Syed Ahmad had taken post in a strong place called Balakote where Sher Singh proceeded to attack him. The Syed left his position to receive the attack and was overpowered.... The Syed's body was identified and was burnt by the Sikhs."

In a subsequent letter, Wade reported, "A dispatch arrived from Kuer Sher Singh that Syed Ahmad having with a force of two or three thousand men consisting chiefly of peasantry of the country established himself across the *nullah* at Malakote (Balakote?). He advanced about noon on the 8th inst., aided by some zamindars of that part of the country, with the force of Pratap Singh Attariwala, Ratan Singh Gharchaker and other Sardars amounting about 5 thousand men and crossing the *nullah*... took the enemy by surprise and investing them on all sides drew their swords from the scabbards and killed Syed with five hundred people taking their tents and baggage, an elephant, several swivels, swords, the rest of the party seeking their safety in fight."[97]

Finally, we have the brief but very important eye-witness account of Alexander Haughton Gardner, a European soldier of fortune, who happened to be present at the site. He was earlier in the court of *Mīr* 'Alam Khan with his 'trusty band of Khaibaris' when Shah Isma'il arrived there to seek the Khan's help against the Sikhs. He decided to join the Shah and marched towards Balakote. The latter had marched ahead quickly in his anxiety to 're-join his master' (Sayyid Ahmad)' and Gardner was left one march behind, and was further delayed 'by the mistake or treachery of a guide'. He arrived on the scene 'just an hour too late,' and saw the battle raging in full fury. He was 'literally within a few hundred yards of the Syed' and saw him falling down fighting. He describes the scene as follows: "I well remember the scene as I and my Yusufzai and Khaibari followers came in view of the action. Syed Ahmad and the *Moulvi* (Shah Isma'il), surrounded by the surviving Indian followers, were fighting desperately, hand-to-hand, with the equally fanatical Akalis of the Sikh army. They had been taken by surprise, and isolated from the main body of the Syed's forces, which fought very badly without their leader. Even as I caught sight of the Syed and the *Moulvi*, they fell down pierced by a hundred weapons.... Those around him were slain to a man, and the main body dispersed in every direction."[98]

A comparative study of the these different sources shows that the version given in the *Tawārīkh-i-Hazāra* enables a better understanding of some of the events of the battle. It explains the sudden crucial decision of Sayyid Ahmad to move out of the entrenched positions across the lowlands near the foot of Matikot. It was probably the sight of the two falling standard-bearers of the Sikhs which made the Wahhabis rush out, thinking that the Sikhs were about to retreat. Mehr writes that the decision was surprising, and it has been regarded by some as the cause of the Wahhabi's defeat. But he defends it by saying that the previous plan was abandoned possibly because the Sikhs started advancing from the south also and started a cannonade across the river. He admits that this explanation has no facts in support, but is the most likely one under the circumstances. The reason stated in the *Tawārīkh-i-Hazāra* is another, more likely one. Wade's account provides some additional information and refers to an initial reverse suffered by the Sikhs and the casualties sufffered by them.

Gardner's account of the last moments of the battle also confirms the broad sequence of events— that as the battle progressed, Sayyid Ahmad and some of his followers who had pushed ahead in the enemy's ranks were surrounded and isolated, and they all fell fighting to a man.

We also get some idea of the number and composition of the troops on the two sides, their arms, etc. Sher Singh had the advantage of a large number of troops and a cannon. Sayyid Ahmad's men numbered around 3000, while Sher Singh's men numbered some 5000. We also get the interesting information that while the former consisted mostly of the local peasantry aided by the 'Hindustani' (British Indian Muslims who had migrated), Sher Singh's troops were accompanied by the zamindars' contingents. The main weapon used on both sides were the swords, but there were some guns too on both the sides. The Sikhs probably had a larger number of guns, and had the decisive advantage of a cannon. Sayyid Ahmad's body bore multiple marks of gunshot wounds.

As for the date of the battle, three different dates, 6, 7 and 8 May (1831) have been given in three different accounts. The last mentioned date is the most acceptable one, as it is given in a source nearest in time to the date of occurrence.

The events concerning the last moments of Sayyid Ahmad's life are shrouded in mystery. This had led to a controversy regarding his actual end. He was last seen fighting in the thick of a pitched, hand-to-hand battle, and then disappeared. Nobody actually saw him falling down. It led a section of the Wahhabis to believe that Sayyid Ahmad had not died but 'disappeared', and would reappear at a future date. The Wahhabi sources are silent on the point because those who were around Sayyid Ahmad at the time did not survive. But the other two sources are quite definite about his death, though they differ in regard to the manner of the death and the disposal of the body.

It is clear that Sayyid Ahmad certainly died in that battle.To the survivors of Balakote and to a great many of his followers, however, it was a bitter and sudden shock, difficult to absorb. They had sacrificed all their earthly belongings and suffered untold hardships for the achievement of a mission under his leadership. Now by a sudden and stunning turn of fortune all that was on the verge of being lost.

The theory of 'disappearance' has to be viewed against this background. It was essentially an emotional reaction, an inability to believe in the death and removal of their cherished leader from the scene of his earthly operations. It also represented, symbolically, a fervent belief, not necessarily in his actual life but in the continuance of his mission.

The death of Adolf Hitler and Subhas Chandra Bose are contemporary examples. Their deaths, too, were shrouded in mystery. In spite of a thorough enquiry into the death of the former, aided by latest scientific methods of investigation, and the repeated finding of the Government of India, in the case of the latter, belief in the survival of these two leaders still persists among a section of their compatriots. If political leaders could inspire such persistent devotion and loyalty, one can imagine the fervour and attachment generated among his followers by one who was not only a religious and political leader but the very personification, to them, of all that was noble and ideal.

Wilayat Ali, in particular, has been criticised both by some English[99] and Indian[100] writers for the propagation of the 'theory of reappearance' of Sayyid Ahmad. The step has been depicted as one motivated by a desire to keep alive the ebbing fortunes of the movement, and to maintain his own leadership of it. Actually, this belief was a momentary emotional reaction. The services of Wilayat Ali and his brother Enayat Ali to the movement were too substantial to be supported by such a weak prop of doubtful advantage.

The intensity of belief in this 'doctrine' diminished with the passage of time. A document[101] dated 1845, specifically states that by the time Enayat Ali first assumed the leadership of the movement (1844), belief in this 'doctrine' had ceased to be a matter of cardinal importance. People could believe in it if they were so inclined, but there was no pressure to do so, nor was there any stigma attached to those who did not believe in it. The same transformation of attitude also occurred in the case of the author of Sawāniḥ, who was earlier a believer in this doctrine but with the passage of time had lost faith[102] in it. Mahmud Husain, taking Wade's remarks about Sayyid Ahmad's body having been burnt by some Akalies as correct, suggests that since the body was not discovered, the theory of 'dis-appearance' came into vogue.[103]

V. Effects of Sayyid Ahmad's Frontier Campaigns

Sayyid Ahmad's activities on the North-western Frontier and his campaigns against the Sikhs and the Pathan chiefs have either been neglected or altogether ignored in most of the general works on the history of the Sikhs, and the Punjab.[104] The foregoing account, however, shows that the threat caused to the Lahore *Darbār* was not insignificant.

The defeat and death of Sayyid Ahmad brought great relief to the *darbār*. Wade, in his above-mentioned report wrote, "Ranjit Singh is elated with joy at a victory which relieved him of a constant source of agitation and inquietitude to his government. He ordered a Royal Salute to be fired and the city of Amritsar to be illuminated in honour of the event." The messenger bringing the happy news was awarded "a pair of golden bracelets valued at Rs. 300/-, besides a turban and a pair of shawls." A letter was despatched to the Kunwar (Sher Singh) acknowledging the receipt of his dispatch and the important services he had rendered and promising an additional *jāgīr* to him after his return. Faqir Imamuddin, governor of Govindgarh, was at the same time ordered to fire a salute of two guns from that fortress. The Government of India also instructed[105] their Political Assistant to offer the congratulations of the Governor General to His Highness (Mahārājā Ranjit Singh) on the 'final extinction' of the commotion excited by that individual (Sayyid Ahmad).

The most substantial result of Sayyid Ahmad's work was the establishment of a strong base in the independent tribal area. It suffered a setback after his death but was revived and activated by his followers, and made stronger and better organised. Another important, if unintended, repercussion was in regard to the Sind area.

Ever since the Treaty of 1809, Ranjit Singh had been casting his eyes towards Sind, particularly Shikarpur, which provided a connecting point between the overland trade route from Qandahar to Central Asia and the Indus riverine route from Punjab to the sea. The British Government in the beginning confined itself to watching the Sikh moves in this connection without having any definite policy of its own. P.N. Khera in his brief but brilliant work has succinctly summed up the position thus : "The decade from 1820 to 1830 was, with one minor exception in 1825, marked by what may be called non-interference coupled with keen watchfulness. From 1825, when Ranjit Singh's army was well-organised, until the early years of Lord William Bentinck's period, when the British Government changed its policy of non-interference and developed further interest in Sindh in pursuit of a peaceful commercial projects, Ranjit Singh could have attacked Sind and probably seized a portion of that country without inviting even a British protest, let alone British interference."[106] In fact, the British were not then interested in Sind. Realising this Ranjit Singh even made preparations for the projected advance on the plea of demanding tribute which the *Amīrs* paid to the Afghan ruler, to which Ranjit Singh claimed succession. His plan was, however, thwarted owing to the emergence of a new danger in the N.W.F. Province. "A formidable foe of the Sikhs, the fanatic Syed Ahmad, offered armed opposition and engaged the whole attention of the Sikh ruler for several years. Thus though the Sayed was finally defeated and killed by Kunwar Sher Singh in 1831, he had indirectly saved Sind from falling into the hands of the 'infidels'." [107] By 1831, when Ranjit Singh was relieved of this danger he found that the English attitude towards Sind had changed.

To conclude, Sayyid Ahmad was deeply moved by the prevailing socio-religious and political conditions, and was convinced of the urgent need for reforms. This need had been felt and the call for reforms given by others before him, particularly by Shah Waliullah. In fact, the impact of the latter's ideas upon Sayyid Ahmad is quite evident.

Basically a fundamentalist in his ideas, Sayyid Ahmad was considerably influenced by *Sūfi* ideas and practices. His *Sirāt-i Mustaqīm* is somewhat on the lines of the Indo-Persian *Malfūz* literature. It discusses various spiritual matters and procedures for contemplation, but also dwells upon a topic not generally discussed in such works—*jihād*. He conceived of it both in a moral and physical sense. Further, a happy combination of spiritual enlightenment and practical efficiency distinguishes him from the Sūfis in general. It was this which enabled him to give a practical shape to the ideas of Shah Waliullah and to organise and lead a powerfful movement over a wide area and for a long time.

Sayyid Ahmad showed awareness of the increasing domination of the British. As he wrote, "the rulers and statesmen had fallen into obscurity" and the "foreigners from distant lands had become masters of the times and territories and vendors of merchandise had attained sovereignty."[108] He realised the importance of controlling the levers of political power for implementing his reforms. He rose from a comparatively humble status and strove consistently for the fulfilment of his mission. He perhaps intended returning to his spiritual pursuits on the completion of his mission. In fact, there is a Garibaldian trait in his character.

Sayyid Ahmad's sincerity and dedication is evident from his numerous letters.[109] He was the acknowledged head of a well-knit organisation and held command over a large area, yet he never assumed any temporal power for himself. He drew a clear distinction between the office of an *Imām* and a *Sultān* and reiterated his intention to restore the administrative powers and functions of the ruling chiefs after the completion of his task: the removing of socio-religious evils and the driving away of the *firangis*. As he wrote in one of his letters addressed to Yar Muhammad Khan of Peshawar, "I have neither the desire for obtaining rank, dignity and false prestige, nor the wish for gaining powers of administration, nor did it ever occur into my heart to amass wealth."[110] That this oft-repeated profession was not just a customary pose of humility is evident from his conduct after the fall of Peshawar. His rejection of the earlier offer of Mahārājā Ranjit Singh for the grant of an independent principality in the trans-Sutlej area,[111] in return for cessation of hostilities is another instance in point. Sayyid Ahmad's concept of the State has some interesting features. It envisages the co-existence of the secular authority of the *Sultān* and the religious authority of an *Imām*. The former was to function under the general supervision of the latter.[112] The theory, however, remained in an embryonic stage during his lifetime.

NOTES

1. Situated on the banks of a small river Sai, it was a place of long antiquity, founded by the Bhārs after whom it was originally called Bharauli or Barauli. The prefix Rai was a corruption of Rahi, a village three miles to the west, after which the *pargana* was earlier named. It was wrested from the Bhārs by Ibrahim Shah Sharqi (1400-40) who fortified it and encouraged Muslim settlements. The area formed a part of the Awadh kingdom and it came under

British control after the annexation of Awadh (1856) and was included in the new Salon district. See H.R.Nevill, *Rai Bareli*, district gazetteers of the United Provinces of Agra and Oudh, vol. XXXIX, Allahabad, 1905.

On the eve of the annexation of Awadh, when Sleeman visited Rai Bareli, it formed a part of the Shunkarpoor estate which belonged to Rana Beni Madho, a large landholder. Sleeman found the place healthy, and its water good, and commented on the possibility of its selection as a cantonment (Sleeman op. cit., vol.I, pp. 244,247-48.)

2. *Makhzan-i Aḥmadi*, (K.B.D.P.L., ms. copy) f. 9b. The earliest biography of Sayyid Ahmad written by his nephew and junior contemporary Sayyid Muhammad 'Ali, it is a primary source for his early life.
3. The *Makhzan* (f. 29) refers to a *risāla, Ḥuqiqatu's Salāt*, written by him. Ghulam Rasul Mehr, *Sayyid Ahmad Shahid*, (Urd.), Lahore, n.d. (hereinafter cited as Mehr) vol.I, pp. 418-19 lists some other pamphlets written by him. There is also the *Sirāt-i Mustaqīm*, based on his observations, which bears testimony to his learning.
4. *Makhzan*, f. 11.
5. Ibid., f. 14.
6. O'Kinealy's article, "A Sketch of the Wahhabis in India" cited above, C.R., vol. I, 1870, p. 85.
7. Muhammad Jafar Thanesari, *Sawāniḥ-i Aḥmadī*, Delhi, A.H. 1309 (1891), p. 4.
8. *Makhzan*, ff. 53-52b.
9. For a biographical account see, Prinsep, H.T., *Memoirs of a Pathan Soldier of Fortune, Nawab Amir Khan of Tonk*, Calcutta, 1832.
10. Mehr, 1, p.82, suggests an earlier date, A.H. 1224, but A.H. Nadwi, *Sirat-i Sayyid Ahmad Shahid*, (Urdu), vol.1, Karachi, 1975, p. 105, mentions this date on the basis of the *Waqri*, 'which is more reliable.
11. *Supra*, pp. 14-15.
12. *Makhzan*, 25b - 27b.
13. *Waqāi'* (Tonk ms. No. 1478), ff.16-16b.

    Hunter indirectly confirms this account. He writes that when Amir Khan entered into an alliance with the British he had an army consisting of 52 battalions of disciplined infantry, 150 guns and a numerous body of Pathan cavalry. After the treaty with the British, his Artillery, excluding 40 guns, was purchased and some of his troops enlisted by the British. The rest were disbanded (see, Hunter, *Imperial Gazetteer*, XIII (Tonk), pp. 337-38).
14. Not much information is available in English on their lives and careers. Mir Shahamat Ali's article in the J.R.A.S., vol.XIII, 1852, gives a brief biographical sketch of Shah Ismail and an English

translation of one of his well-known treatises, the *Taqwīyatu'l Imān.* See also p. 372, note 15, below.

15. During one such tour he visited Lucknow at the invitation of the Wazīr of the Awadh. Wilayat 'Ali, who later played a leading role in the revival of the movement, was then studying at Lucknow. Both he and his teacher, Ashraf Ali, met Sayyid Ahmad more out of curiosity than an intention of taking *Bai'at* but they were deeply impressed and took *Bai'at* then and there.
16. S.M., pp. 111.
    The strong epithets used by Sayyid Ahmad for certain types of Sūfis in these extracts is indicative of his very strong feelings on this matter.
    I am deeply indebted to my friend, Professer S.A.A.Kazimi, formerly Head of the Department of Arabic, Patna University, for help and suggestions in translating these extracts.
17. Ibid., p. 112.
18. Ibid., p. 114.
19. Ibid., p. 124.
20. Ibid.,pp. 126-27.
21. Ibid., p. 132.
22. It was presented as an exhibit in the Patna trial of Shah Ahmadullah, vide *infra,* Appendix I. Copy of the original text in Persian is extant and belongs to Zaid Saheb, a member of the family. The special manuscript copy of the *Sirāt-i Mustaqīm,* referred to in the Bibliography also contains its copy. See also Nawab Waziru'd Dawla, *Wasāya al-Wazīr 'alā Tariqatu'l Bashīr, wa'l Nadhīr,* Muhammadi, Tonk, A.H. 1284 (1867-68), pp. 42-43.
23. See Wasāya-i Wazīr, cited above, pp.42-43, wherein the aims and objectives of the Muhammadi Order have been explained in the words as of Sayyid Ahmad himself.
24. *Sawānih,* p. 23.
25. S.M., p.174.
26. Ibid., p. 137. *'Hindustān .. dar īn juzv zamān ke san ek hazār wa dō sad wa sī olh* (A.H. 1233/1817-18) *ast ke aktharash darīn ayyām Dāru'i Ḥarb gardīda.*
27. Ibid., pp. 168 ff.
28. See S.M., p. 164.
29. A *fatwa* (considered opinion by an *'Ālim* on a religious/legal question referred to him for opinion) had been given stating that Ḥajj might not be undertaken if there was some danger to the lives of the intending pilgrims.
30. *Makhzan,* f 52b; *Waqāi'* (Tonk ms. 1478) f. 105.
31. The important particulars about this journey have been taken from the *Makhzan* which is the primary source of information on the

topic, its author being a member of the *Ḥajj* party.

32. The K.B.O.P.L. *ms.* copy gives the date as A.H. 1238 (f. 56b), which is obviously a copyist's mistake. The date of entry into Makkah is given on another folio (86) as 28 *Sha'bān*, 1237, and the date of return to India as 1238 (f. 102b). Obviously, the outward journey commenced in 1236, not 1238.
33. Persons from such far-off places as Sylhet and Chittagong had gone to Calcutta to offer *Bai'at*.
34. *Waqāi'* (Tonk ms. no. 1478) ff. 166-167b.
A similar complaint was made at Patna too on the arrival of the party there.
35. Muhammad Malihabadi, *Mathnawī-i Bēnazīr*, (Tonk ms. no. 1480/2, f. 489).
36. The party consisted of 850 persons of whom 693 were adults, including some women, for whom fare was paid, and 57 *miskīn* (indigent persons) and 100 children for whom no fare was charged. Originally the fare was calculated @ Rs. 16/- per adult, but later the shipowners demanded an additional sum for freight. Finally, it was fixed at Rs. 20/-, the total amount paid for 693 persons being Rs. 13,860/-. The female passengers were accommodated in the lower decks (*dewsa*) of three ships, for which an additional sum of Rs. 1200/- was paid.
The party carried some 6000 maunds of foodgrains; 4000 mds. of rice @ Rs. 8 per md., 100 maunds of *āta* (flour) at Rs. 2/- per md. and 600 mds of *masūr* pulse (it was preferred because it could be cooked with less water and less firwood.) The foodgrains were packed in 2350 double-knitted jute *bastas* (bags) purchased for 1-$^{1}/_{4}$ annas per bag. Cartage for carrying the bags from the city to the ships was 2-$^{1}/_{4}$ annas per bag, and sewing the bag's mouth cost $^{1}/_{4}$ annas per bag. Each bag bore the number 127, it being the numerical value in *Abjad* system of Sayyid Ahmad's name. Each rice bag contained 2 maunds and each adult was allotted two bags for the journey, the children's ration being half of that. Water was carried in metal containers which were distributed among the different ships carrying the party. *Waqāi'* (Tonk ms. no. 1478) ff. 166b-167, 192b.
These statistics, apart from their intrinsic value, give us an idea of the organisational ability of the leader of the party.
37. An important catonment town situated six miles to the west of Patna. The party had also visited the famous *Khānqah* town Phulwari Sharif, situated nearby. Sayyid Ahmad and Abdul Hayy held discussions with the *Sajjādah Nashīn*, Shah Nematulah (Hakim Shuaib, *Diwan-i Fard*, Supplement, Kanpur, A.H. 1332, p. 42; Mehr, 1, pp. 206-7).

38. At Monghyr some pistols and guns, including a four-barrelled one, were purchased, and a local *Mukhtār*, Zakiu'd Din took *Bai'at*. Sayyid Ahmad also went to the nearby village Surajgarh where a large number of Sayyids and Pathans from the neighbouring villages of Akbarnagar, Uren and Bilthu assembled and took *Bai'at*. Among them was Inayat Husain of Uren who continued giving financial help till much later.
39. At Bhagalpur, the party laid anchor at Barari ghat but stayed in the boats and did not go into the town. Only Shah Ismail met the *Sajjādah Nashīn* of the famous 17th century *Khānqah* of *Maulāna* Shahbaz.
Sayyid Ahmad's visits to two of the important *Khānqahs* of the area and the meetings with the *Sajjādah Nashīns* might have been accidental but deserve notice.
40. Mehr, op. cit., Nadwi, op. cit.
41. Both Mehr (1, p.207, note) and Nadwi (op. cit., pp. 241-42) place the event during the outward journey but in the *Waqāi'* itself, on which their accounts were apparently based, this fact has not been specifically mentioned. In the *Waqāi'* the events of both the occasions have been mentioned at one place, and in some cases the events of the return journey have been recorded after adding the word *tukmila* (supplement). Abdul Rahim who was directly connected with the events, places the *Bai'at* of the family members during the second journey. He belonged to the family and could not have made a mistake about this important event.
42. Elahi Bakhsh (1786-1858) was the son of Shaikh Hidayat Ali of village Mehdawan, near Maner. He had held a high post in the service of the Nawabs of Murshidabad, and had received some *jāgīr* on his return home. He married *Bibi* Latifan, daughter of Shah Muhammad Mui'zz and a sister of Shah Muhammad Husain (note 44 below). He had taken *Bai'at* on the hands of Wilayat Ali and was one of his ardent followers. He was a noted philanthropist and a lovr of books (part of whose collection, particularly the books on Medicine as Philosophy, was extant until recently). He was a noted physician, and distributed medicine free. He had a good military training, too. Three of his sons, Ahmadullah, Faiyyaz Ali and Yahya Ali played important roles in the history of the movement. See also, T.S.
43. Fath Ali was the son of Waris Ali, and was connected with the famous saintly family of Makhdum Sharafu'd Din Maneri. He married the daughter of Hidayat Ali of Mehdawan, and after her death the daughter of Rafiu'd Din Husain Khan, a wealthy gentleman of Patna City. Like his brother-in-law, Elahi Bakhsh, three of his sons, Wilayat Ali, Enayat Ali and Farhat Husain, played impor-

tant roles in the histroy of the movement. He wanted to accompany Sayyid Ahmad to the Frontier but was persuaded to stay back on account of his advanced age. See also T.S.

44. He was influential personage in the town. Three of his daughters were married to the three sons of Elahi Bakhsh, Ahmadullah, Faiyyaz Ali and Yahya Ali, respectively.
45. The *Waqāi*'notes the very interesting case of some Tibetan Muslims meeting Sayyid Ahmad at Patna and desiring to accompany him for *Ḥajj.* Asked about Muslims in that area they said there was 'some trace of Islam' in the region up to the 'second' and 'third' Tibet but none beyond that. They were advised to go back to their land and preach Islam. They agreed and took *Bai'at.* On the return journey Sayyid Ahmad again met some Tibetans and on enquiry he was informed that some preaching had started there (*Waqāi*'Tonk ms. no. 1478, ff. 151.52).
46. See Appendix I for the text of the *Sanad* of *Khilafat,* a rare surviving document of its kind.
47. O'Kinealy's article cited above, C.R. vol.L, 1870, pp. 82-83. Emphasis mine.
48. *J.R.A.S.* Bombay branch, vol. XIV, 1880, p. 353.
49. *Makhzan,* f. 109b.
50. Ibid., 110.
    The party was first put up at the *Chabutra Kothi.* It now houses the Rajasthan government's Arabic and Persian Research Institute (APRI), which, fittingly, is the repository of one of the most important collections of materials on the movement.
51. Mehr, 1, p. 287. See Appendix II for the text of the significant letter Sayyid Ahmad wrote subsequently to Raja Hindu Rao.
52. The place, the commercial centre of modern Tonk, still bears this name. It also contains a historic mosque built by the *Sādāt-i Qāfila* in 1269 (1851-53) of which the chronogram reads;
    شد بنا خالصاً لوجہ اللہ and yields the date 1269 (1852-53). A large well was added to the mosque two years later of which the chronogram reads : . بکفتا مشرب خلق آشکار است
    During the time of Nawāb Ibrahim Khan (1867-1930) some descendants of the Wahhabi families joined the Khilafat movement and having thus incurred the displeasure of the Nawāb moved out of Tonk. Others still live there. I owe this information to Hakim Muhammad Imran Saheb of APRI, Tonk.
53. The Yusufzai area comprised lands extending to the plains of Peshawar and some situated in the hills to the north of Amb. It was inhabited by several Pathan tribes divided into the following smaller units—Usmanzais, Kamalzais, Razais, Omarkhel,

Khudukhel. The Sikhs controlled the area by stationing troops in the plain north of Attock.

54. A *pargana* in the Peshawar district, inhabited by the Mahmudzais. The actual village where Sayyid Ahmad stayed was Charsaddda.
55. *Waqāi'*, Tonk ms. no. 1480. f.11; also see letter of Sayyid Ahmad, quoted in *Sawāniḥ*, p. 249.
56. A village on the western bank of river Kabul in the Peshawar district. It is inhabited by the Khataks.
57. L. Griffin, *Ranjit Singh*, Oxford, 1892, p. 211.
58. It is situated 17 miles east of Attock, on the right bank of river Indus. A place of considerable antiquity, it was a ferry centre for crossing the river.
59. A well-known trading centre of tobacco, situated in Campbellpur district, seven miles away from the river Indus.
60. Quoted in *Sawāniḥ*, pp. 248-50; see also Shah Ismail, *Mansab-i Imāmat*.

    The decision was criticised by some as unjustified and as an assumption of dictatorial power. But it was a necessary step if the movement was not to be lost in a welter of petty skirmishes.
61. It was the chief town of Khudu Khel tribal area, to the north-west of Mardan, and the headquarters of Fatah Khan. The town was destroyed by the British forces during the military expedition of 1858, *vide infra*.
62. A plain area, situated in the Manshera *taḥsīl*, Hazara district.
63. Situated on the left bank of the Siran river, south-west of Balakot.
64. Situated on the eastern bank of Swat river, in lower Swat.
65. *Waqāi'*, Tonk ms. f. 155 b.

    The Bais clan of the Rajputs was the dominant land holding group in Rai Bareli district. They had migrated to the area in early 13th century dispossessing the Bhars. Raja Abhai Chand was the chief who had led this process; see *Rai Bareli* District Gazetteer. The case of this Rajput, Raja Ram, shows that probably some Rajputs of the area had accompanied Sayyid Ahmad, or had joined him there later.
66. *Waqāi'*, Tonk ms. f. 230 b.
67. Sayyid Ahmad's reply is true to his character, but subsequently the attitude of the Wahhabis changed. For Wilayat Ali's comment on the use of modern arms, see *infra*, p. 386.
68. Mehr (vol.II, p. 136) refers to some family papers of Yar Muhammad seized after the battle, which included a *'farmān'* of Mahārājā Ranjit Singh ordering that followers of Sayyid Ahmad be driven out and some fine horses belonging to Sultan Muhammad be sent to him.
69. Situated on the right bank of Indus, opposite Tarebela.

70. Situated in the Buner territory on the western bank of Indus, under the Mahabun mountain range.
During the post-Balakote period, Sittana became the chief centre of the Wahhabis, or the 'Hindustanis', as the English records refer to them. Its chiefs remained steadfast in their support to the movement.
71. Apart from the three *taḥsīls* of Manshera, Abbottabad, and Haripur, the Hazara district comprised a tract known as Feudal Tanawal. It occupied the centre of the western half of Hazara.
72. The principality of Amb lies on the right bank of Indus. Amb is also the name of the chief township in the territory.
73. It is situated like a wedge between Kashmir on the east and the tribal areas to the west. River Kunhar is the main stream in the valley.
The village Kawai is situated on the left bank of Kunhar.
74. Phulera is the chief village of the estate bearing that name. It is situated on a small elevation, a mile from the right bank of river Siran, 10 miles west of Nowshera.
75. Allard and Ventura, two European soldiers of fortune, joined the service of Mahārājā Ranjit Singh in 1829. The former received a command in the cavalry and the latter in the infantry; their annual salary was fixed at Rs. 50,000. The services of Ventura continued longer than Allard's. Following the first Anglo-Sikh war a clause was included in the treaty that no foreigner will be employed by the Sikhs without the permission of the English (M'Gregor, op. cit., vol.I, pp. 190-91).
76. *Waqāi'*, Tonk ms. f. 342b-343., also see *Sawāniḥ*. op. cit., p. 145; Mehr, II, p. 202.
77. *Waqāi'*, Tonk ms. ff. 23-24 b, 189.
78. Ibid.
79. An Islamic land tax, amounting to 1/10 of the produce.
80. *Waqāi'* (1480). ff. 472-79.
Further details are noted to the effect that the area then under Sayyid Ahmad's control covered the territories of the Sima (plain) area and Tanawal, and it was inhabited by four Pathan clans, Khundukhel, Azar. Usmanzai and Amzai. The *'ushr* (in kind) for the *rabi* crop of wheat and barely 7 lakh maunds — 3 lakh from *pargana* Sadua, 2-$^{3}/_{4}$ lakh from *pargana* Gandef, and the rest from *mauḍaḍ'* Khabal and others.
81. He had taken *Bai'at* at Sayyid Ahmad's hands during his visit to the town. He accompanied Sayyid Ahmad to the Frontier. On the conquest of Peshawar (1830) he was appointed to the responsible post of *Qāḍī* and *Muḥtasib* there. He suspected the hostile design of Sultan Muhammad, and had informed Sayyid Ahmad about it. He

along with many other posted at Peshawar were assassinated in a surprise attack.

82. The chief village in the valley of the same name in Manshera *tehsil*. It lies on the left bank of Siran river.
83. Balakote, an important town in Manshera *tehsil*, Peshawar district, is located at the southern end of the Kaghan valley covering the north-eastern corner of the *tehsil*. River Kunhar flows near it (Mehr II, 367).
84. Mehr, II, pp. 368-414; Nadvi, op. cit., 11, pp. 411-59.
85. See Tonk ms., pp. 1478, ff. 503-19; no. 1480, ff. 484b - 487.
86. The *Manzūra*, or, to give its full title, *Manzūratu's Su'adā'fi Aḥwāl-i Ghuzāt wa's Shuhadā'*, also called *Tārikh-i Ahmadia,* was written by Sayyid Jafar Ali Naqvi (1795-1871). Belonging to the Gorakhpur district, he had joined Sayyid Ahmad a little before the battle of Balakote (1831) and was the chief *munshi* of Sayyid Ahmad. See also Bibliography.
87. *Tawārikh-i Hazāra,* Commonwealth Relations Office Library, London, ms. copy dated 1854, ff. 78b - 86b. See also Bibliography. Surprisingly the work has remained unnoticed. Even Mehr and Abul Hasan Nadvi who have made a painstaking survey of the relevant source materials in Persian somehow missed it.
88. For Dept. Pol.Cons. nos. 39-41, dated 17 June 1831.
89. A sub-sect of the Sikhs, noted for its uncompromising religious and militant fervour.
90. Mehr adds (Ibid., pp. 439-40) that the present grave at Balakote was constructed later after a thorough enquiry into the events that it is situated at the spot from where the body was dug out.
91. This is by far the fullest list of the Sikh chiefs accompanying Sher Singh. Several of these names are not mentioned in any other source.
92. He was the son of Sardar Hari Singh, and was deputed with a small force to join Sher Singh (*Zafar Nāma-i-Ranjit Singh*, p. 193). This explains why he was anxious to tackle Sayyid Ahmad first. The Sayyid's presence at Balakote posed a threat to his father's *jāgīr*.
93. Actually, the ms. gives the year as 1837, but it is a copyist's mistake. The Vikram Samvat, 1887 mentioned alongside, corresponds to 1830-31, not 1837.
94. This is highly improbable. Mutilating a dead body is regarded as a sin. No follower of Sayyid Ahmad would have treated his body in this manner.
95. Diwan Amarnath, author of *Zafar Nāma-i Ranjit Singh* writes that Sher Singh ordered an expert painter to prepare a painting of Sayyid Ahmad. It was sent to the Lahore *darbār*, where it was seen

by the chronicler himself (Sitaram Kohli, ed., *Zafar Namah-i Ranjit Singh,* Lahore, 1928, pp.193, 195).

96. Letter, Camp Desoohah, 17 May, 1831, forwarding extracts from the news writers' report dated 10 May, 1831.
97. Letter, Camp Mookerian, dated 18th May, 1831, forwarding report, dated 14 May, 1831.
98. Pearse (ed.), *Memoirs of Alexander H. Gardner,* pp. 17-72.

    Gardner adds sarcastically that though he was quite close to where Sayyid Ahmad was fighting, he did not see the 'angles descend' and 'carry him to Paradise,' as many of the 'Syed's followers' later remembered to have seen.

    Having failed in his objective of joining Sayyid Ahmad's force, Gardner withdrew to 'the hills' with his followers and the Sikhs did not follow him. He later arrived at Bajapur, pretended to be a Muslim, and jotted down the account of the engagement and kept it hidden in a copy of the *Qur'ān.*
99. C.R. vol. LI, pp. 186, 322; I.M., pp. 61-64.
100. M. Ubaidullah Sindhi, *Shāh Walīullāh aur unkī Siyāsī Taḥrīk,* pp. 159-61, 195.
101. *Vide infra,* p. 132, n. 1.
102. *Sawānih,* pp. 179-80.
103. Muhmud Hussain, "The Mystery of Syyid Ahmad Shabid's Death" *Journal of Pakistan Historical Society,* 1955, (1), 167-73.
104. The relevant Persian and Urdu sources, such as the *Manzūra,* and the *Waqāi',* so rich in details have not been used by such writers.
105. For Dept. Pol. Cons. No. 44, dated 17 June, 1831.
106. P.N.Khera, *British Policy Towards Sind up to the Annexation, 1843,* Lahore, 1941, p. 8.
107. Ibid., 9; also see below, chap.III.
108. Sayyid Ahmad's letter to Raja Hindu Rao, App.II
109. There are several collections of the letters of Sayyid Ahmad both published and in manuscript. I have used a ms. copy of the letters, entitled *Khutūt wa Fatāwa,* belonging to the Patna University Library Manuscript Section (hereinafter, P.U.Ms. Supplement (see Bibliography, Section A).

    Masud Alam Nadwi had obtained a copy of it in the Asafiyah Library, Hyderabad, but surprisingly, did not use it his book, P.I.T.Mehr obtained it from Masud Alam Nadwi and utilised it extensively.

    All references to Sayyid Ahmad's letters are from this ms. copy; see pp. 23, 28, 30, 79, 102, 108-09 etc.
110. Letters (P.U. ms.).
111. *Supra,* pp. 68-69.
112. *Cf.* Shah Waliullah's ideas on this point, *supra,* pp. 35-36.

Chapter III

The Post-Balakote Phase, 1831-43

1. The Remnant Group on the North-Western Frontier

The battle of Balakote was a great blow to the Wahhabis, but after a brief period of chaos and despondency Shaikh Muhammad Wali Phulti[1] was elected Amīr and took *Bai'at* from all those present. Although the great majority of Sayyid Ahmad's followers were present with him at Balakote, there were some others who had been deputed to different places. Prominent among them were Muhammad Qasim Panipati[2] and Nasiruddin Manglori.[3]

They now gathered together and the party wandered around for some time, seeking the help of different tribal chiefs in an attempt to recoup and reorganise themselves. But the chiefs only wanted to use them—an armed, disciplined and battle-scarred party—for the extension of their own power and influence.

The first halt of the Wahhabis was at Nandhiar,[4] but on finding the attitude of its chief suspicious and non-cooperative, they moved over to Panjtar. There too, however, difficulties arose, and they moved on to Amb at the invitation of its chief, Painda Khan. He gave them the fort of Jassi and some connected lands in the neighbouring territory of the chief of Agrore.[5] Apparently, this gesture of help was actually an attempt to kill two birds with one stone. There was a long-standing enmity[6] between him and the chief of Agrore. Now by setting the Wahhabis on the borders of Agrore he hoped to create a conflict between the two. He very nearly succeeded in his designs. The Wahhabis having realised his intention gave up his hospitality and proceeded to their old benefactor, Sayyid Akbar Shah of Sittana. For the next three years they stayed at Sittana[7] (1838). It gave them a much-needed period of respite. Shaikh Muhammad Wali divided the party into two groups, entrusted with two different tasks. He himself proceeded to Takhtbund in Buner and brought the family members of Sayyid Ahmad to Sittana. They wanted to join the other members of the family staying in Sind. Muhammad Wali, directed his efforts towards this end which he completed some time in 1836-7. He did not take any part in the wars that followed. That was done by the other party under Nasiruddin Manglori.

Even after the Wahhabis had got temporary shelter at Sittana they were faced with the intrigues of some of the tribal chiefs. The tribesmen of the plains had turned against them since the uprising of 1830. The Sikhs, their most powerful opponent, were also there. Moreover, an attempt was made to strike them at a sore spot by disturbing the passage of the caravans from British India bringing in valuable material support. The caravans passed through the territory of Fatah Khan who started obstructing and looting them. The Wahhabis struck back and attacked Manara,[8] a village where an incoming party from India had been intercepted and looted. Another erring village, Topi, was also attacked but the Wahhabis suffered a serious reverse, and Nasiruddin, the leader of the party, was killed. Thus ended one phase of the post-Balakote period. The next one was to begin under the leadership of another Nasiruddin,[9] of Delhi. In the brief interval, *Mīr* Aulad Ali[10] was elected the *Amīr*.

II. The Sind Party under Nasiruddin of Delhi

Nasiruddin was elected Amīr at a rather difficult time. The Wahhabis had suffered losses in petty skirmishes against one local chief or another, and the hostility of Fatah Khan had affected the flow of men and money from India. However, the new leader had some advantages too. He was connected, with the prestigious saintly family of Delhi and his election provided a much-needed encouragement to the followers of the movement.

He migrated to Delhi in 1835, and travelling through Tonk, Ajmer and Jaipur, reached Sind in 1837. During the course of the journey he was joined by various parties of volunteers, and at Tonk he received financial help from the Nawāb. On reaching Sind, he first stayed at Pirkot, the centre of the Hurs, where the members of Sayyid Ahmad's family were living, and then proceeded to Hyderabad where he met the Amirs of Sind. They entertained him but did not extend much help. His arrival seems to have aroused the suspicion of Lieutenant Colonel Pottinger,[11] the British Resident at Kutch. Under his advice Nasiruddin and his party were ordered to leave

Sind, but some influential persons intervened on their behalf and they were allowed to stay for some time more.

The original plan of Nasiruddin was to proceed to the North-Western Frontier, but in view of the situation in Sind he decided to stay on there.[12] He addressed letters to some of the ruling chiefs in British India and to other persons for help. The response was encouraging and men and money came in from different parts of the country, particularly Bengal and Bihar where extensive missionary work was going on under the leadership of Wilayat Ali and Enayat Ali. The former's name is repeatedly mentioned in Nasiruddin's letters of this period.[13] Later, in course of the investigations into the Hyderabad Conspiracy,[14] it was found that Nawab Mubarizu'd Dawlah, the brother of the Nizam of Hyderabad, and the leader of the conspiracy, who had taken *Bai'at* at Wilayat Ali's hands, had sent some emissaries to Nasiruddin at Shikarpur. They had reported back to Mubarizu'd Dawlah that Nasiruddin was expecting 'the Bengal Army.'

The Amirs of Sind occupied a politically precarious position during the period.[15] Hedged between the powerful kingdoms of the Sikhs and the Durranis on the one hand and the Company's territory on the other, they were afraid of aggrandisement from each. Their policy was improvised and opportunistic. Shikarpur formed part of the Durrani empire but subsequently the Talpurs of Sind gained control over it. With the decline of the Durrani kingdom, the Amirs had withheld tribute, but apprehended a renewal of the demand. When Shah Shuja set out for the reconquest of Afghanistan and passed through Shikarpur, the Talpurs had paid him a sum of rupees 5 lakh. After his return, he raised the question of the arrears of tribute. In desperation, the Amirs even thought of handing over Shikarpur to the Sikhs in order to save themselves from Shah Shuja's demand.

Ranjit Singh, after he was checkmated in the south-east by the Anglo-Sikh Treaty of 1809 sought to extend his power towards the south-west-Sind.[17] He had even settled Abdul Nabi, a representative of the Kulhoras,[18] from whom the Talpurs had wrested Shikarpur, on his south-western border with a view to setting him up against the Talpurs in future. With remarkable political foresight Captain C.R. Wade, the British Political Agent at Ludhiana, had drawn the attention of the Government of India, immediately after the battle of Balakote, to the fact that the Sind area might next engage the attention of Maharaja Ranjit Singh. "The Sikhs", he wrote, "having finally achieved the extinction of the Syed who had afforded employment for their arms for the last five years are now speculating on the future field of their exploits.... It is in the direction of Shikarpur therefore (to the acquisition of which from the Sindhians, Ranjit Singh has often looked with anxious eyes) or the possessions of the Nawāb of Bahawalpur, situated to west of Sutlej, that he is now likely to send his troops. About five years ago the Maharaja demanded from the envoys of the Amirs of Sind present at his Court the payment of tribute which the Amirs had been in the habit of paying to the Government of Afghanistan on the plea that since the dismemberment of the Cabool Empire he had acquired the greatest share of that throne and had succeeded to its share.'[20]

The Amirs were not in a position to oppose the Sikhs openly and directly but they found a convenient ally in the Mazaris,[21] who were a tribe of Baluchis carrying on border warfare with the Sikhs. They enjoyed the tacit support of the Amirs and some other elements in the Sind society. The Amirs also induced the Wahhabis to help them against an apprehended advance by Maharaja Ranjit Singh. As a precautionary measure before such an advance the Sikh governor of Multan had occupied the border fortress of Rojhan (August, 1836) and put a Sikh garrison there.

The English had their own designs in regard to Sind. They wanted to explore the region in order to have an idea of its commercial possibilities and strategic importance. They got an opportunity when Alexander Burnes[22] of the Bombay Army was deputed in 1830 to carry through Sind the horses and other presents which had been sent by the British monarch to Maharaja Ranjit Singh. Actually, it was to serve as a probing mission. "His overt object was to get the Indus opened to British trade, but he was also to look well about him, to learn what he could of Sind politics, to explore the great river of which we then knew little and try to make friends with the chiefs along its banks. Burnes's mission was highly distasteful to the Amirs of Sind who had no wish to open their country to foreign traders and distrusted all overtures from a power known to them only for its territorial greed. 'The mischief is done', said a Baluchi officer, 'the English have seen our country.[23]

The Amirs tried to thwart the Burnes mission by various excuses. Their opposition was resented both by the English and the Sikhs. Maharaja Ranjit Singh took it as a personal affront since the mission was, ostensibly, to carry the royal presents to him. He wrote to the Amirs to grant passage. The latter, while explaining to the Sikh ruler their reasons for opposing the route, wrote that "the object of the Burnes' mission, as given out, was a mere pretext, that the carriage which he was bringing was full of gold *mohars* for the purpose of being given to Syed Ahmad, the Mahārāja's enemy.[24] The Amirs were cleverly trying to dissuade Mahārāja Ranjit Singh by a plea which was very likely to be acceptable, but it proved to be ineffective. Pressured by a military demonstration by General Ventura the Amirs finally agreed to let the mission proceed. The young envoy was allowed to pursue his way up the Indus to the Sikh *darbār*. Two years later (June 1832) Col. Henry Pottinger concluded the treaty, which opened the Indus for irrigational and commercial purposes to the English.[25]

On their part, the English were apprehensive of the intention of Ranjit Singh towards Sind but did not want the Amirs to encourage the Mazaris in their guerilla war with the Sikhs for fear that it might provide the Sikhs with an excuse for a more direct interference in Sind. Mahārāja Ranjit Singh was equally suspicious of the political designs of the English in Sind. Capt. Burnes on his arrival at the Sikh *darbār* was closely questioned on the point. Burnes tried to explain that the main object was of the English policy in terms which, he thought, would allay the suspicious of the Sikh ruler, and counter the rumours, current in the Sikh *darbār*, that the English had captured Shikarpur.[26] Commenting on the reply of Capt. Burnes, C.R. Wade expressed his dissatisfaction. In his opinion, Capt. Burnes could have better reiterated the observation of the Governor General-in-Council that the main object of British policy was the establishment of mutual understanding as well as the preservation of peace and harmony among all the neighbouring powers, "an observation which had the merit of declaring what the wishes of the Government are without exhibiting them in a selfish form which is not of course likely to be pleasing to the Maharaja whose co-operation, in our view, I have been desired to secure by no other means than those of conciliation."

The British, while wary of Mahārāja Ranjit Singh's designs, were reluctant to antagonise him openly. They realised the value of his help in meeting the apprehended threat of a Russian advance in Central Asia. It was to meet that eventuality that they had given political asylum to the two exiled rulers of Afghanistan, Shah Zaman and Shah Shuja. They wanted to use them in extending their own influence at Kabul and in countering the Russian advance. It is evident that both the British and the Sikhs had aggressive designs on Sind, and were watching each other closely. In fact, it is difficult to determine as to what extent annexation of Sind by the British was hastened by apprehensions of their being forestalled by the Sikhs.

Such was the political situation in Sind when Nasiruddin arrived there. He found the Mazaris a valuable ally, especially as they were carrying on a guerilla war with the Sikhs and the English. This indicates the attitude of the Wahhabis in regard to their allies. They wanted to keep away from such Indian powers as were under the influence of the British, directly or indirectly. Nasiruddin settled in the territory of the Mazaris, situated on the border of Khairpur, corresponding to the south-western portion of what later constituted the Dera Ghazi Khan district. In November 1837, he tried to recover the fort of Rojhan from the Sikhs but in the ensuing battle of Rojhan and Kan he suffered defeat due to the defection of the Mazaris who made peace with the Sikhs through the mediation of Dewan Sawan Mal, the Sikh governor of Multan. The Mazaris, like the Frontier tribesmen, neither had the resources nor the organisation to fight consistently against the Sikh *darbār*. At the first major repulse, as also due to inducements offered by Sawan Mal, they made peace with the Sikhs, leaving the Wahhabis in the lurch. The latter came to be regarded as a source of political embarrassment by the local chiefs whose help they sought and they were ultimately forced to leave Sind and proceed to Afghanistan. Nasiruddin had been in correspondence with some of the chiefs there.

In Afghanistan, the relations between Dost Muhammad Khan, the Afghan ruler, and the English were heading towards a crisis.[27] On the eve of the first Anglo-Afghan War, Dost Muhammad Khan thought it to be useful to obtain the services of the Wahhabis. On his invitation Nasiruddin with a party of 1000 persons moved towards Kabul. He himself stayed at Dadur but sent forward a detachment of 300 picked men to the Amīr. They were deputed to assist in the defence of Ghazni.[28] They fell fighting when the citadel was stormed by the British force. Once again, Nasiruddin's action showed that the Wahhabis were eager to join hands with any power fighting against the British. "They were always happy", remarks Hunter, "to get a chance to inflict a blow upon the English infidels." Nasiruddin and the survivors[29] reached Sittana after a strenuous march toward the end of 1840. A small party of Wahhabis under Aulad Ali was already there. On his arrival, Nasiruddin was elected Amīr, but died soon after, and was buried at Sittana. While the movement was thus passing through a lean period in the non-British tribal area, its activities were being extended and strengthened over a large part of the British Indian territory.

III. Organisational and Missionary Activities of the Wahhabis in British India

Sayyid Ahmad had migrated to the North-Western Frontier tribal area due to some ideological and strategic considerations. But he had no intention of cutting off all connections with British India. On the contrary, he realised the vital importance of organisational and missionary activity in that area. He himself had undertaken extensive missionary tours in northern India, and he wanted that work to be continued and to be extended to other parts. He entrusted this task to some of his chief followers, such as Wilayat Ali[30] and Enayat Ali[31] of Patna, Muhammad Ali of Rampur, Muhammad Qasim of Bombay, *Hāfiz* Qutubuddin and Sayyid Aulad Husain of Qannauj.[32]

On arriving in British India through Sind, the party proceeded to the respective areas of their work. Muhammad Ali first went to Hyderabad and then to Madras where he arrived in July 1829 and took up residence in the *madrasa* of *Maulawī* Abdul Rab, son of Abdul Ali. He gathered a large following, including Nawab Muhammad Alam Khan Tahawwur Jung whom he later appointed as his *Khalīfa.*

Wilayat Ali proceeded[33] to the Deccan region and lived at Hyderabad for some time. His preachings received a good response, and many persons took *Bai'at* at his hands, including Zanul Abedin and Muhammad Abbas, two erudite *'Ālims* attached to the 'Court' of Nawāb Mubārizu'd Dawlah (1830-57). Later, Nawāb Mubārizu'd Dawlah himself took *Baiat* at the hands of Wilayat Ali. Through him, Wilayat Ali was able to approach other highly-placed persons and establish contacts with the Indian units of the army. This part of his work, resulting in what came to be called the Hyderabad Conspiracy (1839) has been studied separately,[34] but it may just be mentioned here that the work of infiltration in the rank of the army, which was an important plank of the internal organisation of the Wahhabi Movement, was started by Wilayat Ali during this period. With Hyderabad as his base, Wilayat Ali travelled to other parts and he visited and worked in Bombay and Surat.

On hearing of the disaster at Balakote, Wilayat Ali returned to Patna, where his father, Fath Ali had died at about the same time. Muhammad Ali Ramouri also returned to his home-town from Madras. It seems that the Wahhabis in British India wanted to assemble at some central place to take stock of the situation after the death of Sayyid Ahmad.

During the next two years, Wilayat Ali took several measures for strengthening the movement. He deputed Enayat Ali to eastern Bengal and appointed Shah Muhammad Hussain, earlier appointed *Khalīfa* by Sayyid Ahmad, to lead the Friday congregational prayers and deliver the *khutba* (sermon delivered before the congregational prayer at the local mosque at *maḥalla* Nanmohian, Patna city). Muhammad Husain was also directed to visit other places in Bihar, such as Chapra, Muzaffarpur and Darbhanga and organise the activities there. Wilayat Ali himself led the prayers in another important local mosque known as Fakhru'd Dawlah's mosque.[36] Meetings were also held in the ancestral house at *maḥalla* Sadiqpore, Patna City, in which the *Qur'ān* and *Ḥadīth* were taught and explained to the people in simple language, and lectures delivered on theological and other topics. The idea was to make the people understand for themselves the commandments of God. The emphasis was on the direct reading and understanding of the *Qur'ān* and the *Ḥadīth*, and not being dependant on the *'Ulama* and the *Ṣūfiyā* as some sort of intermediaries. The Urdu translation of the *Qur'ān* by Shah Abdul Qadir, son of Shah Waliullah and some *risalas* of Shah Ismail were obtained from Delhi, printed locally and distributed among the members of the gatherings, which included some women also.

The work of printing had its own problems. Publishers were not always easily available, and some even refused to publish such works. On the refusal of one such press, the *Matba'-i Ḥussainī*, Lucknow, Wilayat Ali got one of his disciples, Badiuzzaman of Burdawan, to purchase a type-press for rupees ten thousand. Thereafter, many other publishers took to the printing of such religious tracts for it turned out to be a profitable line.

Wilayat Ali's daily routine was an exacting one. It began with the dawn prayer, after which he gave lessons to some selected students of an advanced stage. Others of a lower stage were sent to take lessons from Yahya Ali,[38] Fayyaz Ali and Akbar Ali. Larger groups were taught after the midday prayers. During such sessions some topic of *Tafsīr* (exegesis) or the *Ḥadīth* was selected for discussion. A copy of the book containing the lesson was given to all those present, while Abdullah, son of Wilayat Ali acted as the reciter who read out the lesson aloud.[39] These sessions continued till the afternoon prayer. Other works of a more confidential nature were probably attended to in smaller gatherings later in the evening, or at night.

Wilayat Ali also went out on tours, meeting people in different walks of life—farmers in their fields, weavers at their spinning wheels and householders at their doorsteps.[40] He often stayed at a particular place for long periods, concentrating on the initiation and training of a person, and then entrusting him the work of organising a local centre. Wilayat Ali initiated and trained a large number of talented and dedicated individuals who headed the numerous 'local centres' all over the country. These centres continued working till long after the migration of Wilayat Ali and Enayat Ali to the North-eastern Frontier and their death there. This would be evident from the subsequent history of some of these centres, particularly of Malda in Bengal and of Hyderabad.[41]

Similar work was done by Enayat Ali[42] in the districts of northern and eastern Bengal. It was reported to the Government as early as 1843[43] that a band of Mullahs was moving about in the districts of Baraset, Jessore, Pubna and Rajshahi preaching a religious war against the Sikhs, the "allies" of the English, and "endeavouring to procure recruits and money for that purpose." The leading man of that party was "a native of Patna, called Enayat Ali."[44] The reports added that while their efforts at enlisting recruits had not met with much success, the collection of funds was proceeding more satisfactorily.

Another report, stated that besides Enayat Ali, Karamat Ali[45] and Zynoodeen (Zainul Abedin) of Hyderabad were also preaching in those districts; their appeal for recruits was receiving an encouraging response, and they had fixed Narayanpore, near Jungipur in the district of Murshidabad, as their rendezvous, where the followers were to collect before proceeding to the North-West.[46] Enayat Ali had been "making use... of the topic of a religious war and the resurrection of Syed Ahmad as a pretext for calling for aid."[47] The magistrate of Bhagalpur (Bihar), on being asked to report whether groups of men were passing through his district towards the North-West, had informed that men from the districts of Baraset, Jessore, Mymensingh and Rajashahi had passed in different groups, numbering 800 or 900, stating that they were proceeding to Makkah.[48]

Significantly, it was pointed out by the local police officials to the higher authorities of the Government that the Muhammadan population in the eastern districts (of Bengal) contained a large number of *'Faraizis,'* that is Wahabbis,[49] "strongly united, very fanatic, under control of particular leaders *inimical to our government*", and that they "required to be most carefully watched for if there is any danger of an outbreak in these provinces it is from the excited religious fanaticism of this sect."[50] It goes to the credit of the local police officers that they discerned the close similarity between the ideas of the Fara'iḍis and the larger group of the Wahhabis.[51] As we shall see presently, it was the groundwork done by the Fara'iḍis which facilitated the work of the Wahhabi missionaries in Bengal.

The Government, in a consolidated reply to all these reports of the local police officer, while expressing their disinclination to "attend much importance to the preaching", directed him to use a guarded mixture of advice and admonition in conveying to the leaders in particular and the people in general that they would be held responsible for any 'outrage' or 'breach of peace' into which they or their followers might be involved. The magistrates might adopt a similar procedure in their respective districts and might, on occasion, give a well-timed warning to the people of the consequence of "riotous assemblage and tumult". They were directed to submit weekly reports on such activities and the Superintendent of Police was to visit such of those as appeared to be most "obvious to suspicion". The people in general were also to be placed on their guard against unusual meetings and "extraordinary collections of Mohammedans". The Superintendent was finally directed to "report frequently to the Government on the results of the inquiries into the subject."[52]

During the period Wilayat Aliproceeded on an inspection tour of Bengal. He visited Calcutta and then left for Bombay[53] on way to Arabia for the performance of *Ḥajj*. Before returning to India he visited Yemen, Yasir and Muscat, and met the famous scholar of *Ḥadīth, Qāḍī* Shukani, from whom he obtained a certificate of proficiency in *Ḥadīth* and brought some of his works to India. Returning to Calcutta, he again visited some of the districts of Bengal to supervise the work being done there. He met Enayat Ali and they returned to Patna. At Patna Wilayat Ali met Zainul Abedin and Muhammad Abbas, who had probably left Hyderabad in the wake of the arrest and trial of Nawāb Mubariz'ud Dawlah, their patron. They were deputed to Orissa and Allahabad for organisational work there.

The activities of Wilayat Ali, Enayat Ali and others is typical of the missionary and organisational work of the Wahhabis. The importance of this silent, mundane work in sustaining the movement hardly needs any emphasis. It resulted in the development of a civic and corporate spirit among the followers of the movement, and the adoption of a civil disobedience campaign. As O'Kinealy in his above-mentioned article observes, "those who were not in a position to abandon this country and join in a *jihad*, were recommended to resist passively, and refrain from all intercourse with their *Kafir* rulers, *to form as it were a power within the Government, and totally opposed to it.* Assistance should not be demanded from the infidels, their courts which decreed interest, should be avoided, and all complaints between brother and brother should be decided by the local leaders....[54]

The centre of this newly organised corporate life was the village mosque which also served as the collecting point for local contributions both in cash and kind. The *Imām* of the mosque, besides his religious duties, was also entrusted with the judicial work of deciding disputes among the followers. People were forbidden to take their cases to the government courts and persuaded to get them settled in their own corporate bodies. An important locality with a larger mosque was selected as a higher unit with jurisdiction over a larger area. An *Imām* with a kind of appellate authority in judicial and other matters requiring consultation was appointed. This was a system which resembled closely, and drew heavily upon, the working of the Farā'iḍis in Bengal. Before passing on to the next phase of the activities of Wilayat Ali and Enayat Ali, we may examine briefly the origin and development of the *Farā'iḍi* Movement and the connected Baraset Rising.

IV. The Fara'iḍī Movement and the Baraset Rising

The founder of the *Farā'iḍī* Movement was *Ḥājī* Shariatullah (1781-1840). He belonged to a small landholding family of district Faridpur, Bengal. He had his early education at home and later went to Arabia for *Ḥajj* in 1799. He stayed there for about 20 years. On returning home, he took to preaching and travelled extensively in the districts of Bakerganj, Faridpur, Dacca, and Mymensingh. He preached a firm belief in monotheism, and denounced the *Bida'āt.*

In this, as in many other respects, the Farā'iḍī Movement had much in common with the Wahhabi Movement, but there are points of differences too, particularly in regard to the matter of *taqlīd*, or the following of any one of the four schools of Islamic jurisprudence (the *Farā'iḍīs* being followers of the *Ḥanafī* school). Another difference often unduly stressed was about the permissibility of holding the *'Eīd'* and congregational Friday prayers in British India. The *Farā'iḍīs* believed that such prayers could not be lawfully held in British India, which was a *Dāru'l Ḥarb*; whereas the Wahhabis while agreeing on British India being a *Dāru'l Ḥarb* had not stopped holding the congregational prayers there. These differences apart, both the Wahhabi and the *Farā'iḍis* had a common fundamentalist root and approach.

Ḥājī Shariatullah's chief objective was socio-religious reforms, but his programme of work brought him into conflict with the local zamindars who happened to be non-Muslims. His work was further consolidated during the time of his son and spiritual successor Muhsinuddin Ahmad, commonly known as Dūdū Miyān (1819-62), under whose leadership it became more political and militant. Basing himself on a verse of the *Qur'ān*,[56] that the earth belonged to *Allāh* alone, Dūdū Miyān gave the call that all land belonged to *Allāh*, and that those who cultivated the land had the right to do so on payment of some taxes to the Government, but the so-called proprietors of land had no rights to collect any kind of rent from the cultivators. This was a call which was bound to receive a wide welcome and support from the cultivators in the area who happened to be mostly Muslims. It is this which explains the largely rural base and the agrarian character of the movement in Bengal.

The local cultivators were[57] being oppressed by the newly created class of the zamindars and the British Indigo planters. Dūdū Miyān worked chiefly among them, and welded them into an effective organisation. He appointed *Khalīfas* and agents at local and higher levels to administer the affairs of the members of the community. The *Khalīfas* performed the duties of both a religious and secular character. Apart from imparting religious training and supervising the performance of *far'āiḍ*, they also acted as the social and moral mentors, and administered justice. The *Farā'iḍis* revived the age-old *Panchāyatī* system. These activities naturally aroused the suspicion and hostility of both the zamindars and the planters. They got Dūdū Miyān involved in a number of criminal cases.

In 1847 Dūdū Miyān and his followers were convicted of setting fire to the indigo factory of one Andrew Anderson Dunlop at Panchagarh. A series of cases and counter-cases between the parties ensued during 1847-57, but finally the conviction was set aside by the *Sadr Nizāmat 'Adālat,* Calcutta. On the outbreak of the rising of 1857, Dūdū Miyān was kept in a sort of preventive detention at Calcutta.[58] He was regarded as a potential source of danger because of the large number of his followers and because in some police records he had been described as a Wahhabi, with whose activities the Government was quite familiar. He was released in 1859, and died shortly after in 1862. The leadership devolved upon his sons, but the movement got splintered and since the time of the leadership of Abdul Ghafur (1852-63) lost some of its reformist zeal.

The Baraset Rising,[59] led by Nisar Ali, better known as Tītū Mīr, had similar aims and objectives, but it was closer to the Wahhabis' thinking.

Nisar Ali or Tītū Mīr belonged to a family of modest means in village Chandpur, 24-Parganas district of Bengal, but he was connected by marriage to one *Munshī* Amīr, a respectable landholder.[60] Tītū Mīr had a chequered career during his youth. He later came into contact with a member of the Delhi royal family and accompanied him to Arabia for *Ḥajj.* He met Sayyid Ahmad there, and returned to India, 'a powerful preacher of the faith'.[61] Like Shariatullah, he took to preaching on his return from Arabia. He settled at Haidarpore and began to propagate his ideas. He was a strong supporter of the cause of the oppressed peasantry. Very soon he gathered a following of several thousand men, and 'teachers' of his 'sect' were sent all over the country.[62] His activities were naturally opposed by the zamīndārs, who "exerted all their power to check the growth of an association which treated them with disrespect, and exhibited a power of combination which might hereafter seriously affect their interests".[63] His preachings were also opposed by a section of the Muslim cultivators who felt aggrieved with some of his teachings which denounced some of their cherished customs and social practices.

The combination of agrarian discontent and sectarian differences was building up an explosive situation. The districts of eastern Bengal, where the influence of the *Farā'iḍis* was strong[64] were in a disturbed state in the beginning of 1831, and clashes had occurred in some villages. In August 1830, it was reported to the Joint Magistrate, Baraset, that one Punjab Malik, a Wahhabi, had been fined and imprisoned by his Zamīndār for destroying a well-known Muslim shrine during the month of *Muḥarram.* Another zamīndār, Kishen Ray of village Poorna, situated on the bank of Ichchamati river, had imposed illegal and discriminatory fines upon the Muslim tenant, particularly the followers of Tītū Mīr. These fines included the 'beard-tax' of rupees two-and-a-half per head, and other heavier impositions, such as an impost of rupees five hundred and one thousand on the construction of *kachcha* and *pucca* mosques, and of rupees fifty for giving up a Hinduised name.[65] While the zamindar was able to impose and collect this fine on Poorna, he was opposed in the neighbouring village of Sarfrazpore. A large number of Tītū Mīr's followers were present there and when the zamindar's men arrived to collect the fine they beat them back. The zamindar retaliated by sending another party, and a riot ensued. Some acts of communal frenzy were committed, some house were plundered and a mosque burnt. Complaints and counter-complaints were filed in the *thāna* but finally both the parties were acquitted. The matter, however, did not rest there. The zamindar began harassing Tītū Mīr's men.

The zamindar "fraudulently exercised his power to arrest for arrears of rent in order to harass his opponents; he instituted fictitious suits against them in the Civil Court and had them arrested in execution of decrees."[66]

The situation was heading toward a more violent clash. The followers of Tītū Mīr were joined by one Miskin Shah and his followers. They raised contributions, gathered a large number of men and fortified themselves with a bamboo stockade in village Narkulbaria. They attacked Poorna and plundered it. (November, 1831). Acts of communal frenzy again occurred; a Brahmin was killed, a temple defiled and a native Christian named Smith was assaulted.[67] More significantly, the insurgents "openly proclaimed the extinction of the Company's rule.[68] They advanced into the Nadia district and attacked Lowghatta and other villages.

It may be noted that the affected area, comprising Baraset and Nadia districts, was "studded with Indigo factories, and was not very far from the Government Salt Agency at Bagundi. "While the Government officers failed to realise the gravity of the situation, the indigo planters felt more concerned about the disturbances. One Piron, an assistant at an indigo factory near the "headquarters of the rebels' informed his employers at Calcutta, in November, 1831, that unless repressive measures were taken "serious danger to the Government would ensue." His employer, Storm, made representation to the magistrate of Baraset and the Lieutenant-Governor, but it did not produce much effect. Meanwhile reports of continued disturbances were received from the magistrate of Baraset and Nadia, and the Government took some steps to "quell the rebellion". A detachment of Calcutta militia was sent to Bagundi (November, 1831), and Alexander, an employee of the Agency, was directed to join it there, and proceed to Narkulbaria. He took with him the *darogha* of Basirhat and some *barkandazes* (matchlock-men). Taking a rather contemptuous view of the fighting qualities of the600-strong insurgents led by Ghulam Masum, Alexander advanced upon their position but was defeated. The *jama'dār* of the Calcutta militia, 10 sepoy and 13 *barkandazes* were killed. The *darogha* of Basirhat and Kalinga *thāna* were wounded and taken prisoner. Alexander himself 'ran for his life', pursued by 'the insurgents with drawn swords,' and escaped with great difficulty. According to the account in the *Manzūra,* the officers had been instructed to arrest the rebels, not to shoot them down. On meeting the rebels they first fired blank shots, but the rebels were undeterred and attacked them with swords and *lathis.* Many of the militiamen were killed, or took to flight. The District Magistrate advanced alone towards the rebels in a move to surrender, but was pursued and took shelter by crossing the river.

Following the defeat, complete panic prevailed at the Agency. The treasures were put on a boat and sent via Sunderban to Calcutta under the charge of Alexander. Other factories in Nadia district were attacked, and the police declared themselves to be unable to meet the situation. The magistrate collected the available police force, and accompanied by a planter, Andrew, of Rudrapur factory, sailed down the Ichchamati with a party of 300 to tackle the situation. On reaching Badurreah factory, they found that it had been plundered and they also heard about the reverse suffered by Alexander at Narkulbaria. After some initial hesitation, they advanced upon Narkulbaria (the Europeans riding on elephants), where they found "the insurgents about a thousand strong, drawn up in regular order, and led by Titu Mir." They were attacked by Mīr's men. Several *barkandazes* were killed and the rest of the party ran toward the boats. On reaching the opposite bank, the Europeans ran to their elephants which were a mile off and retreated to the Mulnath factory, some 36 miles away. One elephant, several boats and other materials were captured by the rebels, who then proceeded to attack the Hugli factory. Its manager was arrested and brought before Tītū Mīr who "demanded immediate and unconditional obedience to their authority." The manager "wisely assented" and promised 'to sow indigo for them as rulers of India.'[69] The rebels moved on northwards towards Krishnaghur, issuing proclamations to the zamīndārs and authorities calling upon them to acknowledge their supremacy and supply provisions. They appeared to be in control of the area for the time being.

The Government now seemed to have realised the gravity of the situation and took urgent steps. In March 1832, a detachment consisting of 10 regiments of the native Infantry, a troop of horse-artillery with two guns, and some troops of the bodyguard, was directed to join Alexander at Baraset. They advanced upon Narkulbaria, which was reached on the 18th March 1832. In the final round of the struggle which followed, the insurgents gave a good account of themselves. To quote O'Kinealy again, "The troops advanced firing on the insurgents, who received the attack boldly, and it was not until successive volleys had told on them severely that they broke up and retreated into the stockade, leaving sixty or seventy men killed and as many wounded. The stockade was carried by storm."[70] Tītū Mir fell fighting, and 350 of his followers including Ghulam Masum were taken prisoners. They were later on put on trial at Alipore. Ghulam Masum was sentenced to death and another 140 were sentenced to varying terms of imprisonment.

Thus ended the brief but stirring Baraset Rising of 1832. The government, while expressing astonishment at the 'temerity' and "extravagance" of the insurgents contented themselves with the remark that the insurrection was 'strictly local' and was caused by factors "which had operated only in a small extent of country." It also took comfort from the fact that "no person of wealth or consideration in the country joined the insurgents."[71] This assessment was, however, rejected by some keen contemporary observers and the press. O'Kinealy writes, "Even now, after the lapse of forty years, one cannot read the history of the insurrection without astonishment at the apathy displayed by the Government. In 1822 Sayyid Ahmad had preached war against the non-Musalman rulers of India without any impediment. Liberal supplies of men and money were openly forwarded to him from Bengal.... Government must have been well aware of his conquests in the Punjab. Yet when his followers, trusting to their strength, rose in open rebellion within thirty miles of Calcutta, the disturbance was treated as inexplicable and the rebels were treated as men devoid of intelligence and incapable of design."[72]

The *Hindu Patriot* of 2 August 1870 remarked, "Such sects as the Faraizis and Wahabbis, even if impotent themselves for any great movement, may gather all the discontents, hatreds, ambitions... which under the present none too very wise, however beneficent and brilliant rule, must be numerous enough.... The Faraizis, though a Bengal sect are heard of outside in Native States.... This bespeaks of great neglect."[73]

The rising has been characterised as communal by some modern writers,[74] and it has been seen almost exclusively in Hindu-Muslim terms. A third, and in many ways a more important party, however, was also involved—the British Indigo planters. The area was 'studded' with indigo factories and a Salt Agency was not far away. The declaration by Tītū Mīr's men of the cessation of the Company's rule, and their asking the manager of the Hooghly factory to sow indigo for them as the new rulers, are points which have not received the attention they deserve.

The unnoticed account given in the *Manzūra* refers to the role of the planters in the suppression of the rising. It states that after the defeat and killing of the 'Raja' (zamindar) and his son by Titu Mir's men, a British indigo planter proceeded with some men for the former's help but he was also killed. On hearing of this, an English businessman went there but met with the same fate.

Further, the persistent representation by the local planters to the government shows that they regarded Tītū Mīr's activities as detrimental to their interests. The initial effort against the 'insurgents' was led by the planters themselves, and it was only when it failed that the government troops took over and finished the job.

The "ruthless Indigo system" in the Indigo district of Bengal drew the attention of some Christian missionaries too, and they did something on their own to alleviate the distress of the cultivators.[75]

The Baraset Rising was essentially the work of peasants and cultivators harassed by the twin depredations of the planters and the newly-created class of zamindars.[76] Even Colvin, the local magistrate, who was by no means favourably inclined towards the "insurgents", felt constrained to make the following remark on the role of the zamindars: "The powers possessed by the zamindars enabled them to exercise a petty jurisdiction among their ryots and to make petty exactions on all kinds of pretexts."[77]

Finally, it would be wrong to view the *Farā'iḍī* Movement and the Baraset Rising in isolation. These have to be examined in the wider background of the growth of the Wahhabi Movement in India and the agrarian unrest in many parts of Bengal. Although the *Farā'iḍī* Movement began independently, it had much in common with the Wahhabi Movement. Both drew inspiration from a common source and had similar objectives.[78] It is not without significance that many of the contemporary British officials and observers regarded the activities of the *Farā'iḍīs* and the Wahhabis as interconnected, if not identical.[79] In fact, the *Farā'iḍīs* prepared the ground for the wide, positive response to the Wahhabis' activities in many parts of Bengal.

Notes

1. He was one of the early adherents of Sayyid Ahmad. He had been directed to devote more time to military training, and had acquired proficiency in gunmanship. After migrating to the Frontier he had been put in charge of the commissariat and financial matters. He probably belonged to the family of Shah Ahlullah, brother of Shah Waliullah.
2. He lived and worked for some time in the Kaghan area after the battle of Balakote. He was one of those who advocated the idea about the 're-appearance' of Sayyid Ahmad. He was subsequently arrested by the English and died in prison around 1852.
3. He belonged to Manglor in the Shahjahanpur district, U.P. He was elected Amīr after the battle of Balakote, and sustained the movement during the critical years immediately following the battle of Balakote.
4. It is situated in the Swat area between the Daishi, Konsh and Bhogarmang valleys.
5. Located in the Manshera *taḥṣīl*, at the foot of the Black Mountains.
6. The sister of Painda Khan was betrothed to Abdul Ghafur Khan, chief of Agrore. When the former was defeated by Sayyid Ahmad, his family, including the sister, fell into the hands of the Wahhabis. They were handed over, in good faith, to Abdul Ghafur Khan, who while returning the others held back Painda Khan's sister and married her. Painda took it as an affront.

7. H.W. Bellew, op. cit., p. 94.
8. It was a village situated on the bank of the river Indus, and was washed away in the great flood of 1841.
9. An *'Ālim* of repute, he was a descendant, on his mother's side, of Shah Rafiuddin, brother of Shah 'Abdul 'Aziz. He had his early education at Delhi and Calcutta and lived and worked mostly at Delhi. He rendered assistance to the Frontier centre from there. Later he migrated to the Frontier in 1835 and was elected Amīr there, around 1838. He died at Sittana in 1840.
10. He was a resident of village Surajgarh in the Monghyr district, Bihar.
11. He was the Political Agent at Kutch, and was instrumental in concluding the Agreement of 20 April 1839, which opened the Indus to the British for commercial use. Later, he became an Agent in the Court of the Amirs of Sind and played an important role in the annexation of Sind.
12. Naisruddin was advised during his stay at Tonk by Nawab Wazir' Daula to make Sind his centre, (Mehr, IV, p. 148).
13. Mehr, IV, pp. 171-72.
14. *Vide infra,* pp. 191.
15. The following account is based on the reports submitted by Captain Wade; see Dept. Pol. Cons. no 65-69, dated 20 December 1837. Also see Khera, op. cit., pp. 6-55; Cunningham, op. cit., pp. 285-300.
16. Cunningham, op. cit., p. 285.
17. Khera, op. cit., pp. 25 ff.
18. The family enjoyed spiritual eminence and its scions had served as *Sūbahdārs* of Sind under the Mughals. They asserted their independence around 1711 with the help of some Baluchi tribes.
19. Belonging to the Maari tribe of Baluchistan, the Talpurs had earlier served the Kulhoras with distinction, but overthrew the latter in 1783. Upper and Lower Sind was occupied by different members of the family.
20. For Dept. Pol. Con. no. 41 dated 17 June, 1831.
21. Khera, op. cit., pp. 27-28.
22. His brother, James Burnes, a doctor, had treated Murad Ali, the chief of Hyderabad. This connection might have been of some use in getting the permission from the otherwise reluctant Amir.
23. L.J. Trotter, *Lord Auckland,* Oxford, 1893, p. 40.
24. Khera, op. cit., p. 12.
25. Ibid., App. VI, pp. 69-70.
26. Pol. Cons. no. 66, dated 20 October, 1837.
27. See, Kaye, J.W., *History of the War in Afghanistan,* London, 1878.

28. *I.M.*, p. 21; *C.R.*, vol. 51 (1870), p. 384; *J.I.H.* August 1938, pp. 251-68.
29. The distinction between this party and the other one on the Frontier, the remnants of Balakote, under Nasiruddin Manglori, should be borne in mind. Their activities overlap to some extent.
30. For biographical details, see T.S. and *Sawāniḥ*; also chapter IV.
31. For biographical details, see T.S. and *Sawāniḥ*; also chapter IV.
32. He was the father of the famous Nawab Siddiq Hasan Khan of Bhopal *vide infra*, pp. 352-54.
33. At the time of his departure, Sayyid Ahmad gave a pair of his personal apparel to Wilayat Ali as *tabarruk* (sacred relic) and 6 *tāka* (rupees) to meet the expenses; *Waqā'i*, Tonk ms. 1480, ff. 110-1.
34. Vide infra, pp. 191-93.
35. It remained closely associated with the activities of the Wahhabis at Patna and Abdul Rahim, the author of *Tadhkira- Sādqa* lies buried in its compound. An enlarged, mosque has now been built on the site.
36. *Sawānḥ*, p. 160; T.S. 115, 269.
37. It is situated in *maḥalla* Macharhatta, Patna City. Its present inscription, dated A.H. 1202 (1787-88) records its renovation by Nawāb Fakhru'd Dawlah Firuz Jung of Murshidabad; perhaps the original mosque was built during the time of Nawab Fakhru'd Dawlah, the last centrally appointed *ṣūbahdār* of Bihar (c. 1727-35).
38. For biographical details about him and the two others, who were all the sons of Elahi Bakhsh and brothers of Ahmadullah, the chief accused in the Patna Conspiracy Trial at Patna (1865), see T.S.; also *passim.*
39. *Sawāniḥ*, p. 162.
    This invite comparison with what Shah Waliullah writes in *Anfāsu'l 'Ārifīn* about some of the methods of teaching *Ḥadīth* prevalent in Arabia. In one of these, meant for beginners and those slightly above them, as the text was being read aloud by a student, the teacher gave explanatory comments where necessary on points of philology, jurisprudence and *isnād.* The beginners were thus trained for understanding the standard text. There was another method in which the teacher or one of the students read aloud the text while others listened. No explanatory comments were made. The idea seemed to be to let the students go through a kind of rapid reading course of the standard text. For finer points of discussion, they were referred to the standard works of *Tafsīr.* See S. Manazir Ahsan Gilani, *Hindustān Mein Musalmānon Ka Nizām-i Ta'līm wa Tarbiyat*, Delhi, 1944, pp. 234-38.
40. T.S. p. 166. Among the place visited by Wilayat Ali during this

period, was Biharsharif, the seat of the *dargah* of the famous 14th century Sufi saint, *Makhdūm* Sharafu'd Din Maneri.

41. See chapter V and IX.
42. Like Wilayat Ali, he too was accompanied by some persons who had migrated earlier, and he was given some *tabarruk* and expense-money by Sayyid Ahmad, *Wacā'i*, Tonk, ms. 1480, f. 112.
The same source adds that Enayat Ali wanted to stay on but Sayyid Ahmad bade farewell to him, saying that he would have occasion to participate in many other events later.
43. Govt. of Bengal, Judl. Dept. Cons. nos. 21-24, dated 29 May 1843. Earlier, on the basis of O'Kinealy's article it was stated in general that Enayat Ali worked in eastern Bengal, but these police reports, studied for the first time, provide more specific information. It may also be added that the Wahhabi sources, such as the S.A. or the T.S. too are silent on this phase of Enayat Ali's work.
44. Letter from W. Dampier, Suptd. of Police, L.P., to F.J. Halliday, Secy, Govt of Bengal, Judl. Dept. no. 581 dated 23 March, 1843.
45. Karamat Ali (1800-73) belonged to Jaunpur. He was well-versed in Islamic theology and sciences, and was one of the leading followers of Sayyid Ahmad. Travelling mostly in boats he did extensive missionary work in the interior areas of Bengal and in Assam. He later developed differences with the Wahhabis and the Farā'iḍis on several important doctrinal points, including the questions of *taqlīd* and the system of *pīrī-murīdī*. He was a prolific writer, and wrote over forty books and tracts, including some polemical tracts against the Wahhabis and Farā'iḍis.
46. Letter from W. Dampier, Superintendent of Police, Lower Provinces, to F.J. Halliday, Secy to the Govt. of Bengal, no. 680 dated 5 April 1843.
47. Ibid., no. 714, dated 10 April 1843.
48. Ibid., no. 736, dated 13 April, 1843.
49. This was not just a casual remark of a local police officer based on his impression. The same opinion was expressed in a well-researched memorandum on Wahhabism and the Wahhabis prepared by T.E. Ravenshaw, magistrate, Patna, at the time of the trial of Ahmadullah in 1865. Ravenshaw succinctly remarked that "perhaps a Wahabee may be defined to be an ultra Ferazie, particularly on the subject of *jehad*"; *Selection*, p. 140.
50. Letter from W. Dampier, Suptd of Police, L.P. to F.J. Halliday, Secy to Govt of Bengal, no. 680, dated 5 April, 1843. Emphasis added.
51. *Vide infra*, pp. 115 ff.
52. Letter from Secy to the Govt. of Bengal to W. Dampier, Suptd of Police Lower Provinces, no. 348 dated Fort William, 24 April, 1843.

The Government seemed to be trying to put up a brave face before the local officers. While refusing to attach importance to these proceedings, it nonetheless gave detailed instructions to meet the situation.

53. Badiuzzaman and Enayatullah were appointed *Khalīfas* at these two places respectively.
54. C.R., vol. L, 1870, p. 393. Emphasis added.
55. For a well-researched account of the movement, see Muinuddin Ahmad Khan, *History of the Faraidi Movement in Bengal* (1818-1906), Dacca, 1965.

    The term *Farā'iḍī* is derived from *Farā'iḍ*, the plural of *Farīḍah* or the obligatory duties enjoined upon the Muslims. The movement was so called because it strictly emphasised the performance of the *Farā'iḍ*, an uncompromising belief in monotheism and the discarding of *Bida'āt*.
56. "Unto *Allāh* belongeth whatsoever is in the heavens and whatsoever is in the earth." (Verse 4: 131 and 132).
57. For details, see Khan, op. cit., pp. 30-40.
58. Khan, op. cit.
59. An early brief account of the rising is given in Thornton, E., *History of India*, London, 1843, vol. V, p. 179 and a longer one in O'Kinealy's article, C.R., 1870, pp. 177-84; see also, I.M. p. 45.

    For a recent re-appraisal of the earlier account see J.A.S.P., 1959, 4, 113-33.

    Abhijit Dutta, *Muslim Society in Transition: Titu Mir's Revolt* (1831), Calcutta, 1987, examines the rising in the larger context of social and agrarian unrest in western Bengal, and makes use of source-materials in the Bangali language, including Biharilal Sarkar's *Titu Mir*, but his assessment of Tītū Mīr's personality is uneven and inconsistent in parts.

    An unnoticed Persian source-material is the account given in the Supplement of the *Manzūra*, Punjab University Library Lahore, ms. copy. Thanks to my friend Dr. Muhammad Muiz of the Iqbal Academy, Lahore, who very kindly sent a copy of the extract to me, I have been able to use it here.
60. Khan, op. cit., p. lxvi; O'Kinealy's article cited above.
61. I.M., p. 45.
62. Selection from Bengal Government Records, vol. xlii, (hereafter cited as Selections) p. 140.
63. O'Kinealy's article, p. 177.
64. The *Farā'iḍīs* were strong and influential in the districts of 24 Paraganas, Jessore, Pubna, Malda, Faridpur, Dacca and Chittagong and they were estimated to number 80,000; *Selections*, pp. 140, 141.

65. Biharilal Sarkar, *Titu Mir,* quoted in Khan, op. cit., pp. 21, 27; also Abhijit Dutta, op. cit.
66. O'Kinealy's article, cited above.
67. According to the *Manzūra,* after the raja (zamindar) had been defeated and killed a British planter and a businessman went with some of their men to the zamindar's aid but both of them met with the same fate.
68. O'Kinealy's article, cited above, p. 179.
69. *C.R.,* 1870, p. 183.
70. Ibid.
71. Ibid., p. 184.
72. O'Kinealy's article.
73. As quoted in O'Kinealy's article cited above.
74. S.M.R., pp. 37-38; Hardy, op. cit.
75. On this, see Abhijit Dutta, *Christian Missionaries on the Indigo Question in Bengal,* Calcutta, 1989. The records examined relate to a period after the Baraset Rising.
76. See S.B. Chaudhuri. *Civil Disturbances During British Rule in India,* Calcutta, 1955, p. 50.
77. Govt. of Bengal, Judl. Dept., O.C. no. 5, dated 3rd April, 1832.
78. Khan, op. cit., pp. lxlll-lxvl, mentions some differences between the Wahhabis, the *Farā'iḍis* and the followers of Tītū Mīr's men on some minor doctrinal points but he too agrees that Ḥājī Sharatullah's programme of work was 'almost similar' to that of Tītū Mīr's men. He also states that Dūdū Miyān was influenced by the socio-economic aspect of Tītū Mīr's activities but adds that by the time that influence came to be felt, after 1840, Tītū Mīr's impact had dimmed.
79. *Vide supra,* p. 111 and note 2.

    As early as 1829, Sayyid Ahmad had sent some of his chief followers for working in different parts of India. Enayat Ali had been working in Bengal, and his activities there had drawn the attention of the local police officers (*supra,* pp. 109-11).

Chapter IV

Revival and Consolidation of the Movement

1. *The Imārat of Wilayat Ali and Enayat Ali*

Describing the situation after the death of Sayyid Ahmad, Hunter remarked, "Again the fanatic cause seemed ruined. But the missionary zeal of the Patna Khalifas and the immense pecuniary resources at their command, once more raised the sacred banner from the dust. They covered India with their emissaries, and brought about one of the greatest religious revivals that has ever taken place."[1] The remark brings out the crucial role of the Patna Khalifas, specially Wilayat Ali and Enayat Ali, in reviving and consolidating the movement.

A detailed biographical sketch of both the brothers has been given by the author of the *Tadhkira-i Sādqa* and it may only be briefly noted here that they were the sons of Fath Ali of the Sadiqpore family and were born in A.H. 1205 (1790-91) and A.H. 1208 (1793-94) respectively. After the traditional early education at home, Wilayat Ali[2] had been sent to Lucknow where he studied under Ashraf Ali of the *Firangi Mahal,* and where he had met Sayyid Ahmad and taken *Bai'at* at his hands. Enayat Ali,[3] too, after studying at home, studied under the guidance of Muhammad Musafir, a well-known scholar of *Ḥadīth* at Patna.

Wilayat Ali and Enayat Ali had migrated to the North-Eastern Frontier along with Sayyid Ahmad and had later been deputed by him to organise the activities in British India. Both of them worked in British India as well as the North-Western Frontier during the next two decades, and their activities were broadly of two different kinds. In British India, as we have seen above, they extended the activities of the movement to the southern and eastern parts, and helped build up an elaborate system of supply of men and material which sustained the movement till after their own time. They also initiated the important work of establishing contacts with the Indian units of the Company's army, leading to 'conspiracies' in various cantonments stretching from "the Sutledge to Calcutta".[4] On the North-Western Frontier, they re-organised the affairs of the Wahhabi State which had been established during the time of Sayyid Ahmad and attained some notable successes against the British during 1850s. This phase of their activities is referred to as the *Imārat* of Wilayat Ali and Enayat Ali.

The generally anarchical conditions prevailing in the Punjab during the period preceding and following the first Anglo-Sikh war (1845) may be briefly stated, as setting the background to the activities of the Ali brothers on the Frontier. According to the terms of the treaty of the 9th March 1846,[5] the Sikhs ceded to the English the Jalandhar *doab*, and agreed to pay a cash indemnity of 15 million rupees. Since the treasury was short of cash, the whole of the mountainous area between the rivers Beas and Indus, including Kashmir and upper Hazara, was also ceded to the English in lieu of rupees 10 million as indemnity. The balance was to be paid at the time of the confirmation of the treaty. Out of the ceded areas, the lands to the west of Ravi and east of Indus were sold to Gulab Singh, the governor of Hazara and Kashmir for seven-and-a-half million *Mānakshāhi* rupees. Upper Hazara, it may be noted, was included in that area. In the lower Hazara area various local Pathan tribes, convinced of the utter breakdown of the Sikh government, were in a state of revolt, and striving for freedom from Sikh control. Even in upper Hazara, Gulab Singh was far from exercising any effective control over the new-acquired areas. He could reach it only after obtaining effective control over Kashmir. But the governor of Kashmir, Imamuddin, on secret instructions from Lahore, refused to give charge to Gulab Singh.[6] So, for all practical purposes, both Kashmir and upper Hazara were out of control, and seething with revolt. At both these places there developed centres of opposition to the Sikh government led, in upper Hazara, by Enayat Ali, and in lower Hazara, by Sayyid Akbar Shah.

To restore some semblance of order in the financial and administrative affairs of the newly-acquired areas, James Abbott had been posted at Hazara. At the same time, Henry Lawrence, the Resident at the Lahore *darbār*, moved with a small force to Jammu, from where he sent Herbert Edwardes to Imamuddin. The latter was won over, and induced to hand over Kashmir to Gulab Singh.

It was during this troubled period that Sayyid Zamin Shah,[7] son of Hasan Ali Shah, and the chief of the Kaghan valley, invited Wilayat Ali to come over and resume the task for which the circumstances appeared to be favourable. Wilayat Ali recalled Enayat Ali from Bengal who came over to Patna with some two thousand followers. In order to avoid suspicion over such a large assemblage and movement of men, the party was broken into small batches and each batch moved out of Patna after some time. The move started in July 1843 and the whole party took some five months to leave. Enayat Ali,[8] himself started later, and reached the Frontier towards the end of 1844.

The events after the arrival of Wilayat Ali and Enayat Ali have been briefly mentioned by two modern writers. Bellew [9] writes that Fatah Khan Panjtar had turned against the Wahhabis and was harassing their small bands settled in Sittana. Enayat Ali and Maqsud Ali had been sent from Patna with large supplies of men and money. They were joined by Aulad Ali at Pakhli and they occupied the area and levied tributes. The other writer, O'Kinealy[10] writes that Muhammad Qasim of Panipat who was in the Sind party of Nasiruddin,[11] moved to Kaghan were Zamin Shah and his brother Naubat Shah, the chiefs of Kaghan, became his disciples. He also invited other *'khalifas'* in India, and responding to his call Enayat Ali proceeded from Patna. He was accompanied by Zainul Abedin and many others. There were several encounters with the Sikhs, including the one in support of Najaf Khan of Kaghan who had ben deprived of his possession. Soon after a misunderstanding developed between Muhammad Qasim of Panipat and Zainul Abedin over the question of the re-appearance of Sayyid Ahmad and the latter returned to Calcutta. This had an adverse effect upon the morale of the followers of the movement but the perseverance of Wilayat Ali and Enayat Ali overcame all the obstacles and within a short time rendered the movement strong and effective again.

More authentic information on the subject, unnoticed by writers in English, is available from a rare contemporary letter.[12] Narrating the state of affairs in this area, the letter[13] begins with the statement that after the dispersal of men (following the battle of Balakote) and the loss of hope in the "re-appearance"[14] (of Sayyid Ahmad), it was decided by the *'ulamā* and wise men of "this state", the migrants from Hindustan, and the rank and file that someone from among those present should be elected the Amīr. It was resolved that, setting aside all discussions about the re-appearance of Sayyid Ahmad or otherwise, they should gird up their loins and devote themselves exclusively to the propagation of God's Word. Thereafter, following the capture of Balakote in the month of *Dhīqa'da,* A.H. 1261 (November, 1845) all the *mujāhids, mullas,* and *sardārs* of 'this country' took the *Bai'at* of *Imāmat* at the hand of Maulana Enayat Ali. After assuming command, he started appointing soldiers. He took the rein of affairs in his hands and brought everyone, including Zamin Shah of Kaghan, under his control. Balakote had been captured from the Sikhs shortly before this, and in *Muḥarram* 1262 (December, 1845), an attack was made on Garhi Habibullah. Fatahgarh was then besieged for a month, and captured. Owing to the weakness of the central government at Lahore, many of the Sikh garrisons were abandoning the forts in the outlying areas. Enayat Ali had sent messages to some of the Sikh commanders calling for their surrender. Some of them replied in conciliatory terms, while others reacted haughtily. Within a short time, however, twenty-two forts, in the areas of Pakhli, Dhamtaur,[15] Orish,[16] Tanawal and Hazara surrendered and large quantities of arms and other materials were captured. Many wealthy money-lenders were also arrested.[17]

Meanwhile, with the arrival of a Sikh garrison in Pakhli there was a change in the attitude of the tribesmen. They called upon the Wahhabis who went to collect the tithe from them to defeat the Sikhs first. Enayat Ali sent a force, composed partly of salaried soldiers and some 60 Wahhabis, under *Munshī* Shujauddin towards Nowshera and another force, comprising 200 men under Maqsud Ali to Muzaffarabad to help Sultan Husain. There followed a major battle against the Sikhs, which occurred between July and September, 1846. A large Sikh army, comprising 900 *sawārs* and 5000 infantry, was assembled on the slopes of the mountains on both the sides. There were some 12000 tribesmen who were outwardly with the Wahhabis, but secretly in league with the Sikhs. They were waiting to loot the Wahhabis camp as soon as the Sikhs, so they hoped, would be victorious. The encounter began after the noon prayer, and was heralded by a severe bombardment from the Sikh side. The flag-bearer of the Wahhabis, Muhammad Umar, was hit in the arm by a bullet and on seeing the standard fall the tribesmen thought that the Wahhabis were defeated. But the standard was kept aloft, the Wahhabis rallied, and the Rohillas made a concerted attack. The Sikhs could not stand it and retreated, hotly pursued by the Wahhabis. Their stores, worth more than a lakh of rupees, were looted by the tribesmen. Owing to the slushy ground (it being the rainy season), and the tall *shālī* grass, it was not easy for the Sikhs to beat a hasty retreat. They were pursued by the tribesmen, who, on seeing the Wahhābī victory, had turned against them, and killed them in order to loot their arms and other possessions. The hunting down of the Sikh stragglers continued for three days. The Sikhs, although strong and able-bodied let themselves be looted by men who were physically no match for them. Among the hypocritical chiefs, who had sided with the Sikhs, Nawab Khan Tanawli,[18] Madal Khan [19] and Muhammad Ali were produced before Enayat Ali, but were pardoned on the intercession of their loyal chiefs, such as Amir Khan.[20]

The account then moves on to another topic— the arrival of Wilayat Ali on the Frontier and his election as the Amīr. Wilayat Ali, it states, arrived rom Patna in September, 1846. He was accompanied by Yahya Ali,[21] Faiyyaz Ali and Akbar Ali, brothers of Ahmadullah,[22] and a large number of volunteers and considerable arms and stores. Enayat Ali sent an advance detachment to receive him at Mankali, the border outpost of the Wahhabi state. At Nowshera, the local commander *Dārogha* Riyasatullah came out and fired a gun salute; Maqsud Ali too joined in with his detachment. The next halt was at Libberkote,[23] where Zamin Shah and Amir Khan had been sent to welcome the august guest. Enayat Ali himself, with his personal standard and a posse of Rohilla soldiers, advanced one stage to receive his elder brother. The meeting took place in the plains of Uttarsisa.[24] It was a happy occasion, and everybody celebrated it with thanksgiving to God. After the midday meal, the party moved on to Fatahgarh, now renamed Islamgarh, the capital of the Wahhabi state, where the local chiefs assembled to pay their homage and tribute. Enayat Ali also took *Bai'at* at his brother's hands, who assumed the leadership. Wilayat Ali, in a graceful gesture, asked all those present to continue treating Enayat Ali as their chief as before.

The concluding portion of the letter extends an invitation to the "Hindustani and Bengali brothers", assuring them of a warm welcome, and of gainful employment there. It was pointed out that an employment there was better and more "meritorious" than that under the kafirs'. Finally, it states that those who could not migrate for some reason could extend financial support.

Soon after [25] the arrival of Wilayat Ali on the Frontier, the Wahhabis clashed with the British authorities in the battle of Doob Pass.[26] The

British, as stated above, were actively helping the Sikhs and Gulab Singh to restore their power in the disturbed Frontier region. Henry Lawrence, the British Resident at Lahore and under him a group of energetic young officers, such as Abbott, Edwards and Taylor were in fact laying the foundation of British rule in that area. Having helped Gulab Singh get possession of Kashmir, the British thought it advisable [27] to send a detachment of their own soldiers along with the Sikh army under the command of Diwan Karam Chand to march from Kashmir down to Lahore, restoring order on the way. While the Wahhabis were preparing to meet this force coming from Muzaffarabad side, a false impression was created that a Sikh force was also coming from the Pakhli side. The threat of a double-pronged attack unnerved the local adherents of the Wahhabis, and they defected. Left alone, and faced by a force consisting of 10 regiments, the Wahhabis, including Wilayat Ali and Enayat Ali, surrendered after a brief encounter. They were forced to return to their native place, Patna and execute bonds of good behaviour before the local magistrate there.

These events have been mentioned by the authors of both the *Tadhkira-i Sadqa*[28] and the *Sawāniḥ Ahmadi.*[29] Both of them had played a leading role in the movement and had much direct information about the events connected with it. Their books were, however, published after the movement had been suppressed and after they had suffered long terms of imprisonment. They have tried at some places to underplay the anti-government aspect of the movement but in this particular case they have stressed the leading role played by the British officers and their detachment. Both of them state that the Wahhabis had been fighting against Gulab Singh and had achieved some success. Gulab Singh had first sought to come to some agreement with the Wahhabis, but failing in that effort he had turned to the British for help. The British had got a letter written to Wilayat Ali and Enayat Ali, saying that Gulab Singh had entered into an agreement with them and by virtue of it he enjoyed their protection. Fighting against him would be tantamount to fighting against the British government and they shoud desist from it. Soon after, two officers, Lumsden and Vans Agnew, were sent to help Gulab Singh. They succeeded in winning over some of the supporters of the Wahhabis, including Zamin Shah.[30] The position of the Wahhabis was rendered weak, and they wanted to go over to Swat.

To go there they had to pass through some territories under British control. They obtained a written assurance of safe passage from Lumsden and Vans Agnew. But when they reached that area they were surrounded and arrested. The assurance was revoked on the plea that it had been given by local officers without the permission of higher authorities. The Rohilla soldiers were furious at the treachery and wanted to fight, but Wilayat Ali counselled restraint. The Wahhabis were sent to Lahore, where John Lawrence,[31] the chief commissioner welcomed them, but persuaded them to surrender their arms. The Rohilla soldiers were dismissed and paid out of the proceeds of the sale of arms. The Ali brothers were entertained to a feast, given some money for the return journey and sent back to Patna. On reaching Patna they called upon the commissioner, at whose *kothi* (official residence) a very large number of the towns people had gathered to see them. The commissioner asked them to execute security bonds for two years' good conduct.

Mehr [32] rejects this version on account of certain mis-statements from which it suffers. He points out that neither had Punjab been fully annexed by the British till then, nor was Lawrence the Chief Commissioner at that time. Sayyid Akbar too had not ben crowned King of Swat, and the Hazara area was not under the control of the British. Mehr is quite right in pointing out these inaccuracies, but we have to keep in mind the fact that both the authors of the *Tadhkira-i Sādqa* and the *Swāniḥ* were presenting a general account of the activities of Sayyid Ahmad's followers and that their knowledge of the general history of the period was, at best, limited. At the time the two works were written, the post of commissioner was in existence and it is not unlikely that they overlooked the technical difference[33] between the two posts of Resident and Chief Commissioner. As for the areas not being under the control of the British, since the negotiations in this case were carried on by the British officers, the Wahhabis might have got that impression, and in any case the *de facto* political dominance of the British in that area was fairly evident.

A modern writer has pointed out the primary role of the British in quelling the revolt in Kashmir and in restoring the nominal power of the Ṣikh *darbār* and Gulab Singh. The writer draws attention to the "remarkable spectacle of the English Agent marching at the head of the Sikh troops, supported by the English forces to wrest Sikh territory from Imamuddin."[34]

More recently fresh information has come to light, on the basis of the correspondence between Lord Hardinge, Governor-General at the time (1844-48) and Ripon, President, Board of Control, regarding the political situation in the Kashmir and Hazara area on the eve of the first Anglo-Sikh war.[35] Hardinge felt concerned about the fast disintegrating power of the Sikh government and the "revolts in the Muslim majority areas of Multan, Kashmir, and the territories lying between the river Indus and the Afghan border". Hardinge felt anxious about the possibility of a Muslim state or states emerging in the area, as it would "excite and revive Mussalman hopes throughout India". He wanted to bolster up Gulab Singh's power and resources by giving him additional territory wrested (after the war) from the Sikhs. Ripon, however, like most other senior officials, did not share these apprehensions entirely. The point to note here is that the revolt against Sikh authority in the area (the Wahhabis are not mentioned specifically, but it is clear that the activities of Wilayat Ali and Akbar Shah formed part of the general picture) was viewed by Hardinge from a wider angle and construed as a threat to the imperial interests. He wanted either a direct intervention in the Punjab or help to the British protege, Gulab Singh. He was for a policy of fighting the Muslim insurgents (the Wahhabis included) by proxy, so to speak.

Finally, the leading role played by the British officers in this affair is confirmed by the statement[36] of a participant in the events, as also by some contemporary English records.[37] The statement is worth reproducing, as it enables us to see the situation as the Wahhabis viewed it and also because it has been completely ignored. It reads :

> "After the Sikhs escaped, six battles were fought in Muzaffarabad and about 1200 of the Sikhs went up to the hills called Doab (sic); these Sikhs were sent by the English for at *that time the English had possession of Lahore.*[38] At that time Moulvi Wilayat Ali and the rest were defeated, and the *sardārs* of Kaghan, viz., Naubat Shah, Zamin Shah and others, joined the Sikhs, and they plainly told Wilayat Ali, 'We cannot support you any more'. Abbott was then at Hazara and he *directed a Sikh sardār* (whose name I do not recollect), *to fetch us down the hill, promising to let us go and telling him to take charge of us and also stating that if we sold the arms which we had with us he would pay us their value. We received Rs. 12000 for the guns, zambooraks, camels*

> *etc...* We were then about 400 men. On reaching Beer ka Durah we met Mr. Abbott, who accompanied us to Balakote, where there were 12 regiments belonging to the English, and no end of men at Hazara. At this place, Mr. Abbott asked Wilayat Ali, 'Now where will you go ?' He replied, 'To Sittana'. Mr. Abbott replied 'You better come to Hazara and meet the Lord *Saheb*[39] and you can do as he commands.' *They were then helpless, and obliged to go to Hazara and had to encamp close to the fort.* After some days, the Lord *Saheb* sent for Wilayat Ali, Enayat Ali, Maqsud Ali, Fyaz Ali and Yea (Yahya) Ali. When they entered the tent, they were asked *whether they were not inhabitants of Sadiqpore in Azimabad, whether they were not English subjects and whether or not they paid revenue to government.* 'Why have you come to this country', they asked, 'According to our faith we must fight with the *kaffirs.* The Sikhs[40] were our enemies and therefore we came to fight them.' But *the Lord Saheb said, 'That country belongs to the English.* What will you do now?' They said, 'We will go to Cabool.' But the Lord Saheb said, 'That country is *yagistan* (independent) up to Cabool. *If you go there, you will again plot and fight with the English. For this reason I cannot permit you to go there.'* He then ordered that we should return to our homes. On this we dispersed. Moulvi Wilayat Ali, Enayat Ali, Maqsud Ali, Fyaz Ali, and Yea Ali returned to their respective homes at Azimabad, and were bound down under *moochulka* (security bond) not to leave Patna for four years. I went to my home in Hajipur and built a house there, and married at Dinapur.

In view of this authentic corroboration, the version of the *Tadhkira-i Sādqa* and the *Sawāniḥ*, in spite of minor inaccuracies, has to be accepted as substantially correct.

On return to Patna, the Ali brothers were asked to give written guarantees of good behaviour and were "bound down on bail of ten thousand rupees not to leave the city of Patna for four years."[41] They did not, however, remain inactive. Wilayat Ali resumed his preaching tours and the supervision of organisational work. He also maintained correspondence with Aulad Ali, who had managed to escape to Sittana at the time when the Wahhabis had surrendered. Wilayat Ali had, meanwhile, been invited to the North-Western Frontier by Sayyid Akbar Shah. Enayat Ali, on the other hand, slipped off to his favourite field of work in the interior areas of Bengal. His treasonable activities there, including enrolling of 'Crescentaders', was brought to the notice of the district authorities of Rajshahi in 1850,[42] and he had to return to Patna, where he was again bound over a security of one thousand rupees.

On finding that the suspicion of the government authorities had been aroused, the brothers decided to wind up their personal affairs[43] and to start on their second, final migration. They set off separately from Patna towards the middle of 1850. The local magistrate reported that in view of their unauthorised departure he could "seize the party who was their security," but added that such a step might *"cause some stir in this evil and degraded city"*[44] and sought government's order for it.

Some of the other important members of the family, such as Yahya Ali, Fayyaz Ali and Abdullah, along with a party numbering 250 men and women, set out from Patna with Wilayat Ali. Only his younger brother Farhat Husain,[45] was left to look after the home front. Marching in easy stages, halting at different places and delivering lectures, the party reached Delhi after about a year, and halted in a house near the well-known Fatahpuri mosque. They stayed there for two months, and Wilayat Ali's public discourses attracted wide attention.[46] Among the important persons who attended the lectures, delivered in the *Jāmī'* mosque and other mosques in the city, were the famous Urdu poet Momin and Imam Ali, the tutor of *Zeenat Mahal,* the chief queen of Bahadur Shah II. Imam Ali also took *Bai'at* at Wilayat Ali's hands and spoke about him to the King, who expressed a desire to meet him. Wilayat Ali with a party of seventy-five persons went to the Palace, where a *darbār* was held in the *Dīwān-i-Khās,* and he delivered a lecture there. He began his lecture with a verse from the *Qur'ān* relating to the transitoriness of worldly life. It was a moving address, delivered in contravention of the Court etiquette that only pleasant topics, like the blessings in Paradise and not admonitory ones, like the punishments in Hell, were dwelt upon in the presence of the King.[47] Wilayat Ali, and the party accompanying him, were then taken around the imperial buildings by the Resident. The King wanted them to stay on for some time more, as the month of *Ramadān* was at hand. But Wilayat had become somewhat suspicious on account of the close questioning by the Resident about his antcedents and the purpose of his journey.[48] Taking leave, he immediately left the city, crossed the Jamuna and marching by quick stages, reached Ludhiana where he halted at

Khanna ki Sarai, waiting for Enayat Ali. The two brothers met in November 1850, and proceeded on to the North-Western Frontier.

The journey was uninterrupted; only at one place, Khabal,[49] near Sittana, were they intercepted and some baggage and a few camels were captured by the police, but these too were subsequently returned on the orders of the Deputy Commissioner, Peshawar, to whom they had been forwarded. Indeed, the long stay of Wilayat Ali at Delhi, his audience with the King and his being shown around the palace by the British Resident, in spite of his past career and the recorded proceedings of the magistrates indicate a total lack of cooperation between the diffferent government authorities. O'Kinealy expresses astonishment at "the great gulf between the rulers and the governed; how little care is taken to know anything of even the most dangerous sect. The war of Syed Ahmad, the rebellion at Baraset, the resistance and subsequent surrender of the fanatics at Hureepur were forgotten as soon as over; and the Government awoke when it was too late to find that the Patna Maulvis had returned to Sittana to disturb and agitate the minds of the hilly tribes."[50]

There are some references to a difference of opinion having developed between the two brothers during this period. It related to the defection of Jahandad Khan, chief of Amb, who was collaborating with the British and obstructing the caravans coming from India. Enayat Ali wanted immediate action against him, but Wilayat Ali advised caution and restraint. O'Kinealy attributes this to Wilayat Ali's wide travels in British India, which had given him a better idea of the power and resources of the British government. He did not favour premature encounters for it would forewarn the government about their activities and lead to the suppression of their numerous centres working all over British Indian territory. Enayat Ali, on the other hand, was impatient of waiting which he thought smacked of a lack of faith. The differences, led to a virtual division among the Wahhabis, the Bengali recruits following Enayat Ali (who had worked among them) and the rest backing Wilayat Ali.[51] The situation was saved by Wilayat Ali offering to relinquish the leadership and by Enayat Ali, in a reciprocal gesture, accepting the leadership of his elder brother and moving out from Sittana to Mangalthana. This happened around November, 1851.[52]

The difference of opinion was not about the main objective but the line of action and it was partly temperamental too. Enayat Ali was bold, impetuous and sharp-tempered.[53] He was eager to have it out with the British and when his efforts were thwarted by the defections of local chiefs or other causes, he chafed and got annoyed. Yahya Ali, who enjoyed the confidence of both the parties, made some efforts for a conciliation but did not attain much success.[54] In retrospect, it appears that Wilayat Ali's was the more reasonable approach. He showed an appreciation of the important factor of resources. One can only speculate on his line of action in future, had he been alive at the time of the Rising of 1857. He might have taken advantage of it to strike some blows against the government, but that was not to be. He died on the 5th November, 1852 and was buried at Sittana. Jafar (*Sawāniḥ*, p. 167; see also T.S.) gives a chronogram recording the month and year of his death which is translated into English as under:

Wilayat Ali, a guide to the true religion. As in the month of Muḥarram (15 October - 13 November), he was laid to rest;

Say the year of his death by adding (the number of) the first letter[55] of the word *Āh* (i.e. *alif*, = 1)

To (the number of the letters in the words "He travelled to the Holy Paradise". (i.e. 1268 +1, or 1269).

Enayat Ali returned to Sittana and was elected Amīr. Although he had bowed to his elder brother's wishes, he was convinced of the correctness of his own line of action. The first round of direct encounters with the British forces in the area took place during the next six years under his leadership.

II. Early Encounters With The British Forces

Following the annexation of the Punjab, the Hazara area came under the control of the British by virtue of an exchange of territories with Gulab Singh and James Abbott became its first Deputy Commissioner (1849). Abbott gave early attention to the existence of a 'remarkable nest of emigrants from Hindoostan,' whose activities, he thought, might prove to be dangerous in case of trouble from the south, or from the Durranis in the west. He also came into conflict with Sayyid Zamin Shah of the Kaghan valley, a staunch supporter of the Wahhabis. Apparently, the cause of action against the Sayyids was the complaint of their Gujar tenants against their high-handedness, but that was only a pretext. The real reason was Abbott's suspicion that the Sayyids were in league with the Wahhabis, who were stirring up some other tribes, such as the Dhunds, to rise against the British.

During his investigations in the matter, Abbott was "perhaps, too ready to listen to the tales told by the Saiad's enemies."[56]

A force, comprising six regiments, six guns and numerous tribal levies was sent against the Sayyids, who were defeated. Zamin Shah was exiled and the Kaghan valley brought under British control. The matter, however, did not end there; the British subsequently came into conflict with other tribes and with the Wahhabis, the so-called 'Hindustani fanatics.'

After taking over the administration of Hazara, the British in their characteristic thorough manner set up several administrative departments under the overall control of the Board of Administration, Punjab. One of these was the Department of Salt, which prohibited the import of the Kohat salt from across the border. Two local officers of the department, Carnac and Tappe, took upon themselves the task of investigating the route through which the prohibited salt came. It was reported to them that it passed through the trans-Indus portion of Amb, which bordered on the independent tribal area of the Hasanzais. During their investigation, they went perilously close to the Hasanzai area, against the express wishes of their superiors.[57] They paid the penalty and were killed by some unknown tribesmen, suspected to be Hasanzais. The murder was attributed to motives of greed and robbery but actually economic factors were involved. The Hasanzais suspected that the two officers would extend the salt line to their area, and would thus affect their trade in salt. They considered it to be an encroachment on their livelihood. The British suspected Jahandad Khan, chief of Amb and their ally, to be in collusion with the tribesmen and asked him to hand over the Hasanzais who happened to be in his territory at the time. He complied with the demand but it provoked the Hasanzais, who declared war upon him and seized the border outposts of Chamberi and Shinglai.

Abbott pressed the government to avenge the death of Carnac and Tappe, which he considered to be necessary for maintaining the government's prestige among the tribesmen. The Governor General-in-Council was, however, at first reluctant to take any steps, not because of "an indifference to the fate of these gentlemen"[58] (Carnac and Tappe), but because engaging in hostilities proposed by Abbott would place them in a "worse position." After much hesitation, and owing to the pressure of Colonel Mackeson, Commissioner Peshawar, who in this instance supported Abbott, a force consisting of detachments of the Guides and some police were sent against the Hasanzais (December 1851). Thus started the first Black Mountain expedition,[59] which later developed into the first important military encounter between the British and the Wahhabis. The British force ascended the Black Mountain range, chastised the Hasanzais and burnt their villages.

The easy success of the military expedition, about which the authorities were hesitant in the beginning, took the government by surprise. They were fulsome in their praise for Colonel Mackeson, who also expressed surprise at the easy victory and commented that the government "shall have all the credit with Jahandad Khan of having assisted him effectively in his extremity."[60] But he also expressed doubt as to whether Jahandad Khan deserved the help and how long he would benefit from it. The remark proved to be prophetic, for on return from the Hasanzai expedition the British force found itself faced with a new adversary, the Wahhabis. Considering this to be a good opportunity for gaining the wider sympathy of tribesmen, which was vital for the success of his mission, Enayat Ali had started working among the neighbouring tribesmen, exhorting them to rise against the British and help their fellow tribesmen, the Hasanzais. He did not receive an encouraging response but went ahead with his own force. The British tried to dissuade the Wahhabis from helping the Hasanzais but Enayat Ali contemptuously turned down the advice, declaring that "he had come to die."[61] Jahandad Khan's outpost of Kotla was attacked and occupied. The government again hesitated in sending a force against the Wahhabis. Colonel Mackeson candidly writes, "I hesitated much whether I would interfere at all in the Kotla business. Nothing but a confidence from seeing the ground, that we could well protect our crossing and recrossing and reduce the (Wahhabi) garrison to extremity ... induced me to venture to send a force across."[62]

Finally, on the 6th January, 1852, a force[63] under Major Abbott advanced to re-occupy Kotla. It was situated in village Ashra at an elevation of about a thousand feet on a spur of the mountain. The British force, in conjunction with that of Jahandad Khan, advanced from three sides. The former, crossing the Indus, advanced from the front side, while Jahandad's men cut off the line of retreat. The Wahhabis were caught between two forces superior in arms and numbers. Fighting a spirited rearguard action, in which they lost some 70 persons, including the commander Karam Ali of Dinapur, they withdrew from Kotla. Sittana, their chief centre, now lay exposed to a British attack, but the force contented itself with the re-occupation of Kotla.

Some information about the Wahhabis of Sittana, their organisation, resources, etc., is available in the papers relating to this campaign.[64] It appears that the Wahhabis numbered some 600 men and that Wilayat Ali was "formerly the director of all their proceedings," but since his death, a year ago, the leadership had devolved upon Enayat Ali. Four of the brothers of Sayyid Akbar Shah of Swat lived with them and enjoyed considerable influence among them. Monetary help was received from the Nawab of Tonk, who used to send between twenty to forty thousand rupees a year. Nawab Nasiru'd Dawlah of Hyderabad also sent some money. The principal source of revenue, however, was the contribution collected by the volunteers from all over the country. The amount thus collected varied from time to time, but it was considerable. One year, one person alone, from Bengal, had sent Rs. 40,000. Then there was cultivated land, measuring 900 *bighas*, given by Akbar Shah. There were some forty persons owning their own lands; the proceeds of all these lands were put in a common fund.

The party did military exercises regularly; they had some carbines and horses. The usual word of command was *Allah-o-Akbar* (Allah is Great). Their food comprised mainly of bread and pulses.

After the battle of Kotla Enayat Ali moved to Nawaggi in Chumle territory and also toured Swat and Buner areas. He urged[65] Sayyid Akbar Shah and the *Akhund*[66] to join hands with him, but the latter did not show much enthusiasm for the alliance. He probably discerned a threat to his prestige in the increasing influence of the Wahhabis. The *Akhund's* attitude made it dificult for Enayat Ali to do much from Sittana and he moved on, at the instance of Sayyid Abbas, to Mangalthana, situated in the Khudukhel territory on the spur of the Mahabun Mountain, west of Sittana.

Enayat Ali worked among the Yusufzais living in the plains bordering Peshawar and Mardan and tried to organise them against the British. Attempts were also made to infiltrate into the ranks of the Indian units of the army. It appears that the Mubarakkhel tribe accepted the leadership of Enayat Ali (December, 1855) and on their invitation he reached Nagrai in January the following year. Soon afterwards, a messenger from British India, Waziruddin, arrived from Patna with some money.[67]

Enayat Ali's general activities during the period have been summed up in the following words: "He (Enayat Ali) laboured to organise his followers and fired them *with a hatred of the English Kafirs.* The crescentaders were drilled daily, sometimes twice a day, and those on parade were taught to recite songs extolling the glories of *jihad.* On Fridays after the jumma prayers they listened to sermons... exhorting them to wait patiently until the time appointed for subjugation of British India would arrive."[68]

The rising of 1857 provided Enayat Ali with better opportunities to step up his activities in the Peshawar district and to organise raids on some of the border villages and the neighbouring military stations. The Wahhabis and the neighbouring clans were kept under control from the great fort of Mardan. It was garrisoned by the Corps of the Guides but after the Rising of 1857 the Corps had come to form a part of the Punjab Movable Column and was substituted by the 55th Native Infantry. The men of this regiment revolted in the middle of May, 1857 but were attacked and dispersed by a force under Colonel Nicholson and Mardan came to be garrisoned by the 5th Punjab Infantry and two Guns of the Peshawar Mountain Battery under Major Vaughan.[69] Some of the men of the mutinous 55th N.I. had proceeded to Swat where they expected to join Sayyid Akbar Shah. Akbar Shah's death just on the day of the rising at Meerut had, however, brought about a reversal of the situation in Swat. They did not receive the expected welcome there due mainly to the opposition of the *Akhund.* A peculiar form of dual government prevailed there under which power was shared equally by the king and the *Akhund,* with the latter exercising a greater influence by virtue of his religious eminence. Till the time of Sayyid Akbar Shah the relations between the two were good. After the death of Akbar Shah, the *Akhund* opposed the succession of his son, Mubarak Shah, and got him expelled from Swat. Mubarak Shah took refuge at Sittana and later moved to Panjtar, close to Mangalthana where Enayat Ali was staying. Mubarak Shah met Enayat Ali and they planned an attack on the fort of Mardan, commanding the Yusufzai plain. It was at this time that the mutinous units of the 55th N.I. had been dismissed from Swat due to the opposition of the *Akhund* and they were on the lookout for some other anti-British centre of activity. They proceeded to Mangalthana where they received a warm welcome from Enayat Ali's men.

In the neighbouring principality of Panjtar, a dispute had been going on between its chief, Muqarrab Khan, and some of his subjects, particularly the Totalis.[70] The chief of Chinglai, Mubariz Khan, was also against Muqarrab Khan, and had invited Enayat Ali after the Rising of 1857 to join him in attacking some of the adjacent British areas. The first attack was made on Nawakilla, a village close to Chinglai, and another one, Shaikh Jana. The initial attack was successful and both the villages were occupied. But a relieving force was sent from Mardan by Assistant Commissioner Horne, under the command of Major Vaughan of the 5th Punjab Infantry and it re-occupied Shaikh Jana (July, 1857). Seven of the villagers were executed as a punishment.

A fortnight later Enayat Ali led an attack upon Narinji. He had some men of the 55th N.I. and some *sawārs* from Pantjar with him. The village, although situated in British occupied area, was on the extreme border, and was difficult to reach, being located on the upper reaches of a precipitous hill. Enayat Ali, however, succeeded in occupying the strategic village. The British authorities promptly took counter-measures.

On July 18th, 1857, a force [71] under Major Vaughan again set out from Mardan to recover Narinji. The action was heralded by a bombardment of the village; the infantry then advanced in a skirmishing order. After a tenacious resistance by the Wahhabis the force occupied the lower reaches of the hill. The Wahhabis' losses included fifty wounded, including some sepoys of the 55th N.I. whose bodies were identified by the British force from their uniforms and arms. The British losses were 5 killed and 25 injured.[72]

Narinji had only been defeated, not captured. Enayat Ali had not lost hope; the people of Narinji were with him and refused to give him up when demanded by the English. Mubariz Khan and Alam Khan, brothers of Muqarrab Khan, were procuring men from Buner to come to the aid of Enayat Ali. Chumla had sent seven standards (including about 200 men) and promises of aid had also been received from Swat.

On the 3rd August, a larger British force [73] assembled at Shewa and proceeded to Narinji. A detachment was sent by another road a mile-and-a-half ahead of Narinji, to go up the hill by a secret path and attack the enemy's rear. A cannonade was opened with the two 24-pounder howitzers and Mountain Guns. The Wahhabis had no matching guns but returned fire from their matchlocks from their position on the heights. After half-an-hour of bombardment, the assault began. The Wahhabis fought bravely but had to give way to a superior force, attacking from two sides. Enayat Ali withdrew from Narinji to a safer place up the hill. The village was completely destroyed. "Not a house was spared, even the walls of many were destroyed by the elephants. The towers were then blown up under the direction of F.S.Taylor ... of the Engineers, and the village was soon a mass of ruins."[74] Three prisoners taken captive were subsequently executed.[75]

The period following the battle of Narinji was one of great difficulties for the Wahhabis. The success of the British in some of the recent engagements had affected the loyalty of some of the tribesmen who began harassing them. The leaders in British India, Shah Muhammad Husain and Ahmadullah had been put under preventive detention by the Commissioner of Patna, William Tayler.[76] That had affected the flow of aid. After the rising of 1857 a stricter watch was kept on the Indus ferry *ghāts*, and it had become more difficult for messengers to come across.[77] In spite of all these difficulties, however, Enayat Ali continued his anti-British activities till the very end of his life.

In October, 1857, a night attack was led by Shariatullah with the help of the people of Shaikh Jana and Narinji (who in spite of the two punitive expeditions against them were still with the Wahhabis) against the village of Nawakilla where Horne, the Assistant Commissioner of the Yusufzai area was camping. A large booty fell into the hands of the attackers. Horne himself barely escaped with his life.[78] This was the last encounter with the British during the lifetime of Enayat Ali. The ceaseless activities of the past thirty years, the last two of which had been spent under very trying circumstances,[79] had taken its toll, and after a short but severe illness Enayat Ali died at Mangalthana towards the end of March, 1858.

No successor was chosen immediately after his deadh. Enayat Ali's son, Abdul Majid, was not considered fit on account of a natural disability of stammering. A triumvirate was formed, with Ikramullah, Nurullah and Mir Taqi,[80] with Nurullah acting as the senior member. Ikramullah died in a battle shortly afterwards.

III The Wahhabi State on the North-Western Frontier

During the lifetime of Sayyid Ahmad himself, the Wahhabis had been able to establish an independent state on the Frontier. Now as a result of the efforts of Wilayat Ali and Enayat Ali its position was consolidated. The English sources are quite silent about the particulars of the state founded there, nor are the Wahhabi sources of much help in this regard. The lone but very important exception is the letter, cited above,[81] written by the men from Bihar and Bengal to their relatives at home. It gives detailed information about the boundary, income, army, civil and judicial functionaries of the state. An English translation of the relevant portion is given below :

1. *Boundaries:* The boundary of 'Islam' (viz. the Islamic state) was fixed at Nowshera which is adjacent to Sikandarpur in Hazara. Cannon, falcons (?), camels, horses, tents, much wealth and heavy items of equipage came into the possession of the *Mominīn*; smaller items of the equipage (encampment) were left with the (local) tribesmen. As the Islamic army returned victorious, all the 'countries' (areas) such as Jadun, Tanawal, Nandhiar, Alai, Adras (?), Bhogarmang, Pakhli, Dhamtaur, and Kandi agreed to the payment of *ushr* ($^1/_{10}$th of the produce) and accepted our suzerainty. Earlier, tributes had been demanded from the chiefs of the Kunhar valley, Bhogarmang, upper and lower Pakhli, and Kandi; it was hard on them but finding themselves helpless they agreed to pay. By the grace of God, collection of tributes from (the areas) all around is going on. Rewards, gifts and *Ma'āfī* (rent-free assignment of land) and *jāgīrs* are being granted to people according to their respective merits.

About a thousand Rohillas have been recently recruited. In addition to these more than 10,000 are employed in this manner; they have been given lands on the condition of rendering service in times of war. Further, it is the practice in this country that whenever a (tribal) chief goes anywhere for fighting; one arms-bearing man per house accompanies him. In this manner, in addition to the salaried soldiers, there are, by the grace of God, 30,000 troops but out of these only the salaried soldiers are dependable and brave.

2. *Salaries of soldiers.*[82] The salary of a foot-soldiers is from Rs. 6 to 10 (monthly), that of a marksman and *Havalder*, from Rs. 9 to 12, and that of an ironsmith Rs. 30/-. These remunerations have been fixed according to the rate prevailing in the 'country' (area).

3. *Distribution of Work.* (The following are the names of the different functionaries and officers). *Dārogha* Riyasatullah, officer of Manshera[83] fort; *Ḥājī* Gadai Rampurwalia, *Muḥassil* (Collector of Revenue). Manshera, *Munshī* Shujauddin, *Thānadār* of Mankali Tower in Jadun country; Ramzan Ali Khan Azimabadi, resident of

Dhanki, district Patna, Officer (in-charge) Balakote Fort; *Munshī* Ghulam Ali Patnawala, *Munshī* (writer) of the above-mentioned fort; *Ḥājī* Najju Azimabadi, *Muḥassil* of the Revenue of that fort; Yahya Ali, (in-charge of) the Commisariat *(khidmat-i-raftī ?);* Malik Ahmad Ali of Irki,[84] who is a relative of Khairat Ali, trooper, and *Miyān* Muhammad Ali Azimabadi, *Jama'dārs* of the soldiers at the Main Gate of Fatahgarh fort; *Ḥājī* Shamsher Khan of Sahebganj,[85] *Jama'dār* of the Bodyguards; and Bahadur Kahn, of Sahebganj, *Muḥassil* (Collector of Revenue), Fatahgarh. Abdullah Azimabadi has been appointed for giving training to the troopers. He holds (military) exercises daily after the dawn prayers. Salahuddin holds the charge of the Armoury and Stables; Nazir Raihanuddin is in charge of executive matters and the Superintendent of Prisons. Badruddin Burhanwala (?) is the Protector of Treasure, and Maqsud Ali is the commandēr-in-chief of the army. Sufi Muizuddin holds charge of the stores and Nazim Faridpur of grains; and in a like manner there are different posts (which) have been given to the people of Hindustan and of Bangala.

4. *An account of the criminal laws and punishments. Hudūd* and *Oisās* are prevalent in accordance with the *Shara'*. If a poor man absents himself from one (of the five) prayers, he is fined five seers of grains, if it is a chief he has to pay one rupee. The same rule is applicable in the case of the Friday (congregational) prayer. Highway robbers are executed and hung up so that the others may take a warning. Mulla Asad *Akhundzāda* has been appointed *Muftī* in the Kanhar Valley, and the post of Censor of Public Morals has also been assigned to him. Hundreds of students have been placed under him to go round the villages and houses inquiring about those who are performing the prayer; those who do not know how to offer prayers are trained (to do so). (They are also ordered) to restrain people from performing the 'prohibited' practices on the occasions of marriage and mourning and impose fines upon them. The fines realised thereof are appropriated for meeting the expenses of he maintenance of these students. Muhammad Hāji *Akhundzāda* has been appointed Qādī in the Kunhar Pass and Muhammad Husain *Akhundzāda, Akhundzāda* Danawala, the *Wā'zir* (preacher) in Pakhli.

5. *Account of the Darbar.* Rajas, *Salātīn* and *Sardārs* are always in attendance upon *Hadrat Maulāna* (Wilayat Ali). No one, whether a *Rāja* or a Sultān can enter into the Fort without a permit. The *Risāladārs* and *Jama'dārs,* on being called for, present themselves along with a trooper to offer salutation. Eight gunners are always in

attendance upon the Maulana and no one dare speak (in his presence, without permission). Shaikh Imamuddin, the *sūbahdār* of Kashmir, has followed the path of friendly relations, and has appointed two runners *(harkāra)* for the sending of letters; accordingly, two or three letters each month, expressing love and friendly relations, are received from him. When God granted victory *(to Maulāna)* in Nowshera, Shaikh Imamuddin gave rewards to the messenger for bringing the happy news and got cannons fired and expressed much jubilation (over the victory). Letters of Dost Muhammad Khan and Muhammad Akbar Khan from Kabul, in which they express feelings of sincerity and cordiality, and have also avowed for maintaining agreement and alliance, reach him frequently.

It is but with the grace of the *Imām* (Sayyid Ahmad) that such an alliance with the *Sardārs* and Khans of this country has now so firmly been secured. Such a situation did not exist before the battle of Balakote, even in the time of the *Imām.* If given a little thought (pondered upon), it would appear that this too is one of the signs of the nearness of the re-appearance. Now, the matter concerning the *Imām* of the Time is like this; when the *mujāhidīn* reached the Kaghan Pass some claimed that they had sighted him (the *Imām*) in veil, but some people, in spite of (cases of) supernatural feats, refused to accept these visitations, and the visitations stopped. After the lapse of a year and after much beseeching and bewailing, the visitations restarted. After two months some Maulavis again expressed denial and the visitations stopped. However, good tidings communicated through Mulla Abdul Qadir are received even now, and events taken place accordingly. Works done according to such tidings (instruction) are successfully achieved. All such tidings are in accordance with the Book and the *Shariat,* wisdom and consultations. No action is taken against the injunction of the *Qur'ān* and the *Ḥadīth* or against the (principle of) consultation with the *Mominīn.*

Account of the (amounts of) Tributes. The details of the revenues are like this. Tribute from Kanhar Pass, Rs. 16,000/-; Tribute from Bhogarmang Pass, Rs. 5,000/-; tribute from Kandhi, Rs. 7,000/-; tribute from Pakhli, Rs. 26,000/-. The tribute from Dhamtaur is in two parts, that from the territory area of the Salar (tribe) Rs. 30,000/- and that from the territories of Hasanzais and Mansur, Rs. 30,000/-. The tributes from Muzaffarabad, Rs. 40,000/-; that from Karna, Rs. 10,000/-; from Nandhiar, Rs. 20,000/-; from Alai, the same amount. Apart from the lands for the *jāgirdārs* and (other) servants, *'ushr* is due from Alai, Nandhiar and Muzaffarabad, and that too is not less than the sum of *Khirāj* (from those areas). The arrears of the amounts of *Khirāj* is being collected; the collection from Kanhar Pass and Kandi has been completed, that from Bhogarmang Pass is about to be completed, and that from Pakhli too will, God Willing, be completed in a week or ten days. Collectors have been deputed to various places. The collection from Alai has been completed, and on completion of the revenue from Pakhli, the work of collecting (arrears) from Muzaffarabad and Nandhiar will commence. God Willing!

It appears from the foregoing account that a small republic with a considerable income, a large army and a skeleton staff of civil functionaries had been established in the Hazara area. Apart from the territory under its direct control, it claimed the allegiance and received tributes from the chiefs of such areas as Jadun, Tanawal, Nandhiar, Bhogarmang, Pakhli, Dhamtaur, Dares (?), the Kunhar valley, Kandi, Muzaffarabad, Alai, etc. The amount of tributes received from some of these areas is mentioned and it adds up to a total of over two lakh rupees. An equal amount was collected as *'ushr* (land-tax amounting to 1/10th of the produce). Friendly relations had been established with the ruler of Afghanistan and some other chiefs.

The army naturally occupied an important position, since the state was engaged in constant hostilities with the British authorities, and often the tribes. There was, first, a standing army of the Rohilla soldiers; then there were some 10,000 men who had been given lands on condition of service in case of a war. There was also the local custom under which a tribal leader going out on a war was accompanied with one arms-bearing man per house (of the area under his jurisdiction). In all, leaving aside the regulars (who, it is realistically noted, were more dependable), there were some 30,000 soldiers.

The salaries of the infantry and artillery ranks are given as ranging between rupees six to ten (monthly), and rupees nine to twelve, respectively. Interestingly enough, the ironsmiths got a much higher salary of rupees thirty. This indicates both their importance and scarcity. The tribesmen were noted since an earlier period for their skill in manufacturing guns of different calibres, the ironsmiths must have been very useful to the Wahhabis in the manufacturing of country-made guns and other arms.

Among the functionaries mentioned are commanders of forts, officers in charge of armoury, stores and stables, collectors of revenue, *Qādis* and *Muḥtasib*. Criminal laws and punishments were in accordance with the *Shari'at*.

Two rather novel administrative arrangements were made. The first related to the imposition of fines on those who did not perform the five daily prayers or the Friday congregational prayers. The second was about the appointment of a sort of apprentice supervisors, assisting the *Qādī* in training people as to how to offer prayers and in restraining and penalising those who indulged in the prohibited practices on occasions such as marriages and mournings. Such apprentice supervisors were paid out of the fines imposed by them. The linking of the their payment to the fines imposed by them was not a sound arrangement. It might well have made them more prone to levy fines, which in turn might have caused local opposition.

The document gives us a view of the state as it was at a particular period of time. We do not know much about its earlier phase, or its working over a long period of time. It is evident that the administration evolved by the Wahhabis was rudimentary and improvised. This was inevitable to some extent. Circumstances did not allow them time to work out a comprehensive system of government; the shadows of war and rebellion hung over the state all too frequently. The situation was conditioned mainly by the exigencies of war. Hence, only two sets of non-combatant officers could be introduced. Other civilian departments, such as health, education etc. could not be established. One can only speculate on the shape of things, had more time and peaceful conditions been available to the Wahhabis.

IV. Wilayat Ali and Enayat Ali: An Assessment

For over a quarter of a century, Wilayat Ali and Enayat Ali worked ceaselessly over an area of the country stretching from Peshawar to Rajshahi. We know of at least five journeys made by them between Patna and Peshawar: this was in addition to the travels inside Bengal, in the Deccan and in the tribal territories on the North-Western Frontier. All this, one has to be reminded, at a time when the railways were yet to be introduced in the country.[86]

These long journeys across the length of northern India were not always safe, especially for people like Wilayat Ali and Enayat Ali who had been arrested and bound down on bail on more than one occasion, or for the recruits hailing from the interior areas of Bengal whose language, dress and food habits made them easily identifiable. But the rigours and risk of the journeys had been considerably reduced by the chain of 'hospices' set up all along the Grand Trunk Road. This too, as we shall see presently,[87] owed much to the organising genius of Wilayat Ali and Enayat Ali and the discipline and dedication of their followers.

The range and variety of their activities is remarkable by any standard. To begin with, there was the work of preaching both at the headquarters and while travelling. The gatherings were varied: they could be small, simple groups of housewives and uneducated agriculturists and artisans, or consist of educated persons, the *'ulamā*, etc. But they were uniformly characterised by a 'learning and eloquence' which was acknowledged and admired even by their critics.[88]

The preaching was supplemented by the distribution of printed tracts of religious and social importance. This work had its own problems. In the midst of all this, Wilayat Ali, and to a smaller extent Enayat Ali managed to find time for writing *risālas* themselves.[89]

As the Amīr, duties of an altogether different kind had to be performed. Relations with the tribal chiefs was a matter requiring much tact and patience. Apart from the normal administrative work such as appointment of soldiers and officers and correspondence with the tribal chiefs, they had to look after the procurement of arms, supplies, etc. Finally, there was the active duty on the battlefields.

Recounting all this does not imply an emphasis on their role as individuals. The revival and consolidation of the movement was the result of the direct and indirect support of the followers. Wilayat Ali and Enayat Ali provided the leadership, and coordinated the different types of works—organisational, missionary and military—needed to keep the movement going. It is to this multi-faceted nature of their work that Hunter felt constrained to pay tribute. He wrote, "Indefatigable as missionaries, careless of themselves, blameless in their lives, *supremely devoted to the overthrow of the English infidels, admirably skilful in organising a permanent system for supplying money and recruits*, the Patna Caliphs stand forth as the types and exemplars of the Sect. Much of their teaching was faultless, and it had been given to them to stir up thousands of their countrymen to a purer life and truer conception of the Almighty."[90]

The period of their leadership constitutes a significant phase in the history of the movement, which now came to be characterised by a policy of open confrontation with the British government. The reformist base, as propounded by Sayyid Ahmad was there but greater stress now came to be laid on such work as the collection of men and money for the armed struggle and establishing contacts with the Indian units of the army. The stress on the 'obligation' of fighting the foreign rulers becomes a constant theme in the writings and preachings of the Wahhabi missionaries.

Wilayat Ali and Enayat Ali challenged the might of the British government, and constantly fought against its forces in the North-Western Frontier area. They also tried to take some advantage of the situation created there by the rising of 1857. The material resources available to them and their followers were, however, very scanty. It was therefore natural that they could not achieve any important military success. But such a success is not the only, or even an important, criterion for judging the significance of their efforts. One has also to take note of the spirit of sacrifice and the feeling of patriotism which moved them.

Notes

1. I.M., pp. 49-50.
2. He has been described as a man of average height, fat, fair complexioned with a beard and close-knit eyebrows (T.S. pp. 110 ff). After his first wife died childless, he married the daughter of a Hyderabad nobleman during his stay there. Abdullah, the leader of the Wahhabis in the Ambeyla campaign was born of this marriage. Later, in pursuance of the Wahhabis' advocacy of the practice of widow-remarriage, he married the widow of Elahi Bakhsh, a relative.
3. He has been described as a man of average height and fair complexion, with a beard, a broad chest and narrow waist (ibid., pp. 147 ff).
   After his first marriage, he too married a widow in the family, a daughter of Shah Muhammad Husain. She lived and worked with him in the rural areas of Bengal. His son, Abdul Majid, worked with him in the N.W. Frontier and the latter's diary has been quoted as an important source of information for the events following 1860 (Mehr, IV, pp. 276, 494 n.).
   Abdul Majid's grandson, Muhammad Muslim, formerly of St. Columbas' College, Hazaribagh, was a noted Urdu writer and poet, and he translated into Urdu the first edition of this book.

4. Letter from Commissioner, Patna, to Secretary Government of Bengal, no. 1002, dated 8th January, 1846.
5. Cunningham, op. cit. App. XVII, pp. XIV-XVI.
6. Ibid., pp. XIV-XXV.
7. He died in 1871. His brother, Naubat Shah, was also a supporter of the Wahhabis.
8. He was accompanied by Aulad Ali of Surajgarh, who had returned from the Frontier after Sayyid Ahmad's death to arrange for reinforcements.
9. Bellew, H.W., *A General Report on the Yusufzais,* Lahore, 1864, p. 95.
10. C.R., 1870, p. 189.
11. *Vide supra,* p. 96.
12. P.H. ms., Supplement p. 220-28.
    The letter, dated 9 *Dhīqa'da,* A.H. 1262 (12 October, 1846), is written jointly by some of the Wahhabi volunteers hailing from different parts of Bihar and Bengal to their relatives at home. It was a sort of a general report sent to the followers of the movement in British India, keeping them informed of the events on the Frontier and inviting them to join in. Similar reports must have been sent to other parts, but this is the only one of its kind, so far as I know. It covers the period 1845-46.
13. The following five paragraphs present a summarised translation in English of the letter. The concluding portion, covering pages 223-28 have been presented in a later portion of this chapter.
14. On this point, see *supra,* pp. 86-88; *infra,* p. 161.
15. It is a large village, five miles east of Abbottabad, on the right bank of the Dor river. Formerly it gave its name to the whole area.
16. It is one of the plain tracts in the Hazara district, situated to the south of the Mangal tract. The Abbottabad cantonment is situated at its southern edge.
17. The letter says that the events up to this period had been seen by Mamariz Khan (?), the messenger from Tonk, who had since returned.
18. He was the son of Sarbuland Khan, and was known as the chief of Shangeri.
19. He was the younger brother of Painda Khan of Amb, who had assigned the *jāgīr* of Phulera to him. He died in 1878.
20. He was the son of Habibullah, the chief of Garhi Habibullah, who gave his name to the Garhi (fort). He died in 1868.
21. For further details, see chapter VIII.
22. For further details, see chapter VIII.
23. Situated between Nowshera and Uttarsisa.
24. Situated between Nowshera and Garhi Habibullah, 9 miles from the latter.

25. The account given in the letter under reference comes to an end at this point. The narrative has been resumed on the basis of other sources, such as the *Tadhkira-i-Sādqa* and *Sawāniḥ*, supplemented by Bellew's *report* cited above.
26. It is a well-known pass situated at an altitude of 5000 feet between Garhi Habibullah and Muzaffarabad.
27. Letter from Lumsden dated 6 February 1847 to his father in England, quoted by Mehr, IV, p. 262.
28. pp. 215-17.
29. pp. 123-4.
30. T.S., pp. 123-4, Mehr (IV, 265) rejects this version about Zamin Shah defecting, but the statement is confirmed by a contemporary account, *vide infra*, pp. 141-43.
31. The Resident, not Commissioner, at the Lahore *darbār* at this time was Henry, not John Lawrence. The confusion might have been caused by the common surname of the two.
32. Mehr, IV, p. 255.
33. According to the terms of the Treaty of 1845, H.M. Lawrence was appointed Agent to the Lahore *darbār*. In December 1846, the designation was changed from Resident and Agent to Governor General. That designation continued till March, 1848, when it was changed to Resident and Chief Commissioner Cis and Trans Sutlej States (*Lahore Political Diaries*, vol. III, Preface). It is too much to expect Abdul Rahim, quite innocent of English, to bear in mind these fine distinctions.
34. R.R. Sethi, "The Revolt in Kashmir," *Bengal Past and Present*, vol. XLVI, pp. 112-21.
35. See the very illuminating paper, based on the unpublished Ripon Papers, by S.S. Bal, "British Interest in Creating the Dogra State of Jammu and Kashmir," Progs vol., I.H.C., XXIX, Part II, 1967, pp. 40- 50.
36. Statement of Abdullah, son of Jan Ali, of Hajipur, before the Assistant Commissioner, Rawalpindi on 12th October, 1869. Abdullah was a disciple of Wilayat Ali and Muhammad Ali and had taken part in the battle of the Doob Pass.

    The statement forms an enclosure to the letter from J.H. Reily, D.J.G., Police, to the I.G. Police, L.P. no. 207, dated 13th October, 1869. Reily was then investigating the activities of the Wahhabi centres in British India, vide, chapter IX.
37. *Lahore Political Diaries*, vol. III, p. 70. The entry specifically refers to the guarantee by Vans Agnew, but adds that it was for safe passage to Hindustan, not Sittana.
38. Emphasis mine.

39. H.M.Lawrence, who was the Resident at the Lahore *darbār*, and Agent to the Governor-General.
40. This was a convenient subterfuge to conceal their real objective. That the British themselves were well aware of their actual objective is evident from the reply of the 'Lord *Saheb.*'
41. O'Kinealy's article, cited above.
42. A little later, the magistrate reversed his opinion about the nature of Enayat Ali's activities, and informed the magistrate, Patna accordingly, but the latter, being more familiar with the family's background, did not take notice of it.
43. Enayat Ali, who was in Bengal at the time, took some time in disposing of his personal property before leaving Patna.
44. Letter from T. Tucker, Magistrate Patna to C. Beadon, Secretary Government of India, dated 18th August, 1852. This is an unintended testimony to the respect and support enjoyed by the brothers in the city.
45. He was the father of Abdul Rahim, the author of the *Tadhkira-i-Sādqa*.
46. O'Kinealy's article cited above, p. 382.
47. T.S., pp. 126-27. At another place it is stated that the youngest son of Wilayat Ali, Muhammad Hasan who was then aged 5 years was also present on the occasion. The king asked the boy as to what he read and Muhammad Hasan replies that he read the *Qur'ān* and recited some verses from it. The King was very pleased (ibid., pp. 153-54).
48. *Sawāniḥ*, p. 223; *T.S.*, pp. 126-27.
49. It is situated on the right bank of the Indus, opposite Tarabela.
50. *C.R.* 1870, pp. 382-83.
51. Ibid., p. 383.
52. Mehr, IV, p. 275, on the basis of Abdul Majid's diary, cited above.
53. *T.S.*, pp. 132-33.
54. This information is given on a marginal note by Abdul Ghaffar Sahib in his copy of the *T.S.* (p. 32). As mentioned in the Bibliography, these marginal notes have a value of their own.
55. Chronograms are compsed according to the Abjad system under which each letter of the Arabic script has a number attached to it; the total number of the letters in the (usually) last verse, or the indicated words of the verse, yield the year in the Hijri era.
56. H.G., p. 155.
57. For Dept.Pol.Cons. no. 92, dated 15 October, 1852.
58. For Dept.Pol.Cons. no. 91, dated 15 October, 1852.
59. The Black Mountain range is spread over the north-western border of the Hazara district. The Indus skirts its northern extremity and

then turns due south. Between the river and the crest of the Mountain the slopes are inhabited by the Yusufzai tribe, of which the Hasanzais are a subdivision.

The Mountain consists of a main ridge, running north and south, with an average height of 8000' above sea-level. A number of tracks run up to the crest 'which branch off roughly at right angles from the main watershed.' The tracks are thickly wooded and difficult to ascend.

The Black Mountain occupies an important place in the history of British military expeditions. to the North-Western Frontier, especially those directed against the Wahhabis. Several campaigns were fought there in 1852, 1868, 1888 and 1891. For details see Paget & Mason, op. cit.

60. For Dept.Pol.Cons. no. 166, dated the 28th January, 1853
61. Ibid., no. 162.
    On subsequent occasions too such a situation developed, when the Wahhabis, or the 'Hindustanis', hailing from distant areas in British India fought in defence of a Frontier tribe under attack from the British while the neighbouring tribesmen themselves remained indifferent spectators.
62. Ibid., no. 163.
63. It consisted of: Mountain Train Battery, two Guns, 1st and 3rd Sikh Infantries, two Regiments of the Dogras of the Kashmir Army, six wall pieces and six *zamboonaks*.
64. For Dept. Pol. Cons. no. 116, dated 24th March, 1853. The information was obtained from a Wahhabi prisoner of war brought to Peshawar by Dr. Lyell, Assistant Surgeon attached to the Guide Corps. Paying a tribute to the sense of loyalty and honour of the prisoner, Lyell added that the information was elicited only after a government agent had wormed his way into the prisoner's confidence.
65. Mehr, IV, p. 290, writes about this period on the basis of the diary of Abdul Majid, cited above. He saw the diary at Asmast, a centre of the Wahhabis on the Frontier in later years.
66. Born in 1794, his actual name was Abdul Ghaffar. He was an influential religious leader in the Yusufzai and Swat areas. His attitude towards the Wahhabis varied at different periods. In the beginning he supported Sayyid Ahmad but became cold and unhelpful during the crucial years 1857-58. Later, he supported them again during the Ambeyla campaign (1863). For further details, see Bellew, op. cit., pp. 102-07; Oliver, *Across the Border*, pp. 280-88.
67. The British authorities had got a letter circulated at the time that those among the Wahhabis who were willing to surrender would be

pardoned and allowed to return home, while those who refused would be punished severely. The offer was ignored.

68. C.R., 1870, p. 396. Emphasis added.
69. Nevill, H.L., *Campaigns on the North-West Frontier*, reprint, 1984, p. 39.
70. For details, see Paget & Mason, op. cit., pp. 84-89.
71. See Paget & Mason, op. cit., pp. 87 ff.
    The force consisted of Peshawar Mountain Battery, four guns; 2nd Punjab Cavalry, one Troop; The 4th Infantry, 300 bayonets; 5th Infantry, 400 bayonets; mounted police, 40 *sawārs*; Multan levies, 100 *sawārs*.
72. Paget & Mason, op. cit.
73. Ibid., p. 89.
    The force consisted of 24-Pounder Howitzers, two guns, Peshawar Mountain Train Battery, 4 guns; 27, 70 and 87 regiments, 500 bayonets each; 5,6 and 16 Punjab Infantry, 400, 200, and 150 bayonets, respectively; 21 Native Infantry, 50 bayonets; 2nd Punjab Cavalry, 150 sabres, Police and levies, 225 Mounted, 100 Foot.
    The strength of these two British forces gives some indication of the authorities' alarm over the situation, as also their determination to tackle the Wahhabi opposition in earnest.
74. Paget & Mason, op. cit., p. 89.
75. The execution of prisoners of war was an extraordinary measure, to say the least. They could not have been executed on the plea of being 'rebels', for they were working for an independent state.
76. *Vide infra*, pp. 220 ff.
77. The letters of Nathoo Khalifa (*infra*, p. 208) which were written at about this time refer to letters not being allowed through (letter from Deputy Advocate-General, Peshawar, to Commissioner Patna, dated 29th March, 1858; enclosure 1).
78. Bellew, op. cit., p. 198.
79. The disruption of the supplies from British India had put the Wahhabis in a very difficult situation (T.S.) pp. 134-40; Abdul Majid's diary cited above.
80. Bellew, op. cit., p. 198.
81. P.U. ms. supplement, pp. 223-25; see also *supra*, p. 132, n. 1.
82. This portion has not been noted by Mehr.
83. Manshera is a large town and the headquarters of a *taḥsīl* bearing that name.
84. In the district of Jahanabad, Bihar.
85. In the district of Santhal Parganas, Bihar..
86. The railway was opened in 1853, the earliest line being from Bombay to Thana. It was followed the next year by one from

Calcutta to the Raniganj coal-fields and a short stretch in the Madras Presidency.

87. *vide infra,* pp. 174, 180.
88. Hunter's article in S.R., vol. XL, 1860, pp. 130-31.
89. *Vide infra.*
90. *I.M.*, p. 68. Italics are mine.

Chapter V

The Organisational Base of the Movement

I. Organisational Structure, Preaching and Collection of Funds

The information about the internal organisation of the Wahhabi movement is scanty and scattered. Leaving aside the rather brief account given by Hunter about the working of the Wahhabi district centres and itinerant preachers,[1] which relate mostly to a particular area and a particular period of time, we do not have much information on the point. The government records, otherwise copious in their references to the Wahhabi 'preachers' and 'fanatics', are markedly silent about the internal organisation. Nor are the earlier Wahhabi sources, in Persian and Urdu, very helpful though bits and pieces can be culled out. This has to be supplemented with what is available in the family papers and, for the later phase, in the records of the Wahhabi trials. A rough outline of the organisational set-up can thus be drawn. Such an attempt is very essential because it is mainly with reference to the organisational base of the Wahhabi movement that we can understand the wide range and long continuity of its activities.

The outline of the movement was worked out by Sayyid Ahmad himself and the main planks of the organisational activities— touring, preaching, initiating 'volunteers', etc., remained constant over the period. Sayyid Ahmad worked along these lines while he was in British India, and even after his migration he took care to depute some of his more trustworthy followers to India for continuing the work.[2] They not only continued it but extended it in new directions, the most notable being the attempt to establish contacts with the Indian units of the army and to spread discontent among their officers and men. In fact, it was in this field that the Patna leaders made their chief contribution and left their imprint.

The organisational work was guided and controlled from the headquarters at Patna, but there was some decentralisation too, with the heads of the 'district centres' enjoying considerable powers. A well-trained set of secret agents and couriers and a system of secret correspondence with codes and cyphers provided the link between Patna and the outlying centres. An unobtrusive but very efffective system of collection and transmission of funds was also worked out. These constitute the main aspects of the internal organisation of the Wahhabis.

(i) Central Organisation at Pana

Sayyid Ahmad had appointed a number of *Khalīfas* (deputies) during his lifetime. Among those belonging to Patna were Shah Muhammad Husain, Wilayat Ali and Mazhar Ali. They in their turn were authorised to appoint their own *Khalīfa,* and thus the chain continued. Each *Khalīfa* was assisted by a committee of advisers. A family document [3] listing the *Khalīfas* and their advisers is available. It gives the following names:

1. Muhammad Husain, assisted by a committee consisting of Akbar Ali, Faiyyaz Ali, Yahya Ali, Waizul Haque and Maqsud Ali;
2. Wilayat Ali, Amīr; Enayat Ali, 'Minister of War', Farhat Husain, 'in-charge of finance and recruitment of volunteers';
3. Farhat Husain, (*Khalīfa* of Wilayat Ali) Amīr; Yahya Ali, Ahmadullah and Abdul Rahim, advisers;
4. Yahya Ali (*Khalīfa* of Farhat Husain) Amīr; Abdul Rahim, in-charge of finance, Ahmadullah and other surviving advisers mentioned above;
5. Ahmadullah, Amīr; Mubarak Ali, in-charge of finance, Iradat Husain, adviser, names of other members not known;
6. Mubarak Ali, Amīr; Muhammad Hasan, in-charge finance;
7. Muhammad Hasan, Amīr; (no other names given in the document);
8. Abdul Rahim (probably after his return from imprisonment in the Andaman Islands) Amīr; Muhammad Ibrahim, Abdullah of Ghazipur and Abdul Aziz Rahimabadi,[4] advisers.

The list is in accord with what we know of the subsequent history of the movement and the careers of the different Amīrs. It is also evident that though the persons concerned were linked by family ties, succession was not confined to family members and was influenced by seniority in the service of the movement and not by age and rank. For obvious security reasons the committee's composition and working were not based upon written regulations, but it worked on the basis of tacit understanding as it consisted of a set of dedicated men.

Among the *Khalīfas,* Yahya Ali was an outstanding one, and it was his organising genius which ministered to the varied requirements of the chief centre. His duties included public ministrations in the mosque, lecturing the students on doctrinal points, corresponding with the district centres, supervising the vast secret arrangements for the transmission of money and materials to the North-Western Frontier, etc. He was assisted by Abdul Ghaffar, whom Hunter refers to as 'the lay brother' and 'the bursar', in the management of the temporal affairs, such as the board and lodging of the volunteers.

Taking their que, probably from the *Qāfila* at Tonk, the earliest place of refuge after the disaster at Balakote, the Wahhabis referred to their Patna headquarters as the Qāfila in their secret correspondence, while the British officers often referred to it as the 'caravansarai' of rebels and traitors. A graphic account of the large complex,[5] subsequently razed to the ground by the orders of the government,[6] is given by Hunter[7] in the following words : "In the Mussalman quarter of the ancient city of Patna, there is an alley called Sadiqpur Lane much frequented by travellers. On the left side of the alley is a group of buildings in the Moorish style with considerable frontage and running back some distance from the lane, their exteriors have that mournful dilapidated look which the brick and stucco buildings permanently assume after the first wet season and which present such a squalid contrast to our preconceptions of the gorgeous East. The prominent edifice of the group is a mosque of very plain interior in which public prayer is held every hour of the day and a Khutba or lecture is delivered every Friday. These Friday lectures in the Sadikpur mosque are different from those in the other mosques in the City. They are vehement harangues, exposing the inefficiency of works without Faith, warning the hearers of great spiritual dangers and urging them to cultivate the Inward Life. They contrast the simple worship of Prophet with the cumbrous rituals, the endless mummeries, bowings and genuflexions of the mosques and bitterly inveigh against those who by tradition have rendered the written words of no

GROUND PLAN OF THE HOUSE BELONGING TO MOULVEE AHMEDOOLAH AND THE KAFILA ATTACHED TO IT IN MUTIALLA SADICKPORE, THANA SADICKPORE IN THE CITY OF PATNA

THIS HAS BEEN REPRODUCED FROM THE SKETCH GIVEN IN SELECTIONS OLD SPELLINGS HAVE ACCORDINGLY BEEN RETAINED.

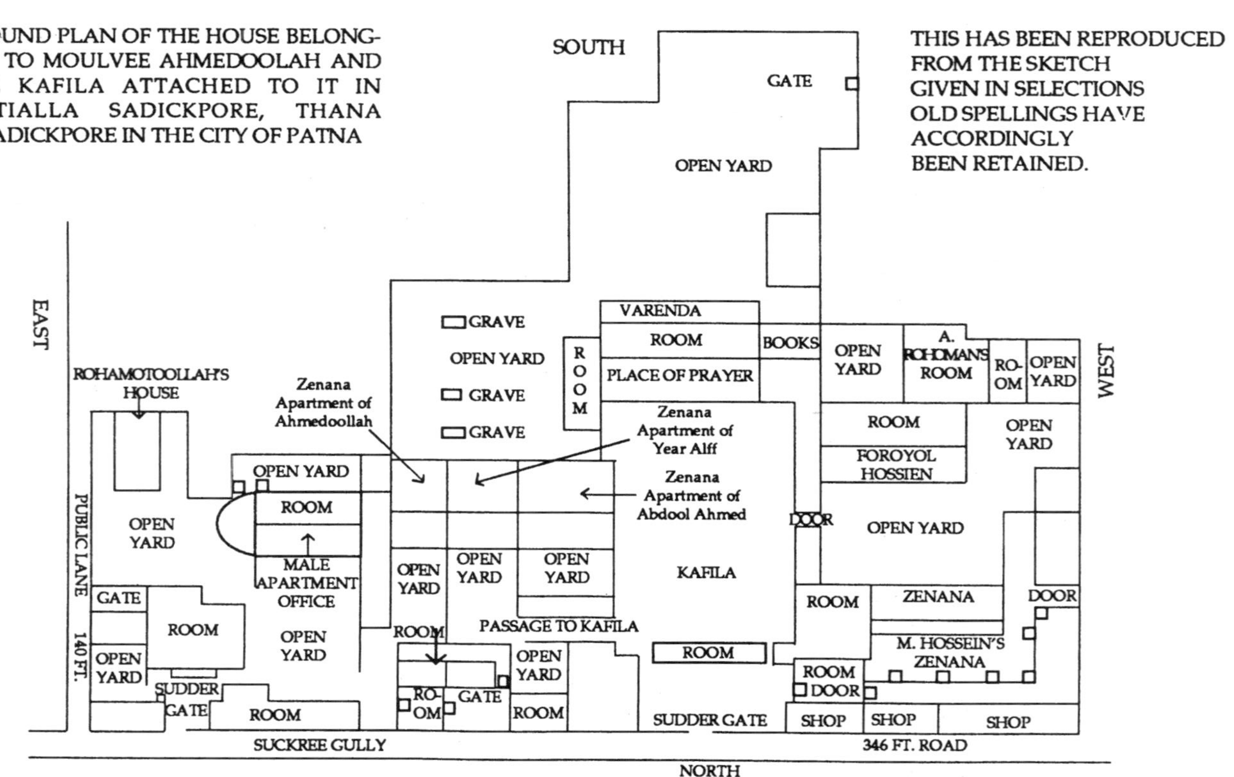

effect. The *Moulvis* of the other city mosques, while forced to acknowledge the learning of eloquence of the Sadikpur Lane preachers, denounce them as rejectors of the holy Sacrament...." The description is finally completed with an account of the surrounding buildings. "Around the mosque are dwelling houses of the priest and their *zenana* with a small college for the students of reformed theology, a hospice for pious travellers and several little white shrines in which repose the bones of the Wahhabi Saints."

It was to this *Qāfila* that a constant flow of volunteers from different parts of the country and belonging to different social groups kept pouring in. They came for receiving instruction in doctrinal matters as well as training for combat duty on the battlefronts. Care was taken in the selection of the volunteers, who were assigned duties according to their aptitude and social and educational background. Thus, the youths of high promise were trained in the "theology and dialects of Islam", as Hunter puts it, while men of humbler capacity were given a brief training and sent forthwith to the Frontier. There were other instances where not much doctrinal training was required. Theirs was to be a more active duty on the battlefield. Their zeal and enthusiasm was carefully aroused. As a perceptive early writer remarks, "The zeal of the fanatics for their religion and their hatred for the Sikhs, *which they also transferred to the successors of the Sikhs, the English,* was so great that recruits and money flowed abundantly into Sittana from British India many years after the apostle, Syed Ahmad, had perished."[8]

(ii) Itinerant Preachers.

They were the self-effacing workers who travelled all over the country, spreading their message in the interior areas and collecting funds. the climatic conditions and the age-old tradition of wandering *sanyasis,* rendered feasible and attractive this system of itinerant preachers. Hunter gives a beautiful pen-portrait of a typical Wahhabi preacher on his march: ... the Wahhabi missionary's lonely life renders him an object of interest to the villagers upon his route. Throughout many months of the years he enters the doors of no human dwellings. He comes from a distant Province, and during the long journey he admits no companion, save perhaps a faithful disciple, to interrupt his self-communion. His serenity of demeanour and indifference to external surroundings make him visibly a different being from ordinary men. It is not surprising, therefore, that the villagers cluster around him and forget for a moment their disputes about water-courses or their long-standing boundary feuds".[9] These teachers took pains to see that there was nothing in their teaching to excite the suspicion of the authorities. Their teaching was a guarded mixture of advocacy of socio-religious reforms and that of the struggle against the foreign rulers. In many villages the sectarian differences, traditions and usages were too deeply embedded and the disappointed preacher often had to 'shake off the dust of obdurate hamlets from his feet'.[10] But his message also struck a favourable response in many a home.

Where circumstances appeared to be favourable, the preacher often settled down as a village teacher, married locally and thus helped form the nucleus of a local centre. He took care to select an individual and train him intensively and then moved on, leaving the local man as a trustworthy deputy. Other villagers were 'initiated', and often persuaded to accompany the preachers. During the long journeys they were prevailed upon to attend to the call of the hour. A war was waging on the Frontier, volunteers were needed there, it was the highest service one could render, the choicest eminence one could achieve. Wouldn't they take the chance of a lifetime which had come their way? There could hardly be any other answer to such repeated exhortations during the months of living together. Hunter somewhat ruefully remarks, "They (the wandering missionaries) have enveloped the whole of Bengal in their mesh and converted many thousands of useful British subjects, first, into vagrant fanatics and then, into bitter traitors to the Crown."[11]

(iii) District Centres

The local and district centres were spread over many parts of the country. Very little information is available about their number or functioning but the history of one such centre at Malda (Bengal) can be reconstructed on the basis of the details given by Hunter[12] and the information available in government records of police investigations in the 1860s. About 1841, Abdul Rahman, a resident of Lucknow and one of the *Khalīfas* of Wilayat Ali, came to Malda during the course of his preaching tours, and having married and taken up a job as school teacher he settled down there. His job enabled him to meet different social groups and to exercise his influence over the young. He carried on the dual task of collecting contributions and enlisting volunteers and forwarding them to Patna. In this work he was ably assisted by one Rafique Mandal, a local cultivator whom he appointed as 'tax-collector'. Their work continued undistrubed until 1853, when the authorities became suspicious. Rafique Mandal's house was searched and some papers, 'proving the seditious character of his trade', were discovered and he was arrested. He was, however, released soon after because of what Hunter calls the official policy of 'contempt towards petty conspirators.' After his release Rafique handed over the work to his son Amiruddin who proved to be a worthy successor. Under him the Malda centre grew in importance and became the favourite rendezvous of all the district chiefs in Bengal, and served as a safe halting place for many of the Patna leaders during their tours of Bengal. Hunter records that its jurisdiction extended to the Murshidabad and Rajshahi districts,[13] and that in one single Wahhabi outpost on the Frontier, containing over 400 men, more than 10 per cent had been sent from areas under his jurisdiction.[14] The leaders were finally arrested in 1869 and the centre was dispersed.[15]

(iv) Preaching and Publication

Preaching played a key role in the work of the Wahhabis. The training of preachers and printing and circulation of religious and non-religious tracts was among the more important works carried on at the headquarters and the district centres. The Wahhabis realised the great importance of carrying their message directly to the people, orally through the itinerant preachers and in writing through booklets and pamphlets. They exhorted the people not to participate in 'sinful' practices, such as the taking out of processions on the occasion of *Muharram*, visiting the tombs and *dargahs* of saints or supplicating the saints' help in solving their problems, and not to indulge in wasteful expenditures on marriages, mournings, circumcision and *'aqīqa* (shaving off the hair on the head of a new-born child), etc. Another common topic was the great need and merit of joining the *jihād*. Long poems were composed on the merits of this work.

The tracts were written in simple conversational style, keeping in view the reading public for which they were meant. Most of these were written in Urdu, some in Persian and a few in Arabic. Some were bilingual too, with the Arabic/Persian text on one half and the Urdu translation or commentary on the remaining half of the page or along its borders. We know of Wahhabi pamphlets in Bengali and in

Hindi too.[16] The tracts were distributed among the sepoys and obviously not all of them knew Urdu. Keeping in mind the fact that many such tracts were proscribed by the government or got otherwise destroyed, it can be assumed that many more pamphlets must have been produced in Hindi and other Indian languages.

Thus, over the years the Wahhabis produced a large body of missionary literature. This has been examined separately in a following chapter, and only a couple of general remarks may be made here. This literature possesses both historical and a linguistic significance. It constitutes an important, not fully utilised, category of source-material on the history of the movement. It provides direct information on some new aspects of the Wahhabi leaders and their objectives. One can also look at it as a specimen of early Urdu prose-writing in eastern India.

(v) Collection of Funds

For collection of funds, several villages were grouped into 'fiscal centres', each under a 'tax-collector'. Under him there were sub-collectors for each village. Populous villages had, besides the tax-collector, a chief priest who led the public prayers in the mosque, a lay chief who was a sort of general manager, and a 'Dak Sardar' who arranged for the messengers who carried the letters and money to the Frontier. The chief tax-collector made annual tours of his area to see that the required amount had been collected. In between the tours they also received regular periodic instalments of funds collected by the local men, and sent them on to Patna where a register was maintained of the receipt of such amounts.[17]

The preachers emphasised the great merit of donating generously for the movement and recommended it specially to those who for some reasons could not migrate and participate in active duty on the Frontier. That their appeals received a wide response is evident from the statement of a British Indigo Planter in the North-Western Provinces (modern Uttar Pradesh) that his Muslim employees kept regularly a portion of their wages as contribution to the Wahhabi fund. The more daring among them took periodical leave and went to the Frontier for active duty. Between 1830 and 1846, the Muslim bailiffs of these Indigo Planters often urged the necessity of 'joining the cresentaders (Wahhabis) on the Frontier as a ground for one month's leave.[18]

Contributions were accepted both in cash and kind. Full use was made of the religious injunction of *Zakāt,* and the old, well-established practice of distributing the skin of goats, sheep and cows, etc., sacrificed on the occasion of Baqr'īd and other special occasions such as *'Aqīqa,* for gathering the funds.[19] The skins thus collected were processed and sold.[20]

Another more frequently used method was the *muthiā* system under which each household was treated as a unit and was expected to set aside one *muththī* or a handful of grain out of the quantity of daily consumption. Such small savings did not put any strain even on the poorer people[21] and at the same time, enabled large quantities of grain to be gathered and stocked. The grain or their sale-proceeds were periodically sent to Patna. It may be of interest to note here that the efficacy of this system was recognised and recommended for adoption at a much later period by political leaders, including those of the early Indian National Congress party. Surendranath Bannerjee, while moving a resolution for raising a National Fund for the constitutional rights' agitation observed in a meeting held at Calcutta in July 1883: "How do the Wahhabis raise their funds? I speak of the Wahhabi reformers and not the Wahhabi rebels, so you need not be afraid.[22] They do it in this way. Every householder puts by a handful of rice before he takes his meal, and these handfuls are all collected in course of a week, and then they are taken to a mosque for the Wahhabi missionary to come round and take them. In this way a fund is raised for the maintenance of the Wahhabi Mission."[23]

(vi) Transfers of Money and Materials :

The amounts thus collected were carried to the North-Western Frontier through a chain of hospices established along the full length of the Grand Trunk Road. Hunter pays tribute to the efficacy of the system and the dedication of the nameless people engaged in the work. "The Great North Road," he writes, "was divided into suitable sections, and the Wahabi traitors on their way to our Enemy's Camp journeyed in safety through strange provinces in the full assurance that at the end of each stage there were friends on the look-out for their arrival. The Wahabi agents in charge of the hospices were men of diverse ranks of life, *all devoted to the overthrow of the British Rule,* and each the head of a local committee of traitors. Yahya Ali must have displayed a very deep knowledge of character in selecting these men for neither fear of punishment nor hope for reward has induced a single one of them to appear against their leader in the hour of his disgrace and at this moment, although it is known that a chain of asylum like that of Thanesar connected Patna with the Punjab Frontier yet no one came forward and put his finger upon the particular spots."[24]

The difficult and dangerous work of carrying the money was done by a host of secret agents and couriers.[25] The assorted collection of cash was converted into gold *muhrs* or guineas in order to make the consignment lighter and more easily manageable. The gold *muhrs* were often sewn in the jackets and shoes of the carriers. The Calcutta office of the famous hide merchants Amir Khan and Hashmatdad Khan was very helpful in the converting of assorted cash into guineas. The services of some bankers in Delhi were also utilised. During Sayyid Ahmad's time Delhi was a more important place for this work, and the chief agent there was one Ishaq,[26] whose name was recommended to the Patna leaders by Sayyid Ahmad in a letter. Later Patna became the chief centre for this work and the money came to be sent through Thaneshwar and Rawalpindi.

The secret agents proceeded sometimes alone, in disguise and often in groups with other bigger caravans. They proceeded slowly and in stages, staying at the hospices referred to above. The journeys, however, were not always safe, as Hunter's description quoted above would have us believe. Sometimes prior information about an agent's errand leaked out and he still had to brave the hazard. Once Pir Muhammad, an agent of Sayyid Ahmad's time, was on his way to the Frontier with a promisory note of Rs. 3000/- and 1000 gold *muhrs* in cash. This information somehow reached Maharaja Ranjit Singh, and he ordered General Ventura to be on the look-out for the messenger. He was arrested and the hidden money on his person was found. He was beaten up and put under arrest. The Wahhabis, who too had their own means of getting information, came to know of this. *Ḥakīm* Mughisuddin of Saharanpur, who was acquainted with *Begum* Samroo, the widow of the German soldier of fortune, William Reinhardt, got a letter written by her to General Ventura, and Pir Muhammad was released.[27] He returned to the Frontier after many other vicissitudes.

Money was also sent by *hundis.* Cash money was deposited with bankers in Delhi and in Peshawar who arranged for payments in the Frontier area after deducting a 12 per cent commission. The rate charged was exorbitant, but the firms were dependable, and there is hardly any instance on record of money being held up or mislaid.[28] Drafts of small amounts were preferred as they could be easily cashed. Sometimes, instructions were given to the bankers to keep aside some amount for being paid to the dependants of the messengers left in India. Special care was taken to look after them.

It is a striking fact that there is no recorded instance of the messengers defaulting in the payment of the huge amounts entrusted to them. Another important fact, often overlooked, is that the work of converting the cash into gold *muhrs* or of getting the *hundis* prepared was done through Hindu bankers.[29]

The names of the banking houses, Ramkishen Futtuh Chand (Delhi), Lall Chand Kurum Singh (Benaras), Manohar Dass (Patna), Samunt Ram and Shew Buksh (?), and of two bankers Moti and Santu of Manara (North-Western Frontier) are mentioned. Of the last-named bankers, one particular transaction is recorded in the *Waqā'i*.[30] It states that once a draft issued by a *mahājan* of Amritsar was received by that firm. It demanded a commission of 16 per cent. The Wahhabis offered 8 per cent, and finally settled at 12 per cent. The firm asked for 16 days to get it confirmed by the Amritsar *mahājan*. This was, however, just an excuse. They got it confirmed through the *mahājans* at Hazru. The Wahhabis came to know of this, and asked the banker to pay out of the total amount, a sum of 200 in cash and clothes worth Rs. 300/-. Later, when the stipulated period was over the firm sent a messenger asking the Wahhabis to collect the remaining amount. They took the remaining Rs. 700/-, Rs. 500/- in cash and the balance in clothes. The firm owners were very pleased with the profitable transaction and assured the Wahhabis that they could use their services whenever they liked.

Some idea of the large amounts of money thus transferred by the Patna leaders can be had from the fact that during the three years, 1865 to 1867 (when the Ambeyla campaign was on) a sum of Rs. one lakh was transferred from Patna through one banker, Manohur Dass alone.[31]

(vii) Code words, cyphers and aliases used in the secret correspondence[32]

Code words for intimating the amounts transferred or acknowledging the amounts received, were in use since the time of Sayyid Ahmad. As far as possible, direct use of the names of the persons concerned was avoided. Literary references and similes and allusions were used to convey a secret meaning. Code words and figures were also used. One such code figure seized during the investigations in the Hyderabad Conspiracy case could not be decoded in spite of the best efforts of the police authorities.[33]

The attention of the Government was drawn on several occasions to the existence of a network of 'treasonable correspondence' with, and supply of men and money to, the Wahhabi 'colony' on the North Western Frontier, of which Patna was the chief centre.

James Abbott, the Deputy Commissioner of Hazara drew [34] the attention of the Board of Administration, Punjab, as early as 1849 to the "existence of a remarkable nest of emigrants from Hindoostan who bring with them their own arms and means of subsistence and sit down at Sittana," which was a rallying post of all who hoped to "see a successful *ghazwa*" (battle). He also referred to the secret smuggling by these emigrants of "gold on their persons and letter in bamboo canes." Nawab Wazir Muhammad Khan of Tonk was also reported to be sending large sums of money annually. The number of the emigrants in the previous two years was 60 or 80 but it had increased steadily till thousands more were expected. In subsequent letters[35] James Abbott repeatedly drew the Board's attention to the continued collection of men at Sittana from different parts of India, particularly Rajputana and Rohilkhand. They came via Attock, "disguised as beggars and students." The ragged garments were cast off on reaching Sittana. Godowns were also being constructed in Sittana where large supplies of wheat, brought on camels, were being stored. Abbott was apprehensive "of the existence of these enthusiasts in the strong country of Hazara," where they could always be used as a nucleus for anti-government activities in the event of trouble from the Sikhs or the Durranis. He thought that in the event of fresh trouble in Punjab, Hazara might be selected as the theatre of the first outbreak. "The elements of strife are numerous, the ground is high and distant from the capital, and the consummate judgement which selected Multan would not be slow to perceive the points of parallel." He advised the establishment of armed posts along the Indus to cut off the sources of supply to Sittana, but the Board did not share the apprehensions of Abbott. It did not agree to the establishment of such armed posts in forward areas without suitable means of communication. It perceived no grounds for an insurrection at Hazara,[36] and observed 'All the enemies of the British Government have recently been signally defeated. The people of Hazara, fickle and faithless as they are... the time has not yet come for a religious war, whatever the fanatics, may preach or whatever a few desperadoes may determine." The difference over policy between the man on the spot, Abbott and the Board of Administration continued, with increasing bitterness, until Abbott had to leave charge in 1858. Actually, however, Abbott's assessment turned out to be more correct and the Board of Administration were disillusioned in their fond hope of continued loyality from the 'people of Hazara, who had received nothing but favours from our hands.'

In 1852 Patna again figured as a supply centre for the Wahhabis on the Frontier. The Government of Bengal, like the Board of Administration, Punjab, did not share the apprehension of the local magistrate and contented itself with drawing up a Minute, dated 26th August, 1852, which admitted that "a correspondence exists between the persons of Patna and the fanatics in Swat and Sittana" but considered it sufficient to instruct the magistrate to watch the situation, and in the event of "armed men being assembled" to take proper measures" for upholding of the Government's authority."[37]

It was this system of the supply of men and money from British India which kept the Wahhabi centre on the Frontier alive. The Government was occasionally informed about its existence, but seemed not to realise the true nature of the threat caused by it. The hard knocks suffered by the government forces in the Ambeyla Campaign forced it to give more serious attention to these 'centres of sedition.' Many of their leaders and workers were arrested and tried for treason and the centres were practically rendered harmless. After that, even though the Wahhabis continued to be active on the Frontier, their strength and effectiveness was gone. Once the flow of the vital supplies from the fertile Gangetic plains were stopped, the sapling of the Wahhabi centre shrivelled on the hot barren rocks of the North-Western Frontier.

II. Wahhabis' Contacts with the Indian Units of the Army

Besides spreading their influence among the civilians, the Wahhabis also tried to establish contact with the Indian units of the army. During the period 1839 to 1857 several such attempts were made and from the more important recorded instance discussed below it would appear that the Wahhabis had developed a somewhat standard form of what the authorities call 'tampering' with the army units.

The formation and growth of the Indian units of the East India Company's army, the so-called Sepoys, is an absorbing subject in itself.[38] They played a vital role in building up the British empire in India. It was the French, and mainly Dupleix, who first gave practical shape to the 'profitable' idea of raising Indian units to form a part of the French army in India, to be used in promoting French interests by taking part in the wars between the Indian powers. It was Clive, rather then Dupleix, who made full use of this brilliant idea of his political adversary. During his visit to Bihar in 1758 he, 'not unmindful of military matters,' raised a small unit consisting exclusively of men of the Shahabad district who were noted for their robust physique and martial spirit. These units were trained along European lines and were commanded by a band of European officers who did their work with a perfection surpassing even the imagination of the promoter of the idea. Various factors, including years of fighting together, had developed a peculiar spirit of camaraderie between the European commanders and the Indian ranks, and they formed an effective military organisation.

Indian history in the 19th century provides many examples of Indian units raised from one part of the country being trained to fight in another part. The role of the Bengal Army, first, in the Kabul War and, later, in the Anglo-Sikh wars and then, as if to underline the irony of the situation, the crucial importance of the services of the Sikh Regiments in suppressing the rising of 1857, of which the Bengal Army sepoys were the standard bearers, are two of its more striking examples. The biographer of Lord Lawrence, one of the main architects of the recovery of Delhi in 1857, praises the policy pursued by Lawrence. "Availing himself of the hostility which he knew to exist between the different races in the Punjab," Lawrence's biographer remarks, "he enrolled 3000 Pathans (during the second Anglo-Sikh War), thus following the reverse of the process which afterwards stood us in such good stead in the Mutiny."[39] With the passage of time and probably due to a fuller realisation of the role they had played in building up the British empire, as also owing to many local grievances fanned by religious considerations, discontent grew among the sepoys, resulting first in minor risings and conspiracies and culminating in the great conflagration of 1857, which nearly brought about the end of the empire built up by the sweat and blood of the sepoys themselves.

It is to the credit of the Wahhabi leaders that they realised very early the great importance of the sepoys. They constituted the chief instrument of the British power in India and if they could be neutralised half the battle would have been won. Realising this, the Wahhabi agents repeatedly brought home to the sepoys the full extent of the power wielded by them and the dependence of the British government on them. From the instances discussed below, it would be clear that they worked all over the country. They did not know which unit would next be sent against them. So the agents were deputed to all the military stations "from the Sutledge to Calcutta"[40] who tried to win the support of as many units as possible. Where simple preaching and appeal to patriotism failed, monetary inducements were tried.

Some of the earliest efforts were made, surprisingly, in the south. Wilayat Ali had lived and worked for some time in Hyderabad[41] and among the persons who had taken *Bai'at* at his hands was *Nawāb* Mubarizu'd Dawlah, brother of the Nizam of Hyderabad, Nasiru'd Dawlah (1830-57). Wilayat Ali had established contacts with some other highly-placed persons and the Hyderabad Conspiracy[42] was a result of this phase of his activities.

The adherents of Mubariz had been working among the 'native' troops stationed at Hyderabad and other places in the south. Several Indian ruling chiefs including that of Kurnool were involved in these activities.[43] The Raja of Satara, the princes of Jodhpur, Udaigiri, Bhopal and Rampur were in correspondence with the organisers. Some of them had their own personal grievances against the British authorities, but a general anti-British sentiment was shared by them all.

Taking advantage of the departure of the British troops to Afghanistan, the adherents of Mubariz had planned a rising. Reporting the matter, Fraser, the British Resident in the Court of the Nizam, had enclosed the statement[44] of one Haji Sayyid Ismail, an employee of Mubariz. It stated that military training was being undertaken by Mubariz himself and his followers and referred to Mubariz's intention to 'move out,' collect men and 'slaughter the English in order to possess himself of the country and the government. His followers had gained the confidence of some officers and soldiers in the guise of *faqirs*, and were endeavouring to 'seduce' the sepoys to Wahhabism and "conjointly with it in all probability to sedition."[45] A ceaseless flow of intelligence reports was reaching Mubariz from his agents. They reported that the men of the regiments were of one mind and were looking forward to Mubariz's moving out, in order that they might join him.[46] Mubariz had prepared two seals engraved with the legend, "Protector of Established Religion, The Defender of the Faith and of Mussalmans," and "Mubarizu'd Dawlah, the Nā'ib of the Martyred Syed Ahmad."[47]

According to another statement,[48] Mubariz in response to an appeal from Nasiruddin, the leader of the Wahhabi remnant group in Sind, had sent his envoys Asif, Qasim and others to Sind to report on the condition of the Wahhabis there and on the attitude of the Sind Amirs towards them. The envoys who were the disciples of Wilayat Ali consulted[49] him by post about their mission and on his advice had proceeded through Bombay and Karachi to Shikarpur, where Nasiruddin was staying at the time.[50] They sent their report from there, mentioning among other things the approach of 'the Bengal Army.'

The conspiracy was discovered by the suspicion aroused by the large influx of men from north India, Kabul and Persia in the Madras Presidency. A Sikh who was arrested informed about their activities, and the matter was reported by Stonehouse, Magistrate of Nellore to the government of Madras.[51] The latter, while forwarding the report to the Government of India, observed as follows; ".... a considerable number of Muhammadans in different parts of India had embraced Wahabism, among whom are persons who from rank and position exercise considerable influence over their brethren; that they have actively been engaged for some time past in making proseyltes, raising men and money for the prosecution of a war against the Infidels, that there can be little doubt that their ultimate objective has been *the overthrow of British power in India and that with this view they had been endeavouring to make converts among the Native Army.*"[52]

Enquiries were conducted against Mubariz by the British Resident, Fraser,[53] who reported to the Secretary, Government of India that it had been established, *inter alia,* that Mubariz had entertained 'treasonable designs' not only against his sovereign (the Nizām) but also had hostile intentions more specifically directed against the British Government as manifested by the extraordinary pains he had taken to tamper with the allegiance of the Native Infantry, especially at Secundarabad and Nagour. Fraser added that he had no objection to the Wahhabis' "normal missionary activities" but their political intrigues, in whatever guise had to be curbed. He thought that the

Nizam was committing a mistake in viewing his brother's activities from a religious angle only, and advised that the Nizam should be informed of the full extent of the treasonable activities of his brother (the enquiry had so far been carried on at the Resident's initiative) and his consent obtained for confining Mubariz as a state prisoner in the Golconda Fort. He also advised against his own role, and that of the Nizam, in the matter being made public, for it might precipitate a rising.

Mubariz was tried by a commission of enquiry[54] consisting of British officers and some Indians, and he was sentenced to life imprisonment and lodged in the Golconda Fort where he died after 14 years in 1854. His adherents, most of whom were Wahhabi *moulvis* were arrested, pending further enquiries.

The conspiracy has to be viewed in the background of an apprehended Russian advance in Central Asia and the attempt to induce the Nizam to in effect abrogate all his powers to the British. Fraser himself, writing much later, has thus stated the ultimate aim of the Company's Court of Directors in regard to Hyderabad: "... only one thing was wanting to give us the power of reforming the administration, viz., the formal assurance of His Highness that he would abstain in future from interfering in public affairs. *This abstinence has, for most part, been practised but were an assurance of this nature given it could be beneficial to the highest degree by including all ministers to solely look to the Resident.* [55] The main objective of Mubariz's adherents was to counter this projected increase of political control over the affairs of the state.

The Government of India, however, did not see any dangerous portent in the situation. The Governor-General, Lord Auckland, remarked that "he was not one of those who believe that there exists any universal and active spirit of aversion in India to British supremacy."[56] The same attitude had been shown by the higher authorities at the time of the *Fara'idī* Movement and it typifies the official attitude to these apparently isolated events. It shows a lack of awareness of the wider religious and political unrest of which these were the symptoms.

The ramifications of the Hyderabad Conspiracy were wide and even spread to the south. During the investigations, it had been found that there existed a network of Wahhabi agents[57] working in different civil and military stations in Madras and other places down south. Their activities were reported to the Government by the Officer Commanding at Vellore.[58] He reported that Wali Muhammad the *Muftī* of the district court and Hubbullah, the *Sadr* of the Collector's court, used to receive a Persian newspaper, *Suttarah Akhbar*, printed by one Rajab Ali at Calcutta. Rajab Ali was a *khalīfa* of Muhammad Ali Rampuri who had earlier been expelled from Madras for treasonable activities in the Carnatic area. His newspaper gave prominence to the news about the impending war between Dost Muhammad and the British, and prophesied that the former would soon drive out the British from India. Another person, *Maulawī* Mudin (Mubin?), the head-priest of the mosque near the Fort and other followers of the above-mentioned Muhammad Ali used to address the gatherings after the evening prayer and preach *jihād*. Similar speeches were delivered in the three other mosques in the city, the Fort mosque, the Subby Street mosque and Piran Sahib's mosque. In the last mentioned mosque the head-priest was a discharged trooper. In a subsequent letter the same officer reported[59] to the Madras government that a certain Cowda Mian, who was in the habit of addressing the sepoys of Palaverum, was frequently present in the officers' quarters on the pretext of playing chess. He also reported the publication of a pamphlet containing seditious material by a person known as *Baṛa Sāḥib*.[60] In another letter dated 10th June, 1930, the same officer had enclosed a list of the *khalīfas* or agents of Muhammad Ali Rampuri who were working in the civil and military stations in the south.[61]

III. The Patna Conspiracy (1845)

A wider and better organised attempt was made in Patna in 1845 in which the Wahhabis again figured prominently. Kaye has briefly referred to it,[62] and more recently K.K.Datta has discussed it at greater length.[63] In both these cases, however, the episode was examined as part of the larger story of the Rising of 1857, and the antecedents of the main figures involved were not closely examined in the light of the original documents.[64] It is to the credit of Kaye that in spite of his large canvas he takes note of this episode, but he candidly admits that "to what dimensions the conspiracy really extended and from what central point it radiated, is not known, and now will never be known."[65] Datta, whose work is specifically about Kunwar Singh and Amar Singh examines the event from the angle of Kunwar Singh's participation in it to which a reference[66] is made in a letter of the local magistrate. As for Saif Ali who played a leading role in the conspiracy, Datta remarks, "He (Saif Ali) remained till the last a mysterious personality."[67] The point about the Wahhabis being the main organiser of the attempt could not, therefore, be fully appreciated. The following brief account of the events, based upon the statement of Peer Bakhsh, the Regimental *Munshī,* who later turned approver and disclosed the full story,[68] will make this point clearer.

Towards the end of 1845, it was reported[69] to the Government that there existed a 'widespread conspiracy' to promote disloyalty among "the native officers and sepoys" stationed at Dinapur. Tracing the events leading to it, Peer Bakhsh stated that in September 1845 he had met Rahat Ali,[70] a wealthy local zamindar, for some loan. Saif Ali was also present on the occasion and was introduced to Peer Bakhsh. In December next, Saif Ali met Peer Bakhsh in the Regimental Line on the pretext of selling books. He also introduced him to one Khwaja Hasan Ali,[71] and later all three of them met in the upper storey of the house of the Khwaja in Patna. The Khwaja asked Peer Bakhsh about the condition of his employment, the pay, etc., and then exclaimed, "Oh, Munshi, Hindustan has become a place of battle,[72] and what tyranny is taking place in the jails[73] ... the Magistrate of Bombay has closed the way for the men of Islam to proceed to Mecca."[74] The latter thereupon enquired about the Khwaja's intention, to which the latter replied that he wanted to be introduced to "those who are high in the Army such as *Soobadars* and *Jamadars.*" At this stage the Khwaja asked a man to bring Rs. 100 tied in a handkerchief and gave it to Peer Bakhsh who deposited it with Saif Ali. The Khwaja asked the *munshī,* to also "persuade the *sardars* of the Regiment to engage with us and not to let this be known to the *Sipahis* for the present." On being asked as to whether similar attempts had been made to contact other regiments, the Khwaja mentioned Kanpur, Benares, Allahabad, Sugauli (Champaran district) and Doranda (Singhbhum district) as the places where they were working. He added that if the *sardārs* would accept this "entertainment" he would give them one month's pay, and that he had powers to spend up to Rs. one crore. He did not want the *sardārs* to be present "on our side" and fight, but expected them to be on his side when there would be a "rebellion." On being asked whether he was in charge of arrangements up to Kanpur and further up, he replied that "beyond that (Kanpur) there is someone else managing." The *munshī* said that Durga Prasad, the Pandit of the regiment, would perhaps be of greater use to them in establishing contact with *sardārs.*

Saif Ali then asked to be introduced to the Pandit and Peer Bakhsh spoke to Durga Pandit and Bhikhan Jamadar. Durga Pandit promised to speak to the *sardārs*. He later informed Rahat Ali and Saif Ali that he had communicated their message to the *sardārs*. Saif Ali accompanied him to Dinapur and asked him to call the Havaldar Major. He offered Rs. 75/- to the havaldar who refused to accept it. Meanwhile the Pandit came and stated that "he had done much endeavour" and that while "some persons were assenting, others were not." Saif Ali give him Rs. 10/- and promised further rewards including feeding 40 Brahmans and a cash gift of Rs. 10/- to each one of them.

After a fortnight the Pandit again visited Peer Bakhsh and informed him that the *sardārs* had agreed to take the money. Mooti Misra and Ram Swaroop, *Jamadar* and *Soobadar* respectively of the 4th Company were starting for Gaya and they wanted their shares to be paid at Patna near the Golghar. Peer Bakhsh, Saif Ali and Khwaja Hasan Ali met and finalised the arrangements. They brought two hundred rupees, laid out rupees eighty-two (being the actual amount of the pay of the Havaldars) in two handkerchiefs and proceeded to the *Golghar* in two separate *ekkas* (horse-drawn carriages). On reaching there, they learnt that the two *sardārs* had gone to meet the magistrate. Saif Ali and Peer Bakhsh waited at the gate and when the two *sardārs* came out, the later gave them the money (these two had divulged the plan to the magistrate and were receiving the money on his instruction. This was not known to Peer Bakhsh at the time he was giving the statement). On their return to Dinapur, Bhikhan Jamadar also demanded his share, and was given thirty-two rupees. Then the Pandit told Saif Ali that one Kewal Tiwari *Soobadar* wanted money for five other *sardārs*. Saif Ali did not have that much, and returned to Patna to bring it. Meanwhile, Peer Bakhsh, who had some enmity with Kewal Tiwari, suspected foul play on the part of the latter and conveyed his suspicion to Saif Ali. Saif Ali wanted him to leave but he stayed on. The following Sunday, Peer Bakhsh was arrested.

Additional information regarding the "tampering" with soldiers in other places in Bihar is also available in these papers. Peer Bakhsh had stated in an earlier statement that the 66th Native Infantry had agreed to accept money, and the 7th Irregular Cavalry at Sugauli had been contacted through Baqar Ali, "*Kotegusht Darogha*" of Patna City.[75] Sums of rupees 16,60 and 101, corresponding to the pay of native officers and privates of the irregular cavalry, had been found tied in a piece of cloth in the house of Rahat Ali.[76]

The end of the enquiries and the trial was rather peculiar. Peer Bakhsh turned approver and was pardoned. Durga Prasad Pandit and Bhikhan *Jamadār* were tried and sentenced to three years rigorous imprisonment and dismissed from service. The commander-in-chief intervened[77] in the matter, as he considered the punishment to be too light, and it was altered to a sentence of death for the Pandit and life-imprisonment for the *Jamadār*. Curiously enough, the Commander-in-chief intervened once again and the original sentences were restored. Rahat Ali was released as Peer Bakhsh modified his earlier statement. Khwaja Hasan Ali, after remaining untraced for one year was put on trial but Peer Bakhsh refused to identify him as the person concerned and he too had to be released.

Saif Ali just disappeared and nothing was heard of him. He was a key figure[78] in the whole episode. He had taken the lead in meeting the sepoys, had visited the Regimental Line and handled the cash. It is therefore surprising that the point about his identity, clearly mentioned in the records, has been missed by the writers on the topic. The Superintendent of Police who had earlier in his letter dated 16th March, 1846 given vague clues about Saif Ali being an agent from "the North-West" came out subsequently with the more specific and crucial information that Saif Ali was "the agent of the son of the celebrated Mohammadan Sardar Amir Khan, now holding the *jagir* of Tonk."[79] The connection between Waziru'd Dawlah and his father Amir Khan of Tonk and the Wahhabi Movement hardly needs any elucidation. Once this major fact has been noted, many other oblique references in the records become clearer. Thus, for instance, the reference to emissaries from the North-West,[80] on the quotation from the *Qur'ān* in Peer Bakhshs letter to Rahat Ali: "Leave your Homes. Fight in the Path of the Almighty," and the reference in another letter to the well-known work, *Anwar Suhaili*,[81] for certain lessons—all these indicate unmistakably the Wahhabi technique. The emphasis, unlike in 1857, was not on an immediate uprising, but on remaining neutral for the time being. This too was in accordance with the Wahhabi strategy. There are clear references to the fact that the conspiracy had spread beyond Bihar and that "others were managing it beyond Kanpur." Only the Wahhabis with their all-India network of anti-government activities could probably be this other party.

Rahat Ali, was another important figure. He was known for having organised anti-government demonstration against Land Resumption Proceedings in 1829.[82] We do not know for certain as to whether he was a Wahhabi, but during subsequent police enquiries against a suspected Wahhabi leader, Muhammad Umar of Patna, it was found that some close relatives of Rahat Ali holding high positions in the government were Wahhabis.[83]

As some of the contemporary officers very perceptively remarked, the origins of the conspiracy could be examined in two parts: the existence of local discontent and the channelising of that discontent into anti-government agitations, and carrying it into the ranks of the army units. The Commissioner Patna observed that the "emissaries, who it is alleged have been sent to every division of the Army from the Sutledge to Calcutta would naturally ascertain all local causes of discontent in order to foment them and to make the acquaintance of persons who from their known character of intrigue would be likely to aid in the subversion of our power. To the Mohammedans they .... held out the hope of restoration of the family of Timoor to the throne of Delhi, and to the Hindus the fear of conversion to Christianity."[84] Rahat Ali was exactly such a local person of known anti-government background. He was, therefore, chosen as a local collaborator by the "emissary from the other parties to the North-West." Saif Ali represented this other party. He was the connecting link between the local leaders and those from outside. That this outside party was the actual organiser of the conspiracy is testified to by the investigating police officer who observed that "the plan (of conspiracy) came down from above," with the emissary Saif Ali.[85]

Malleson, one of the authoritative historians of the Rising of 1857, also mentions this conspiracy as the work of the Wahhabis. Discussing the causes of discontent in Bihar and recounting the long history of the Wahhabis' activities in Patna, he indirectly refers to the conspiracy in the following words, "a plot had been hatched by a band of conspirators, when cash had been distributed to the sepoys, a scroll discovered containing the names of one hundred of the principal families—a city (Patna) which was the headquarters of two notorious vice-regents (Wilayat Ali and Enayat Ali) of the great prophet (Sayyid Ahmad)."[86]

Another attempt to "tamper with the allegiance" of the Indian troops was made in Rawalpindi in 1852. A number of letters were intercepted in the house of Muhammad Wali, a regimental *munshī* of the 4th Native Infantry stationed there. The *munshī* acknowledged himself to be a disciple of Sayyid Ahmad.[87] The letters recovered from him and written in the familiar Wahhabi style included many from Akramullah in Sittana to Hussain Ali Khan of Dugber Toli,[88] Patna City. The letters reported the arrival of Indian volunteers in Swat and gave detailed instructions for the guidance of future parties on their way to the Frontier. It was stated, further, that the volunteers and the ammunition were sent to Swat via Meerut and Ludhiana. The arms were deposited in Meerut with one *Qādī* Muhammad or Sarfraz Ali. The Agent in Ludhiana was Abbas Ali, who lived near the local Abdul Qadir's mosque.[89]

The Deputy Commissioner, Rawalpindi wrote to the magistrate of Patna and Meerut and the Divisional Commissioner, Ludhiana to search the houses of the persons named under their respective jurisdictions and to seize papers found in their possession. Abbas Ali of Ludhiana was arrested and some additional letters incriminating one Abu Abdool Rahim of Patna were found in his possession. Philip Goldney, the Deputy Commissioner of Ludhiana also wrote to the Magistrate, Patna to enquire about the person who "was connected with the Swat leaders." The Magistrate of Patna accordingly made enquiries and searched the house of Husain Ali. He reported[90] that the search was a mistake, for Husain Ali was only a *khānsāmān* (steward) of Ahmadullah and the letters were addressed to his house merely as a blind. The real addressee was Ahmadullah. The magistrate had no authority to search his house which in any case would have required the "assistance of the Military." Ahmadullah had received prior information about the enquiry from a *hakīm* of Lahore, who arrived in Patna two days before the letter from Rawalpindi,[91] and he had destroyed the papers. The magistrate went on to remark that the sect (of the Wahhabis) was on the increase in the City. Meetings were held on Fridays in which "the tenets of the sect were explained and converts made." What was more ominous, Ahmadullah had assembled five hundred men and had declared that if government would take harsh measures and suppression, he would raise the standard of revolt. Matters were sufficiently serious to deserve the attention of the government. As regards Abu Abdool Rahim, mentioned in Goldney's letters, the magistrate remarked that there was no such person. He, however, suspected that the person involved was Abdullah, the eldest son of Wilayat Ali and that the above mentioned name was merely a blind.

Neither the Board of Administration, Punjab, nor the Government of Bengal shared the apprehension of their subordinate local officials. The Governor of Bengal contented himself with drawing up the Minute dated 26th August, 1852, referred to above.[92] In a separate letter [93] to the Board of Administration, Punjab, the Secretary to Government of India, while reiterating the sentiments expressed in the Minute of the Lt. Governor of Bengal added that Patna undoubtedly was the headquarters of the Wahhabis in India. *"Letters had been found there and parties of volunteers had proceeded from there to the Frontier Colony."* The Governor-General in Council also directed that an "example should be made of the Regimental Munshie of the 4th N.I." who had been the channel of the anti-Government correspondence.[94] Hunter correctly assesses the significance of this attempt at Rawalpindi and observes, "In 1852 they deemed their plans ripe for execution. Money and men from our territory had been poured into the Sittana Camp, and treasonable correspondence with our troops was seized by the Punjab authorities. Their leaders made a skilful attempt to tamper with the 4th Native Infantry stationed at Rawalpindi, *conveniently near the Fanatic Colony; and one of the first Regiments which, on their invading our Province would have been sent to act against them.*"[95]

The next attempt was made further up in Peshawar in 1857. Once again, letters written by some Wahhabis in Patna were intercepted in the possession of Shaikh Karimullah, *Nā'ib* of the 64th N.I. stationed at Peshawar. Karimullah was the son of Shaikh Qudrutullah, of village Irki in district Gaya. A number of his relatives were occupying different positions in the other units.[96] The letters were written by one Shaikh Nathoo on the eve of the Rising of 1857. Karimullah used to pass them on to the Wahhabis at Sittana and also spread the message among his own men. Translations and abridged versions of these letters were sent to Patna to locate the writers.[97]

This event has to be viewed in the context of the political conditions in the Hazara area on the eve of the Rising of 1857. The district lay on the border of the Yusufzai tribal area which was in a state of ferment. Mubarak Shah, the dispossessed chief of Swat who felt aggrieved with the British, was staying in the neighbouring Panjtar. Not far from it was the Wahhabi headquarters at Mangalthana, where

Enayat Ali was eager to utilise the crisis of 1857 to strike a blow against the British while their hands were tied in other areas.[98]

It should be remembered that the Rising of 1857 had already taken place and the conflagration was spreading fast from one military station to another. In the Peshawar Division, the leaders of the Movement of 1857-58 and the Wahhabis were working simultaneously but separately and the different units were reacting differently to the influence of these two groups. Thus, for instance, the 51st N.I. was greatly exercised over the 'cartridge affair',[99] with which, as we know, the Wahhabis had nothing to do. But several other units, such as the 55th N.I. (with detachments at Mardan and Nowshera), the 69th N.I. at Peshawar and the 10th Irregular Cavalry were definitely under Wahhabi influence. As reported by Edwardes, the Divisional Commissioner, the 64th N.I., the 10th Irregular Cavalry and the Hindustani Fanatics in Swat and the neighbouring hills,"[100] and that two "Hindustani Moulvis"[101] (agents of the Wahhabis) in the Collectorate of Mardan were the hosts of "emissaries who passed to and fro". The official account of the British military expeditions sent against the Wahhabis on the North-Western Frontier is more forthright on the point. It states, "the only portion of Peshawar district in which advantage of the Sepoy Mutiny was taken by the people to disturb the country was on the Yusufzai border and this was *principally due to the pressure of the Hindustani Fanatics* who were supported by contributions of men and money from traitorous princes and individuals in Hindustan."[102] The subsequent action of the 55th N.I., after they had broken out of their station, confirms this, for they headed straight to Swat and then to Mangalthana, the Wahhabis' centre. The sudden death of Akbar Shah, the king of Swat and a staunch supporter of the Wahhabis, however, completely changed the situation in favour of the British.[103]

Two autoritative historians of the Rising of 1857-58 felt constrained to remark that if only the Swatis under their religious leader, the *Akhund*, had joined hands with the sepoys of the 55th N.I. and the Wahhabis, other tribes might also have joined in and the British would have been overwhelmed.[104] That, however, did not happen; many sepoys of the 55th N.I. were chased out due to the opposition of the *Akhund* and a few of them managed to move out to Mangalthana.[105] The reason why they acted separaely[106] from the other larger movement is another entirely neglected topic which has been discussed in the following chapter.

To sum up, the Wahhabis worked steadily and silently all over the country, both among the civilians and the army ranks. They wroked at different levels and through different mediums—preaching, pamphleteering and personal contacts. That showed an awareness of the crucial significance of the Indian sepoys in the Army, the value of winning over their allegiance and failing that, their neutrality. That their effort failed, or was nipped in the bud, does not lessen the significance of the attempt.

NOTES

1. *I.M.*, pp. 70 ff.
2. *Vide supra*, pp. 105 ff.
3. It is available in the private papers of Abdul Gafffar Sahib of Sadiqpore family and is copied in the copy of *T.S.* belonging to him. See Bibliography and p. 394.
4. He was a student of Maulawi Nazir Husain of Delhi, and had a large number of *Ahl-i Ḥadīth* followers in the districts of north Bihar and in Bengal. Much later, when the leaders of the Silk Letters Conspiracy were organising an anti-government force, *Junūdu'llāh*, he was to be included in it.
5. See the sketch of the buildings on p. 134.
6. The site is now occupied by the building of the old Patna City Municipality, Sadiqpur, Patna City (now the city circle of Patna Municipal Corporation).
7. Hunter's article, 'The Indian Conspiracy', in *C.R.*, vol. XL, pp. 130-31.
8. *J.R.A.S.*, Bombay, vol. XIV, 1880, pp. 363-64. Emphasis added.
9. *I.M.*, p. 72.
10. *C.R.*, vil. XL, p. 133.
11. Ibid.
12. *I.M.*, pp. 78-81.
13. Ibid., p. 80, note 3.
14. Ibid., p. 80.
15. *Vide infra*, pp. 331-32.
16. *Vide infra*, p. 378.
17. *I.M.*, pp. 81-82.
18. Ibid., p. 20.
19. Ibid. Also see Government of Bengal, Judicial Proceedings. no. 168, dated November, 1868.

20. This is still one of the recognised methods amongst the Muslims for donations to the orphanages and other charitable institutions.
21. *Selections*, p. 138.
22. This distinction between the Wahhabi reformers and rebels was probably made purposely, otherwise the authorities might have objected to the advocacy of a method used by 'rebels'.
23. Printed Report of the Proceedigs of a National Fund Meeting held on the 17th July, 1883. Sen Press, Calcutta, 1883. I am thankful to my friend Dr. J.S. Jha, formerly Director, K.P. Jayaswal Research Institute Patna, for drawing my attention to this information.
24. C.R., vol.XL, 1864, p. 134. Italics are mine. He wrote this in the wake of the Ambala Trial (*vide infra*, chap VIII) in which Yahya Ali was one of the chief accused.
25. For list of secret agents, see *Selections*.
26. *Mehr*, III, p. 53.
27. *Mehr*, III, p. 93-96.
28. One of the witnesses in the trial of Ahmadullah at Patna (1865) had stated that out of the three *hundis* of Rs. 2500, 1000, and 500, given on 10 April, 1863, which were drawable at Delhi, the last one of Rs. 500 had not been cashed. The judge, discussing the statement, had remarked that it was not clear from the records produced in support of the statement that the *hundi* had not been cashed. That, the judge added, was not material. What had been established was that *hundis* for these amounts had been given, see *Selections*, pp. 98-99.
29. *Selections*, p. 71; see also *Mehr*, III, pp. 62 ff.
30. Tonk ms. no. 1480/1 ff. 108-109b.
31. *Selections* , p. 98.
32. See Appendix III for a list of some such terms.
33. Sec. Cons. no. 15, dated 12 June, 1839, Appendix B. The message in cypher is as follows (the figures are in Arabic numerals):

81169	169161	161911	616961
11696	116966	161911	116961
11696	116911	169116	1691161
112116	11611211	991169	169611

34. For Dept. Sec. Cons. no. 44 dated 29th September, 1849.
35. Ibid. Letters from James Abbott, Dy. Commissioner Hazara, dated 19th and 31 July, 1849.
36. Ibid. Letters from H.P.Burn, Dy. Secretary, Board of Administration, to Abbott, Dy. Commissioner Hazara, dated 9th August, 1849.
37. For Dept. Pol.Cons. no. 86 dated 15 October, 1852.

38. See A. Broome, *History of the Rise and Progress of the Bengal Army*, London, 185 , pp. 199ff; see also J.W. Kaye, *History of the Sepoy War in India*, London, 1872, vol. I, pp. 200ff.
39. R. Bosworth Smith, *Life of Lord Lawrence*, London, 1883, vol. I, p. 253.
40. *Infra*, p. 203.
41. *Vide supra*, p. 106.
42. A useful but isolated account of the conspiracy was published by Nanigopal Chowdhury, "The Wahhabi Conspiracy in Hyderabad, 1839-40," *Progs. vol. I.H.C.* 1956, vol. XIX.
43. For Dept. Sec. Cons. no. 23, dated 10 July, 1839.
44. Ibid., enclosures.
45. Ibid., no. 113, dated 10 July, 1839.
46. Ibid., no. 23 dated 10 July, 1839.
47. Ibid., no. 113, dated 10 July, 1839.
48. Ibid., no. 21, dated 10 July, 1839.
49. Mehr, IV, p. 183.
50. For Dept.Sec. Cons. no. 21, dated 10 July, 1839.
51. Ibid.
52. Ibid., no. 20, dated 10 July, 1839. Emphasis added.
53. Fraser was helped in the inquiry by his assistant, Malcom, and a Persian Muslim who was the representative of Bombay merchants at the Nizam's court and who was later recommended for an award of Rs. 2000/- (plus Rs. 1000/- for expenses) for his services in this connection.
54. See H. Fraser, *Our Faithful Ally, the Nizam*, London, 1865, pp. 241-42. The Commission was convened in June 1839 and closed its proceedings in April, 1840.
55. Ibid., p. 238. Emphasis added.
56. Sec. Cons. no. 12, dated 2 June, 1839.
57. It is customary to appoint a *Maulawī* and a *Pandit* in each regiment. Often, the Wahhabis worked through these regimental *Maulawīs* and *Pandits*.
58. For Dept. Cons. no. 23, dated 10 July, 1839; extracts of a letter from the Officer Commanding, Vellore, dated 6 June, 1839.
59. For Dept.Sec. Cons. no. 23, dated 10th July, 1839; letter dated 15th June, 1839 from Officer Commanding, Vellore.
60. It may be noted here that in the circle of his close associates and in their correspondence the Wahhabis referred to Wilayat Ali as *Baṛe Ḥaḍrat* and Enayat Ali as *Manjhle Ḥaḍrat*.
61. For subsequent happenings see the portion about Hyderabad Conspiracy, *supra*, pp. 191-93.
62. Kay, op. cit., vol.I, pp. 303-10.

63. K.K.Datta, *B.K.S.*, Patna, 1957, pp. 59-69.
64. These papers (Judicial Proceedings, Government of Bengal, dated 14 January, 11 Feb, 210d. 1846), were discovered in the Patna Commissioner's office by Dr. Jatashankar Jha and myself while we were collecting materials for the preparation of the *Biography of Kunwar Singh and Amar Singh* in early1950s.
65. Kaye, op. cit., p. 304.
66. This was denied in a subsequent letter from the Magistrate, Patna, to Secretary, Government of Bengal, no. 68, dated 30th January, 1846.
67. Datta, op. cit., p. 64.
68. Deposition of Peer Bakhsh under Act V of 1840 on 7th June 1846.
69. Letter from E.S.Lillie, Magistrate Patna, to Secretary, Government of Bengal, dated 26th December 1845.
70. He was known for his anti-government activities since a long time, *vide infra*, pp. 202-03. See also B.K.S., pp. 62-63.
71. He was employed in the Gwalior state for some time, and had acted as its *Wakil* at Calcutta. He was a man of means.
72. Echo of the *Dāru'l Ḥarb* theory of the Wahhabis.
73. This has, perhaps, a reference to the disturbances in Bihar jails following the introduction of a new mess system; vide *B.K.S.*, pp. 63,66.
74. A ship carrying passengers for *Ḥajj* was quarantined at Bombay at the time. That perhaps led to the rumour about interference with the performance of *Ḥajj*.
75. Letter from Officiating, Magistrate, Patna to the Secretary, Government of Bengal, no. 43 C dated the 20th January, 186, enclosure; ibid., no. 16, dated 14th January, 1846.
76. Ibid. Also letter from C.A.Lushington, Joint Magistrate, Patna to Magistrate, Patna dated 25th December, 1845.
77. Letter from Lt.Col. R.J.H. Birch, Judge Advocate-General, to Captain Cotton, Judge Advocate-General, Dinapur, dated Simla, 30th May, 1846.
78. Both the Magistrate, Patna and the Superintendent of Police, Lower Pronvinces, in their letters addressed to the Secretary Government of Bengal dated 3rd January and 6th October, 1846 respectively, stressed this point and remarked that his arrest would have thrown more light on the affair.
79. Letter from Superintendent of Police, Lower Provinces to Secretary Government of Bengal, no. 2261, dated 6th October, 1846.
80. It has been assumed that the reference to the North-West concerns the Anglo-Sikh war. But it may also be noted that this was the time when Wilayat Ali and Enayat Ali were fighting against the Sikh

forces, aided in some cases by the British on the North-Western Frontier.

81. He was the son of Salamat Ali, a zamindar, and belonged to village Neora near Patna. A brick tower built by him there, with holes made for firing from guns, still stands.
82. *B.K.S.*, p. 63.
83. *Infra*, p. 343.
84. Letter from Commissioner, Patna to Secretary, Government of Bengal, no. 1002, dated 8th January, 1846.
85. Letter from Superintendent of Police, Lower Provinces to Secretary, Government of Bengal, no. 2414, dated 27th October, 1846.
86. G.B.Malleson, op. cit., vol.I, pp. 547 ff.
87. For Dept.Pol.Cons. no. 88, dated 15 October, 1852.
88. A mahalla in Patna City, situated very close to Sadiqpur.
89. For Dept. Pol.Cons. no. 86, dated 15th October, 1852; see also letters from J.R.Carnac, Deputy Commissioner, Rawalpindi.
90. Ibid.; letter from H. Tucker, Officiating Magistrate, Patna, dated 19th August, 1852.
91. This throws some light on the question of the Wahhabi accomplices in the goverrnment, and the alertness of their organisation.
92. *Supra*, p.187.
93. For Dept.Pol.Cons. no. 92, dated 15 October, 1852.
94. It is not known as to what actual punishment was given to the *munshī*.
95. *I.M.*, p. 22. Emphasis added.
96. To mention some of them: Qadir Ali, Shaikh Makhdum, Shaikh Aulad Ali, Shaukat Ali and Affzal, in the 18th Irregular Cavalry; Babar Ali, Muhibb Ali and Rahat Ali in the 7th *Risāla* at Jullundur.
97. Letter from Deputy Advocate General, Peshawar to Commissioner, Patna dated 29th March, 1858.
98. *Vide supra*, p. 155.
99. Letter from H.B.Edwardes, Commissioner, Peshawar to R. Montgomery, Judicial Commissioner, Punjab, no 64, dated 23rd March, 1858. Edwardes quoted a letter written by men of the 51st Regiment to "the whole of Herriot Regiment" (64th N.I.), expressing their discontent with the "cartridge affair", and inviting them to join hands with them. Edwardes stresses the importance of this document as expressing the sentiments of one regiment to another on the quetion of the 'Mutiny'.
100. Edwardes' letter referred to above, vide *Punjab Government Records* (Mutiny period), vol. III, pt. II; also see Kaye, op. cit., vol. II, p. 496.
101. They both fled on the night the force from Peshawar arrived to disarm the units. One was later arrested and hanged.

102. Paget and Mason, *Records of the Expeditions against the North-West Frontier Tribes since the Annexation of Punjab.*
103. *Supra*, p. 155.
104. Kaye, op. cit., vol. II, p. 48; Holmes, *Indian Mutiny*, p. 318.
105. Subsequently, they fought under the leadership of Enayat Ali at Naranji', *vide supra*, pp. 155-56.
106. Their separate identity, as also their inluence on the course of events has not been fully appreciated; cf. Kaye, op. cit., pp. 455 ff.

Chapter VI

The Wahhabis and the Movement of 1857-59

The century following the battle of Plassey (1757) witnessed the gradual expansion and consolidation of the British Empire in India. At the same time, it was characterised by a number of conspiracies, risings, and generally anti-British movements. Among the last-mentioned, the Movement of 1857-59 and the Wahhabi Movement stand out as the two most formidable ones. Whereas the former has been the subject of some near-contemporary authoritative studies[1] supplemented by a few more valuable works in recent years,[2] the latter has not received adequate attention, to put it mildly.

An isolated and very brief account of only that phase of the Wahhabi Movement which relates to the years 1857-59 has been given by some of the standard historians of the Movement of 1857. But this account has been given out of its proper context. The origins of the Wahhabi Movement, its aims and objects, organisational set-up, and other similar points have been left out altogether. What is more important, the significance of the continuing activities of the Wahhabis has not been brought out, much less stressed. When the great conflagration of 1857 occurred, the Wahhabis had already been active for about three decades. This fact, however, has hardly been mentioned, with the result that in the general histories of the Movement of 1857-59 the Wahhabis are made to appear as an inexplicable and incongruous factor. Which group did they represent? Why was it that they were actively fighting against the British in the North-Western Frontier area,[3] but engaged in a diffferent kind of activity in, say, Bengal and Bihar? How did they manage to survive the ruthless and the thorough suppression of the other movement? These and other connected questions are left unanswered. Some of the historians of 'the Mutiny' were, perhaps, conscious of these gaps.

Malleson, for example, tried to offer a partial solution by including a brief appendix on the Wahhabis. But an appendix is hardly the place for treating a subject like the Wahhabi Movement. Among the recent works, a notable exception is K.M. Ashraf's incisive study[4] of the role of the Wahhabis during 1857-59. Ashraf has very correctly stressed two generally neglected points about the Wahhabis — that they were the only people at the time who were not only armed with "a consistent anti-British ideology" but also had "the backing of a network of organised centres spread all over northern India ...." He has discussed the role of the Wahhabis at Delhi, and , more briefly, at some other places, but perhaps the limitations of a rather short article prevented him from attempting a more detailed, comparative, analysis of the role of the Wahhabis in British India and in the North-Western Frontier.

While it is beyond the purview of the present work to go into a detailed analysis of the nature and extent of the Movement of 1857-59, a few points of comparative interest between the two movements may be noted.

Taken as a concerted military blow the Rising of 1857 was the most formidable single challenge faced by the British in India. Though it was the result of a long-standing and varied discontent, it was not pre-planned.[5] It flashed across the firmament of Indian history with the brilliance of a meteoric flight. The Wahhabi Movement, on the other hand, was a more sustained sruggle spread over more than half a century, and passing through different phases of intensity. It too had its share of battles fought against the British, but these were, unlike those in 1857-59, the results of a well-organised plan of action. One weakness of the Rising of 1857, which contributed in no small measure to its unsuccessful end, was the absence of a unity of purpose, and a co-ordinated plan of action.[6] The whole of northern India was, as it were, divided into separate theatres of war, each with its own leader. While it is true that the anti-British motive was active in all these cases, and that there was some degree of contact between the different leaders, yet, by and large, the fact remains that the struggle was divided into small and often isolated fronts.[7] As against this, the Wahhabis had an efficient, centralised organisation. Secondly, the Movement of 1857-59 was essentially an attempt from inside the country to drive out the British. Undoubtedly, there was widespread civilian support for the rising, and in some parts of the country, such as the Shahabad area in Bihar and in Awadh, it assumed the proportions of 'a national revolt' [8] yet it was primarily a rebellion from inside.

The leaders of the Rising of 1857 did not have any clear programme of action for the future. British rule practically ceased to exist in many areas during the period, but no alternative administration was evolved in those areas. This was due partly to shortage of time, no doubt, — the British rule was restored quickly enough— but the lack of a well-worked-out plan of action was also an important factor. The Wahhabis, on the other hand, aimed at comprehensive social reforms. The political aspect was only to be a part of the wider social programme.

The Wahhabi Movement since its inception was influenced by the doctrine of *Hijrat.* This concerns the point as to whether British India could be regarded as a *Dāru 'l Harb* or not. There was much difference of opinion among the *'ulamā* on this, and without going into the finer points of the religious arguments, it may be said that it was postulated that if a country formerly under 'Islamic rule' was conquered by a non-Muslim power, or when the internal conditions there became such as to render the performance of one's religious duties impossible, that country became a *Dāru 'l Harb,* and it became the duty of a Muslim living there to migrate to a *Dāru 'l Islām,* or one where there were no impediments to the performance of their religious duties. A struggle against the *Dāru 'l Harb* is to be carried on from outside its territories.[9]

Since the time of Sayyid Ahmad the Wahhabis on the Frontier were in control of an independent state and had an army to defend it. The Wahhabis in their writings and speeches stressed the need for migrating from British India, particularly for those who for various reasons could not directly participate in the struggle against the British.[10] The struggle was to be waged as between two states, from outside British India.[11] This point is crucial to an understanding of the Wahhabis' attitude towards the Movement of 1857-59, and their differing role in the areas outside British India and those inside it, particularly in Bihar, their chief centre at the time.

In Bihar, the existence of a group of 'Wahhabi agitators' had been reported to the Government from time to time. On the eve of the rising the situation had become more explosive. Tayler, the Divisional Commissioner, Patna had reported that in spite of the outward calm the city was tense and the people's pent-up feelings ready to burst out. The news of the military risings at Meerut and Delhi

(May, 1857) had made the authorities only more apprehensive. There was a rumour of a rising at Dinapur on the 7th June. A letter inviting the *Nujeebs* (volunteers, corps), guarding the treasury and the Commissioner's residence, to join the rising, had been seized by the government, and its bearer executed. The authorities had taken several preventive steps—additional force was raised, six companies of Captain Rattray's battalions had been transferred to Patna, and government's treasures from the outlying districts had been transferred to Patna.

Anti-government activities were being pursued in the town by several groups of persons. There was, first, what Tayler called the Lucknow group, (active since the annexation of Awadh, 1856) whose leades were Masihuzzaman, Pir Ali and Mahdi Ali, a police *darogha* in the town. Then there was the Delhi group, whose leaders were Maulawi Ali Kureem, an educated wealthy zamindar of Patna[12] and Waris Ali, a police *jama'dār* of *thāna* Bandaraj, Muzaffarpur district. Finally, there were the local Wahhabis, whose leader was Farhat Husain.[13] The leaders of these groups were trying to co-ordinate their activities, and there was an active exchange of correspondence between them.[14] Masihuzzaman had written to Pir Ali to contact Ali Kureem and the family members of Wilayat Ali and Muqsood Ali (the Wahhabi leaders on the Frontier) as their cooperation was considered valuable. Pir Ali was directed further that, 'if in the family of Velayut Ali or Muksood Ali you are on friendly terms with anyone you think is able for our work, you may inform me. I think *we should not disagree with any caste, and even with Hindoos,* for we should try and get our work done, for in disagreeing there are countless disputes. For my part. I am on (friendly) terms with the Wahhabis, with those who are weak and wavering, and with many even of the Shias and Rafzees."[15]

In a detailed report, characterised by deep political insight, Tayler drew attention to the activities of these groups, with particular reference to the Wahhabis, whom he considered to be potentially more dangerous. "Although I have believed," wrote Tayler "that in carrying out a great anti-Christian league—which we are.... warranted in regarding this Movement to be—all sects would be willing to merge their own sectarian differences for the time being and to make common cause against the Nazranees, there were yet two special quarters from where danger might be looked for at Patna—partisans and adherents of the Lucknow party ... secondly from the numerous and fanatical sects of the Wahhabees. In addition to this was the great danger to be expected from the mass of the townspeople if an outbreak occurred." He adds, "To each of these separate points" he aimed "a separate blow."[16] Mahdi Ali of the Lucknow party was arrested. The townspeople were disarmed—5000 arms having been produced voluntarily and deposited in the *thana* and everybody was forbidden to come out of his house after 9 o'clock in the night. As for the Wahhabis, their leaders were put under a sort of preventive detention. In spite of these preventive measures, however, a rising led by Pir Ali occurred in Patna on the 3rd July 1857,[17] some three weeks before the revolt of the Native Infantry at Dinapur, which marked the beginning of the general upsurge all over Bihar.

Since we are concerned here specially with the role of the Wahhabis, we shall examine the incident[18] of the arrest of the Wahhabi leaders a little more closely. A striking characteristic of the Wahhabis, Tayler pointed out, was their complete subservience to their *'pir'*. Without writing a single line, a Wahhabi leader could convey a confidential message from Patna to Lahore in an incredibly short span of time, and an order from the chief would be met with 'unquestioning acquiescence." He therefore decided to "take possession of their leaders, more as hostages for the good conduct of the whole brotherhood *than from any expectation of having sufficient evidence to punish them*" (italics are mine). He was, however, afraid of arresting them openly, for it might have lead to resistance. So he thought of an unorthodox plan. He issued a circular letter to 'respectable natives' of the city, asking them to come to his house to discuss preventive methods to be adopted in case there is any outbreak of trouble. The next morning (19th June, 1857), the gentlemen, including Ahmadullah, Muhammad Husain[19] (*Khalifa* of Sayyid Ahmad) and Waizu'l Haque,[20] presented themselves. Chairs were placed for them around the dining table, and after they were seated Tayler entered the room, accompanied by the Collector, Captain Rattray, Hedayat Ali, and some others. The "supposed consultations" were gone through, while Tayler was all the time "inexpressibly amused" at the demeanour of the three intended victims, who "perhaps knew something of the coming arrest." He, however, admired their fortitude. When the meeting was over, the three Wahhabi leaders were 'politely' requested to remain seated, and then after the others had left, Tayler announced their arrest, explaining that although he had no positive proof of their guilt he thought it to be a necessary preventive measure. The *Moulvis* took the blow "with a wonderful presence of mind and a politeness of manner worthy of all admiration." They were despatched under the escort of the Sikh Regiment to the Circuit House where they were detained. Tayler was particular to drop in a parting threat. He told Ahmadullah that he had not arrested his father, Elahi Bakhsh,[21] who was an old and invalid man, but made it clear to Ahmadullah that the temporary concession was strictly dependent upon the good behaviour of his followers. "Remember .... his (Elahi Bakhsh's) life is in your hands, your's in his," Tayler said.

Tayler was quite happy about what he had done, and in the controversy which subsequently developed he justified his action strongly. "To this day," he asserted, "I look at the detention of these men as one of the most successful strokes of policy which I was able to carry into execution." But his critics compared it to the murder of William H. Macnaghten by Akbar Muhammad during the Anglo-Afghan war. In retrospect, it is clear that from the government's point of view the action had served its purpose. The arrest of these leaders did temporarily upset the Wahhabis' arrangements for the transmission of money to the Frontier, where acute privations prevailed. But Tayler was completely wrong in his assertion that his action not only prevented the Wahhabis from participating in the Patna Rising of the 3rd July, but forced Elahi Bakhsh, the father of Ahmadullah, to convey prior information to the government about that rising. In maintaining this, Tayler was being guilty of grave, possibly deliberate, withholding and misrepresentation of facts. Throughout the letters which he wrote during the period, he maintained that the information was lodged by Elahi Bakhsh, father of Ahmadullah.

The actual informer of the rising had, however, gone to Louis, the Magistrate of Patna, and not to Tayler. The Magistrate, who had taken down the informer's statement, gave the following report :

> Statement of Ilahi Baksh son of Sufdar Ally, of *mouzah* Darwah, *thanah* Barh, July Ist (1857). There are arms and men collected at the house of Pir Ali Khan, a bookseller in *thānah* Khajekallan. I have been sent to give this information by *Moulvi* Ilahee Buksh who heard it from some persons whose names I do not know.[22]

It is thus clear that the informer was a person named Ilahi Bakhsh, belonging to Barh, who said that he had come from Elahi Bakhsh (father of Ahmadullah). There is no evidence to judge the veracity of his statement. It may very well have been a case of incriminating one's enemy by making a false complaint against him. Such cases abounded in the atmosphere of false incrimination and witch-hunting prevailing in the city.[23] The informer might have been a pawn in the hands of some opponents of the Sadiqpur family. Or, probably, being a man of rather obscure family connections, whose words might not have carried much weight with the authorities, the informer might have quoted the name of Ahmadullah's father, a prominent local gentleman, to add weight to his testimony.

This contention would be appreciated better if we take into consideration the family history of the Wahhabi leaders of Patna. Having dedicated their lives to the mission, and sacrificed all their material possessions, they were not likely to be influenced by such small personal considerations. Elahi Bakhsh, in particular, was the father, of not only Ahmadullah, but also of Yahya Ali, Faiyyaz Ali and Akbar Ali. The latter three had been fighting against the government on the Frontier since a long time, and their activities were well known. Moreover, Elahi Bakhsh's nephews, Wilayat Ali and Enayat Ali, were 'proclaimed rebels'. *If the life and safety of Elahi Bakhsh was to be dependent, in the eyes of the government, on the 'good character' of his sons, it was already forfeit* on the above count. The actions of *one of his sons* could not have mattered much either way. A man who had willingly sent three of his sons, and many more of his nearest relatives, to fight against the British (knowing full well the risks involved to their lives, and his own) was not likely to flinch at the prospect of a supposed danger to the safety of one of his sons, against whom there were no charges at all. It is simply inexplicable why a man, a considerable number of whose family-members were deeply involved in anti-government activities, whose wealth had been at stake in his struggle against the government, would give information to an offficer of that very government about a rising which was to take place against it. The doubt increases when we find that Tayler deliberately made use of the strange coincidence that the name of the actual informer and that of Ahmadullah's father happened to be the same. Louis, in his letter to Tayler, had specifically drawn the latter's attention ('to prevent confusion') to this particular fact. Tayler, however, passed off the name everywhere as that of Ahmadullah's father. He was clearly doing this in a vain attempt to justify Ahmadullah's and the other Wahhabis' arrest. Tayler seems to have ignored the wider ideological influences under which the Wahhabis worked. He failed to realise that their attitude would have remained the same even if no preventive arrest of their leaders had taken place. Their action in this matter was based not on superficial personal considerations, but on impersonal factors of principles and policies.

The Wahhabi state on the Frontier, and their district centres inside British India were the two pivots around which the movement revolved. Each had a particular role assigned to it, which was strictly adhered to. The main task of the latter was the assembling and training of recruits, and the transmission of money and materials. The Wahhabis must have realised that if the activities of the district centres were too openly displayed, it would attract the attention of the government. They would be suppressed, and the supply lines would be cut. It is this consideration which explains the apparently contradictory situation that while one group of Wahhabis under Enayat Ali were waging war on the North-Western Frontier during 1857-58,[24] the others, inside India, were comparatively quiet. The leader at Patna then was Farhat Hussain, younger brother of Enayat Ali, and his attitude towards the British was not different from that of his elder brother. The only reason why he acted differently was the iron-discipline of the organisation, which had assigned to him a different task.

Among the more recent writers on the movement of 1857-59, only R.C. Majumdar [25] and S.N. Sen[26] have briefly referred to the significant point that the Wahhabis as a group kept themselves aloof from the developments during 1857-59. Majumdar recalls that the Wahhabis had "turned against the British when they succeeded the Sikhs as ruler of the Punjab," and they had "carried on a relentless campaign against the British from their remote seat at Sittana." He, therefore, finds it "not a little curious that this violently anti-British militant organisation should have practically kept aloof from the great revolutionary movement of 1857". He goes on to add that the Wahhabis of Sittana "could have rendered great service to the cause of the Mutiny by attacking the British in the North-West." That would have hampered the flow of men and money from the Punjab to Delhi.

It will be noted that Majumdar has made the remark, about the Wahhabis keeping aloof, applicable to all the Wahhabi centres, and, secondly, he takes it that the Wahhabis on the North-Western Frontier did not take any advantage of the situation arising in the wake of the rising. Neither of these two assumptions can be substantiated. As shown above,[27] Enayat Ali had joined hands with the rebellious men of the 55th N.I., who led across the border, and fought several engagements against the British. The bare details of the Sittana campaign,[28] clearly indicate the magnitude of the threat posed by the Wahhabis right in the middle of 1858, and the seriousness with which it was viewed by the British. It is, therefore, not correct to maintain that the Wahhabis on the North-Western Frontier "kept aloof."

In another connected work of his, published a little later,[29] Majumdar has taken note of the anti-British activities of the Wahhabis on the North-Western Frontier, and though he has referred very briefly to Enayat Ali's occupation of Chinglai and his attack on Narinji [30] he still maintains that the Wahhabis kept "almost quiet" during the crucial period of the rising. He also refers to the present writer's explanation of the differing role and attitude of the Wahhabis in and outside British India during the period, but he does not find it to be incompatible with his own explanation, to which we will turn presently.

Majumdar's remark is true only to the extent that if the whole of the Punjab had risen against the British in 1857, not only would Lawrence not have been able to gamble with the forces in Punjab, but the entire course of events would have been different. But the whole of Punjab was not a Wahhabi sphere of influence, though they had pockets of strong support in some areas there. One has to look at some other factors in the situation prevailing there. It has been rightly pointed out that a variety of motives—often contradictory—led the three major communities in Punjab, the Hindus, Muslims and Sikhs, to remain, "on the whole, loyal."[31] We may also recall here a significant remark of Bosworth, the biographer of Lord Lawrence about the policy adopted by the latter of playing off one section of the population in the Punjab against another.[32]

As for Sen,[33] he too, after correctly noticing the point that the Wahhabis as a group did not take part in the rising, makes this remark applicable to all the Wahhabi centres. He goes a step further and refers to a Minute of the Lieutenant-Governor of Bengal, dated the 30th September, 1858, to the effect that "Nothing was at any time proved or even alleged against the Wahhabis" (of Bengal).

An account of the Wahhabis' activities in Bengal and Bihar during 1840s has already been given.[34] At the other end of the country, officers from Hazara had reported about the existence of a "remarkable nest of emigrants from Hindoostan" and to their "treasonable activities."[35] The Lieutenant-Governor himself had recorded in an earlier Minute, dated the 26th August, 1852, that "a correspondence exists between persons in Patna and fanatics in Sittana and Swat" and that it was "expedient to watch the conduct and the proceedings of the parties implicated."[36] To hold in the face of all this that the Wahhabi kept aloof does not carry much conviction.

To conclude, although both Majumdar and Sen are correct in stating that the Wahhabis as a group kept aloof from the developments during 1857-58, they have not viewed the Wahhabi position quite in its entirety. Majumdar has explained the attitude of the Wahhabis purely in religious terms. He writes that they kept aloof because they "did not like to co-operate with the Hindus."[37] This would be too narrow and negative an explanation. It is true that *Dāru'l Ḥarb* and *Dāru'l Islām* were religious concepts, but, as shown above, the Wahhabis did not insist strictly upon the doctrine of *hijrat*. The number of people who did actually migrate at any given time was not very large. Secondly, it seems to have been clearly understood that those who remained in British India and extended support from there were rendering very crucial help to the movement.

The appraisal of the political situation by the Wahhabi leaders was influenced by other, political and military, considerations as well. And as things actually turned out, their appraisal may not be regarded as short-sighted and incorrect. By keeping low inside British India they survived the great storm of 1857, and were able to render valuable help to the Wahhabi state on the North-Western Frontier during the British onslaughts in 1858, 1863 and subsequently. That the lease of life obtained by them proved to be a short one, and that the superior and better-organised British resources, which enabled them to meet the challenge of so many scattered "centres of revolt" all over northern India, would have enabled them to meet the additional, Wahhabi, challenge as well, is a different matter. Material and technological superiority was a crucial advantage possessed by the British, and it would not have been substantially affected by the actions of the Wahhabis during 1857-58.

A mistaken notion seems to have prevailed in some quarters that it would somehow detract from the anti-British character of the Wahhabi Movement if it was maintained that the Wahhabis in British

India did not take much part in the Rising of 1857. This notion is based on a double fallacy. Firstly, it ignores the history of the Wahhabi Movement before 1857, and presumes that the character of the Movement has to be judged on the basis of the activities of its followers during 1857-59, and, secondly, it is assumed that the Wahhabis inside British India were somehow different from those on the Frontier. On the contrary, both these groups, were well-integrated, working under a centralised organisation. The same set of persons closely inter-related, worked in and outside British India. In fact, the same persons—Wilayat Ali, Enayat Ali, Yahya Ali and many others—worked alternately at the two places. The open struggle on the Frontier was not possible for some of the centres in the British area of control. The more substantive, if less spectacular, work of procuring resources, however, was continued by these centres.

Many amongst us are apt to look with admiration at the exploits of a daring pilot carrying on bombing missions on enemy territory and feel inclined to emulate his feats. But how many of us give a thought to the ceaseless toil of the groundcrew without whose silent and prosaic labours such flights would be unthinkable? If they were to be negligent in one small detail of their work, let alone ceasing work altogether, where would the pilot and his plane be? Such was the role of the Wahhabi centres in British India, particularly Bengal and Bihar.[38]

Notes

1. To mention only a few, Kaye, *op. cit.*, Malleson, *op. cit.*, G.W. Forrest, *History of the Indian Mutiny*, Edinburgh & London, 1904-12.
2. S.N. Sen, *op. cit.*, R.C. Majumdar, *The Sepoy Mutiny and the Revolt of 1857*, Calcutta, 1957 and *History of the Freedom Movement in India*, vol.I, 2nd rev.ed., Calcutta, 1971; K.K. Dutta *Biography of Kunwar Singh and Amar Singh*, Patna, 1957, P.C. Joshi (ed.) *Rebellion 1857, A Symposium*, P.P.H., 1957.
3. *Vida supra*, pp. 148 ff.
4. K.M. Ashraf, "Muslim Revivalists and the Revolt of 1857," P.C. Joshi (ed.), *Rebellion 1857, A Symposium*, P.P.H., 1957, pp. 71-102.
5. Sen, op. cit., p. 405.
6. Ibid., Foreword, pp. XV-XVI.
7. Ibid., p. 402.
8. Ibid., pp. 409, 411. K.K. Datta, *op. cit.*, p. 112.

9. Nawab Siddiq Hasan Khan, *Mawāi'du'l 'Awāi'd,* 1882, p. 34; see also his other work, *Tiqsār-i Jiyūdu'l Aḥrār min Tizkār-i Junūdu'l Ahrār,* hereafter referred to as *Tiqsar.*
10. See C.R., 1870, pp. 385 *ff.; I.M.,* and *infra,* chapter X.
11. Nawab Siddiq Hasan Khan, *Tiqsar* in which he states the point, often neglected that Sayyid Ahmad chose not to wage war inside (British) India but migrated outside to fight.
12. For an account of his career and activities, see my article, "Maulawi Ali Kurim, a scholar-soldier of Bihar during the Movement of 1857-59," I.H.R.C. Progs. vol., XXXIII, pt. II, 1958, pp. 9-15.
13. Younger brother of Wilayat Ali.
14. J.S. Jha, "The Patna Conspiracy of 1857," *I.H.R.C. Progs. vol.* XXXII, pt. II, 1956.
15. Ibid. This is corroborated by the *Tadhkira-i-Sādqa,* which mentions Pir Ali's contacting Farhat Husain and seeking his cooperation in the contemplated rising. The latter, however, declined for reasons to be discussed presently.
16. B.K.S., p. 83.
17. We are not concerned here with the details of the rising, but its main events may be briefly noted. The anti-government activities of the diffierent groups culminated in a rising in the town on the 3rd July 1857. It was precipitated, probably before time, due to apprehensions about the exposure of the plan. Dr. R. Lyell, the Principal Assistant to the Opium Agent in Bihar, was shot dead, but the situation was controlled by Captain Rattray's force. Pir Ali, the leader of the rising, was arrested the next day and after a mere show of trial he was hanged 'within three hours after sentence.'

    Tayler, who let loose a reign of terror in the town, and who tried Pir Ali felt constrained to admire the courage of conviction and idealism displayed by the condemned prisoner. He writes that on being asked as to whether Pir Ali could do anything to make it worthwhile to spare his life. The prisoner replied; "There are some cases in which it is good to save life, others, in which it is better to lose it." He then taunted Tayler with the repression he had exercised and concluded by saying, "You may hang me or such as me every day, but thousands will arise in my place and your object will rever be gained." (For detail, see William Tayler, *Our Crisis,* 1858, K.K. Datta, *B.K.S.* pp. 70-88; J.S. Jha's article cited above).
18. The account is based on Tayler's own version, *vide, Our Crisis.*
19. *supra,* p. 58 n.5.
20. He had incurred the government's displeasure earlier for opposition to the activities of Christian missionaries, and had been imprisoned. He went to Arabia subsequently, and died at Makkah.

21. *Supra*, p. 58 , n.3.
22. Letter from J. Louis, Magistrate, Patna to W. Tayler, Commissioner, Patna dated the 21st July, 1857, Mutiny Records (Bundles) in the Divisional Commissioner's Office record room, now transferred to the State Archives, Bihar.
23. Some idea can be had from the letters of the local officers. Louis, in his letter referred to above wrote, "I had come utterly to distrust spies and underhand information, not only from being misled by one of your (Tayler's) *goindas* (informer) ... but also from what I heard afterwards of the doings of this spy; armed with a *perwanah* (order) from you (Tayler), levying contributions on many respectable Hindoos and others in the city .... Much mischief resulted from such powers being placed in the hands of unscrupulous persons." Louis also refers to the case of another informer of Tayler who had misled him into searching the house of a 'Wahhabee Moulvie' on the 20th June (1857) from where 'nothing whatever was found' after the strictest search, and the magistrate learnt subsequently that the spy had been an *Amin* (revenue official to whom 'the Wahabee gentleman had once refused an unjust demand of rupees 5/-).

    The Divisional Commissioner, who succeeded Tayler had this to say about the *goindas*; "*Goindas* in this country are much more formidable to innocent men from whom they extort money by threats of accusations than to criminals who can generally secure their silence by bribery or intimidation." (Letter from the Commissioner, Patna to the Secretary, Board of Revenue, dated 22nd September, 1857.)
24. *Supra*, pp. 154-57.
25. R.C. Majumdar, *The Sepoy Mutniy and the Revolt of 1857*, 2nd ed., Calcutta.
26. Sen, *op. cit.*, p. 248.
27. *Supra*, p. 155.
28. *Infra*, pp. 233 ff.
29. R.C. Majumdar, *History of the Freedom Movement in India*, 2nd. rev. ed., Calcutta, 1971, vol.I, pp. 248-49.
30. Majumdar's bare mention of thee activities does not bring out the full magnitude of the struggle, nor the exact time-sequence.
31. Talmiz Khaldun, 'The Great Rebellion' in P.C. Joshi, *(ed.)*, *Rebellion 1857: A Symposium*, PPH, 1957, p. 32.

    For some perceptive comments on the nature of the Wahhabi Movement and its indirect influence on the course of events at Delhi and some other places at this time, see K.M. Ashraf, "Muslim Revivalists and the revolt of 1857," *ibid.*, pp. 71 *ff.*

32. *Vide supra*, pp. 189-90.
33. Sen, *op. cit.*, p. 248.
34. *Supra*, chapters, III and IV.
35. *Supra*, p. 185.
36. *Supra*, p. 187.
37. Majumdar, *The Sepoy Mutiny and the Revolt of 1857*, p. 59; ibid., *History of Freedom Movement*, vol.I, p. 249.
38. Writing about the respective importance of these two different types of works, Mehr remarks, 'The trials of this field of work (organisational) are in no way less than those of the field of battle. On the contrary, I would say that it is easier to die swiftly in the raging fire of the field of battle than to pass the slow-winding hours of the long, unending, day in constant worries and ever-present risks. These warriors (the Wahhabis of Patna) lost their hearths and homes, spent their days in the dark dungeons of prisons and the terrible wastes of the Andaman Islands, they cheerfully accepted eternal separation, from one another, so much so that even in deaths the brothers (Ahmadullah and Yahya Ali) were denied the grace of having their tombs together; and yet their resolve was never shaken, their steps, never faltered. Mehr IV, p.372, translated into English by me.

Chapter VII

The British Campaigns Against the Wahhabis on the North-Western Frontier

Even before the annexation of Punjab (1849) and the extension of their hold to the Frontier tribal areas, the British had started feeling concerned about, what they regarded as the declining Sikh rule, and the developing resistance movements in that area. As we have shown above,[1] these resistance movements were led both by the tribal chiefs and the Wahhabis, and the British authorities had been extending indirect help to the Sikhs, and more particularly to Gulab Singh, in suppressing these revolts. This was the background to the early phase of the British clash with the Wahhabis. The clash became more acute and direct after the annexation of the Punjab.

The Wahhabis had been fighting against the British since 1852, and the Rising of 1857 presented them with better opportunities of continuing their struggle. The significance of this development was not lost upon the chroniclers of the British military expeditions to the Frontier area. Paget and Mason[2] drew attention to this point by remarking that, 'The only portion of the Peshawar district in which advantage was taken of the Sepoy Mutiny by the people to disturb the country was on the Yusufzai frontier, *and this was principally due to the presence of the Hindustani fanatics, who were* supported by contributions of men and money from traitorous princes and private individuals in Hindustan.' Between 1850 and 1857 the British Government had sent as many as 16 military expeditions against the Wahhabis on the Frontier.[3] On account of the exigencies of the Rising of 1857, when the entire military resources of the Punjab were at stake under the tireless direction of Lawrence upon the recovery of Delhi, the authorities had been meeting the situation on an adhoc basis, but with the easing of the situation it was decided to tackle the Wahhabi challenge in earnest.

Two of the most powerful and protracted campaigns— that of 1858 (the Sittana campaign) under the command of Sir Sydney Cotton, and that of 1863 (the Ambeyla campaign) under the command of General Chamberlain, followed in quick succession.

The Campaign of 1858

A powerful expeditinary force,[4] under the command of Sir Sydney Cotton, was organised with the express object of destroying the Wahhabi centres at Sittana and Mangalthana.[5] The force, having assembled in the village of Salim Khan, started on the 25th April, 1858. This attack coincided with a period of set-back in the history of the Wahhabi state on the Frontier. The chief supporters of the Wahhabis, the Sayyids, had just suffered a reverse in an encounter with the Usmanzais which will be described presently.

The tribesmen, as on some earlier occasions, had turned hostile on seeing a punitive expedition being sent against the Wahhabis. The first tribe to disown their own chief (let alone the Wahhabis), were the Khudukhels. They attacked Panjtar and drove out Muqarrab Khan. The English forces, arriving at Panjtar on 25th April, found it already deserted, and set fire to it. The destruction of Chinglai also took place on the same day.[6]

The next move concerned Mangalthana. The Wahhabis had decided on concentrating all their strength at Sittana and had withdrawn from Mangalthana, but Muqarrab Khan, on being driven away from Panjtar, had sent his family to seek shelter in the abandoned fortress. Its destruction was considered essential by the English as "it would render the chastisement of the Khan (Muqarrab) more complete and memorable,"[7] if this remaining fortress was also destroyed. It enjoyed a great prestige among the tribesmen and was considered impregnable, being so embedded in the mountains as to be all but inaccessible. It was the pride of all the tribes around, and such was the prestige attached to it that its reduction alone was considered enough to overawe the tribes. Cotton, the leader of the expedition, gives the following account of this important Wahhabi citadel.

"Mangalthana stands on the chief spur of the Mahabun mountains and was the headquarters of Enayat Ali who so perseveringly endeavoured (1857-58) at Narinji and other places to raise the Yusufzai in rebellion ... it consists of the two villages, upper and lower. The lower consists of 30 or 40 houses and is occupied by Syeds ... upper Mangalthana stands upon a plateau in the midst of three crests, which are themselves outworks when held by the Garrison, but as soon as carried by an enemy command the place. On this plateau stood first the fortified house of Enayat Ali with the enclosures for his Hindusthani followers, secondly, the fortified house of Syed Abbas and thirdly, (Syed) Akbar's citadel, a white masonry tower, the whole having 30 or 40 houses. The fortifications had been laboriously constructed by large stones and timber, the Hindusthani fanatics and the thieves flocking to Akbar's citadel must have lived there in considerable enjoyment and security and it is easy to understand the prestige that surrounded them."[8] The prosperous settlement was destroyed[9] on the 29th April and its fortifications razed to the ground. The troops, having halted overnight amidst the ruins of their own making, left the next day and returned to Salim Khan.

In between the brief interval of the sack of Mangalthana and that of Sittana, there occurred an event, which although traceable to a much earlier period, had a direct bearing on the destruction of Sittana and, in fact, rendered it easier.

Between the territory on the right side of the Indus and the British frontier outpost of Topi, in the Yusufzai plain, lies a narrow strip of land by the side of the river and under the shadow of Mahabun mountain. Situated outside British India, this land belonged to the Usmanzai tribe. It contained, besides a few other hamlets, the villages of upper and lower Kyah and Khabal and upper and lower Sittana. Sittana had, a long time ago, been given as a rent-free grant to Sayyid Zamin Shah of Takhtbund in Buner, a religious recluse of great eminence who had been expelled from his own area owing to a feud. His grandsons, Umar Shah and Akbar Shah, had taken part in the activities of the Wahhabis earlier, and the latter had acted as the treasurer of Sayyid Ahmad. He had also invited the Wahhabis to Sittana and let them settle there. He had been elected leader of the revolt against the Sikh *darbār* in Lower Hazara in 1846-47, described earlier. When Hazara passed under British control, he went back to Swat and was elected the King there. During his absence Umar Shah was the chief of Sittana. Both he and Akbar Shah had collected some tithe from the villages of Kyah and Khabal as a measure of their political overlordship and also with a view to defraying the cost of the Wahhabi centre there. The Usmanzai resented this levy but found themselves powerless to oppose it, especially as the local people of the two villages supported the Sayyids. Now, on the eve of the Cotton expedition, they saw a good opportunity to drive away the Sayyids.

Edwardes, the Commissioner of Peshawar, was forcing agreements[10] from the Frontier tribes pledging themselves not to give protection to the Sayyids or the Wahhabis. Accordingly, the Usmanzais attacked Sittana on the 30th April, 1858 and in the ensuing battle Umar Shah was killed. Thus the way for the subsequent British victory was paved, for the leader of resistance, Umar Shah, was already dead. Mangalthana was destroyed because the tribesmen had turned against their own leader, Muqarrab Khan; now Sittana was to be destroyed because the Usmanzais had already broken the back of the resistance right on the eve of the attack.

The English army under Cotton proceeded against Sittana on the 4th May, 1858. Having crossed the Indus, the British advanced from the south, while the levies of Jahandad Khan of Amb took position on the northern hills. According to the author of the *Durr-i-Maqāl,*[11] the local tribesmen had informed Mubarak Shah of the advance of the British upon Sittana, and the former finding himself unable to offer resistance retreated with his family members to Malka, some 35 miles up Sittana on the northern slope of the Mahabun mountain. Only a small party of the Wahhabis, numbering forty, and some Jadun tribesmen, remained behind in Sittana. They took position on a hillock called Shah Noor-ki-Lari, some distance ahead of Sittana and awaited the arrival of the English. The leader of the party[12] was Ikramullah, one of the members of the triumvirate. The result was a foregone conclusion but the small band of Wahhabis fought well. Neville[13] quotes an account from the authoritative records of British campaigns against the Frontier tribes, which is one of calm and resolute behaviour of the Wahhabi warriors fighting against heavy odds and against a much larger force. "The fighting of the Hindusthanis was strongly marked with fanaticism, they came bodily and doggedly on... in perfect silence without a shout or word of any kind. All were dressed in their best for the occasion, mostly in white but some of the leaders wore velvet cloaks."[14] Another writer also comments favourably on the spirited resistance of the Wahhabis which was in striking contrast to the much vaunted fighting qualities of the tribesmen. The latter "escaped as best as they could, but the Hindusthanis stood to a man... The fight was short, desperate and decisive, and in the end everyone of these brave warriors was either killed or captured."[15] Some 30 of the Wahhabis including their leader were killed.[16] The English also suffered some losses. Sittana, like Manglathana, was mercilessly destroyed. Elephants were used to bulldoze all structures. Fortifications were blown off. Trees were cut down and the barks of those which could not be cut were scrubbed so that they might not grow. Punitive expeditions were also taken against some other tribes, like the Jaduns, and they were sworn, as also the Usmanzais, not to let the Wahhabis come back and settle in Sittana again. Apparently, the English had done everything possible to blot Sittana out of existence but they had not reckoned with the steadfastness and perseverence of their foe.

After the battle of Sittana the Wahhabis were invited by the Sayyids to Malkae, which also belonged to them, but had been lying practically uninhabited. Now, with the settling of the Sayyids and the Wahhabis, a prosperous[17] habitation quickly grew up there.

The Wahhabis were now under the leadership of Nurrulah and Mohammad Taqi, the remaining two of the triumvirate. They once again began the painful task of picking up the lost threads, and organising anew the centre from scratch. The crisis caused to the Wahhabis by stopping supplies from Patna eased with the release of Ahmadullah and the other leaders. At about this time Maqsud Ali, who had left for Patna earlier to arrange for reinforcements, also returned to the Frontier after a perilous journey via Meerut, where he was arrested, but was later released. He also visited Peshawar[18] where he stayed for about three months and made arrangements for supply of men and money through the usual channels and for circulating some proclamations. He had left Patna early in 1859 and reached the Frontier the next year. Meanwhile, Nurullah had, died on his way to Kabul to meet the Amir of Afghanistan. We do not have any details about the purpose of this journey, but it is relevant to recall that the Wahhabis had rendered valuable services to the Amir in the first Anglo-Afghan War. This journey might well have been to seek his help in this hour of difficulties for themselves. After Nurullah's death, Maqsud Ali was elected leader, but he, too, died shortly afterwards, in 1862. There were two likely leaders after his death. Abdullah,[19] the son of Wilayat Ali, and Ishaq, the son of Maqsud Ali. The former was elected Amir because of his greater experience and better knowledge of military affairs. Ishaq was elected to the next higher post of treasurer.[20] The period of Abdullah's *Imārat* covers some four decades and the most important development of the period was the Ambeyla Campaign.

The Ambeyla Campaign, 1863

The Ambeyla Campaign[21] was the biggest and best-organised single campaign led by the British against the Wahhabis. It represents a major escalation in the British effforts to root out the Wahhabis' centre. Hunter, comparing the earlier, pre 1850, efforts with the subsequent expeditions including this one, points out that whereas 16 expeditions, involving 33,000 regular troops, were sent between 1850 to 1857, 23 expeditions, involving 60,000 regular troops, were sent between 1850 and 1863. In terms of both men and money, it represented a supreme effort by the British to root out the Wahhabis against whom it was solely directed. In some of the previous campaigns the objects of chastisement were both the Wahhabis and the tribesmen, the former often getting involved because of their help to the latter. On this occasion, the roles were reversed. The expedition was aimed against the Wahhabis primarily, but was prolonged because the latter succeeded, only for a brief priod, in making the tribesmen join the resistance.

The origin of the war is to be found in the continuation of the conflict between the Sayyids and the Usmanzais,[22] referred to above. Following the withdrawal of the Sayyids and the Wahhabis from Sittana, the Usmanzais re-occupied the village and brought the fields under cultivation. Mubarak Shah, the leader of the Sayyids, had not, however, given up his claim to the ancestral patrimony of Sittana. He had been planning for its re-occupation ever since his exile. He first sought the aid of the Jadun tribes for this and they agreed.[23] With their help, as also that of the Wahhabis, he constructed a fortified tower, known as Siri's tower, situated between Kyah and Sittana, and from there he organised raids on Sittana and the other villages. He succeeded soon in driving away the Usmanzais from their newly-acquired fields by these harassing tactics. They even sent word to Mubarak Shah that they were withdrawing and that he could get Sittana cultivated by his own men and take tribute from them. Mubarak Shah also started levying *octroi* duty on all merchandise passing through Sittana territory. His aim in pursuing such harassing tactics was to overawe, generally, the Usmanzais and make them retreat. He very nearly succeeded in his design, but soon after some unscruplous elements joined his party and the Siri's tower gained notoriety as a den of wayside robbers and lawless men who took refuge there and carried on petty raids, robberies and kidnapping of wealthy merchants[24] on the border villages.

This was the state of affairs when Mahmud Shah, the son of Umar Shah and cousin of Mubarak Shah, arrived in Sittana. On the death of his father, he had received a nominal employment under the English as a *resaladar* or head of a unit of irregular cavalry.[25] He served first in the Musgrave's Horse Column[26] and then in the Lahore police. He had received the appointment through the recommendation of Jhanadad Khan, the ally of the English, who was also related to him. The British had a political motive also in employing him, for it was hoped that this would keep him away from the Frontier and disturbing the peace there. After the rising of 1857, during the course of which he was sent to Delhi and Lucknow, his *resala* was disbanded and, having refused a regular employment[27] as a Cavalry Officer in the Frontier force, Mahmud Shah applied to the government for Sittana being reassigned to him. The Lieutenant Governor refused his application on the plea that Sittana was outside British India and that they "could not give what did not belong to them."[28] The prince then applied in April, 1863 for permission to take possession of Sittana himself without seeking English aid. This too was turned down, with the strange order: "Tell him nothing of the kind would be listened to." The attitude of the English towards Mahmud Shah was exasperatingly equivocal. They were neither willing to give him back his ancestral property nor would they allow him to do so on his own, and feeling disgusted, Mahmud Shah left with his men, and returned to Sittana. He returned there at a time when Mubarak Shah had been active, as mentioned earlier. Mahmud Shah represented a moderate policy and had been striving for a peaceful transfer of Sittana to himself. The English refusal, however, forced him to join hands with his cousin, who had been carrying on a more active policy.

Among the Usmanzais, too, there were two parties, one favouring the return of the Sayyids, and the other, trying to oppose it with the help of English. On the occupation of Sittana by the Sayyids, the latter group fled to the British outpost of Tarabela opposite Khabal, and complained to the British that the Sayyids and the Wahhabis were on the warpath. The panic spread among the people of Amb, and its young chief Akram Khan son of Jahandad Khan, also fled. The local British officers exaggerated the supposed aggressive designs of the Wahhabis and sent reports to that effect to the government. This is clear from the fact that the English themselves suspected in the beginning that the anti-Sayyid group of Usmanzais were deliberately creating a panic to bring about the intervention of the British.[29] The Deputy Commissioner, Hazara candidly admitted that "the inhabiting of Sittana may be the primary object of the Movement though of course there are manifold rumours of other designs on the part of the Syeds, the Usmanzais holding that their object is ravaging of Kyah and Khabal and Mohammad Siphan (Minister of Amb) anticipating the attack and plunder of Umb."[30]

The genesis of the Ambeyla Campaign has been traced at some length in order to bring out clearly the respective roles of the Sayyids and the Wahhabis, as also the aggressive policy of the British. The Wahhabis were indebted to the Sayyids in more ways than one. Sittana belonged to the Sayyids, and the Wahhabis considered their efforts to re-occupy it as justified. They gave them tacit support, and some limited assistance, but did not participate in the series of raids, robberies and general depradation carried on by Mubarak Shah's men with the deliberate object of terrifying the Usmanzais and making their strength felt by the British, the supporters of the latter. The respective roles of the two have, however, been misunderstood by most of the English writers[31] on the subject, who represent the campaign as one of retaliation by the British, initiated, reluctantly, against the lawless activities of the Wahhabis. The man on the spot, the Deputy Commissioner, Hazara drew a sharp distinction between the activities of the Wahhabis and the tribesmen.[32] The former represented a political threat, whereas the petty raids and robberies were the result of the activities of some of the desperadoes from outside, who had taken shelter in Siri's tower. The Deputy Commissioner wrote, "*The Hindoostanees themselves withhold their hands from all murder and robbery;* it is necessary that this point should be clearly noted. *It is not known that any of their members have ever participated in kidnapping and murder of our Hindoo subjects.* They form undoubtedly a centre of political intrigue and occasionally despatch Ghazis to lie in wait to murder infidel *Firanghees* (Christian)... Our immediate concern with them at present is that it is from their presence and support that Mubarak Shah derives his strength and importance ... it will be very necessary, in the event of operations being undertaken, and of its not being found possible to destroy them entirely, to guard against their making any fresh settlement near our border ..."[33]

It is, thus, clear that the Wahhabis were regarded as a potential source of political threat, and the petty raids of some desperadoes, largely unconnected with them, was considered a good reason to root them out. The provincial government of the Punjab were bent upon a war of aggression, and in their eagerness to proceed ahead with their design they even failed to keep the Government of India, or the Commander-in-chief, fully informed. In fact, the expedition was taken against the advice of the Commander-in-chief.[34]

Finally, it has to be remembered that the dispute between the Sayyids and the Usmanzais related to an area which lay outside British India, in the independent tribal area. The British had refused Mahmud Shah's request for help on this very plea, and yet when he took steps independently the principle of non-intervention was given a go-bye, and under the pretext of protecting their feudatory, the Chief of Amb, from a supposed threat the British intervened.

After much discussion[35] between the civil and military authorities regarding the different routes of march, and the respective military advantages of each, it was finally decided to march through the Chumla valley, advance up the comparatively easy and accessible side of the Mahabun mountain fortress. The entrance to the Chumla valley was (from the side of the Yusufzai plains) through a narrow pass at whose other end stood the village, Ambeyla, giving its name to the pass. It was a narrow pass with a rocky and jungle-infested track, some nine miles long.

The plan of advance was based upon an important presumption, the neutrality, if not active support, of the Bonair tribes, whose lands were separated from the valley by a narrow belt of very low hills. Ambeyla itself belonged to them. Thus the British forces were to march perilously close to the borders of a powerful tribe about whose history and political inclinations the British knew very little. What was even more of a risk, was the decision not to inform the Bonairs of the intended march. In their anxiety to keep the route secret, the British did not consult even those tribes who were friendly to Bonairs, and who knew better about the likely reaction of the Bonairs to the proposed stealthy march by the side of their territory.[36] It was considered inadvisable to consult the Bonairs, for it was most likely that they would object, and moreover, the plan itself would have been betrayed and the element of surprise, so vital for its success, would have been lost. It was proposed to enter the pass and take position in the Chumla valley suddenly and quickly, so that the Bonairs might be presented with a *fait accompli*. The whole thing, it was expected, would be over in about two weeks. Accordingly, on the 19th October, 1863, when it would be too late for the Chumla or other tribes to make preparations ... for the impending march of the troops,"[37] Taylor, the Commissioner of Peshawar accompanying the troops, sent a proclamation to the Bonair tribe explaining that the expedition was against the Hindustanis and that they need not have any apprehension. In the opinion of James, who succeeded as Commissioner of Peshawar, it was an unwise step and likely to have the opposite results.

As he observed, it was unlikely that a "a brave race of ignorant men would pause to consider the purport of a paper they could not read, when the arms of the supposed invaders were glistening at their doors."[38] Moreover, the English had reckoned without Abdullah,[39] the leader of the Wahhabis. As a counter-step, he too issued a proclamation,[40] exhorting the tribes, to oppose the advance of the British troops, and explaining to them the real danger of the situation. The proposed objective, just then, were the Wahhabis but how long, it asked, would it take for their turn to come? The enemy was 'deceitful and treacherous', and would possibly lure them with gold but they should be on their guard.

Detailed information about the strength of the 'Grand Army' of the British authorities, and of its progress, is available in some works,[41] but similar information about the Wahhabis is very meagre. Only one writer[42] provides some information about the Wahhabis' military strength and organisation at this time. It appears that there were between 1200 and 1400 volunteers belonging mainly to the Bengal Presidency, Awadh, Central and Northern Provinces (modern Madhya Pradesh and Uttar Pradesh) and the lower Punjab. The recruits were drilled daily, and were well-supplied with arms. They had a couple of small cannons, and there was a foundry at Malka. The fighting force was divided into ten companies, each under a commander. A list of the different *Jamā'at* (groups), the name of its commander, the number of men constituting the group, and the number of percussion muskets, and flintlocks possessed by each one of them is available. It may be of some interest to reproduce it here:

1. The *Jamā'at* of Miyan Usman: 120 men, 20 percussion muskets and 10 flintlocks.
2. The *Jamā'at* of M. Shariatullah: 150 men, 30 percussion muskets, 10 flintlocks.
3. The *Jamā'at* of Abdul Ghaffar: 130 men, 30 percussion muskets, 20 match locks.

4. The *Jamā'at* of Qaim Khan: 130 men, 6 percussion muskets, 20 matchlocks. (This was the oldest *Jamā'at*, called the Hindi *Jamā'at*, and was composed exclusively of the Hindusthanis.)
5. The *Jamā'at* of Najaf Khan: 130 men, 15 percussion caps, 20 matchlocks. Half of them were Bengalis and the rest Hindusthanis.
6. The *Jamā'at* of Naimuddin: 125 men, mostly Bengalis, 6 muskets, 30 matchlocks.
7. The *Jamā'at* of *Munshi* Taufiquallah: 100 men, 100 muskets, 20 matchlocks. This was called the Nai (new) *Jamā'at*.
8. The *Jamā'at* of *Munshi* Bashiruddin: 100 men, 6 percussion muskets, 20 matchlocks.
9. The *Jamā'at* of Muhammad Ibrahim: 130 men, 4 percussion muskets and 20 matchlocks.
10. The *Jamā'at* of Bahramuddin Bunairi: 40 men, no firearm. This was called the *Desī* (local) *Jamā'at*, comprised of men of Hazara, Bunair and the neighbouring areas.

On the other side, the British Army commanded by a General, comprised some six thousand soldiers, of whom about a quarter were British soldiers. The 'Grand Army'[43] assembled under the command of General Chamberlain and advanced across the Yusufzai plain on the 18th October, 1863. The pass was reached on the 20th. Part of the army entered the Chumla valley and occupied the entrance without much opposition, but this was only the beginning of the trials ahead. The baggage and stores, coming through the pass were cramming and blocking it. Chamberlain, therefore, decided not to move further until the rear position had crossed the pass. By now the proclamation of Abdullah had done its work,[44] and the Bonairs had turned hostile to the British. General Chamberlain wrote in his despatch of October 23rd, "that their conduct (hostility of the Bonairs) has been prompted by Hindustanee fanatics at Sittana, there can be no doubt. Some papers have been intercepted which show that ever since it became known that the present Expedition was being organised against them the Hindustanees have been endeavouring to obtain the assistance of Bonairs by alarming them as to our intention of annexing their country."[45] With the Bonairs turned hostile, the British found themselves trapped. The only line of retreat, down the Pass, was blocked by masses of men, animals and stores still coming up. The British troops were in a deep gorge flanked by mountains on either side, and a powerful tribe assembled on their slopes poised to strike against them. Not only was the main object of the expedition relegated to a secondary place, but the safety of the army itself was in danger. The whole situation had been masterfully exploited by Abdullah. Describing the position, Hunter remarked, "A great political catastrophe was now dreaded. Our Army, wearied out with daily attacks, might at any moment be seized with panic, and driven back with immense slaughter through the pass."[46]

During the next few days up to the middle of November, the British troops remained entrenched in the narrow defile under the constant fire of the Wahhabis and the tribesmen. General Chamberlain asked for reinforcements which were hurriedly sent forward by a panic-stricken provincial government. It was deeply perturbed over the adverse turn of events, especially because it had undertaken the expedition in spite of the objection raised by the Commander-in-chief, some of which were proving only too true. The provincial government felt shamefaced, and in the reports sent to the Government of India they were at pains to explain their failure to foresee the defection of the Bonairs, but for which everything would have been so easy.[47]

The flow of reinforcements continued, so much so that the whole of the Punjab was denuded of forces[48] in an attempt to provide succour to the hard-pressed garrison. The Commander-in-chief himself hurried to Lahore. The reinforcement on the British side was counter-balanced by a steady flow of fresh batches of volunteers from different tribesmen. Abdullah and Sayyid Imra, the uncle of Mubarak Shah, wrote a letter to the *Akhund* of Swat seeking his cooperation and assistance.[49] The *Akhund* responded readily and, by virtue of his religious hold over a vast area, brought forth with him a large number of tribesmen. Other tribes of Chumla and Dir also responded. Faiztalab Khan of Bajour alone brought 300 men. The Afridis and the Usmanzais also sent in recruits. The Expedition, from its original limited objective, had been transformed into a major Frontier war against a coalition of tribes, the like of which had never been seen so far.[50]

During the period many tenacious local engagements were fought in which heavy casualties were inflicted on both the sides. Detailed accounts of these engagements are available elsewhere,[51] but mention may be made here of the encounters which took place at the

Crag Picket, firstly because these are typical of the various encounters, and, secondly, because the Wahhabis figured prominently in these actions. Reconciling himself to virtually a long siege, Chamberlain had occupied two lofty hill-tops on either side of his position in the gorge below, and established pickets there. These were known as the Crag's Picket and the Eagle's Nest. Both were vital points to hold, and both, consequently, witnessed several bloody actions. The Crag Picket alone was attacked and captured four times by the Wahhabis and retaken as many times. The troops from both sides showed remarkable courage and perseverence, but Adye draws out a sharp distinction between the "bold and vigorous attitude" of the Wahhabis and the "dogged resistance" of the British. He also comments on the "discouraging effect" of the prolonged defensive warfare on the latter. Between 30th October and 20th November, several bold and spirited attacks were made on the Crag Picket by the Wahhabis. They captured the hill-top, but were forced out by overwhelmingly large relieving forces. In the third attack on November 13th, so strongly supported was the Wahhabi onslaught that "not only the British Picket, now one hundered and twenty strong, was thrown away, but something like a panic spread among the followers in the camp."[52] The relieving force was unable to "drive out swarms of warriors grimly holding the vantage point." The last attempt on Crag Picket was made on the 20th November, "So determined was the attack that the British garrison was swept from the hill with considerable loss. The position of affairs was so critical that General Chamberlain himself determined to lead the column detailed to assault and retake the Picket.'[53] The peak was retaken, but the British suffered a casualty of 153 men, including Chamberlain himself, who was severely wounded in the arm. A large amount of stores of ammunition fell into the hands of the Wahhabis. Some British were also taken captive.[54]

The provincial government, not fully aware of the situation on the front, still pressed for the accomplishment of the original objective, the destruction of Malka, but Chamberlain did not think it advisable to advance without first securing his flank threatened by the coalition of tribes. Committing himself to a long and wearying war, and in order to have an alternative route for returning to the Yusufzais plain, he ordered the construction of a road over the mountain slopes. Work on another road, forward to Malka, was also taken in hand, to facilitate an advance on it, in case it became feasible. The

Wahhabis were quick to retaliate. The parties of engineers, which were often isolated and spread over different ridges, separated from one another by deep ravines, were attacked and driven away. Parts of the road already built were broken up and blocked with rocks and trees.[55]

By December, about 9,000 regular troops, including picked regiments, like the 93rd Highlanders, were deployed on the Frontier and it "seemed hard to believe that a powerful British Army should thus remain cooped within the pass week after week, harassed by the attack of the enemy, and unable to strike a blow."[56] This was because the British had "underrated the hold which the Fanatical Colony had acquired over the Frontier tribes. Those who had joined them for the sake of Faith were burning with hopes of plunder or of martyrdom, while the less bigoted clans were worked upon by the fear of their territory being invaded by the British."[57] The situation was getting difficult, both militarily and politically. The Commander of the Force, General Chamberlain, had been injured and lay incapacitated. The Governor-General, Lord Elgin, lay on his death-bed in the 'interior hills,' out of touch with the developments and unable to give any guidance. The weight of events lay heavy on the shoulders of a perplexed and somewhat apprehensive Lieutenant Governor. The despatch of General Chamberlain, following the encounter of November 20th, so unnerved the provincial government that they even contemplated ordering a general retreat, but the perseverance of Sir Hugh Rose, the Commander-in-Chief, and the supply of powerful reinforcements, saved this humiliating move. There was also another danger, "Faithful and courageous as our native Frontier Regiments had as yet proved themselves, still it was contrary to the human nature to suppose that they would go on week after week fighting against their own kith and kin."[58] The political situation was even more serious. The entire Frontier was in commotion. Even in Kabul there was considerable sympathy if not active support for the tribal confederates.[59]

Having failed to achieve their object in open battle, the British authorities set in motion political intrigues aided by the never-failing, inducement of the weighty yellow metal. James, the Commissioner and the Political Officer, in particular, started sowing seeds of disunity among the confederate tribes.[60] Hunter candidly admits that "a coalition of mountain tribes is always capricious; and *what our arms had failed to accomplish, dissensions and* diplomacy began to effect."[61] Early in December, James, submitted a Memorandum to Major General Garvock, who had succeeded in command to General Chamberlain, reporting the existence of internal feuds and animosities among the Bonairs. The Bonairs, fighting originally in defence of their homeland, were weary of the war, and divided among themselves. The repeated pressures of James, coupled with monetary inducement,[62] finally succeeded in weaning the Bonairs away. The war, which had begun so encouragingly for the Wahhabis amidst unprecedent enthusiasm and cooperation of the tribes, came to an unsuccessful end largely because of the tribal dissensions. The *Akhund* tried in the beginning to steer clear of the tide of tribal defections, but failed in his attempt and in the end remained a helpless spectator.

In the final stages of the war the Wahhabis were left, practically alone, with a few Bajouries, to face their formidable foe. Abdullah made one final attempt to offer battle with the small band of his own followers in the hope of stirring up the tribal sense of honour, and inducing them to rejoin the battle. He made a spirited speech before the commencement of this last engagement, emphasising upon his followers the transitoriness of life and the honour of dying in battle rather than surrendering. Moved by his eloquence and fired by a selfless zeal, they fought valiantly; their lines "stood unyielding like a wall of steel."[63] A large number of Wahhabis fell down fighting; Abdullah retreated, to appear once more against the British at a later stage.

The battle was over, but the professed object of the expedition, the destrution of Malka, yet remained to be fulfilled. Even after the Bonairs had withdrawn the English remained where they were. They had once taken the neutrality of the Bonairs for granted, and knew what it had cost them. Now, they were reluctant—so panic-stricken were they—to venture out in the Amzai and Madikhel tribal areas, which was necessary if the British troops were to go to Malka. The author of the *Durr-i-Maqāl*[64] dwells upon the fear and hesitation of the British, even after their victory, and depicts how they had to buy the assistance of the Amzais[65] and Bonairs for performing the destruction of Malka. He writes, satirically, of how the Bonairs marched ahead and the "ever-valiant" English made up the rear.

It was James once again who conceived of a novel plan.[66] The actual work of destruction was to be done by the Bonairs, Amzais and Khudikhel tribes, for these latter "having once committed themselves thus openly against the fanatics it was the surest guarantee that they would not readmit them." But to make matters doubly sure, and to see that the destruction was actually carried out, a few British officers were to accompany the party. They started on the 19th December accompanied by Colonel Taylor as the Political Officer. The place was reached on the 21st, and after an overnight stay the work of destruction began. James gives the following account of the place and its destruction. "Malka was situated on an elevated plateau on a northern spur of the Mahabun ridge. It was a much larger and more substantial place than any known in those hills, containing several large edifices, amongst which the Moulvie's hall of audience, barracks for the soldiers, stabling *and a powder manufactory* formed conspicuous objects. There was no regular fortification but the outer walls of the houses were connected and formed a continuous line of defence with posterns; there was also a tower at the gateway. The place was found deserted ... and was completely destroyed by noon" (22nd December),[67] James in his letter, quoted above, also speaks of an attempt by some Amzais to save a large portion of the village on the plea that it belonged to them and not to the Wahhabis, but the plea was overruled and the whole place burnt.

The campaign had cost the British Government heavily, both in men and money. Their losses amounted to 847 killed[68] and wounded or close to one-tenth of the entire force, when it numbered 9000. This was in the Pass alone, and exclusive of men disabled by exposure and diseases. The loss on the other side, including the tribesmen was 3000.[69] The provincial government, while summing up the result of the expedition, observed that on no former occasion had the fighting in the hills been so severe, and of such a sustained character and that on account of the Wahhabis's initiative a formidable combination of tribes had been effected in which their (Wahhabis) counsels have had the ascendancy."[70]

The long time taken by such a large British force in achieving a comparatively limited objective caused a serious damage to their prestige in the eyes of the tribesmen. And even after all this sacrifice, the more farsighted of the English officers and contemporary writers were not slow to realise that the source of opposition had not been finally disposed off. Adye observed. "In retrospect the Campaign was not altogether satisfactory."[71] Hunter bewailed the fact that "Our prison gates have closed upon batch after batch of unhappy misguided traitors; the Courts have sent one set of ring-leaders after another to lonely islands across the sea; yet the whole country continues to furnish money and men to the Forlorn Hope of Islam on our Frontier and persists in its blood-stained protest against Christian rule."[72] James in his letter, quoted above, remarked that "the colony of fanatics so perseveringly hanging on our borders, blemish to our administration has been half destroyed, forced to retreat to more inhospitable and uncongenial regions and will shortly, I trust, be eradicated for ever." That James was sadly mistaken in his trust was to be soon evident from the next series of campaigns—the second Black Mountains Expedition of 1868 onwards.

The Black Mountain Military Expeditions, 1868,1888, 1891

As we have seen above, the first Black Mountain campaign was organised in 1852 in order to enforce British military and administrative presence in the border area between the British administered and the tribal territories. The area was populated, among others, by the Hasanzai tribe which had been defeated, along with its Wahhabi supporters, in 1852.

In 1868 the British government set up a police outpost at Agrore. The Khan of Agrore opposed the move in alliance with some of the clans on the western side of the Mountain. After some local counter-offensives, an expedition was organised in September under the command of Brigadier-General A.T.Wilde.[73] The centre of operations lay to the north of the area attacked in 1852, and punitive action was taken against many villages. It was considered enough to have "'lifted the *purdah*'and let those concealed behind behold the power of the British arms." While returning, the troops, making a circular movement, marched through the northern and western areas in an attempt to overawe the neighbouring tribes. Sporadic border raids, however, continued.

Hostilities betwen the British forces, on the one hand, and the tribesmen and the Wahhabis on the other, commenced again in 1888. The main cause was the continued British efforts to assert their authority, as represented by road-building in the border areas, establishment of police outposts and collection of punitive fines, etc. The British had established a military post at Aghi, the chief place in the district, and had distributed arms among the men of 'friendly' border villages. Skirmishes had been occurring since some time, and in June 1888 'a serious affair' took place, in which two British officers and four men of the 5th Gurkhas were killed. It was a signal for a 'general gathering of tribesmen and increased audacity.' A force under the command of Major-General McQueen[74] was, therefore, sent in September. Proclamations were sent to some of the tribes, the Hasanzais, Akzais, Prari, the Sayyids, Tikariwals, etc. asking for their acceptance of specified terms within a month, and to some others, assuring them of the government's friendly intentions, as had been done at the time of the Ambeyla Campaign. The expedition was divided into Ist, 2nd and 3rd columns and it adopted the same plan of action as in 1852. These columns were to move up towards the crest along the spur of the Black Mountain from the front, while a detachment at Derband was to threaten the rear of the enemy's position. The tribesmen, as on many earlier occasions, were helped by the Wahhabis.

A 'sharp engagement' took place at Towara, on the western side of the mountain. A body of sword-wielding 'Hindustanis' made a desperate attempt to break the advancing British line but almost all of them were shot down by the Royal Irish and the Gatlings. It was noted that more than half of the enemy's troops killed were the 'Hindustanis'.[75] By the middle of October, the Hasanzais and Akzais were forced to submit and pay punitive fines. The settlement of the 'Hindustani fanatics' at Maidan on the right bank of the river (Indus, Kunhar?) was destroyed, "this being the fifth occasion[76] on which this notorious faction had come into collision with the British troops in the past forty years."

During the second phase of the campaign the clans living on the northern slopes were subdued. This portion had been left uncovered in the previous, 1868 campaign, and it was now considered desirable to make the tribesmen there also feel the might of British arms. The tribesmen suffered severe losses because the detachments from the Suffolk and Royal Sussex Regiments were picked marksmen and used their rifles effectively against the enemy. As a result of the Expedition, 222 miles of roads, suitable for pack transport, were constructed, 177 miles of unknown track surveyed, and Rs. 14,000/- were collected as fines.

To consolidate the military gains achieved during the campaign, the British government tried to assert the right to move troops along the summit of the Black Mountain ridge, and in 1890 work was started on the construction of several roads leading from Agrore valley to the crest. This led to the last campaign of the series in 1891 under the command of Major-General Elles. It was largely successful and once again forced the Hasanzais and Akzais to observe the terms imposed earlier. Arrangements were made for the protection of the roads already constructed and the British subjects got the right to enter into tribal territory, just as the tribesmen were also given reciprocal rights. More importantly, the tribal leaders, and the Wahhabis who had assisted them were ordered to be expelled from the Hasanzai and Akzai territories.

The foregoing account of the wars fought by the Wahhabis on the North-Western Frontier against the British government, and the military expeditions sent against them, brings out the magnitude of the threat they presented. They had been working steadfastly among the tribesmen, trying to build up a common front against the government. During the Rising of 1857, the only areas where government posts were attacked, were those where the Wahhabis were active, and in 1858 a military operation had been launched against them. The Ambeyla Campaign of 1863 represented an hour of triumph for the Wahhabis when they succeeded in forging an alliance with a large number of tribes and waged a major war on the Frontier. Even during the post-Ambeyla period, when the Wahhabis had become militarily weak, the Black Mountain Expeditions of the period 1868 to 1891 show that they continued to be politically and militarily active.

Their position had undergone substantial change, and their role during these campaigns was subsidiary. They appeared as allies of the tribesmen under attack. They had become too weak a body of men to represent a serious challenge but they still represented a potential threat. They kept alive a 'forlorn hope' in the hearts of their compatriots back home, and they still had the capacity to organise the persistent anti-government feelings among the tribesmen into a powerful concerted movement. As a writer on the subject remarks, even when the Wahhabis were not directly involved, "they have proved to be at the bottom of most of the tribal complications ... they seem never to lose an opportunity of ill-feeling and to be always ready to join any lawless Khan that could be persuaded into taking the initiative"[77] (against the government). The British authorities, therefore, considered the Wahhabis, even in their weakened state, a threat to the stability of their rule in India, and subjected them to constant military blows ever since the Annexation of the Punjab (1845), which brought them into direct contact with the latter.

To try to maintain in the face of all this that the Wahhabi Movement was directed against the Sikhs, not the British government, is to ignore completely the greater part of its history.[78]

NOTES

1. *vide, supra,* pp. 129.
2. Paget and Mason, *op. cit.,* p. 84. Italics are mine.
3. *I.M.,* p. 23.
4. The composition of the Army was as follows :

	Europeans	non-Europeans	Total
Artillery	131	88	219
Cavalry	16	535	551
Infantry	632	3472	4107
	779	4095	4887

vide, For Dept.Pol.'A' Cons. no. 191, dated August, 1862.

5. A full account of this campaign is given in General S. Cotton's *Nine Years in India,* London, 1868, pp. 218 ff. The author was the commander of the expedition, and described it in details. See also Paget and Mason, *op. cit.,* pp. 90-97. Abdul Haq, the author of *Durr-i-Maqāl,* also gives a brief account of the campaign.
6. *For Dept.Sec.Cons.* nos. 535-55 dated 28th May, 1858; also *D.M.,* p. 26.
7. Cotton, *op. cit.,* p. 227.
8. *Ibid.,* pp. 226 *ff.*
9. *D.M.,* pp. 28-29.
10. Aitchison, *Treaties, Engagements and Sanads* (Ck Sp), vol. II, pp. 415-18.
11. *Ibid.,* pp. 29-30.
12. *Ibid.,* p. 31.
13. H.L.Neville, *Campaigns on the Frontier,* London, 1912, p. 41.
14. Paget and Mason, *op. cit.,* p. 95.
15. G.J.Younghusband, *The Story of the Guides,* London, 1908, p. 77.
16. *D.M.,* p. 33.
17. For details, see *D.M.,* pp. 34-36.
18. Bellew, *op. cit.,* pp. 98-99.
19. He had returned to Patna after Wilayat Ali's death in 1852. He left Patna again after Farhat Husains death some time in 1858, and after visits to Mecca and Afghanistan reached the North-Western Frontier some two years before the death of Maqsud Ali, i.e., around 1860. *T.S.,* p. 147, Mehr, IV, p. 319, mentions the date of his journey from Patna as 1859, but does not refer to his visits to Arabia and Afghanistan; see also p. 248, n.2 below.

20. Bellew, *op. cit.*, pp. 98-99.
21. Colonel Adye, J., *Sittana: A Mountain Campaign on the Borders of Afghanistan in 1863*, London, 1867. A small, rare and out of print book, it gives an informative account of the campaign. The author an Artillery Officer, took part in the campaign. Further, there is the Diary of the Sittana Campaign by A.G.Hartshorne, which was published (for private circulation) in 1864, and of which the Commonwealth Relations Office Library has a copy. There is also an official publication, "Papers realting to the late Disturbances in the North-Western Frontier of India," ordered by the House of Commons to be printed in 1864. It contains the correspondence between the British Indian government and the government in U.K. on the subject.

    Among the non-English sources, *Durr-i-Maqāl*, is the only one of its kind. Its author too was an eye-witness of the events. Storey (section II, Luzac, 1939, p. 674) refers to a printed edition of the book (Patna, 1901) entitled, *Hālāt-i Jang-i Malka wa Sthana*.
22. *D.M.*, pp. 37-47.
23. *For Dept.Pol.'A' Cons.* nos. 140-43, dated September, 1863; Letter from Deputy Commissioner, Hazara to the Commissioner, Peshawar dated 6th July, 1863.
24. In some cases the wealthy traders held up for ransom happened to be Hindus, and the English writers have made much of it. It is to be noted, however, that the Wahhabis themselves were not responsible for these crimes (*For Dept.Pol.'A' Cons.*, nos. 191-93, dated August, 1862, *vide, infra*, p. 245.
25. The British authorities in the Punjab were then employing several groups of irregular horsemen. Recruited on an emergency basis, they kept their own horses and men, and were paid according to the number of horsemen maintained by them—something like the Mughal *mansabdārs*.
26. *For Dept.Pol.'A' Cons.* no. 193, dated August, 1862; Letter from the Deputy Commissioner, Hazara to the Commissioner, Peshawar dated 28th July, 1862.
27. The refusal was on sentimental grounds, of not serving under the English.
28. Letter from the Secretary, Government of Punjab to the Commissioner and Superintendent, Peshawar, no. 543-1/2, dated 15th July, 1863.
29. *For Dept. Pol.'A' Cons.* nos. 140-43, dated September, 1863; Letter from Deputy Commissioner, Hazara, to the Commissioner, Peshawar, dated 6th July, 1863.
30. Letter to the Commissioner, Peshawar dated 3rd July, 1863.

31. *I.M.*, pp. 25-26, Neville, *op. cit.*, p. 50; Adye, *op. cit.*, p. 18; Paget and Mason, *op. cit.*, pp. 102 *ff; H.G.*, p. 168.
32. *For Dept. Pol.'A' Cons.* no. 193, dated August, 1862.
33. *Ibid.*,no. 191, dated August, 1862. Emphasis mine.
34. Adye, *op. cit.*, pp. 29-32.
35. For a summary of these lengthy discussions, see *For. Dept. Pol. Cons.* nos. 14 and 15, dated March, 1864.
36. Adye, *op. cit.*, pp. 22, 27.
37. *Ibid.*, p. 26.
38. Ibid., p. 27.
39. Abdullah (1830-1902), son of Wilayat Ali, was born at Hyderabad. He lived and worked with his father on the N.W.Frontier and then returned to Patna around 1847, where he assisted his uncle Farhat Husain, in the organisational work. He married the latter's daughter and had three sons. On Farhat Husain's death, he set out for *Hajj*, and returned to Afghanistan from where he re-joined the Wahhabis on the Frontier. He was elected Amīr and led the Wahhabis in the Ambeyla war. A good rider and marksman, he also had some knowledge and experience of construction of forts. See also, *T.S.*
40. See text of the proclamation in Appendix no. IV.
41. *Supra*, p. 240, n.3.
42. Bellew, *op. cit.*, pp. 99-102. From the meticulous details given, it appears that the information was collected by a spy specially deputed for the purpose.
43. The composition of the army was as follows :

Regulars	*Punjab Irregular Force*
1/2 Belt, Royal Artillery,	8 Native Mountain Batteries
3 Guns on Elephants.	
71st Highland Light Infantry	8 small Guns on mules back
71st Royal Bengal Fusilliers	Regiments of the Gudies,
20 and 32 Regiments, N.I.	N.I. Ist, 3rd, 5th and 6th Regiments, N.I.
IIth Bengal Cavalry	5th Gurkhas

2 Companies of Native Sappers Guides Cavalry.

In numbers, the composition was as follows:

Regulars		*Irregulars*
Infantry	5150	100 under civil
Cavalry	200	command, and 13 Guns.
Artillery	280	

44. *For. Dept.Pol. Cons.* no. 15, dated March, 1864; Taylor's letter no. 15, dated 21st January, 1864, paras 72-76.
45. Adye, *op. cit.*, p. 41.

46. *I.M.*, p. 35.
47. *For Dept. Pol. Cons.* no. 14, dated March, 1864; Davies' letter to the Government of India, dated 1st February, 1864.
48. *I.M.*, p. 34; Adye, *op. cit.*, p. 55.
49. *D.M.*, pp. 54-57.
50. Adye, *op. cit.*, p. 54.
51. *Gazette of India Extraordinary*, dated 30th January, 1864, pp. 51-74; Adye, *op. cit.*, pp. 44 *ff.;* Younghusband, *op. cit.*, pp. 87-90.
52. Younghusbad, *op. cit.*, p. 89.
53. Ibid., p. 90; *D.M.*, pp. 259-64.
54. *D.M.*, p. 261.
55. An account of the guerilla warfare carried on by the Wahhabis is given in *D.M.*, pp. 196-206.
56. *I.M.*, p. 36.
57. *Ibid.*, pp. 36-37.
58. Adye, *op. cit.*, p. 74.
59. *For. Dept. Pol. Cons.* no., 15 dated March, 1864; James' letter no. 9, referred to above.
60. *Ibid.*, James' Memoranda, dated 5th, 7th, and 14th December, 1863.
61. *I.M.*, p. 37.
62. *D.M.*, pp. 348-49.
63. *Ibid.*, pp. 317-20.
64. *Ibid.*, pp. 330 ff.
65. *Ibid.*, p. 349. The author mentions the exact amount, *400 dinars*, given to them for this work.
66. *For. Dept. Pol. Cons.* no. 15, dated March, 1864; James' letter no. 9, referred to above.
67. *Ibid.*, para 49; italics are mine. Mehr, IV, p. 365, refers to the testimony of Abdul Jabbar Shah, a descendant of Sayyid Mahmud Shah, of Sittana, to the effect that Malka was not actually burnt, but the testimony of the contemporary English records is quite definite on this point.
68. A full list of the casualties is given in *India Gazette Extraordinary*, cited above, pp. 51-79; also see, *I.M.*, p. 38; Adye, *op. cit.*, pp. 70-72.
69. *For. Dept. Pol. Cons.* no. 15th March, 1864; James' letter no. 9, referred to above, para, 66.
70. *Ibid.*, no. 14, dated March, 1864; Letter from H.R. Davies, dated 1st February, 1864, para 114.
71. Adye, *op. cit.*, 91.
72. *I.M.*, pp. 122-23.
73. On account of the 'disquieting news' about the Peshawar border, troops were not drawn from the Frontier garrisons but the stations down-country.

The troops were from: (i) First Brigade, 1st Battalion 19th Foot; 20th Punjab N.I.; 1st Gurkha Regt.; (ii) Second Brigade, 1st Battalion, 6th Foot; 3rd Sikh Infantry; 2nd Gurkha Regt.; (iii) Royal Horse Artillery, 19th and 24th Royal Artillery; Peshawar and Hazara Mountain Batteries; Bengal Cavalry 2nd and 7th Companies; Miners and Sappers. See Paget and Mason, *op. cit.*, p. 45.

74. The troops were drawn from, First Brigade, Hazara Mountain Battery (7-pounder rifled muzzle loaders) 4 Guns; 1st Battalion, Northembcrland Fusiliers; 3rd Sikhs & 5th Gurkhas; 1st South Irish Division Royal Artillery (2.5-inch riffled muzzle loader) 2 Guns; 1st Battalion, Suffolk Regt. 2 Gatlings; 45th Sikhs, Second Brigade; No. 2 Derajat Mountain Battery (7-pounder rifled muzzle-loaders) 2 Guns; 2nd Battalion, Royal Sussex Regt.; 14th Sikhs, Half No.; 3 Company Sappers & Miners; Khaibar Rifles; 2-1st Scottish Division Royal Artillery; 4th and 29th Punjab Infantry, Two Gatlings. See Paget and Mason, p. 591.
75. H.L.Neville, *op. cit.*, p. 98.
76. These previous occasions were 1853, 1857, 1858 and 1863.
77. Oliver, *op. cit.*, pp. 290-91.
78. For further discussion on this point, see chapter XI.

Chapter VIII

State Trials of Wahhabi Leaders, 1863-65

I. The Ambala and Patna Trials

Since 1840 the attention of the government had been drawn from time to time by different local officials to the dangerous and 'seditious' character of the activities of the Wahhabi centres in British India. The apprehension was not shared, or at least not given adequate attention, by the higher authorities in the beginning, but the military expeditions which the government was forced to organise against the Wahhabis on the Frontier from 1852 onwards forced it to view the problem more seriously. In 1858 and even more so in 1863 the government had to organise full-scale military expeditions against the Wahhabi centre on the Frontier. The inter-connection between these military efforts and the police investigations started against the Wahhabi centres inside the country was realised and commented upon by several writers. Thus, Hunter remarks that the trial of 1864 was the natural outcome of the disastrous fanatic war in 1863.[1] Another outside observer of the contemporary Indian scene and public opinion, Routledge writes, "In 1858 Sir Sydney Cotton, with 5000 British troops, stormed the camps of the Wahabees at Sittana and razed the villages of their allies. After this for a time the fire smouldered, and seemed to be extinguished; but it again burst out, and in such a way that the Government decided to attack the propaganda in India itself, from where there was no doubt that money in large amounts was sent to Sittana."[2]

For about ten years since 1863 extensive police enquiries were carried on and a large number of Wahhabi workers and sympathisers were detained and interrogated at different places all over the country, such as Malda, Rajmahal, Patna, Thaneswar, Ambala and Delhi. The enquiries were followed by a long series of trials spread over a decade. These trials were held at Ambala (1863), Patna (1865), Rajmahal, Malda and again Patna (1870-71). Of these, the

Ambala and Patna Trials were the earliest[3] and the most important. They set the pattern for subsequent government proceedings.

The Ambala Trial, 1864:[4]

In May, 1863 Ghuzzan Khan, a Pathan police sergeant posted at *chowki* Panipat, Karnal district, noticed some persons apparently belonging to the eastern provinces, moving up the Grand Trunk Road. On enquiry, he was told that they hailed from Bengal and were on their way to the Wahhabi centre on the Frontier. They invited him too to join, but were arrested and sent for trial. The magistrate found them to be genuine travellers and ordered them to be set free. Ghuzzan Khan felt slighted, and in order to vindicate himself, he sent his son to the Frontier to join the Wahhabis and gather information about them.[5] The dutiful son did his work thoroughly and on return he reported the existence of a well-organised system for the transmission of men and material from British India to the Frontier, in which Thaneswar was one of main depots, and Muhammad Jafar an important leader. Alerted and alarmed, the Punjab government acted swiftly and ruthlessly.

Parson, the Superintendent of Police, Ambala, hurriedly encircled the house of Jafar at Thaneswar in the early hours of the 12th December, 1863. Some letters were found in the house which mentioned the names of Muhammad Shafi, a meat contractor at Ambala and other military cantonments, and some persons of Patna. Although the implications of many of the coded letters were fully understood by the authorities subsequently, the police officers of these places were telegraphically informed to search the houses of the persons implicated and to arrest them. One Abdul Ghafur of Hazaribagh, and a Bengali boy both, present in the house of Jafar, were arrested the same night and taken away. Jafar himself was, curiously, not arrested that night, and escaped to Delhi via Panipat. At Delhi he stayed in the house of a co-worker, Bashiruddin. He met there two persons from Patna named Husaini and Abdulla, alias Muazzam Sirdar, who were carrying gold *mohars* from Patna to the Frontier. Jafar took the money from Husaini and gave it to another person of the same name, of Thaneswar, with instruction to take it to the Frontier. Jafar himself, along with Husaini and Abdulla of Patna continued his eastward journey.[6]

In the meantime Shafi and his nephew, Abdul Karim, were arrested at Ambala. The next evening (December 13) when Parson arrived at Thaneswar to arrest Jafar he learnt of his escape. He at once let lose a reign of terror on the family members of Jafar, who were severely beaten and humiliated.[7] On learning from the younger brother of Jafar that he had fled to Delhi, Parson immediately started for that place, taking Jafar's younger brother with him. In Delhi he missed Jafar by a few hours. The latter had already left for Koil (Aligarh). A telegraphic message was sent to Aligarh to look out for Jafar and his party, and they were arrested there and brought back to Ambala. Husaini of Thaneswar who was carrying the gold *mohars* to the Frontier was also arrested on his way up at Pipli, the *Tahsīl* headquarters of Thaneswar. Having rounded up the implicated persons in the Punjab, the authorities turned their attention to those belonging to Patna.

Among the papers seized at Jafar's house there were some letters written by two persons, namely Elahi Bakhsh and Muhyuddin of Patna. Husaini, when arrested with Jafar had also stated that he had been sent by the above mentioned Elahi Bakhsh to deposit a draft of Rs. 2,500/- with a person named Alauddin, a shoe merchant of Delhi. The other Husaini of Thaneswar, who was arrested at Pipli, was also found to be carrying some gold *mohars* on his person. The number of these gold *mohars*[8] corresponded exactly with the number mentioned in the letter of Muhyuddin (whose identity was established later) to Abdul Ghafur, arrested at Thaneswar.

The Punjab police sent a series of urgent confidential communications[9] to the authorities at Patna to arrest Elahi Bakhsh. There was some confusion in the beginning about his identity. The particulars given by the Punjab police did not tally with those learnt by the magistrate of Patna. The magistrate, to be on the safe side, searched the house of a shoe merchant, named Elahi Bakhsh living in the city on the 18th December and seized all the papers found there. On enquiry the magistrate learnt that Elahi Bakhsh was the son of Karim Bakhsh who was also alive. He was a poor man when had gone to Delhi[10] on the eve of the 'Mutiny' but had returned some time later a rich man and had opened a shoe shop in Machurhatta, Patna City.[11] He imported shoes from Delhi by taking loans from different local bankers. The profits were distributed equally between his bankers and himself. Elahi Bakhsh was arrested and asked to produce two sureties of Rs. 5000/- each. Soon after, the Punjab authorities sent a telegraph that Parson was himself proceeding to Patna to conduct the enquiries. He arrived on the 16th January, 1864.

The letters[12] found in the house of Elahi Bakhsh showed that various amounts of money had been sent from time to time by Elahi Bakhsh (through Husaini) to Jafar, and to different persons in Delhi, ostensibly for purchasing shoes and other merchandise. The most important discovery among these papers was a letter written by Yahya Ali of Sadiqpur to Fukhruddin of Arrah. The hand-writing of this letter was exactly the same as that of the one written by the above mentioned Muhyuddin to Abdul Ghafur. It was thus established that Muhyuddin was none other than Yahya Ali, "the chief of the whole sect and a man of influence." So the enquiries were switched to Sadiqpur. On the 21st January, Alexander the Magistrate, Patna, and Parson along with some armed men, raided the Sadiqpur premises and searched the house of Ahmadullah and Yahya Ali.[13] The former had gone to Calcutta to attend a meeting called by the Lieutenant Governor.[14] All the papers, manuscripts and registers found in the house were seized and taken away. Abdul Rahim was also subjected to a searching cross examination which lasted from morning till evening. One Abdul Ghaffar, who was present in the house and who, on being questioned, declared himself to be a servant of Abdul Rahim, was also interrogated. He stated that Abdul Rahim, his master, had monetary transactions with Elahi Bakhsh in his (Ghaffar's) name. On examining Elahi Bakhsh's accounts it was found that a large sum of money had been withdrawn by Ghaffar from his account with Elahi Bakhsh. It was suspected that these withdrawals (for which no account existed) had been sent to the Frontier through Jafar. A letter[15] was also found in the house of Abdul Rahim, which mentioned, *inter alia,* persons (Yaqub, Nasiruddin, etc.), who were known to be in the Frontier. Both Abdul Rahim and Ghaffar were arrested and were remanded to *hājat,* and after two days sent to jail. Yahya Ali too was asked to deposit a security of Rs. 10,000/-. This was arranged by Abdul Hamid, his nephew and the eldest son of Ahmadullah.

Meanwhile, two other witnesses, Salimuddin and Aminuddin, were brought from Dacca. They testified that they had stayed in the *Qāfila,* the Sadiqpur house, on their way to the Frontier, and that at Sadiqpur, Yahya Ali used to preach the desirability of fighting against the British. They also stated that many others besides them had stayed at the *Qāfila.* On receipt of this information Yahya Ali's bail was cancelled and he was arrested on 8th February, 1864,[16] and put in jail along with Abdul Rahim and Ghaffar. All three prisoners were forwarded to Ambala in early March, 1864. From March till the end of the session trial the prisoners were kept in solitary cells measuring 6'x 4', with a high roof and a small opening high in the wall.[17] The door of this room was opened once in twenty-four hours when a *jama'dār* gave the prisoner a pot of water, some bread and *dāl*, and the sweeper cleaned the toilet. The prisoners were subjected to the most inhuman treatment during all this period.[18]

The preliminary commital proceedings, lasting over a week, were held in the court of Tighe, the Deputy Commissioner, Ambala. The session trial opened in the court of Herbert Edwardes, the Session Judge, Ambala in April, 1864. The judge was assisted by four Assessors — two Hindus and two Muslims. In all, eleven persons listed below faced the charge of waging war against the Queen:

1. Yahya Ali [19] of Sadiqpur, Patna, Age 47 years.
2. Muhammad Jafar, son of Mian Jivan *Lambardar* of Thaneswar, a prosperous businessman, referred to as Peero Khan in code letters. Age 28 years.
3. Abdul Rahim [20] of Sadiqpur, Patna. Age 28 years.
4. Muhammad Shafi, son of Muhammad Taqi. Meat contractor to military contonments, prosperous businessman, turned approver. Referred to as Shafaat Ali in code letters.
5. Abdul Karim, relative and employee of Muhammad Shafi. Age 35 years.
6. Abdul Ghaffar, described as a servant of Abdul Rahim. (Actually, he was a trusted worker of the movement.)
7. Qazi Mian Jan of Comorcolly district, Pubna. Had several aliases and was 60 years old at the time of arrest. Died in detention at Ambala pending transportation to the Andaman Islands.
8. Abdul Ghafur, son of Shah Ali of Hazaribagh. Age 25 years. Arrested in the house of Jafar.
9. Husaini of Patna, son of Meghoo, Patna City. Age 35 years, servant of Elahi Bakhsh.
10. Husaini of Thaneswar, son of Muhammad Bakhsh. Age 25 years. Had fought under Enayat Ali on the Frontier.
11. Elahi Bakhsh, son of Karim Bakhsh. Shoe merchant of Patna City, also acted as Ahmadullah's *Mukhtar.*

The prisoners were accused under section 121 of the Indian Penal Code of waging war against the Queen. We are not concerned here with the legal arguments in the case. These are summarised in the works of two of the accused persons who lived to write about their own arrest and trials.[21] The broad facts of the prosecution case were true enough but the government did not have enough evidence or witnesses to prove the guilt of all the accused persons. The manner in which the witnesses were tutored [22] often under severe beatings and even threats of hanging, further marred the judicial character of the proceedings.

On behalf of the prisoners not much was said in defence. Only Shafi, who was a wealthy man, employed a lawyer in the beginning. Jafar did his own cross-examination and also argued his case. Yahya Ali refused to have any lawyer and also said nothing in his defence. Throughout the trial he kept reciting Quranic verses and also an Arabic quatrain which was to the effect that one should not care how one died, for in any case one had to return to God.[23] Later, Abdul Rahim, on the insistence of Shafi, employed on his own and on Yahya Ali's behalf, a noted lawyer of Calcutta, named Plowden.[24] On his arrival at Ambala, Plowden was not allowed to meet his clients in jail, and his appeal for permission to this effect was rejected by the Judicial Commissioner. It was only after he appealed to the Lieutenant-Governor that he was granted this elementary right of a defence lawyer.

The judgement was delivered on 2nd May,1864. Yahya Ali, Muhammad Jafar and Muhammad Shafi were sentenced to death and the rest to transportation for life. All the properties of the convicts were ordered to be confiscated. The judgement is a very lengthy document, spread over more than a hundred pages of the proceedings. It would suffice to give here a summary of the relevant portions of the judgement, specifying the 'crime' of the prisoners, quoted by Hunter [25] on the basis of the text of the judgement.

Yahya Ali : (He) "has been the mainspring of the great treason which this trial has laid bare. He had deluded hundreds and thousands of his countrymen into treason and rebellion. He has plunged the Government of British India by his intrigues into a Frontier War, which has cost hundred of lives. He is a highly educated man who can plead no excuse of ignorance. What he has done, he has done with forethought, resolution and bitterest treason."

Jafar : "It is impossible to exceed the bitter hostility, treasonable activity and mischievous ability of this prisoner. He is an educated man and a Headman in his village. There is no doubt of his guilty and no palliation of it."

Abdul Ghaffar : 'He managed the whole temporal affair of the hospice, daily lectured the recruits on the high duty of Holy War. What he did, he did with perfect sincerity of heart and at last stood undaunted by his master's side in the dock of Ambala.[26]

Abdul Rahim : "It is proved against the prisoner Abdul Rahim, that at his house these treasons have been carried on. In his presence the Bengali crescentaders were gathered and were lodged. It was his servant who kept the treasure, fed the recruits, and remitted the subscription to the Fanatics ... he has done what in him lay against the State."

Husaini : "It is proved against Husaini of Patna that he is a servant of Ilahi Bakhsh; that he has been employed by him in effecting remittance for treasonable purposes ... that he thoroughly understood the treasonable nature of the service on which he was engaged."

Abdul Ghaffar : "It is proved against Abdul Ghaffar that he was a disciple of Yahya Ali at Patna, that Yahya Ali deputed him to be an assistant of the prisoner Jaffir, in the rebel recruiting depot at Thaneswar, that he did so assist."

Qazi Miyan Jan: "It is proved against Qazi Miyan Jan that he preached and recruited for the Crescentade in Bengal... collecting and remitting funds, forwarding letters, etc. The most treasonable correspondence has been found in his house ...he used four aliases."

Elahi Bakhsh : "It is proved against Ilahi Bakhsh that he has been the channel through which the Patna Maulvis forwarded the funds they collected up-country to Jaffir at Thaneswar to be passed on to Mulka and Sittana."

Husaini : "Husaini of Thaneswar was a confidential agent and go-between of the prisoners Muhammad Jaffir and Muhammad Shafi, in these treasons and that he was seized in the act of conveying 290 pieces of gold from Jaffir to Muhammad Shafi for remittance to the Queen's enemies."

Shafi was originally sentenced to death but on turning an approver he was reprieved and set free after having been in jail for two years. His property, which was confiscated earlier, was not restored.

The sentences were referred to Roberts, the Judicial Commissioner for confirmation. After a prolonged prorogation, to enable consultations with the Home Government,[27] the judgement was delivered on 24th August, 1864. The sentences were slightly modified. The capital punishment awarded to the three accused persons were commuted to transportation for life. The final order of the Lieutenant Governor was passed in September.

The prisoners remained in Ambala Jail from the commencement of the trial till February, 1865. European families living in the cantonment area used to come to see them out of curiosity.[28] Once during this period a warder of the jail offered to let them escape and suffer the punishment which might be given to him for this neglect of duty. The prisoners, however, refused this offer.[29] Commenting on the three most conspicuous features of the trial, Hunter[30] enumerated these as the "admirable sagacity with which so widely spread a treason had been organised; the secrecy with which its complicated operations were conducted; and the absolute fidelity to one another which its members maintained."

Commenting further on the characters and 'crimes' of some of the accused persons, Hunter felt constrained to pay this tribute to the "earnestness" and "conscientiousness" of Yahya Ali and Jafar who "made no pretension to loyalty and sought nothing at our hands... They were earnest, conscientious men, who pricked themselves with the poisonous weapons which a false religion had put in their hands and now that, Laetres-like, they have paid the price of their treachery history may dwell with emotion akin to pity on their fate."[31]

About Shafi, who had turned approver, Hunter remarked, "but for Muhammad Shafi there can be no such feeling. He licked our hand in order to bite it and "he appears throughout the keen sharpsighted, sordid schemer."

Indeed, the whole set-up had been planned with great ingenuity; the genuine and bona fide work had been so cunningly mixed up with anti-government activities that it was very difficult for the authorities to differentiate the two. Elahi Bakhsh, for instance, apart from the money he sent to the Wahhabis on the Frontier, also sent money for the bona fide purchase of shoes for his shop. The fidelity and integrity of the great majority of the workers was also remarkable.

From February, 1865, when the first batch of the prisoners was transferred to Lahore on their way to the dreaded penal settlement of the Andaman Islands (which they reached almost after an year) began a period of nightmarish sufferings and inhuman severities for the prisoners. They were transferred from Ambala to Lahore on 22nd February; the journey between these two places being on foot.[32] Abdul Rahim was detained at Ambala for some time in the hope of using him as an intermediary in arranging the surrender of Abdullah and others on the Frontier. He refused to oblige his captors and was soon despatched to Andaman. Shafi and Abdul Kareem turned approver and were detained at Ambala. The other prisoners were transferred from Lahore to Multan Jail towards the end of October the same year. During the journey the prisoners were chained together and locked in a compartment which was opened only on reaching the destination.[33] They were put on a steamer from a point near Multan and travelled down the Indus to Karachi. During this journey, covering a week, the prisoners were seated together on a wooden plank and an iron chain was stretched through their chains from one end to the other so that they could not stand up from their seats. Even the call of nature had to be attended to in this uncomfortably fixed posture.[34] The total weight of iron handcuffs and chain on the legs of the prisoners during the time was not less than half-a-maund per person.[35] From Karachi they were brought to Bombay where they were put in the dreaded Thana Jail, which was situated in an old deserted Marhatta fort. The prison was known for the severe and harsh punishments meted out to the prisoners, as only the worst type of prisoners were lodged there.[36]

The last leg of the tortuous journey of the Ambala Trial convicts from Bombay to the Andaman Islands began on 8th December, 1865, and they reached the island on 11th January, 1866. On reaching there they joined Ahmadullah of Patna, elder brother of Yahya Ali, who had in the meantime been tried and convicted in the Patna Trial, and had reached the Andaman Islands ahead of them.

The Patna Trial: 1865

During the course of the investigations preceding the Ambala trial, the house of Ahmadullah had been searched, but he was not arrested owing to a difference of opinion between the Punjab and the Patna authorities [37] in regard to the desirability of that step.

Early in October, 1864, the Secretary, Government of Punjab addressed a letter [38] to his counterpart in the Government of Bengal, enclosing two very long letters from the Deputy Commissioner, Ambala, dated 16th & 18th September 1864 on the subject of the complicity of Ahmadullah in the conspiracy against the government. The letters stated that the statements of some of the prosecution witnesses in the Ambala Trial had revealed that Ahmadullah was frequently present in secret meetings addressed by Yahya Ali. It was also proved from the statement of Elahi Bakhsh that some of the money deposited with him (for transmission to the Frontier) had been credited through Ahmadullah, that it was on his orders that various amounts of money were withdrawn and transmitted, and that it was he who had directed the accounts to be maintained by Elahi Bakhsh in the name of Abdul Ghaffar, instead of his own name (Ahmadullah's). Some old records also referred to Ahmadullah's complicity.[39] The Deputy Commissioner, Ambala, advised the Patna authorities to arrest Ahmadullah, particularly on the following counts, viz. for allowing the premises occupied by him and his family as a recruiting centre for the 'Sittana fanatics', for his intriguing at Patna during the 'late Mutinies',[40] for his being the head of a family which had been warned much earlier (1847) by the Board of Administration, Punjab, not to 'disturb the Frontiers' and, finally, for having not only failed to stop these activities in his house but, on the contrary, having encouraged and helped them.

Ahmadullah,[41] as a matter of fact, was already under a cloud since the time of Yahya Ali's arrest and even earlier. The authorities at Patna had strong suspicions about his complicity. In the middle of 1864, when the appeal of the Ambala convicts was pending in the High Court, Plowden, the Defence Counsel, had informed the prisoners about the impending arrest of Ahmadullah.[42] Some self-seeking citizens of the town who felt jealous of Ahmadullah's high social status and official rank had also poisoned the ears of the officers in regard to his complicity.[43] Tayler, the dismissed Divisional Commissioner of Patna and a staunch persecutor of the Wahhabis, still lived in the city. He and Ishree Prasad,[44] a young police sergeant, out to prove his zeal to the government by his exertions in the prosecution of the Wahhabis, offered their services in this connection. The latter in fact, showed such zeal in this lucrative assignment[45] that his services were repeatedly called for by the government in the subsequent Wahhabi trials.[46]

The views of the Punjab Government regarding Ahmadullah's complicity were duly conveyed by the Government of Bengal to the Divisional Commissioner and Magistrate, Patna for investigation, and comments. The Lt. Governor also directed that Ahmadullah be removed at once from the offices he held under Government and that he be debarred from ever again serving government in any capacity.[47] The magistrate was doubtful about procuring sufficient legal proof to establish in a court of law the treasonable designs of

Ahmadullah in "knowingly allowing Bungalles to assemble in his house for purposes which he must have been aware were treasonable."[48] He even submitted that "it would be very much better to let the matter altogether drop than raise the question of his guilt unsuccessfully." Ultimately, he felt that further proofs could be found in the statements of the prosecution witnesses in the Ambala Trial and these could be supplemented with information gathered by local investigations. He, therefore, suggested that investigations should be started. Ahmadullah was arrested in November.

The prosecution of the case was entrusted to Ravenshaw, the magistrate of Patna, then on leave at Simla. He was directed to come to Patna via Ambala after consulting the authorities there. All local officers were instructed to render every assistance to Ravenshaw in his investigation.

The preliminary committal proceedings[49] were held in the court of Monro, the Officiating Magistrate, Patna, and Ahmadullah was charged on 16th January, 1865 with the following:

> "1. That he, on or about the years 1861, 1862 and 1863 attempted to wage war against the Queen ... an offence punishable under Section 121, Indian Penal Code ....
> 2. That he, on or about the same years, abetted the waging of war against the Queen by traitorously furnishing supplies of men and money to fanatics at Sittana engaged in warring aganist the Queen.... an offence punishable under Section 121 and 107 of the Indian Penal Code ....
> 3. That he, on or about the same years, abetted the attempt to wage war against the Queen, an offence punishable under Sections 121 and 109 of the Indian Penal Code.....
> 4. That he, on or about the same years, abetted the collection of men with the intention of waging war against the Queen, or being prepared to wage war against the Queen....
> 5. That he by acts and illegal omission concealed the existence of a design to wage war against the Queen...."[50]

The Session Trial was held in the court of Ainslie the District Judge, Patna, who was assisted by a Board of Assessors. Many prosecution witnesses were brought from Ambala, chief among them being Elahi Bakhsh and Abdul Kareem.

The defence Counsel argued that Section 121 related to attempts to wage war from within the country. He also argued that no one could be convicted of treason except on the evidence of two persons (Section 28 Act II of 1855) [51] and that in this case Ahmadullah was being convicted solely on the evidence of Elahi Bakhsh, whose evidence was not "fit to hang a dog upon." He was sentenced to transportation for life and confiscation of property, a man "with nothing left to fear and all to hope."[52] He also argued that all the prosecution witnesses who now identified Ahmadullah had not done so earlier at Ambala or Howrah. The Judge rejecting all these arguments observed in his judgement (27 February 1865) that it was quite clear that there was a regularly organised system of forwarding men and money to the Frontier for the purpose of carrying on war against the British Government,[53] that among the persons engaged in this 'treasonable' work were some of the very close relatives of the prisoner (Ahmadullah), that the prisoner was appointed "General Manager of the temporalities of the Kafilah:" that "he received monies .... attended Meetings where treason was preached" and that he was a "member of the Committee which organised the treason."[54]

The Judge held the prisoner guilty on the second, fourth and fifth counts. He acquitted him of the first count and considered the second count to be merged with the third. The Assessors also held him guilty of the fifth count. Ahmadullah was sentenced to death and his properties were directed to be confiscated.

The sentence was referred to the High Court for confirmation. The Court [55] having taken into consideration the full proceedings of the Session's Court decided on 13th April, 1865, that the evidence before them was 'sufficient to support the conviction of the prisoner under Section, 121 of the I.P.C., upon the second count. As it did not find from the evidence that the prisoner took a more active part in the conspiracy than the others, who have been convicted and sentenced, it declined to confirm the sentence of death passed by the Session Judge, and directed that the prisoner Ahmadullah "be transported for life and do forfeit all his properties to the Government."[56] Ahmadullah was, accordingly, transported to the Andaman Island. He was sent there via Calcutta and reached the place in June 1865, ahead of the other convicts of the Ambala Trial.

II. The Prosecution's Conduct

The Ambala and the Patna trials were closely interlinked. The prosecution witnesses and the evidence utilised were to some extent the same in both the cases. As regards the men convicted, except Jafar and Shafi, many of the principal accused persons in both the cases belonged to a particular place and were closely inter-related. In fact, with a little more of co-ordination and planning between the officers at Ambala and Patna, Ahmadullah might have been arrested earlier. The magistrate of Patna was not slow to express his distress over this lack of co-ordination.

At the outset, the prosecution was doubtful as to whether it would be able to procure enough evidence to establish the charge. The magistrate of Patna had observed that the "deposition of the witnesses at Ambala" would be the principal proof in the case of Ahmadullah and that the other proofs procured locally would supplement the former. As we have seen above, the "deposition of the witnesses at Ambala" boiled down to the evidence of one man — Elahi Bakhsh, who, as Ravenshaw admitted, was "himself a life convict on a similar charge,"[57] and who throughout the trial was kept in virtual imprisonment by the magistrate and was never allowed to see anyone.

Some of the brutal excesses committed by the police during the investigation of the case, and also later in the jail, are described at length both by Jafar and Abdul Rahim in their works. Widespread and indiscriminate arrests of a large number of people were made with a view to terrorising them into giving evidence against the prisoners. Some of the members of the families of Jafar and Shafi were beaten up in order to elicit information. On arriving at Delhi, in pursuit of Jafar, Parson created a reign of terror in the city. All the gates of the city and the inns were closed, thousands of persons were searched and about a hundred were arrested.[58] Even during the hearing of the case many persons were won over, by intimidation, including threat of arrest and even hanging and also by monetary inducements to give evidence against the prisoners.[59]

The official records corroborate the fact of money being paid to witnesses. On the conclusion of the trial, Elahi Bakhsh was not only pardoned and set free but his house in *Mahalla* Nagla, Patna City, which had been confiscated earlier was restored to him.[60] In addition, Rs. 500/- out of the sale proceeds of his other confiscated properties was also given to him to set up some business again.

Another ten witnesses brought from the Punjab, were also awarded a sum of Rs. 470/- (Rs. 50 to nine and Rs. 20 to one).[61] This was given, ostensibly, as compensation for the "loss of time and absence from other various employments." The magistrate was at pains to emphasise in his report, recommending the above-mentioned rewards, that their detention was 'voluntary', but it is stated in another letter of the same magistrate[62] that during their stay in Patna the witnesses were kept in the magistrate's own compound and were not allowed to go out or meet anyone. It is, therefore, likely that their food was also provided out of the magistrate's establishment. Where then, was the justification for the compensatory allowance? We also know that similar awards had been given in the Ambala case, too.[63]

Also, in the jail, prisoners were subjected to various forms of brutalities. Jafar refers to the sadistic glee with which the jail authorities made preparations, such as purchasing a new silk cord or wooden planks for hanging the convicted prisoners.[64] At the same time, the prisoners were tempted with offers of being released, and better treatment in the jail, for eliciting information from them.[65] Shafi, who had turned approver, was served good food in the presence of other sick or starving prisoners. Jafar also narrates the incident of a young boy, aged 14 years who was tutored by the prosecution to give evidence along a certain line. On coming to the dock the boy forgot his lines and for that he was beaten to death by the police. It was given out later, that he had died of natural causes.[66]

The apparent gesture of mercy by the Judicial Commissioner in commuting the death sentences, was also motivated, according to Jafar, by a desire for revenge. He writes that when the authorities learnt that the prisoners welcomed the death sentence, thinking that they would become martyrs by dying for the cause, they denied them this pleasure, and commuted the sentences.[67] Hunter, incidently, corroborates this contention of Jafar when he applauds the "wise revenge" the authorities took in denying "even to the most treasonable among them (Ambala prisoners) the glory of martyrdom."[68] As regards the Patna Trial, Abdul Rahim refers to the transfer of the Session Judge of Patna on the commencement of Ahmadullah's trial. The transferred Judge was known for his impartiality and independence of opinion.[69] Even after allowance has been made for the fact that these statements came from men who were themselves convicted[70] it is fairly obvious that the prosecution used methods which were extraordinary, to say the least.

The official records also threw some light on the methods and motives of the prosecution. Thus the Magistrate of Patna himself reported[71] to the Commissioner that Elahi Bakhsh was brought from Ambala secretly and was taken down at Khagaul station from where he was brought "disguised as a woman" in an *Ekka* and kept in a bungalow in the magistrate's compound under strict vigilance. No one knew of his presence at Patna until he was produced in the witness box. The other prisoners brought from Punjab were similarly kept confined in the magistrate's compound. During the period of detention at Patna Elahi Bakhsh was kept in charge of three men of the Punjab police force, who too were especially brought down from the Punjab. Later, after the conviction of Ahmadullah, these three police officers were given gratuitous rewards totalling Rs. 400/- for their having been held up at Patna.[72] When it is recalled that it was upon Elahi Bakhsh evidence alone that Ahmadullah was convicted, the manner in which the authorities kept him confined throughout the trial and later compensated him handsomely becomes highly suspicious. About Ishree Prasad, a local minor official, who showed so much zeal in the investigation of the case, the magistrate wrote that he 'could not speak too highly of him.' He was also given a cash reward, besides promotion in service.

III. Life of the Convicts in the Andaman Islands[73]

The penal settlement of the Andaman Islands, popularly known as *Kala Pani,* comprised a group of islands of various sizes, separated from one another by the shallow sea and wide rivers.

Most of the islands were jungle-infested and interspersed with mountain ranges, the highest peak Mt. Herriott being above 11,000 ft. high. There was very little cultivable land, and 'natives' of the island lived in jungles where they had developed small patches of cultivable land. Grains for feeding the convicts and the officers of the penal settlement was brought from Calcutta, which was five days' journey by steamer, and distributed at a uniform rate. Communication between the islands was almost non-existent and supplies of essential commodities scarce. The climate was so "poisonous" that anyone with a wound would die soon after as a result of its getting gangrenous.[74]

In one respect being sent to this penal settlement was better than confinement in other prisons. Except certain classes of particularly dangerous prisoners the rest were not confined to cells. On reaching the islands, the prisoners' chains were cut and they were allowed to live normally once they had done their quota of manual labour as had been imposed on them under the rules of the settlement. Those who were educated were employed in some clerical or technical jobs, for which they were paid. They could also have personal servants if their means permitted. After completing 12 years of imprisonment and on good conduct, a convict could be given a 'ticket'. Such ticket holders enjoyed certain amenities; for instance such a convict could set up a business with the capital he might have saved. He could also own a house, marry a local woman or have his family brought over.[75]

An inhuman practice, formerly in vogue in the island, was the branding of the words 'transported for life' on the prisoner's forehead.[76] The practice was stopped shortly before the Wahhabi prisoners arrived so that they were saved from this torture. Each one of the prisoners was assigned a number and was referred to by it.[77] Another revolting feature of life in the islands was the socio-religious discrimination, a form of the modern aparthied, enforced by the authorities. European and Indian Christian convicts were given preferential treatment. They were not only allowed better bungalows but were also provided with servants, free of cost. Jafar narrates the pathetic story of the Raja of Jagannath Puri,[78] who was sent to the island in 1879. Being dark complexioned, he was put to work with the shoe makers and given food of the poorest kind, while an Anglo-Indian of 'low descent', who had arrived at the same time, was given the most peferential treatment. Unable to bear these indignites and the corporal punishments the unfortunate Raja died soon after.[79]

As stated earlier, Ahmadullah was the first among the Wahhabi prisoners to reach Port Blair. On his arrival, he was met by Akbar Zaman, the kind-hearted Head *Munshī* of the Commissioner of the Island. Zaman was himself a convict sentenced to 20 years' imprisonment for participating in the Movement of 1857.[80] Later he was employed as a *Munshī*. He obtained permission for Ahmadullah' to stay with him and work as his *Nā'ib* (assistant). Ahmadullah lived with him for the next five years, which was a period of comparative ease for him. When Yahya Ali and Abdul Ghaffar arrived in January 1866, Ahmadullah, who had received intimation of their arrival (probably through Akbar Zaman) was ready to receive them. Yahya Ali and Abdul Ghaffar were also taken in by Akbar Zaman as his assistants. Thus, at long last after the fateful 8th February, 1864, when Yahya Ali was suddenly arrested and whisked away to Ambala, the two brothers met together and lived for some time under the same roof. Abdul Rahim who arrived in December, 1867 was employed as a *Ghāt Munshī*. Muhammad Jafar was also gainfully employed. During this period all the Wahhabi prisoners lived in the Ross island, where most of the officials lived.

Yahya Ali, who was gradually getting old and infirm as a result of the protracted severities suffered by him, fell ill in February 1866 and was admitted to the Island's hospital. Abdul Rahim, who was then employed as a *Muharrir* (writer) in the Marine Department and lived in a distant island, used to come daily to attend to him. This was necessary as Ahmadullah was himself too old and weak to go daily to the hospital which was situated at a high ground. After an illness of two weeks, Yahya Ali died on 29th February, 1868 and was buried in the cemetary at Ross island. Some 2500 Muslims living in the different islands as well as many Hindus attended the funeral procession.[81]

In February, 1872 there occurred an event in the penal settlement which shocked the whole country and of which the reverberations were heard till long afterwards. This was the assassination of the Governor-General, Lord Mayo, by a prisoner who was later identified as a Pathan of the Frontier area named Sher Ali. The motive behind the crime and the possible association of the assassin with the Wahhabis, was hotly debated and opinions were sharply divided. Jafar states that the Wahhabis were not in any way connected, but adds that some officers of the Government of Bengal, who were familiar with the background of the Wahhabis, were keen to have their revenge.[82] When the news reached Calcutta this group of officers tried to use it to implicate the Wahhabis.[83] Ishree Prasad of Patna, referred to earlier, who by now was regarded as an expert on the Wahhabis, was sent to the Andaman Islands along with the Commissioner of Police, Calcutta, to try to find out some clues about the presumed Wahhabi complicity. General Stuart, an officer of the Madras Provincial Service, who had joined as Chief Commissioner in October, 1872, being comparatively unfamiliar with the Wahhabis' background, did not encourage this Wahhabi-baiting.[84] Nonetheless, the Wahhabis came to be viewed with greater suspicion, and were removed to more distant islands. They were until then living in the main island where most of the officers lived, and some of them were employed in different offices. Now they were transferred to the outlying jungles-infested islands. Ahmadullah was sent to the Viper

Island where the worst type of hardened criminals were kept. He was appointed a *muḥarrir* in the medical department on a monthly salary of rupees ten and was given a rent-free house. Abdul Rahim was transferred to another outlying island where he was appointed a *muḥarrir* in the hospital.

Ahmadullah was getting old and infirm and had no one to look after him except Abdul Rahim. His request to let his son, Muhammad Yaqin, then living in Calcutta, come and live with him was not allowed. Such an arrangement was permissible and had in fact been allowed in the case of Abdul Rahim. The latter was in a comparatively better position. On completion of 12 years' of imprisonment he had been permitted, under the bye-laws of the penal settlement, to start a business with his savings. He had set up a shop in Aberdeen, near the principal station of the island. His son Abdul Fattah had been allowed to visit him but after living there for over a year had to return due to the unsuitability of the climate. He had sought permission to have his ageing ill uncle (Ahmadullah) with him, but it was refused. He could visit his uncle but could not stay with him. During the next two weeks, he writes, he visited Ahmadullah every day. For this he had to leave his home early in the morning, walk two miles to reach a ghat, ferry across a shallow sea two miles wide and then again walk back to Ahmadullah's place.[85] (His shop was looked after by his son.) One day, on 22nd November, 1881, while Abdul Rahim was on his daily trek he learnt that his uncle had died alone and unattended the previous night. Shocked and distressed, he hurried back to his home to arrange for the funeral. His last request on behalf of the deceased was that he be buried by the side of Yahya Ali, the younger brother who had died earlier but even this harmless request was refused by the local authorities and Ahmadullah was laid to rest in the public graveyard, in Dundas' point, at some distance away from Viper Island.[86]

Jafar quotes a Persian chronogram recording the year of Ahmadullah's death and referring to his imprisonment "in the island by the orders of the Christian government,"[87] English translation of which is given below:

Verses (1-2) When Ahmadullah, a man of God, who sojourned in the islands (Andaman Islands) by the orders of the Christian (British) rulers; (3-4) Passed on from this lowly world to the exalted Heaven in the night of 28th of the month of *Dhu'l Hijja*; (5-6) The

(Invisible) Crier called out the date of his death, "Deliverance of a Momin from the prison of the world."

The chronogram is dated (A.H.) 1299 or 1881-82.

IV. Confiscation of the Properties of the Wahhabis

The material losses suffered by the Wahhabis in the wake of these trials is a topic about which very little is known. Not only the English published works, but the Wahhabi sources themselves are surprisingly reticent[88] on the point.

As we have seen, many of the accused persons belonged to the Sadiqpur family of Patna. The family enjoyed a high social position and many of its members were well-known for their academic attainments. They also possessed zamīndārī rights at different places and owned extensive landed properties. The family was divided into three main branches, [89] headed by Shah Muhammad Husain, Elahi Bakhsh and Fath Ali.[90] Elahi Bakhsh had married the sister of Muhammad Husain and four of his sons had married, respectively, four daughters of Muhammad Husain. The two branches had thus merged into one. Fath Ali and Elahi Bakhsh were also related by marriage ties, the former having married the latter's sister.

Individual members of these branches possessed considerable landed properties. Elahi Bakhsh's properties[91] were inherited by his sons, Ahmadullah and Yahya Ali,[92] among others. Fath Ali's father-in-law was the son of Ruhu'd Din Husain Khan, who held a high post under the East India Company, and had received the title of *Mu'inu'l Mulk Aminu'd Dawla Nāṣir Jung*[93] for having rendered valuable services, and he succeeded to his father's position as well as his *jagirs*. A portion of the estate was thus inherited by Fath Ali. That this portion was quite valuable, is evident from the fact that the share of one of Fath Ali's sons, Enayat Ali, who sold it at the time of his final migration to the North-Western Frontier was, alone, worth above Rs. 20,000.[94]

After the pronouncement of the judgement on the Ambala Trial a list of convicts belonging to Patna was forwarded to the Government of Bengal with a request that their moveable properties be confiscated. An inventory [95] was accordingly prepared. The Lieutenant Governor directed the Commissioner under section 7 of Regulation XIX of 1810 to report as to how the immovable properties were to be dealt with. He also recommended to the Government of India that the "land and house properties escheated within the City be made over to the Municipal Commissioner for the use of the City." In reply to this recommendation the Government of India directed that the premises of Sadiqpur,[96] where the conspiracy had been carried on be made over to the Municipality "with a view to their being razed to the ground [97] and an open market built on this site and to devote a portion of the sale proceeds of the escheated property of the traitors to the Municipality."[98]

A legal hitch[99] developed subsequently in giving effect to this order. It was found that the Sadiqpur premises were divided into two blocks. The larger portion, to the east, belonged to Ahmadullah and Yahya Ali, both convicted, and to Faiyyaz Ali, whose property too was under attachment. This block could be taken over entirely. The smaller block to the west belonged to Fath Ali's sons, Wilayat Ali, Enayat Ali and Farhat Husain. The first named had four sons, Abdullah and Abdul Qadir who were on the Frontier and were 'proclaimed'. The other two, Muhammad Hasan and Hidayatullah were living at Patna and Barh and their shares could not be attached. Enayat Ali had only one son, Abdul Majid, who was 'proclaimed'. Farhat Husain had two sons, Abdul Rahim who was convicted at Ambala, and Abdul Rauf who lived in Patna and whose share could not be attached. In view of this legal complication the Lieutenant Governor recommended that the remaining portion not escheated should be taken over "for public purposes under Act VI of 1857." Compensation for those portions was to be paid out of the sale proceeds of the escheated property and the whole portion was to be made over to the municipality.

The Government of India approved[100] of these recommendations, and the Government of Bengal instructed the local officers to implement them. Under section 2 of Act VI of 1857, Declarations were issued for the acquisition of the following plots of land belonging to the Wahhabi prisoners: (i) land measuring 3 bighas and 11 kathas in all situated in *maḥalla* and *thāna* Sadiqpur, *pargana* Azimabad, district Patna, for construction of a Municipal Market, (ii) land measuring 1 bigha and 1 katha situated in *maḥalla* Sadiqpur for the construction of a slaughter house and a road connecting it to the Municipal Market, and (iii) a plot of land measuring 1250 feet north-south and 100 feet east-west, situated in mahallas Sadiqpur and Tulsi Mandai, for a road from the Municipal Market to Peepulpanty road.[101]

While carrying out the Government orders for pulling down the Wahhabi premises at Sadiqpur, the local authorities did not spare even the family graveyard.[102]

Hakim Abdul Hamid, the eldest son of Ahmadullah, draws attention [103] to some other aspects of the situation and the plight of the members of the family who were virtually thrown on the street. They were forced to leave the premises without taking anything with them. They had to hand over everything which had been found in the house and entered in the inventory prepared earlier. If anything was found missing, they were made to pay for it at rates ten times their value.[104] Ironically, the blow fell on the day of *'Eid*, the festival of rejoicings. To quote Abdul Hamid,

Chun shab-i 'Eīd rā sahar kardand
Hama rā as makān badar kardand;
Māya'-i 'aish sāz'i mātam shud
Eīd mā gharra-i Muḥarram shud.

English translation :

As the day of *'Eid* dawned
All were turned out of the house;
The trappings of pleasure were racked and ruined
Our *'Eid* was turned into the first (day) of *Muḥarram*

Abdul Hamid goes on to express the mute protest of the innocent children :

Ahmadullah būd mujrim-i Shāh
Tiflak-i begunāh rā che gunāh

English translation:

Ahmadullah was the accused before the State
(but) what was the crime of the innocent children?

The Lieutenant Governor while conveying his recommendations about the confiscation and disposal of the Wahhabis' properties had also submitted that it was desirable that the sale proceeds should not be absorbed in the general revenues, but spent for local purposes, as it would be "more becoming". The Government of India, while disagreeing with it as a general proposition agreed that in this particular case the money obtained could be spent on local works.[105]

Accordingly, large amounts of money, obtained from the sale proceeds were released for local public works and as grants to local educational institutions.

The Wahhabi Fund and some works of Public Utility financed out of it

The properties were sold over a period of time and the money obtained was kept in different offices including that of the Magistrate, Patna. These amounts were later transferred to the Accountant General's Office and put under a separate head called 'The Wahhabi Fund'. Even though the properties were disposed of at throw-away prices [106] they yielded a total of Rs. 1,21,948.[107] There were other amounts too, including Rs. 24,000 in cash and Rs. 97,500 in government securities kept under the charge of the Magistrate, Patna.[108] Out of Rs. 1,21,948/-, mentioned above, Rs. 42,119/- belonged to Ahmadullah, and the amount was set apart pending the disposal of a suit filed by his wife, Bashiran Khatoon, claiming that it belonged to her as part of her *mehr* (dower money). The remaining amount of Rs. 79,828/- was spent on useful local public works, among which the following are more notable.[109]

A grant of Rs. 33,407/- was given to the Patna Municipality for constructing a market on the site where the Wahhabis' house stood. This was in response to a proposal [110] from the Municipal Commissioner to construct "single-storied masonry shop-rooms"[111] on three sides of a square area. The fourth side, on the north facing the road, was to be left open for passage. Another Rs. 30,000 was spent on the construction of a road from the Patna City railway station to 'the river station of the Eastern Railway' or the Patna Ghat station. Yet another important public work financed out of the fund was the digging up of the site then known as Sheikh Matha ki Garhi[112] (the present Gandhi Sarovar, Patna City) and its conversion into a public garden. The site was then a 'depression' which was a 'receptacle' for all kind of filth and night-soil. It was dug up to a depth of 27', the earth taken out being used to raise the sides. The primary cost was met from the Wahhabis fund, out of which a sum of £ 4982.16 shillings was sanctioned.

In 1878 a scheme for the expansion and renovation of the Patna College [113] buildings involving an outlay of over one lakh of rupees was taken up.[114] It included the construction of a Wing on the eastern side similar to that on the western side, a science lecture hall and a chemical laboratory, a museum, a staircase and a boundary wall on the road side. Out of Rs. 54,752 spent till February 1880, Rs. 30,000 was allocated from the Wahhabi Fund. Another sum of Rs. 39,501 was subsequently sanctioned (20,000 for the year 1880-81 and an equal amount in the next).[115] Later in 1884 the Mohammadan Education Committee, Patna,[116] which had established a school, Mohammadan Anglo-Arabic School, in Patna City, sought government assistance for the establishment of 'a boarding institution on the Aligarh principle', and laid claim to a share from the Wahhabi Fund. The Committee was given a grant of Rs. 15,000/- which was to be deposited in the Patna Treasury and the school was to get the annual interest. Once the institution was well-established it was to receive the principal amount too.[117]

V. Release of the Surviving Wahhabi Convicts

Attempts to get the surviving Wahhabi convicts released were being made since 1880. In April, 1882 a petition was submitted [118] by Bibi Jamila, wife of Abdul Rahim, before the Governor-General in which it was stated that the Sessions Judge, Ambala had observed in regard to Abdul Rahim that his sentence might be reconsidered after 15 years, provided his conduct had been satisfactory. She prayed that 18, instead of 15 years, had now passed and the case of her husband might be favourably considered. An effort had also been made for the release of Muhammad Jafar. He had learnt English with the help of one Ram Swaroop and acquired some proficiency in it. He had risen to the position of the Chief *Munshī* of Major Prothero, Deputy Commissioner of the southern district of Port Blair, who was satisfied with his conduct. At his instance a suggestion was made to the higher authorities regarding Jafar's release, but it was turned down by the Home Secretary.[119] There was still an apprehension in the minds of some officers about the anti-government potential of the movement. Hunter's well-known book *The Indian Mussalman* had recently been published[120] and had further increased these apprehensions. Jafar writes that on hearing about the book he had specially obtained a copy of the second edition of the book from Calcutta, and on reading Hunter's assessment, that if the Wahhabis were released they would take it as a favour of God, not the Government, and would renew their anti-government activities, he had lost all hopes of release. Hunter had since been appointed 'adviser' to the Governor-General, and his views were bound to influence the Government's decision all the more.[121] Even when a rule was made about the release of life convicts after 20 years, it was not applicable to the Wahhabis who were treated as an exception.[122]

What actually turned the scale in favour of the Wahhabis' release was the fact that during the decade and a half since the Ambala and Patna trials the movement had been rendered weak an resourceless, and had come to be regarded as less of a threat. Even then much consultation went on between the Government of India and those of Punjab and Bengal before the actual release was ordered. The petition of Abdul Rahim's wife was referred to the Punjab government which recommended that in view of the long lapse of time and the changed circumstances not only Abdul Rahim but the other Wahhabi convicts too should be released.[123] The government of Bengal did not share this view [124] and drew attention to the statement of Halliday, the Commissioner of Patna, that three sons of Ahmadullah were living in Patna, and if Abdul Rahim and Abdul Ghafur returned, they "might attempt to cause mischief if opportunity arose.[125] The Superintendent of Prison Andaman Islands, was asked to report on the conduct of the prisoners, and he submitted that their conduct had been extraordinarliy good. Abdul Rahim had not comitted a single 'local offence' during the period, Ghaffar had been fined only once for absence and Jafar had been 'named and warned' once for contravention of some bye-law. The last-named, it was added, was a "remarkably able and intelligent man". Finally, in December 1882, the Government of India resolved that the surviving Wahhabi prisoners "shall now be released and permitted to return to their homes conditionally on police surveillance and subject to such restrictions as to residence as the local Government may see fit to prescribe."[126]

Of the eleven prisoners convicted at Ambala, only Abdul Rahim, Jafar and Ghaffar were still in prison. Amiruddin of Malda and Tabarak Ali of Patna, sentenced to imprisonment for life subsequently, were also released at the time. Masud Gul of Bogra, about whose arrest and conviction no information is available, was also released. Jafar's release was held up for some time because his convict-wife,[127] serving a sentence of imprisonment for life, had not been released. That was done later, in May, 1883, on an application from Jafar. On the eve of his departure, Jafar wanted to convert his house into a mosque and put it under a *waqf* (Trust) for the benefit of the local Muslims, but the permission was not given by the Deputy Commissioner, Birch, on the ground that the mosque might become a centre for Wahhabi 'intrigues.'[128] Jafar finally sailed for Calcutta and arrived there on the 14th *Muḥarram* 1301 (13 November, 1886). While recollecting his 20 year odyssey and checking from a map, Jafar was amazed to find that during the journey from Ambala to the Andaman Islands via Bombay, and then back to Ambala via Calcutta, he had in all travelled 7000 miles, and except for some districts of northern India travelled 'all over the country'!

Abdul Rahim, Ghaffar and Tabarak Ali wanted to return to Patna, but the magistrate opposed their return. He reported that though the "Wahhabi issue was dormant the fanaticism of the sect still exists, the released Wahhabis would undoubtedly be objects of sympathy ... and reference to their supposed wrongs, their conviction and transportation, would inflame feelings."[129] He added that they should be asked to live in some other town, such as Bhagalpur. Patna was a crowded place and effective police surveillance would be difficult. More importantly, the contiguous towns of Dinapur and Phulwari were 'full' of Wahhabis, and it would be difficult to prevent contacts between them. The Government, however, did not agree.

The prisoners were released on the 5th February, 1883 [130] and reached Patna in April next. They were ordered to execute bonds agreeing to report personally to the Superintendent of Police on the 1st of every month and not to move out of town without his permission. The order was enforced strictly during the next seven years after which it was partly relaxed.[131] Masud Gul applied for permission to stay on for six months in order to wind up his affairs. He set sail on the 28th April, 1883.[132]

Abdul Rahim lived till the ripe age of 90, and engaged himself in piecing together the broken fabric of the family's fortune.[133] While some members of the family, notably Abdullah, stayed on, others returned from the Frontier. Showing remarkable resilience, they set out on a new track and carved out new careers. They changed their names, took to learning English and achieved an equal degree of eminence in the new field of their activity. Thus, for example, Hakim Abdul Hamid (1829-19...),[134] poetically surnamed *Parishān*, the eldest son of Ahmadullah, achieved great fame as a physician, while another son Ashraf Ali (1843-1908) became a teacher of Mathematics in the M.A.O.College, Aligarh. Amjad Ali, (1847-1923) son of Yahya Ali, who was educated in the Benaras Hindu University, was appointed a teacher in Philosophy in the same college, and received the title of *Shamsu'l Ulama*.[135] Muhammad Hasan, the son of Wilayat

Ali, took to wider public activities.[136] He was the leading spirit behind the constitution of the Mohammadan Education Committee (1884), whose chief object was the dissemination of secular education along with religious education and the teaching of English. He also founded a printing press and brought out *The Institute Gazette,* one of the earliest Urdu newspapers in Patna.

The other group which had stayed on at the Frontier, and which was led by another son of Wilayat Ali, Abdullah, continued for a long time to be the nucleus of anti-government activities.

NOTES

1. *I.M.*, p. 84; see also *I.A.*, p.4.
2. James Routledge, *British Rule and Native Opinion in India,* London, 1878, p. 69.

   Based on notes taken in 1870-74, the author remarks on various matters of current importance. The Wahhabis were much in news then, and he has commented on the Malda Trial, the assassination of Justice Norman, etc. He also comments on other issues such as public education, agrarian riots, indentured labour sent to the West Indies, and many other topics.
3. For the subsequent two trials at Malda and Patna (1870-71), see the next chapter.
4. Muhammad Jafar Thanesari, *Kālā Pānī* or *Tawārīkh-i-'Ajīb,* A.H. 1302 (1884-85).

   Jafar, a *lambardar* (local revenue officer) of Thaneswar, district, Ambala and one of the main accused in the trial, on his return from the Andaman Islands after an imprisonment of nearly 20 years, wrote this work. It gives a detailed account of the trial at Ambala and the life of the convicts in the Andaman Islands. It adds substantially to the information available in English on the trial.
5. *I.M.*, p. 85.
6. *T.A.*, pp. 3-6.
7. *Ibid.*
8. In the coded language of the letters, the gold *mohars* were referred to as 194 large stones and 96 small (Victoria) stones. The same number of gold *mohars,* wrapped in paper to avoid clinking, were found sewn in the coat of Husaini.
9. *For.Dept.Pol.Cons.* no. 209, dated March, 1864.
10. Elahi Bakhsh in his own statement later said that he and his father had a shop in Arrah, which was looted during the Rising of 1857. They had then shifted to Patna.

11. Government of Bengal, Judicial, Prop. no. 122, dated October, 1865.
12. See texts of these letters in *For.Dept.Pol.Cons.* no. 209, dated March, 1864.
13. Letter from Magistrate, Patna to Commissioner, Patna dated 16th February, 1864.
14. *T.S.*, p. 66.
15. See the text of this letter, quoted in the magistrate's letter dated 16th February, 1864, referred to above.
16. Ibid.
17. *T.S.*, p. 66.
18. *Ibid.*, pp. 67 ff; *T.A.*, pp. 7ff.
19. Yahya Ali (1828-68) was the youngest son of Elahi Bakhsh. He had taken Bai'at at Wilayat Ali's hands and accompanied him to the Frontier. He returned to Patna after 1852 and during the next decade played the most important role of his life as the guiding spirit of the vast secrect organisation for the supply of men and money to the Wahhabi centre on the Frontier.

    He married Hamida Khatoon, a daughter of Shah Muhammad Husain, and had five sons and a daughter from her. He married again subsequently and had a son from his second wife. He has been described as a man of average height, fair-complexioned, bearded and bearing some pox-marks on his face. For further details, see *T.S.* also *infra*, pp. 296, n.1, 302, n.1.
20. Abdu'l Rahim (1836-1923) was the son of Farhat Husain, after whose death he administered the affairs of the headquarters at Patna. He married Jamilu'n Nisa, daughter of Shah Habibu'l Hasnain of Deora, *pargana* Arwal district, Gaya. Arrested at the young age of 23, he was tried in the Ambala Trial, and after about 20 years of rigorous imprisonment in the Andaman Islands, he returned to Patna in 1883, and wrote the well-known work, *Tadhkira-i Sādqa*. Also see *infra*, pp. 312, 313, n.3.
21. *T.A.*, *T.S.*
22. *T.A.*, pp. 9,10,37, etc., *T.S.*, p. 70.
23. *T.A.*, p. 39; *T.S.*, 69.
24. Abdul Rahim writes that he had agreed to work on the fabulous fee of Rs. 21,000 (*T.S.*, p. 69). Muhammad Hasan, youngest son of Wilayat Ali, then only aged 18, and Haji Mubarak Ali somehow arranged for this large sum.
25. *I.M.*, pp. 90-91, 93, 96-7, etc.
26. This observation is Hunter's own, vide p.91.
27. *T.A.*, p. 44.
28. *Ibid.*, pp. 44-45.

29. Ibid.
30. *I.M.*, p. 98.
31. *Ibid.*, p. 95.
32. *T.A.*, pp. 52-53.
33. *Ibid.*, p. 55.
34. *Ibid.*, p. 56.
35. *Ibid.*
36. These particulars have been noted here not just because they are not included in any of the published English works - including Hunter's - but also because they give us an idea of what the Wahhabi prisoners suffered for fighting against the British government. They also invite comparison with the treatment of political prisoners and freedom-fighters later on.
37. Government of Bengal, Judicial Dept. Proceedings, no. 51-56, dated May, 186.
38. Ibid.
39. One report said that at the time when Faiyyaz Ali and Yahya Ali were encamped at Sittana, "Moulvi Farhat Ali, brother of Moulvi Wilayat Ali at Azimabad and Moulvi Ahmadullah ... at their houses, in their villages collecting money from others, send weapons and supplies."
40. It may be recalled here that Ahmadullah's house was searched in June, 1857, by the then Divisional Commissioner, William Tayler, and he was put under detention; *supra*, pp. 220-21.
41. Ahmadullah (1808-81) was the eldest son of Elahi Bakhsh. Like his father, he enjoyed a high social position, and was known to local British officers. He served on various local bodies, and was a member of the Board of Assessors, Income Tax, and the Committee for Public Instruction, Patna. He had also served for some time as a Deputy Collector, and an *Iqrār Nāmah* (deed of agreement) relating to a dispute about the management of the Sikh shrine, the *Harimandir*, bearing his signature, is extant. On an inquiry being made by the Government of India about the literary tastes and reading habits of the residents of Patna, and Oriental books published from there, the local magistrate, Arthur Littledale, considering him to be a good authority on the point, had sought his opinion, and had been informed that "the taste for literature had decreased rather than otherwise" (letter from Magistrate to B.J.Colvin, Commissioner, Patna, dated 2nd August 1858).

    He married the daughter of Shah Muhammad Husain and had six sons and two daughters. Later, he married again, and had a son. His eldest son Hakim Abdul Hamid (*infra.*, pp. 304, 313) was a famous physician and scholar of repute. See also *T.S.*, and *infra*, pp. 298-99.

42. *T.A.*, p. 51.
43. *T.S.*, pp. 47-48; *Shahar Āshob*, pp. 5-7.
44. *T.S.*, p. 48, *T.A.*, p. 10. *ck.*
45. For his services during this and the subsequent trials, Ishree Prasad was promoted to the post of Deputy Collector. He was also given a cash reward of Rs. 2500/- (*T.A.* p. 79); Government of Bengal, Judicial Department, no. 126, dated October, 1865.
46. *vide infra*, chapter IX.
47. Earlier he was removed from the post of Deputy Collector, Income Tax on the reduction of the establishment in that department. After the conviction of Yahya Ali, he was also relieved of the membership of the Patna Committee of Public Instruction.
48. Letter from J. Monro, Officiating Magistrate, Patna to Secretary, Government of Bengal, dated 31 October, 1864.
49. The Government of Bengal got the proceedings of the trial of the case printed in the series Selections of the Records of the Bengal Government. Entitled, *Trial of Moulvie Ahmedollah, of Patna, and Others, for Conspiracy and Treason*, (Calcutta, 1866), it is no. XLII of the series (hereinafter cited as *Selections*).
50. *Selections*, pp. 7-8.
51. *Ibid.*, p. 80.
52. *Ibid.*, p. 83.
53. *Ibid.*, p. 73.
54. *Ibid.*, p. 79.
55. The Bench consisted of Hon'ble C.B.Trevor and Hon'ble G. Loch, Judges.
56. *Selections*, p. 103.
57. *Selections*, p. 165; also p .110.
58. *T.A.*, p. 7.
59. *Ibid.*, p. 37.
60. *Selections*, pp. 165-66.
61. *Ibid.*, pp. 3.
62. *Ibid.*, p. 110.
63. *T.A.*, pp. 37-38.
64. *Ibid.*, p. 47,

    By a curious coincidence it so happened that the sentences of death of Jafar and the rest were commuted; and the rope and wooden plank were used, instead, for the hanging of a European convict sentenced to death in the same jail; *Ibid.*
65. *T.A.*, pp. 49-50.
66. *Ibid.*, p. 38.
67. *Ibid.*
68. *I.M.*, p. 98.

69. *T.S.*, p. 48.
70. It may be pointed out that Jafar, in recording the events connected with his arrest, trial and conviction freely narrates incidents about his own weaknesses and faults. He states that during the period when Shafi was being given good food and the rest were starving, he once stole some *pulāo* from the former. Similarly he once kept Rs. 10/- for himself out of the money sent to Shafi. (He returned it to Shafi after he earned some money in the Andamans). These incidents depict human weaknesses which are understandable. They also enhance the authenticity of Jafar's account.
71. *Selections*, pp. 110-111.
72. *Ibid.*, pp. 3-4.
73. The earliest and in many ways a most autehentic account of the penal settlement of the Andaman Islands is found in a very rare book, entitled *Tārīkh-i 'Ajīb* (History of Port Blair) by Muhammad Jafar, Thaneswari. It was originally prepared at the request of Sardar Bhagat Singh, District Superintendent of Port Blair Police, and with the permission of the Deputy Superintendent, printed in 1879, with some additions in 1880. A second edition, revised by the author was published by the Nawalkishore Press in 1892. The first one hundred pages contain a general account, and some rules and regulations, and the next one hundred pages give conversational short sentences in a number of 'Asian languages'. The other, later, work of Muhammad Jafar with a similar sounding title, *Tawārīkh-i 'Ajīb*, describes the life of the Wahhabi convicts on the islands, and it has been utilised in many books on the subject, including this one. The earlier one, under reference, has remained virtually unnoticed.

    We now have R.C.Majumdar's *Andaman Penal Settlement* (Publications Division), but it does not refer to the earlier history. Majumdar, in fact, seems to be unaware of this valuable work.
74. This account is based on the works which two of the convicts, Muhammad Jafar and Abdul Rahim, wrote on their release *(T.A., T.S.)* supplemented with information available in government records.
75. *Ibid.*, pp. 104 ff.

    Jafar writes that when he was chief *Munshi* of the Deputy Commissioner, Port Blair, he had helped in the compilation of Rules and Regulations for the island. He also translated it into Urdu and both versions were published (p.98).
76. *Ibid.* p. 59.
77. Among the Wahhabi prisoners, the numbers of the following are available, Abdul Rahim (no. 1156) Muhammad Jafar (no. 11450)

and Abdul Ghaffar (no. 11451). This is mentioned in the correspondence at the time of their release in 1882 (letter from Superintendent, Port Blair and Nicobar islands convicts Board department) to Secretary, Government of Bengal, no. 611, dated 15th September, 1882.

Ahmadullah and Yahya Ali had died earlier and hence their names were not referred to.

78. John Beames, (*Life of a Bengali Civilian*, London, 1961, p. 273) who was the Commissioner of Puri at the time (1875-77) writes about the arrest of the Raja of Kharda (not Puri) his conviction and transportation to the Andaman Islands.
79. *T.A.*, pp. 67-68.
80. He was subsequently released and returned to his native place, Agra, when he died in 1904.
81. *T.S.*, p. 78.

    Jafar (*Sawānih*, p. 225) quotes a Persian chronogram recording the year of Yahya Ali's death, English translation of which is given below:

    When Yahya Ali, who was a man of praiseworthy qualities and learning and piety and (also) a *muḥaddith*;
    (When) his pious soul left the association of his body, and set out on the road to Union with Truth;
    The (Invisible) Crier, in sorrow, called out the year (of that event);
    "Allah, his Creator, was pleased with him."
    The chronogram is dated (A.H.) 1284, or 1866-67.
82. *T.A.*, p. 79; see also *infra*, p. 347, n.1.
83. W. Tayler, *Thrity Eight Years in India*, London, 1882, vol.I, pp. 555, 561.
84. *T.A.*, p. 79.
85. *T.A.*, p. 55.
86. *T.A.*, p. 101.
87. *Sawānih*, p. 225.
88. Abdu'l Rahim, for instance, while describing in detail the arrests and trials of his family members and others does not write much about the material losses suffered by them. Jafar too was a wealthy man, but does not dwell much on his financial losses or those of his fellow-worker, Muhammad Shafi.
89. See the family-tree on the opposite page.
90. He was the son of Wazir Ali and the son-in-law of Rafi'ud Din Husain Khan, a high official of the Murshidabad Court and the East India Company.
91. *T.S.*, p. 42. He had received the grant of *mauḍa* Bhuyee (area 400 *bighas*, income, Rs. 15,000) and *mauḍe* Bijay Gopalpur (area 700 *bighas*, income, Rs. 4,000/-) in the district of Patna.

92. The two brothers together owned properties worth an annual income of Rs. 7971-7-10, while Abdul Rahim possessed properties yielding an annual income of Rs. 1395-7-1 (Government of Bengal, Judicial Department, Proceedings nos. 122-127, dated October, 1865).
93. *T.S.*, p. 203.
94. *Ibid.*, p. 137.
95. Government of Bengal, Judicial Department, Proceedings nos. 122-127, dated October, 1865.
96. See plan of the house on the opposite side.
97. The family ms. copy of T.S., which I have used, contains a copy of a letter written by Yahya Ali to his wife on hearing about the demolition of the family houses. It states, ".... I learnt from the letter of Muhammad Hasan (may he live long!) about the demolition of both the houses. My heart was grieved, and I was deeply shocked (to hear this) because these were our ancestral houses, the more so because the recitation of God's name and the performance of His commandments were so often done there. (As such) true *Momins* loved them as their kith and kin."
98. Government of Bengal, Judicial Department, Proceeding no. 126, dated October, 1865.
99. Ibid., no. 34, dated April, 1866.
100. Letter from A.P.Holwell, Under Secretary, Government of India, to A. Mackenzie, Officiating Under Secretary Government of Bengal, dated Simla, 15th May, 1866.
101. Vide Declaration issued by the Chairman, Patna Municipality, 28th May, 1868.
102. Even Abdul Rahim, who generally avoids any harsh comment on the government's actions, wrote this when he visited the site after his return home from the Andaman Islands. "It is difficult to describe in words the sense of shock which I felt on finding this treatment meted out to our dead ones. Even now it makes my hair stand on edge to recall it. I cannot understand why our ancestors' graves were dug up and why that graveyard was confiscated and why our 'just government' acted in this manner (*T.S.*, p. 179)
103. See his short Persian *mathnawī, Shahar Āshob-i Patna.*
104. Ibid., pp. 11, 16.
105. Government of Bengal Judicial Dept. Proceedings no. 39, dated April, 1866, Also Holwell's letter cited above.
106. Abdul Rahim's share, for example, was sold for only Rs. 1364.
107. The total amounts varied from time to time depending upon the withdrawals from and credit to the Wahhabi fund.
108. Enclosure to letter from Magistrate, Patna no. 919 dated 17 September, 1873.

109. These particulars are available in some confidential papers kept separately in the Commissioner's office, Patna. These are not formal letters but office notes and drafts, initialled by pencil. A scrutiny of the contents reveals as to which draft is from whom and to whom.
110. Letter from Commissioner Patna to Secretary, Government of Bengal, dated 27th February,1869.
111. Muhammad Hasan, son of Wilayat Ali, lived in one of these rooms which he took on rent. Later he built a house across the road to the north.
112. W.W.Hunter, *A Statistical Account of Bengal* (Reprint-1976), vol. XI, p. 221.

    In some old records of Jahangir's reign (1605-27) there are references to a *garhi* in the town, *Shaikh Matha ki garhi.* It was renamed Maugles' Tank, after the then Collector, A.C.Maugles, and is now called, the Gandhi Sarovar.

    In the introductory note to the enclosure giving the Indian equivalents of money, weights ad measures, Hunter poined out that one rupee was equal to an amount between 1•8d to 2•, but for conventional purposes it was taken as 2s. The amount taken out of the Wahhabi Fund would thus be a little over Rs. 50,000/- (in late 1880).
113. Established in 1863. The principal at the time was W.J.McCrindle (1867-80).
114. General Dept. (Education Branch) Proceedings nos. 9-12, March, 1880.
115. General Dept. (Education) Memo no. 270, dated 12th April, 1880.
116. It was constituted in 1884, and one of its objectives was the establishment of a school "on the principle of the Aligarh Collegiate School." Its founder secretary was *Shamsul 'Ulama* Muhammad Hasan, mentioned above (no. 111).
117. The school continued to get the annuity until 1940s. The principal amount, now invested in government securities, was due for release in 1987, but it has not been paid as yet for various reasons.

    The *Al-Punch,* an Urdu weekly of Patna edited and published by Maulvi Syed Rahimuddin from the Union Press, Mussalahpur, started on 7 February, 1885, referred in its issue of 18 July 1887 to the government resolution published in the Calcutta Gazette of 22nd June ordering of this grant (See J.S.Jha, *Aspects of History of Modern Bihar,* Patna, 1988, pp. 74 *ff*).
118. *T.A.*, p. 98; *T.S.*, 1964 ed. p. 237.
119. *T.A.*, pp. 96 *ff.*
120. The book was first published in London in 1871, and a second

edition followed soon, the next year. Both the editions were published by Trubner & Company, London.

121. *T.A.*, pp. 96 *ff.*
122. *Ibid.*
123. Letter from Secretary, Government of Punjab to Secretary, Government of India, Home Dept., no. 182, dated 17th June, 1882.
124. Letter from Secretary, Government of Bengal to Secretary, Government of India, Home Dept., no. 754 B, Confidential, dated 7th Octobcr, 1882.
125. Draft Letter from Commissioner, Patna, dated 24th August, 1882.
126. Government of India, Home Dept., Proceedings no. 1871, dated Fort William, 31st December,1882.
127. *T.A.*, p. 104. Earlier, Jafar had married a young Hidu Brahmin girl from Almora who was a fellow-prisoner, and had become a Muslim (*ibid.*,p. 75).
128. *Ibid.*, p. 104.
129. Letter from Magistrate, Patna to Commissioner, Patna, no. 903 C dated 10th February, 1883.
130. Letter from Superintendent, Port Blair to Secretary, Government of Bengal, no. 1184, dated 6th February, 1883.
131. *T.S.*, p. 178. also see p. 181, where he refers to the continuation of this restriction even during his journey for *Hajj*, and to his being asked to report to the British Counsul at Jidda on arrival there.
132. Letter from Superintendent, Andaman and Nicobar Islands, to Secretary, Government of Bengal, no. 98, dated 28th April, 1883.
133. His long life-span (1836-1923) enabled him to see the active phase of the movement, as also the later one, when its adherents turned their attention to peaceful social and educational work. He was the founder of the *Madrasa-i Islāhu'l Muslimīn*, now called *Jāmia Islāhiyya Salafiyya*, which is a residential *madrasa* imparting education in the traditional Islamic disciplines along with some English education and crafts training. It does not seek Government s affiliation, or aid, and is run entirely by donations. Its annual budget is Rs. 4lakhs. Abdul Rahim was the Amir of the *Ahl-i Hadith* of Bihar until his death, and was succeeded by his grandson (daughter's son) Abdul Khabir (see no. 136).
134. After the confiscation of the family residence at Sadiqpur, he had moved but eastwards and set up a dispensary in Khwaja Kalan. He also purchased a house there which was renovated and expanded by his grandson, Dr. Azimuddin Ahmad (Formerly Head of Arabic and Persian Department, Patna College). The family still lives there.
135. For biographical details of all these three, see *T.S.*

A recent writer, basing himself on *Aligarh Institute Gazette*, states that for the first three years of M.A.O. College classes, Siddons and the Mathematics professor had to cover all the subjects, except Arabic and Persian. Then, in 1881, Aligarh hired Maulawi Amjad Ali, M.A., as Professor of Philosophy and Logic. One of the first north Indian Muslims to take a degree, Amjad Ali remained at Aligarh till 1887, when he took the post of Professor of Arabic at Muir College, Allahabad (David Lelyveld, *Aligarh's First Generation*, Princeton University Press, New Jersey, 1978.

136. He also had a prosperous business at Calcutta. He built a new house near the site of the old one, in which his descendants lived until very recently. Close by is the house of Hakim Abdul Khabir (1883-1973). Living a life of simplicity and piety he enjoyed wide respect, and was the *Amir* of *Ahl-i Hadith*, Bihar.

Chapter IX

The Concluding Phase of the Movement

The Ambala and the Patna trials form a landmark in the history of the Wahhabi Movement. The arrest and conviction of so many leaders and workers naturally weakened the organisation and affected its financial resources. It was not, however, the end but only the beginning of the end. In fact, the area of the Wahhabi activities seems to have spread out a little more during the period following these trials. From 1869 onwards the government of Bengal was again engaged in comprehensive enquiries against the Wahhabi centres inside the country, and another series of Wahhabi trials followed. As was revealed by these enquiries and the trial proceedings, the work of preaching and collection of funds continued inside British India while the Wahhabi centre on the Frontier remained active under the leadership of Abdullah. The following account of the concluding phase is accordingly arranged, dealing, respectively, with the Wahhabi activities (i) inside the country and (ii) on the Frontier. In between, there is a section on the controversy about the use and abuse of the term. "Wahhabi", and its discontinuance in official papers.

1. Wahhabi Activities in British India, 1868-1886

Towards the end of 1868 the attention of the Government[1] was drawn to the continued working of some Wahhabi centres, particularly those of Malda and Rajmahal.[2] Wilmot, the Assistant Commissioner at Rajmahal, suggested to Reily, the D.I.G. of Police, Lower Provinces, to depute Nobokishto Ghose, an assistant, Police Department, to village Kaliachak in Malda district which appeared to be the chief centre. Ghose proceeded there and, having stayed there for a week in disguise as a silk merchant, collected a lot of information and evidence which tended to show that contributions were openly made in several villages adjacent to Kaliachak *"for a 'Jehad' or religious war against the English with the intention of restoring the Muhammadan rule and driving the Kafir, the English out of the country."*[3] He also found that

Nazir Sirdar was one of the chief agents for collection in the area. After some time, when Ghose found that his real identity had been exposed and seeing that no useful purpose could be served by his continued stay in disguise, he went to James O'Kinealy[4] the magistrate of Malda, and applied for warrants of arrest against eight persons,[5] suspected to be engaged in collecting funds for the Wahhabis. After their arrest, Reily rushed to Kaliachak and got the accused persons examined before the magistrate and their statements recorded. Some additional witnesses were also examined.

The statements showed that Nazir Sirdar of village Qazigram was the local leader that he had taken an active and prominent part for several years past and that he had also induced several persons of the districts to go to the Frontier. Those who did not contribute were socially boycotted.

The evidence also implicated Ibrahim Mandal as the 'headcentre' to whom all the collected money was forwarded by Nazir Sirdar. Ibrahim Mandal lived in village Islampur, close to the Deputy Magistrate's Court at Pakur, and not far from the railway line. The magistrate of Malda was requested to issue a warrant of arrest against Ibrahim. As a precautionary measure Reily did not proceed direct to Rajmahal, lest Ibrahim got scent and escaped. He sent Ghose by road to Islampur. The latter arrived there in disguise as a Muslim private tutor in search of a teaching job. By chance he met a nephew of Ibrahim who took him straight to the house of his uncle who, he said, was the most likely person in the village to help him. Ibrahim was immediately arrested with the help of two constables who were closely following Ghose. Wilmot, the Assistant Commissioner, and his deputy, Beames also arrived on the spot. They had come from Rajmahal on elephants to help Ghose capture Ibrahim.

Reporting about the information gathered by him, Reily stated that "similar collection and preachings have been general among the Muhammadan population in the other districts and unless active measures are adopted to check this fanatical Movement it was likely to spread." More significantly, he remarked that "this Movement does not include any influential zamindars or landholders." Its supporters were, mainly, the small cultivators and landless *ra'iyyat*. The chief inducement held out to them was the prospect of holding their lands rent-free in the event of success. Naturally, the zamindars were not likely to support such a movement.

This rather scarce reference to the agrarian links of the movement deserves attention. We have seen above as to how the Faraidis and the

Wahhabis worked among, and obtained their main support from, the peasantry in the interior areas of Bengal. This brought upon them the hostility and active opposition of both the zamindars and the indigo planters, of which the Baraset Rising is a very good example. As it appears from the present enquiries, the link had not been broken, and the Wahhabis had continued their association with the small cultivators and the landless *ra'iyyats,* and supported them in their struggle against the zamindars and the planters. As was subsequently reported, two other notable Wahhabis of the area, Rafique Mandal and his son Amiruddin, had also been very active against the indigo planters' exactions.[6] The planters in fact were very apprehensive about the Wahhabis' work among the *ra'iyyats* and of its repurcussion on their interests. They had taken a lead in opposing this combination at the time of the Baraset Rising, and on the present occasion too a local planter, Grey, was actively associated with O'Kinealy in the enquiries, and was found to be of 'great assistance'[7] to him. This long continuity of the Wahhabis' work among the peasantry and the workers of the planters, and in fact, the whole question of the economic under current of the movement deserves greater attention.

It was also learnt that seditious pamphlets were being distributed. The magistrate of Malda reported[8] that out of the many pamphlets seized by the police, he had studied two. On was the *Tafsīr-i-Murādiya,* a commentary on the *Am Sīpārah*[9] one of the most frequently used verses of the *Qur'ān.* The other was a compilation of *Fatāwa* (canonical decrees) on different religious subjects by *Ḥājī* Badruddin of Dacca, one of the most active supporters of the Patna conspirators in Eastern Bengal. It was written in Bengali verse, admirably adapted to attract an ignorant Bengali.

Finally, Reily reported his intention to charge the arrested persons under sections 108 & 122 of the Indian Penal Code for abetment of an attempt to wage war against the Queen. He admitted that although there was no proof of money having passed beyond the custody of Ibrahim Mandal the intention of the arrested persons was established by evidence already recorded.

The provincial government referred the matter to the Legal Remembrancer for his advice in regard to the charges to be framed against the arrested persons. He replied that although it was clear that "seditious preaching of disaffection had been continuously followed in various districts," the difficulty arose from the absence of any proof of the final disposal of the money collected.[10] Drawing attention to the Ahmadullah case he observed that in the former case money had been traced from Patna to the Frontier, unlike in the present case. He expressed doubt whether charges under Section 120 & 122 Indian Penal Code could be framed unless more evidence was forthcoming about the disposal of the money. He also advised that printed copies of the proceedings[11] of Ahmadullah's case should be distributed among all the officers working on the case, as it was a useful guide on the subject of Wahhabis and their organisation.

The Government were faced with a legal difficulty. The above-mentioned persons had been arrested on some *prima facie* evidence, but detailed investigations had to be carried on at several places for gathering actual proof of their guilt. All these persons could not be detained indefinitely unless the Government of India was moved to invoke Regulation III[12] of 1818. This regulation, the precursor of the Defence of India Act, armed the Central Government with certain extraordinary powers for the preventive detention of persons and for holding them in prison without trial for as long as it considered necessary. The Lieutenant Governor, while reporting the matter to the Government of India recommended that only the leaders of the movement be detained and the rest released, but kept under watch. He observed further that although there was no proof that the money which had been collected was going to the Frontier, the village Islampur itself contained families of men who were either at the Frontier or had died there. Their families were being looked after by Ibrahim out of the collected funds. The purpose, in both cases, was virtually the same—helping the Wahhabis. Accordingly, Ibrahim Mandal and Nazir Sirdar were detained and the rest released.[13] Ibrahim Mandal was put in the Rajmahal jail. He was a man of fairly advanced age, but was confined in a very small and damp room and under unhygienic conditions to which even the jail doctor objected.[14] He was later transferred to the Monghyr jail.

Among the witnesses who had given statements at Malda was one Enayatullah, son of Faizullah of village Sheikhpura, district Monghyr. He deposed[15] that his father-in-law was a *Murīd* of *Hājī* Mubarak Ali of Patna who became the *Sirdar* after the arrest of Ahmadullah. Mubarak Ali had sent for Enayatullah in the month of *Dhu'l Qa'd*, 1281 (May, 1864), spoken to him about the task of transmitting money, and had pointed out to him the 'blessings of participating in this work. On further enquiries he had been directed to go to

Rajmahal and meet Ibrahim. The witness stayed with Ibrahim for a fortnight and during that period he saw Nazir *Sirdar* and many others come to Ibrahim and deposit various amounts of money. On the occasion of *Baqr'id* particularly, large sums of money were collected, sometimes as much as rupees fifty to sixty thousand. The cash was converted into gold *mohars*, often with the help of Amir Khan of Patna who had his firm in Calcutta. The amounts were then sent to Mubarak Ali who sent them to the Frontier through secret agents, among whom was one Maula Bakhsh a resident of Maner, district Patna, a "short brown man who spoke Pushtu fluently". He was a most efficient and trustworthy agent.

Enayatullah's statement showed that Patna was the keycentre, and served as the link between Bengal and the N.W.Frontier. Reily tried to get Ishree Prasad, who had proved so efficient and useful in the previous investigations against the Wahhabis, deputed to Patna, but he was preparing for his departmental examination at Monghyr and did not want to be sent away from there. So Ghose was deputed to Patna, but he proved to be so unpopular, and so antagonised the populace of Patna,[16] that the Commissioner asked him to leave Patna at once, and also admonished Reily for having deputed Ghose without consulting him. Reily's defence of Ghose was ignored. Instead, Elahi Bakhsh, then an assistant at Purnea, was called to Patna and given the work of investigation. Subsequently, Ishree Prasad was deputed to Patna to assist Reily.[17] With the arrival of Ishree Prasad enquiries were set in full motion, and it was found that the 'conspiratorial organisation' was spread over practically the whole of northern India. The governments of Punjab and the North-Western Provinces were requested to extend help to Reily and his assistants in the investigations, and the governments of Bombay and Madras were requested to send reports on the state of Wahhabi activities within their states.

Before passing on to the main enquiries carried out at Patna, we may look at the position of the Wahhabis in the Madras and Bombay Presidencies. It had come to the Government's notice that the money meant for the Frontier Wahhabis was often sent to Mecca through Bombay, the main port of embarkation for the *Hājis*, and it was re-directed from there to the Frontier. Reily wanted to know specifically as to whether there was an active link between the Wahhabis of the southern areas and those of Bengal and Bihar. To that question the answer, in most cases, was that no ostensible evidence to that effect existed, but the Wahhabis were active at several places.

(i) Wahhabi Activities in Madras and Bombay Presidencies

In Madras [18] the government had been watching the activities of the Wahhabis for quite some time. In 1866 a man named Muhammad Ismail, formerly a sepoy in the 37th N.I. and 'a zealous Wahhabi missionary' had been confined in Madras under Regulation II of 1819 (the equivalent of Regulation II of 1818 in Bengal). He had been earlier turned out of the Lines in 1852 for preaching sedition. In 1857 he was suspected of similar activities in Guntur. After that he went over to Burma where he continued to preach Wahhabi doctrines to the 'native' troops. He was deported on that account from Thyetmeo (Burma) to Calcutta and was again suspected of seditious activities in Vizianagram in 1863. He was finally imprisoned in 1866 for similar activities in the Northern Circars.

Another noted Wahhabi preacher who had been active in Madras, particularly in the units of the regiments of the Native Infantry stationed in Madras, was a man from Bengal,named Ahmadullah. His activities had alarmed some of the top military authorities. The Adjutant-General, Madras, on instruction from the Commander-in-Chief, Madras Army, circulated an order to all officers commanding stations and regiments in Madras to watch out for a 'bigoted Wahhabi, a native of Bengal (Ahmadullah) whose chief object is to stir up the sepoys to sedition and who is engaged in travelling from place to place where Madras troops are and carrying on seditious communications.'

Ahmadullah was arrested at Raipur in October, 1869. It was reported [19] that he had come to Raipur in the previous year and had been visited by some known Wahhabis. The police were already in possession of the circular of the Adjutant-General, referred to above. They arrested him and he admitted that he had been to Vizianagram in 1860 and met some men of the 11th N.I. Attention was drawn to the fact that the regiment had since been transferred to Raipur.[20] It was further reported that Ahmadullah was the *Pir* of Ismail Khan, a noted Wahhabi who was arrested a few years ago at Berhampur for preaching sedition among the sepoys of the 28th Madras N.I. and was imprisoned for life in the Coimbatore jail. Ahmadullah had also visited Ellore (Godavri district) in 1862, and that Wahhabism there had been on the increase ever since.[21] On interrogation Ahmadullah stated that he traded in clothes, hides and bones. He purchased clothes from Bombay and sold them at various places. That explained his frequent travels. It is fairly evident that he was employing the standard Wahhabi technique of mixing missionary work with genuine business which could be satisfactorily proved if ever the necessity arose. Some additional information about Ahmadullah was received from Ali Kureem of Patna,[22] but the government, for some reason did not want to accept Ali Kureem's offer to furnish information regarding the Wahhabis.[23]

Summing up the general situation, it was stated that the Wahhabis' activities consisted mainly of the propagation of their religious tenets. They brought out a newspaper named *Belchi* (Mattock) in Madras town. This, it was added significantly, "also showed that they must have been in touch with the progress in other places or else they could not have subscribed to an obscure newspaper in a remote city." No overt acts had been committed by them, but *"it was likely that their innate feelings under a forced Christian rule occasionally find expression."*[24]

As regards the Bombay Presidency, it was reported[25] that there were about one hundred Wahhabis in the Presidency town, but there was no evidence to indicate that they were connected with their compatriots in Bengal. In Poona, a man named Barkatullah, of Farrash Khana, Delhi, had preached *jihād* some time ago. 'No Moulvie had ever been heard to preach sedition at Poona in so strong a language as this man did.' He was also warned to keep out of the Lines of a 'Native' regiment. He had left on the pretence of going to Mecca but went instead to Bombay where he stayed with a wealthy Wahhabi named Enayatullah. There were some Wahhabis in the town, in the Sadar Bazar, but they did not tell much about their avocation.

They had set up a mosque in Neriad, but the Bohras had turned them out. In Surat and Broach the Wahhabis were not very influential, because "the tenets of their creed are so opposed to those of the local population." But they came from outside either as casual labourers or as preachers. When the railway bridge near Nerbada was being repaired some of the workmen there were said to have been Wahhabis, who left after the completion of the work. In 1869 a considerable number of Wahhabis had come to Gondhra from Tonk for propagating their creed.

There were some Wahhabi families, mostly weavers, living at Talikote. At Bijapur too there were some Wahhabis belonging to the weavers class, and a Wahhabi Moulvi 'from the direction of Madras' had arrived there.

(ii) Enquiries in Bihar and Bengal

To revert to the enquiries carried on by Reily in Bengal and Bihar, it was learnt from an informant that Khurshid Ali, brother of the late Elahi Bakhsh (approver in Ahmadullah case), who now managed his shop on behalf of latter's infant son, was the person through whom Mubarak Ali transmitted money to Delhi and the Frontier.[26] Elahi Bakhsh's shoe shop, connected with Delhi (from where he purchased shoes and sent money for it), was a convenient point for transmitting funds. Reily commented on the audacity of Mubarak Ali for selecting that very shop which had earlier been searched by the police, thinking that the authorities would not suspect it so soon again. Khurshid's shop was searched and the papers seized. They showed entries of credits of various amounts and transmission of two amounts of Rs. 9,728/- and Rs. 11,914/- in the year A.H. 1284 and 1285 (1867-69). No explanation was forthcoming for these transfers, nor did the extent of the business justify such profits. Both Khurshid Ali and Mubarak Ali were arrested in December, 1868.

It was further learnt that Mubarak Ali had written some letters to one Umeed Ali, a resident of Backerganj (Bengal) who lived in Delhi. Ishree Prasad immediately rushed to Delhi, located and searched Umeed Ali's house and seized the papers. Umeed Ali admitted [27] that he had received letters and money from Mubarak Ali and also forwarded letters to him from the Frontier. He also named some of the Wahhabi agents who carried money to the Frontier, including Tabaràk Ali, (also known as Qadir Bakhsh) son of Mubarak Ali of Patna. Tabarak Ali was arrested at Patna.

Umeed Ali further stated[28] that one day while he was sitting in the shop of Muhammad Amin, several men came to meet Amin, who said that they had come from Prince Firoz Shah,[29] who lived on the Frontier. They had brought letters from Firoz Shah addressed to some Rajas of the Deccan. The Prince had reminded them about promises of help made during the Mutiny of 1857 and asked them to join him at the river Oxus. The letter bore the seal of Firoz Shah which was 'a span in diameter' with the names of all the kings of Taimur's family in a circle and Firoz's own name in the centre. The letters were to be delivered to Prince Izad Bakhsh, brother of Firoz, who lived with his mother in a hut in Delhi and had a cloth shop.[30]

Izad Bakhsh, on being questioned, stated that he was unwilling to receive letters from his brother's messengers, but had agreed to meet them while on his way to Nazir Husain who lived near Phatak Habsh Khan in Delhi. Umeed Ali's statement, thus involved Nazir Husain who, he said, was present when the messengers of Firoz Shah had come. This indeed was an important piece of information, for the person named was the famous scholar of *Ḥadīth,* Maulawi Nazir Husain *Muḥaddith.*

Nazir Husain[31] (c. 1805-1902) was the son of Sayyid Jawwad Ali and belonged to village Bilthua, in district Monghyr. The family claimed descent from a 13th century general of Sultan Qutubuddin Aibak (1206-10), Ahmad Shah Jajneri, who had been sent against Raja Indradaman of Uren. Nazir Husain had gone for higher studies to Patna in 1822 where he lived for some time in the house of Shah Muhammad Husain. Sayyid Ahmad's visit to Patna occurred during this period; and Nazir Husain had listened to his lectures. Probably influenced by these, he had proceeded to Delhi to join the circle of the students of Shah Abdul Aziz. He reached there after the Shah's, death, and became a student first of Maulawi Muhammad Abdul Khaliq, and then of Shah Muhammad Ishaq, the successor of Shah Abdul Aziz. In 1832, he married the daughter of Maulawi Abdul Khaliq,[32] and settled down at Delhi as a teacher of *Hadith.* This was the beginning of a life-long career as a distinguished and dedicated teacher of *Hadith* and other branches of Islamic learning.[33] His students came from all parts of India as also from other countries.[34] Though he sometimes visited Patna and his village-home, he lived mostly at Delhi, and was there throughout the stormy days of 1857-58. He is said to have refused to sign a declaration calling for a *jihād* against the British, but in the light of evidence now available, this appears to have been nothing more than a tactical move.

The search of Nazir Husain's house yielded a very large number of letters, and on being asked as to why he received so many letters, Nazir Husain gave the sardonic reply that it was because the Government had lowered the postal rates![35] Some of these letters were from such well-known Wahhabis as Jafar Thanesari and Tabarak Ali of Patna. There was also a letter written by Nazir Husain to Abdullah, the Wahhabi *Amīr* on the Frontier.[36] Reily recommended the arrest of Nazir Husain under Regulation III, but as he was an *'Ālim*[37] of great repute and influence the Government, in the absence of more concrete evidence against him, was reluctant to take this 'extreme' step. The matter was referred to the Punjab government in whose jurisdiction Delhi lay, and the latter ordered his detention in jail for six months as a precautionary measure, but released him soon after.

In December, 1869, Reily submitted some additional information[38] against Nazir Husain. He pointed out that according to the statement of Abdullah given at Rawalpindi in October, 1869 Nazir Husain was the chief of the Wahhabis at Delhi. Another witness from Rajmahal had stated that he had been induced by Nazir Husain to go to the Frontier. Reily recommended that Nazir Husain should be re-examined and that he confront the witnesses. The papers were again referred to the Punjab government,[39] but no action seems to have been taken against him. He figured again in the subsequent enquiries.[40]

Carr Stephen, the Magistrate of Delhi, who recorded the statements of Umeed Ali and others reported[41] that the clues given by Umeed Ali regarding the Wahhabi agents in other provinces should be followed through and, in the meantime, Umeed Ali be detained and the rest released. He was accordingly arrested along with a few others, including Muhammad Ameen or Aminuddin of Backerganj who had fled to Dacca following the arrest of Umeed Ali.

(iii) Amiruddin of Malda

While at Malda, in connection with Ibrahim Mandal's arrest, Reily had learnt that one of the most influential men there, next to Ibrahim Mandal, was Amiruddin of village Sandipa Narainpur. His activities had continued for a long time and were not unknown to the authorities.

He and his father Rafique Mandal had been active in the agitation against the indigo planters in the area, including Grey, mentioned above.[42] They spared neither time nor money in protecting the hapless *ra'iyyat* against the oppresssions of the planters. Even though they were harassed by the application of rent laws they fought for the protection of the *ra'iyyat* in the courts and elsewhere. Praising the dedication and integrity of Rafique Mandal, then over 70 years old, a contemporary British observer, James Routledge wrote: "Rufeek Mondul at the time the story was told (1871), was seventy years of age, and in his dotage; and though the fire of enthusiasm still broke out, in view of the principles to which he had devoted his life, he could hardly be counted dangerous. There were those, however, who remembered the old man as foremost in the indigo disputes, and spending both time and money in opposition to the exactions of the planters, fighting every battle to the bitter end, even in the High Court and before the Sudder Revenue Board of Calcutta, and never yielding a foot of ground while he was able to maintain it."[43] Reily's assistant, Ghose was sent to Malda, and he arrested Amiruddin on the 30th March, 1869. The magistrate of Malda reported that he was not being charged just then, and that the investigations against him would be treated as a preliminary measure to put the Government in possession of sworn evidence for his eventual prosecution.[44]

Reporting on all these investigations at the different places the Lieutenant Governor, Bengal, in a letter to the Government of India, observed that the "Wahhabi Movement is extensively ramified, and that there are agents stationed at Saharanpur, Jhelum, Roorkee, Dinapur and several other places."[45] He was doubtful whether proceedings could successfully be launched against the suspected persons in the criminal courts. He was of the opinion that there was no provision in the Penal Code, as it existed, for meeting the sort of activities in which the Wahhabis indulged. Hunter, too, comments on the predicament of the authorities in the following words: "The evil is so widely diffused that it was difficult to know where to begin. Each District-Centre spreads disaffection through thousands of families; but the only possible witnesses against him are his own converts who would prefer death to the betrayal of their master."[46]

(iv) Enquiries at Dinapur and Patna

During the next phase of enquiries the spotlight shifted to Dinapur and Patna. It was found that letters had been written from Rawalpindi to Pir Muhammad of Orderly Bazar, Dinapur, and that *Hājī* Din Muhammad of the same place had been posted at Rawalpindi by Abdullah, the leader of the Wahhabis on the Frontier.[47] Din Muhammad's duty was to receive the money sent from Patna and to pass it on to the Frontier. Din Muhammad's letter which was intercepted made allusions to matters connected with illegal transmission of money. Reily drew the attention of the Government to the fact that "in so important a place as Dinapur, where native Regiments are quartered, it was advisable that the whole band of Wahhabi conspirators, should be secured."[48] He applied for the arrest of Pir Muhammad under Regulation III. The provincial government was more cautious and wanted a report from the Commissioner about the man's antecedents. The Magistrate, Patna, while supporting the demand of Reily, reported[49] that Pir Muhammad was a man without any independent income of his own and lived out of the collection charges paid to him for doing the Wahhabi's work. He also quoted the observation of Emerson, the Cantonment Magistrate, that Pir Muhammad was suspected in 1857, and though then looked upon by Tayler as a minor fry he was mentioned as a "likely individual to join in an intrigue with those opposed to the government." He was also the father-in-law of Tabarak Ali, son of Mubarak Ali, both of whom were known Wahhabis and had been arrested. Pir Muhammad was arrested under Regulation III and was lodged in the Digha jail on 14th June, 1869.[50] *Hājī* Din Muhammad too was arrested shortly after this, when he came to Dinapur from N.W.Frontier to pull up the local people for their slackness in the work of collection. While being taken to Delhi under an escort of two constables Din Muhammad jumped from the running train and escaped.[51]

(v) Amir Khan and Hashmatdad Khan

The information given in regard to Pir Muhammad involved many, including the well-known hide merchants of Patna, Amir Khan and Hashmatdad Khan. The authorities had all along suspected them; they were reported to have stood security when Wilayat Ali and the Enayat Ali were asked to execute bonds for 'good behaviour.' Further incriminating evidence including a letter of Amir Khan, had since been discovered.

Among the many who had given statements on the eve of Pir Muhammad's arrest, there was one named Sheikh Jhagroo.[52] His statement is of particular importance as it reveals the *modus-operandi* of the Wahhabis in transmitting money, as also the respective 'areas' of collections assigned to some of the collectors. He stated, *inter-alia,* that money was often remitted through women agents (they were less likely to create suspicion). It was also "a common practice to send men and money with detachment and regiments when they marched. The men (Wahhabi agents) acted as camp-followers on such occasions."[53]

Jhagroo further stated that Din Muhammad and Karim Bakhsh made collections in Hajipur, Aligunj, and Siwan. Abdul Rahman (of Dinapur) in Mainpura, Sultanpur, Shugga (all neighbouring villages), and Khuda Bakhsh in old Dinapur and Leslieganj. Budhye (Sic) Khan and Umdu Khan also collected subscriptions in the adjacent areas.

Following these investigations about a dozen persons,[54] all belonging to Dinapur, Amir Khan and Hashmatdad Khan were arrested under Regulation III. Amiruddin of Malda, who had been arrested earlier was also charged under the same regulation. Hashmatdad Khan and his *Mukhtar*, Elahi Bakhsh, were at Patna at that time but were not immediately arrested lest it put Amir Khan, the senior partner at Calcutta, on guard. He was arrested at Calcutta on the 9th July, 1869 and brought to Gaya Jail but soon after he was transferred to Alipur Jail, Calcutta. Hashmatdad Khan and his *Mukhtār* were arrested subsequently.

Ishree Prasad also learnt during the course of his enquiries that secret letters from the Wahhabis in the N.W.Frontier were addressed to Karamat Ali of Dinapur, who had been posted at Barabanki in Awadh to receive the letters there and to redirect them to the parties concerned in Bihar. Some villages lying within the postal jurisdictions of Bihta, Behea and Buxar (all in Shahabad district) were suspected to contain persons to whom such letters, were sent.[55] The I.G. Police wanted the authority for censoring these letters, but the provincial government disagreed with the necessity of taking this 'extreme course'. When the matter was referred to the Government of India, it supported the chief of police,[56] and the Postmaster General was directed to order the postal officers concerned to censor letters passing through their jurisdiction. Similarly, the Commissioner of Awadh was authorised to censor letters addressed to Karamat Ali at Barabanki. During that period several letters were seized and examined.

Waizul Haque of Patna, who had earlier been arrested by Tayler at the time of the Patna Rising (1857), also came under suspicion, as he had been to Mecca, the place through which money was suspected to have been sent to the Frontier Wahhabis. The matter was enquired into but the Commissioner was not quite satisfied about the allegation.[57]

By now most of the important leaders and other workers in Bihar and Bengal had been taken into detention. It was felt necessary, however, to complete the investigations at other places, particularly the Punjab and N.W.Frontier. The whole organisation was interconnected, and the Government wanted to have as much information as possible before filing a case. In the next round Reily turned his attention to the western side, and himself proceeded to Punjab. This explains the unusual time-gap between the arrests made during

December 1868-July 1869 and the institution of cases during October 1870-March 1871. During the interval many of the arrested persons were transferred from one jail to another to give statements and to contact other suspected persons at different places where investigations were going on.

Reily, on his journey to Punjab (September, 1869) had taken with him a man named Murtaza, a resident of Malda, who had once been with the Wahhabis at the Frontier. Reily had taken him with the express object of pointing out to him such men as he had seen there or whom he knew to be associated with the Wahhabis. Murtaza more than fulfilled Reily's expectations.[58] He pointed out several men in Peshawar as Wahhabi agents. Among them were Mufti Husaini (also known as Muhammad Husain, Ghulam Husain, etc.), Ahmad Ali (of Dinapur) "the well-known *cossid* (messenger) who had so often successfully run the cordon of our police from Patna to Peshawar,"[59] Ghulam Rabbani, the seller of scents and *sharbats* (cold drinks) in the city of Peshawar, Sayyed Khan, *khānsamān* to General Haly, the local Commander, whose arrest 'created a sensation in the city', Faiyyaz Ali, a converted Hindu of Dinapur, and many others. The case of Mufti Husaini is quite interesting. He had been pretending for a long time to be acting as a spy of the Government and he had maintained this pretence so successfully that the authorities never suspected him.[60] When he was arrested and searched he was even found to be in possession of certificates of good character from several high-ranking civil and military officers. It was only after the sudden confrontation with Murtaza that he was finally exposed. Among the papers seized in his house was a letter from one Imdad Ali, once a Deputy Magistrate of Farukhabad in Uttar Pradesh, who had joined the 'rebels' in 1857, fled to the Frontier and was then with Prince Firoz Shah.

In the same month Reily proceeded with Murtaza far up in the tribal areas, "thirty miles as the crow flies," from the border of the Wahhabi centre. From there he deputed a spy to go to the centre and report on the state of affairs there.[61] Meanwhile, Reily got hold of another important witness, Abdullah of Hajipur, who gave a statement before the Assistant Commissioner, Rawalpindi on 12th October, 1869, referred to earlier.[62] The statement gives valuable information about the organisation of the Wahhabis in North Bihar, particularly Tirhut district which, as Reily commented, had not so far been 'touched' by the police authorities, and from where substantial amounts were transmitted. It also gave information about the agents in the Punjab.

Abdullah deposed, *inter alia,* that Ahmadullah of Muzaffarpur, a *Khalifa* of Wilayat Ali, was an influential Wahhabi of Tirhut and contributed Rs. 1,200/- annually. He had several *Murīds,* and sub-agents in the district: Maula Bakhsh and *Hāfiz* Jafar Ali of Mahalla Syudpur, Muzaffarpur, Mustafa Ali of Darbhanga, Abid Husain of village Sheohore (?) district Darbhanga, and Sheikh Subhan Ali of village Mahua (Darbhanga) were some of the local chiefs, who sent money to the Patna centre regularly. The funds from Muzaffarpur and Sherghati (Gaya) were collected by Pir Muhammad. Among the agents who carried these amounts to the Frontier, Maula Bakhsh and Ahmad Ali of Patna and Nizamuddin of Lucknow were the most trustworthy and experienced. Abdul Haq of Surajgarha (Monghyr) brother of Abdul Ghani was another trusted agent.

Among the patrons of the movement, Amir Khan and Zorawar Khan of Patna were the most eminent. The former's contribution amounted to over Rs. 1,200/- annually. He had also given Rs. 7,000/- to Abdullah when he was migrating to the Frontier. An even more important patron of the movement was the Nawab of Tonk. The money was received from the Nawab by Muhammad Ismail[63] and Abdul Rahman, nephews of Sayyid Ahmad and passed on to the Frontier. Abdullah went on to give further information about the agents in the Punjab. One of them was Fakhrullah (Faqir-ullah ?) who had been arrested around May, 1869.[64]

Abdul Aziz, the other agent, was directed to go in hiding and he escaped to Dinapur. Mufti Husaini of Peshawar went over to take his place and lived in the Lal Kothi in Rawalpindi. Another agent there was Alimuddin, the Imām of the Pucki Masjid. His duty was to pass on the money collected from Lal Kothi and other places to the *Cossids* or messengers from across the Frontier. Among these latter was Murad Ali who lived in a deserted cemetery in Hazara, posing as a hermit. In Jhelum,[65] the agent was Muhammad Niaman (sic), who too, sent money through Murad Ali. He had also requisitioned two books, *Sirātul-Mutaqīm* and *Balūghu'l Murām* (a collection of *Aḥādīth*) from Din Muhammad of Patna who had at once complied with the request.

Early in 1870 the Government obtained fresh information indicating a revival of Wahhabi activities in Rajmahal and the adjacent areas. The Commissioner, Bhagalpur reported that Ghulam Shah,

Haji, of Rajmahal had succeeded as the chief after the arrest of Ibrahim Mandal and was continuing his work.[66] He suggested that it would be better if Reily paid another visit to Rajmahal. He also informed that he had directed Wood, the Deputy Commissioner to detain only Ghulam Shah and release the other eight persons arrested along with him in accordance with the Government's policy of detaining only the leaders and not getting lost in a maze of minor arrests and enquiries.

Reily visited Rajmahal and reported that "since my last visit to this part of the country in October, 1868 I find that there is a marked change in these fanatics. They are undoubtedly, much bolder and ready to take the initiative." He noted with concern that the 'dreaded' punishment of social ex-communication was effectively used against those who did not participate either in subscribing to, or co-operating generally with the work of the movement. The threat of social boycott, "the *hooka-pani bund*," as he put it, was a "terrible engine of intimidation" among ignorant rural folks and the Wahhabis were making full use of it. About Ghulam Shah, in particular, Reily noted that he was formerly a resident of Calcutta who became a disciple of Moulwi Abdul Jabbar [67] and was deputed to Rajmahal area some seventeen years ago. He had been living there since then and set up a tailor's shop, but in reality he was one of the most able assistants of Ibrahim Mandal and helped him both in "collecting money and making proselytes." Since the latter's arrest he was the local chief, Maula Bakhsh, a nephew of Ibrahim (who had been arrested along with Ghulam Shah and later released in accordance with the Commissioner's order) was another important Wahhabi worker. He had been active not only in the Santhal Parganas but "preached sedition" in the Malda district also. Reily recommended not only the detention of Ghulam Shah under Regulation III but also stressed the desirability of getting Maula Bux re-arrested immediately.

Reily also visited Malda and reported[68] that village Hanspokhar[69] of the district was another 'active centre of sedition'. He recalled that Government's attention had been drawn to the activities of the Wahhabis of this village as early as 1866. Collections for '*jihad*' were still going on in the village mosque. The local inhabitants carried extensive correspondence with the men of the Frontier centre where a large number of recruits from this village still lived. Amanut Mandal was the local *Sardār*. His arrest, he thought, would put an end to the seditious activities and he recommended his arrest under Regulation

III. He also wanted to "make an example" of the village as a warning to the general inhabitants.

In May, 1870 Reily got information from Lal Muhammad, a prosecution witness in the Ambala Trial, that two men, Sharfullah and Nazir Muhammad of Bogra, who used to give military training to the Wahhabi recruits on the Frontier and had participated in several campaigns against the British, had since returned to India and were residing in their respective villages.[70] He applied for the issue of warrants of arrest against them under Regulation III, but was directed to get the deposition of the above-mentioned persons recorded before a magistrate. If the magistrate thought that a *prima facie* case could be made out against them only then he should take necessary action.

Reily's attention was also drawn to Shahabad district and the adjacent areas. Earlier, while he had been working in the N.W.Frontier with Murtaza, the latter had informed him that the Shahabad district was one of the most important recruiting centres of the Wahhabis. Recruits from that area were known to have gone to the Frontier where "they formed the pick of the Wahhabi sepoys."[71] Reily thought that investigations which had, till then, been exclusively carried out in Patna and Dinapur should be extended to the other parts of the province, and directed Ishree Prasad, in June, 1870 to visit Buxar. Ishree Prasad visited Buxar and a cluster of adjacent villages extending into the Ghazipur district of U.P. He reported[72] that the area was visited by Sayyid Ahmad when he was on his way to Calcutta. In particular, he had visited the village Chowsa Bara which had a large population of Pathans, many of whom had taken *Bai'at* at his hands. Their descendants had maintained the link, and were the followers of the 'Sadiqpur Moulvis',[73] and they sent $^1/_{40}$ of their savings to Patna as subscription.

Another young informant, Muhammad Ishaq,[74] informed him about two other Wahhabis, Musharraf Ali of that village and Muhammad Umar of Dinapur. While not much evidence was obtained from Musharraf Ali, a search of the house of Muhammad Umar yielded letters which had been written to him by different persons, including some employed in Units of the 32 Regiment stationed at Roorkee and Nainital.[75] The writers sought Umar's assistance either for the dependants they had left behind in India or financial help for themselves for going to the Frontier. There were also some who had returned from the Frontier and were stranded on the way back and sought help. All this indicated that he was the leader since the arrest earlier of Pir Muhammad. Muhammad Umar was arrested on 22nd July, 1870 and put in *hājat*, and the Government of India was requested to issue a warrant of arrest against him under Regulation III.[76]

Subsequently, the Government learnt that Muhammad Umar was the nephew (sister's son) of Rahat Ali, a man of well-known anti-government antecedents.[77] This information hastened the pace of further enquiries against him. It was found that he was related to other persons who had taken an active part in the movement of 1857-59. The magistrate also observed that he was well-connected, having relatives in practically all the courts in the province[78] and that powerful influences would be at work to destroy the evidence against him even if he was held in custody. From the absence of further references to him, however, it appears that Regulation III was not after all invoked against him.

The investigations had continued for over two years, but the Government still felt uncertain as to whether the evidence in their possession was sufficient to warrant the successful prosecution of the arrested leaders in a court of law. Many of the arrests had been ordered in 1869 and the prisoners had been in detention continuously since then. Neither had the grounds of their arrest been intimated to them nor had they been charged with any definite crime. Most of the prisoners were men belonging to the lower middle class whose moderate means made it impossible for them to challenge the unwarranted harassment. But two of them, Amir Khan and Hashmatdad Khan, were men of wealth and a high social status, and they did not take this 'oppression' lying down. They challenged the Government's action in a series of legal battles which have made their case the *cause celebre* of its time.[79]

Both the brothers belonged to distinguished Pathan family of Mewat whose origins went back to the times of Babar. They were residents of Alamganj,[80] Patna City and owned a prosperous hide and skin business in Calcutta whose assets were worth over a million rupees. Both were elderly men; Amir Khan at the time of his arrest was 75 and the other was 67 years old, and both were used to a comfortable standard of living.[81] They had been kept in jail for over a year under conditions of acute discomfort. Their prolonged detention, besides affecting their health, was also ruining their business which they could no longer supervise. They had submitted several petitions [82] to the Government during this period requesting it to let them know the grounds for their detention or, alternatively, to put them on trial at an early date. All this had proved unavailing.

Finally they took recourse, in August, 1870 to the last remedy open to them under the law. They moved the Calcutta High Court for the issue of writs of *habeas corpus*. Three of the topmost English lawyers in India at that time, Chisholm Anstey, Ingram[83] and Evans[84] appeared on behalf of the petitioners. The Government was represented by the Advocate-General, Graham and the Standing Government Counsel, Paul. The cases were heard in the court of Justice Norman. The case of Amir Khan was taken up first, but as the facts in both the cases were similar the arguments made in one case were held to have been made in the other also.

The fundamental point raised by the Defence was whether all British subjects had the same right of freedom from arbitrary arrests as was guaranteed in England under the *Magna Carta*, Bill of Rights, and other acts of Parliament.[85] Anstey, made fun of the Standing Counsel, Paul's eulogy of Lord Mayo as "a nobleman who had left ease and comfort at home to give his services to India," and remarked that for this Paul would be "rewarded in the next world as he was sure to be in this." He went on to maintain that Lord Mayo, like anyone else, was bound by the law, and he could not ignore it." In fact, Anstey's speeches were so "fiercely denunciatory of Lord Mayo and his Government" that it was clear he had no hope of the writ being granted to his client.[86] The judgement was delivered on 29th August, and it refused the issue of the writs.[87]

Immediately after the pronouncement of judgement by Justice Norman, Anstey submitted petitions before the Chief Justice and Justice Markby appealing against the judgement. The Chief Justice "refused to receive the petition but directed the Appellants, if so advised, to lodge them to Registrar's Office according to the practice of the Court." He also refused to fix an early date for hearing the Appeal as "one of the Lordships would be engaged."[88]

On the 14th September, Anstey sought leave to Appeal to the Privy Council both against the judgements of Justice Norman and that of the Chief Justice. This, too, was declined on the same date. Thus ended the first round of the legal duel between the Government and an individual claiming his inalienable right of freedom from arbitrary arrest.

A little later the prisoners were released from the Alipore Jail, but were re-arrested at the prison gate itself. This second arrest was under a warrant issued by a magistrate, and they were to be tried at Patna for offences alleged to have been committed there.[89] Commenting on this action of the Government, Routledge felt constrained to remark, "the long imprisonment without trial, the re-arrest at Alipore, and the removal from the jurisdiction of the highest Courts of law to the court of a civilian judge, able and respected though he was as an officer, did not give one the idea of that impartial dignity of law which is one of the best claims of England to her supremacy in India." He went on to express his belief that Lord Mayo, by whatever advice he acted, was primarily to be blamed in this case.[90]

About an year after the judgement, Justice Norman was assassinated on the steps of the stairway of the High Court building. The assassin, named Abdullah, was captured and tried. It was stated in the evidence brought forward during the trial that "the blows ... were given with unerring certainty, indicative of a man who had probably studied the art of murder." The accused did not say much during the trial, was declared to be insane and was sentenced to death.[91]

(vi) The Malda and Rajmahal Trials

The efforts of Amir Khan were successful in one respect. They forced the hands of the Government to expedite the institution of proceedings against prisoners so long held without trial. The trials of Amiruddin and Ibrahim Mandal were taken up first. They were tried in October 1870 at Malda and Rajmahal, respectively. Both were sentenced to imprisonment for life and transportation to the Andaman Islands, and their properties were ordered to be confiscated.

Recalling the perseverance and defiance displayed by Rafique Mandal, when young, in fighting the legal battles against the oppressions of the indigo planters,[92] and his fortitude in the midst of the present trial, Routledge writes: "If such a story had been told of Greece and Rome, or any other nation or race that lived hundreds of years ago, it would have been among the lessons of Oxford and Cambridge - a story termed classical. *That the history* (of these trials) *will some day be read with just pride in India, when India knows its most honourable records, I take to be among the certainties of life.* Can anyone, whatever his views, help feeling for these two men, father and son? Is there an Englishman anywhere who would refuse to petition the Indian Government, or the Government at home, beseeching them, if Ameeroodeen still lives, to find some means for his release? We may be bound, for the safety of society, to punish rebellion, whatever its cause or justification; but are we not also bound by the highest laws to admire such heroism and self-sacrifice as these men evinced? Tried and condemned in a dusky little court, under circumstances of which even Englishmen in India know very little, and Englishmen at home nothing at all, *I think the name and fame of Ameeroodeen, and of his gallant old father would not readily die.*"[93]

Amiruddin arrived in the Andaman in March, 1872.[94] Some of the amenities granted to the convicts in the penal colony had since been abrogated. Amiruddin had to suffer many hardships in the next few years. He was later appointed a teacher in the local *madrasa.* He was released in 1883 along with other Wahhabi prisoners. Pending government's permission to let him live in his home-town he stayed with Abdul Rahim at Patna, and like him had to report to the local Superintendent of Police once every month.

Although Ibrahim Mandal was also sentenced to imprisonment for life, it is not known whether he was actually sent to the Andaman. Jafar is not quite explicit on this point. At one place he makes a general remark that Amiruddin, Tabarak Ali and Ibrahim were all arrested and 'they' were transported to the Andaman, but it is not clear whether 'they' included Ibrahim also, for although Jafar subsequently mentions the arrival of the first two in the island and their release in 1883 he makes no mention of Ibrahim.[95] Another writer states that Ibrahim was not actually sent to the Andaman. He was released along with Amir Khan in 1878 and died in the early years of the present century.[96] This seems more likely.

(vii) The Patna Trial, 1871

The second round of Wahhabi trials began in Patna in March, 1871. In this case prosecution was launched against seven persons charged under different sections of the Indian Penal Code. The accused persons were Tabarak Ali, Pir Muhammad, Din Muhammad, Amiruddin, Amir Khan and Hashmatdad Khan. The last two were charged with the offence of rendering financial assistance to the movement. Mubarak Ali was charged with the offence of collection and transmission of funds. His son Tabarak Ali was accused of having given military instructions and drilled the recruits on the Frontier. The other three were accused of having assisted the rebels in various ways.

The accused persons had been arrested at different times and in different places. Some among them, such as Mubarak Ali had been released in the interval. Others had been frequently transferred from one jail to another all over the Bengal Presidency. Still some others such as the Khan Brothers and probably Tabarak Ali, had been continuously in detention since July, 1869. At the time of the trial they were all brought together and Mubarak Ali, too, was re-arrested.

The commital proceedings were held in the court of D.M.Barbour, Joint Magistrate, Patna. All the accused persons were committed to the Session's Court on 27th March. The session trial commenced in the court of Prinsep, the District Judge, on 29th May, 1871. Over a hundred prosecution witnesses from all over the country were examined in the course of the trial which continued with intervals, till 19th July. Anstey and Ingram, who had appeared on behalf of the Khan Brothers in the hearings for issue of writs of *habeas corpus,* represented them in this case also.

All the accused persons, except Hashmatdad Khan who was released as no *prima facie* case could be established against him, were sentenced to the, by now, standard punishment of transportation for life and confiscation of all properties. Pir Muhammad was released later on appeal to the High Court.

Amir Khan, because of his old age (he was above 80 years of age at that time) and due to the earnest efforts of his relatives was not sent to the Andamans. He was released in November, 1878 on the intercession of the Governor-General, Lord Lytton, after having spent over nine years in jail. He died within days of his release. His brother Hashmatdad Khan, died a little earlier in 1877 . Both lie buried in Patna. The material losses suffered by them were enormous.[97]

Mubarak Ali died as a result of severe beating while under trial.[98] The rest of the prisoners were transferred to the Andaman. Tabarak Ali reached there along with Amiruddin in March, 1872. After suffering severe hardships for a few years he was appointed as a Station *Muḥarir*[99] (clerk), and was released at the time of General Amnesty in 1883 and returned to Patna with Abdul Rahim.

Thus ended the last round of proceedings against the Wahhabis. The Government had done everything possible to root out the movement by arresting and convicting the leaders to long term imprisonment on the far-off convict colony of the Andaman Islands and confiscating all their material possessions. But the flame which had been lit by Sayyid Ahmad was not altogether extinguished. The embers continued to smoulder under the surface and occasionally burst out in sharp flashes.

(viii) The Wahhabis in Bhopal and Rangoon: 1875

On the eve of the visit of the Prince of Wales to Bihar (1875) the Government apprehended trouble from the Wahhabis, and an enquiry was ordered about their organisation and activities.[100]

The enquiry revealed that there were three main centres of Wahhabi activities: Patna, Bhopal and, surprisingly, Rangoon.

Muhammad Hasan, son of Wilayat Ali, and Abdullah, an Afghan national, were among the active Wahhabis in Patna. A son of the former had gone to the Andaman Islands on the eve of the assassination of Lord Mayo and was suspected to be implicated in it. The other agent, Abdullah, owned a fruit shop in *mahalla* Guzri, Patna City, but that was just a front. He was travelling to the different 'native' Indian states on the pretence of selling precious stones. His real object, however, was fund raising. Closely allied to the Patna centre was the one at Surajgarha, the birth-place of Nazir Husain, who was addressed as *Madāru'l Mahām* (chief of the difficult work) was still regarded as a prominent leader of the Wahhabis in India. The arrest and conviction of their leaders had weakened the Wahhabis and they had dispersed their activities over a wider area.

The second centre was Bhopal, whose chief was Munshi Jamaluddin[101] who had married one of the late *Begums* of Bhopal. The other prominent Wahhabis there were Sadiq Hasan, Abdul Jabbar, Abdul Rahman and Ali Karim. The last-named was known to be 'a desperate character.'

It is appropriate to mention here briefly the career of Nawab Siddiq Hasan *Wālā Jāh,* (1832-90),[102] the husband of Shahjahan Begum of Bhopal and the virtual ruler of that state for about a decade from 1871. His was a remarkable personality in many ways. Siddiq Hasan's father, Aulad Hasan, had taken *Bai'at* at Sayyid Ahmad's hand and was appointed his *khalīfa.* Siddiq Hasan himself was a great admirer of Wilayat Ali and Enayat Ali. They and their families had stayed in Siddiq Hasan's house during their visit to Qannauj, and it was at Wilayat Ali's instance that Siddiq Hasan had studied closely the well-known work (on *Hadith*) *Bulughu'l Muram* and later written a commentary on it. Siddiq Hasan had also lived for some time in Tonk where he was given an allowance by Nawab Waziru'd Dawlah, and where he stayed for some time with Maulawi Ismā'il,[103] the son-in-law of Sayyid Ahmad. Later, he had gone to Bhopal, where he was first appointed *Tārīkh Nigār* (Chronicler) in 1859 on a monthly salary of Rs. 75/-. He married the widowed daughter of *Madāru'l Mahām*

Munshi Jamaluddin, the *Nā'ib-i Awwal* (First Deputy or the *Wazīr*) of the state. He gained further ascendancy, and reached the position of the virtual ruler of the state when he married the recently widowed Begum of Bhopal, Shahjahan Begum [104] in 1870.

During the next few years Siddiq Hasan travelled with her to Bombay, Calcutta and Delhi and enjoyed great power and influence. He was on friendly terms with the top-ranking British officials from the Agent to the Governor General. He was also honoured with a special award (*Tamgha-i Majīdī*, second class) by Sultan Abdul Majid, the last Ottoman ruler and *Khalifa*, for his work *Tafsīr-i Fathu 'l Bayān*, and for the help rendered by the state in the war with Russia. Later, he incurred the hostility of Sir Lepel Griffin, the Resident of Indore, and also got involved in the ruling family's internal intrigues. Among the seven charges framed against him two were those of propagating 'Wahhabism' and 'Jihad'. He was divested of his titles (1885) but was allowed to live with the Begum until his death (1890).

Siddiq Hasan was a prolific writer[105] with a wide range of interest, in *Fiqh, Ḥadīth, Taṣawwuf, Tārīkh, poetry*, etc. Of particular interest from our point of view are his writings on the Wahhabis, their doctrinal position, aims and objectives. As early as in the 1880s, he pointed out the fallacy of calling Sayyid Ahmad's followers Wahhabis. Tracing the rise of Muhammad bin Abdul Wahhab of Arabia and the subsequent defeat of the 'Wahhabis' by Muhammad Ali Pasha, he explained as to how his followers in Arabia, like those of Sayyid Ahmad in India, were dubbed 'Wahhabis' due to ulterior motives.[106] The growth of Wahhabi influence in Bhopal during this period is clearly traceable to his position and influence.

As for Rangoon, it was reported that there was frequent correspondence between the Wahhabis there and those of Bhopal. One of Muhammad Hasan's sons was said to have gone there. It would be of interest to recall here the episode of some Tibetan Muslims meeting Sayyid Ahmad at Patna.[107] They had taken *Bai'at* at his hands and were authorised to go back and initiate converts there. On his return from *Hajj*, Sayyid Ahmad too met some men from Tibet at Calcutta and was glad to know from them that his work was being continued there. Again, we find that among the many foreign students of Nazir Husain there were some from China and Tibet.[108] These brief, scattered references to the spread of Sayyid Ahmad's teaching to such unexpected areas deserve to be noted. The men concerned were probably the traders who came in large numbers to

India, and they belonged to the western parts of China with a large Muslim population. Their influence, however, does not seem to have taken deep roots. Difficulties of regular contact and communication prevented its further growth.

(ix) Revival of Wahhabi Activities in Shahabad and Northern Bihar: 1882

In 1880 Badiuzzaman (of Dacca ?) tried to arrange a meeting [109] of the prominent Wahhabis to which Nazir Husain was also to be invited. The latter, aware of the police surveillance, had advised against it being held at Delhi and had suggested some remote village instead. Ibrahim [110] of Arrah suggested Tajpur, a village near Muzaffarpur, as the venue. Thirty prominent 'Wahhabi Maulvis' attended the meeting, of which the chief object was to plan a strategy for 'spreading sedition.' It was also decided to raise funds for various 'sectarian purposes.' Schools were to be opened at Delhi, Patna and Arrah in which the Wahhabi tenets would be taught. Books and pamphlets were also to be printed for distribution. Printed appeals for subscription: were distributed at the meeting and sent to other places. The response was encouraging, and even poor people, such as tailors, washermen and water-carriers had sent subscriptions. Some of the Maulvis present were asked to go out on tours, and Ibrahim himself had travelled to Delhi, Lucknow, Ghazipur, Benaras and Calcutta and delivered lectures there.

Another meeting [111] of the Wahhabis was held at Sirajganj where Nazir Husain had gone under the pretence of attending his niece's marriage. The ceremony provided a convenient excuse for an assemblage of the Wahhabis. Prominent among those who attended were Nazir Husain, Muhammad Husain of Lahore and Ibrahim of Arrah. The meeting had been convened by Ibrahim 'with the object of securing their co-operation and ... proclaiming this country as Dar-ul-Harb.' It was also decided that efforts should be made to send more volunteers and funds to the Wahhabi centres at the Frontier which had become weak due to lack of aid from India. News of the secret meeting had leaked to the authorities, but the magistrate's attempt to take the Wahhabis by surprise failed, and nothing incriminating was uncovered on searching the place and no one was arrested.

Ibrahim in his speeches at Calcutta[112] had stressed that it was incumbent on all Muslims *to resign from Government service,* and that it was better *to work in non-Government jobs at half the wages than to work under Government for double the wages for the same sort of job.*

It was pointed out that Ibrahim used "all the methods of agitation, disturbance, law-suits, raising of subscription, *inciting Government servants to resign in a way which would tell upon the Sepoys.*"[113] It was also reported that Ibrahim was collecting funds "by a sort of income-tax of one pice in the rupee." The *Begum* of Bhopal was one of the prominent contributors to the fund which was being raised ostensibly for financing a civil suit [114] in which the Wahhabis of Arrah district were engaged, but it was really meant for the 'Sittana fanatics'.[115]

It may be added here that Ibrahim played a pioneering role in the re-organisation of the *madrasa* education and the introduction of an institutional sense among the *Ulama.*[116] He established an association, *Mudhākra-i 'Ilmiya,* at Arrah. At its annual meetings papers on educational and cultural topics were read and discussed. He also administered the *Madrasa-i Aḥmadiya* established at Arrah in 1890, with arrangements for the teaching of Englih and a hostel for the boarders.[117] The *madrasa* suffered after Ibrahim's death in A.H. 1322 (1904-05), and was transferred to Darbhanga where it continues as *Madrasa-i Ahmadiya Salafiyya.*[118]

To resume the account, inquiries against Ibrahim were continued in the following year, and it was reported [119] that Ibrahim, along with Abdul Aziz of Rahimabad,[120] district Darbhanga, Azmat Husain, *Mukhtar* of Calcutta, Abdul Rauf, nephew of Abdul Rahim and Latif Husain and his brother, Abdul Ghafoor of Mehdawan,[121] were continuing the collection of funds. The amount collected the year before totalled well over Rs. 10,000. It was distributed by Ibrahim, but it was not known where he deposited it. Of the amounts collected only a very small portion was spent for schools and such other professed objects. The bulk remained unaccounted for and was probably sent to the Frontier.

Summing up, it was stated that the Wahhabis in general were in straitened circumstances owing to the conviction of their leaders in 1870-71, and earlier in 1862-65, but that there was a deep undercurrent of resentment among them against the convictions. This resentment may break out against the Government whenever they may have the power to do so."

This, in fact, was an apt appraisal of the position of the Wahhabis in India in the closing decades of the last century. Relentlesly pursued by the powerful police organisation of the Government, almost crippled under successive blows of conviction and deportation, the Wahhabis and their followers had been rendered practically innocuous. And yet such was the impact of what they had done in the preceding half-a-century that the Government felt apprehensive of even this weakened organisation for a long time after 1870—a year which marks the end of the Wahhabis' struggle in India.

2. Controversy regarding the Use and Abuse of the Term "Wahhabi": Its Discontinuance in Official Documents.

A lively, often vitriolic, disussion has continued, through the medium of books, pamphlets and periodicals on the implications of the term 'Wahhabi', and its application to the followers of Sayyid Ahmad in India. Wahhabis have been subjected to a double onslaught; firstly, from the British officials and others who viewed them as conspirators and rebels, and secondly, from some Indian Muslims themselves who criticised them strongly on the ground of being *ghair muqallid,* and for believing British India to be a *Dāru'l Ḥarb.* Sayyid Ahmad's followers were quick to refute these arguments.

The publication of Hunter's book *The Indian Mussalmans,* gave added weight to the opinion of the first-mentioned group of critics. Hunter maintained that there were links between the reform movement in Arabia led by Muhammad bin Abdul Wahhab and that in India led by Sayyid Ahmad, and that the Wahhabis in India had a moral obligation [122] to rebel against the government. Hunter's thesis was challenged from two distinct quarters. Sir Sayyid Ahmad Khan, in a long review of Hunter's book, asserted that all the Muslims were not anti-British, nor anti-Government, and that there was nothing specifically anti-government in the Wahhabi Movement in India.[123] On the other hand, we have the case of Muhammad Jafar Thanesari, a convict of the Ambala Trial in the far-off Andaman Islands, who on hearing of the publication of Hunter's book managed to procure a copy from Calcutta and refuted some of the points made in it.[124]

As regards the criticism of the other group, the Wahhabis wrote extensively on the various points in their own defence. An early and fairly exhaustive example of such writings is Murtaza Khan Rampur's work, *Dāfi'u'l Fasād Nāfi'u'l Ibād Qāṭi'u'l Shirk wa'l Bid'āt.*[125] The writer maintains that Sayyid Ahmad himself was a *Ḥanafi,* had taken *Bai'at* at *Shah* Abdul Aziz's hands in the *Naqahbandi* Order, and that he had praised all the four *madhāhib* in the *Sirātu'l Mustaqīm.*[126]

Nawab Siddiq Hasan Khan *Wālā Jāh* of Bhopal was another such writer.[127] Giving a resume of the career and activities of Muhammad bin Abdul Wahhab, he pointed out that there was no link between his ideas and activities and those of Sayyid Ahmad. There were only four recognised *madhāhib* among the Muslims, and the Arabian reformer Muhammad bin Abdul Wahhab was the follower of the *Hambali madhhab.* If his so-called followers in India were to be called after him, they should be called *Muḥammadī* rather than Wahhabi. None of the Arabian reformer's books had been published in India, nor were any one of these taught in any *madrasa* in India. How could, then, his influence spread into India ? The use of the term 'Wahhabis' in relation to the followers of Sayyid Ahmad was uncalled for; in fact, it was a sort of religio-political abuse.[128] Fazal Rasul Badauni was the first person who used 'Wahhabi' in a derogatory sense, and gave it currency.[129]

Continuing, he pointed out that Sayyid Ahmad himself had not used the term Wahhabi in his writings or utterances, nor did his followers call themeselves Wahhabis, unlike the *Shīa's* who insisted on using it to distinguish them from the Sunnis.[130] A more apt term for Sayyid Ahmad's followers was *Ahl-i-Ḥadīth.* In the sense of a follower of the *Ḥadīth,* the term was as old as Islam itself, whereas the term Wahhabi was used for extraneous purposes. This was also indicated by the fact that Wahhabi did not have a common, widely accepted, meaning; it had acquired new meanings in different parts of the country. To the followers of Fazal Rasul, a Wahhabi was one who did not worship the *pīrs* and the tombs, and disowned all *Bid'āt;* in Lucknow, Kanpur and Delhi, a Wahhabi was not a follower of the Ḥanafī *madhhab,* or any particular *madhhab,* but followed the *Qu'rān* and the *Ḥadīth;* in Bombay a Wahhabi was not a disciple of Shaikh Abdul Qadir Jilani, did not cry out *'al 'Idroos'* on boarding a ship, and did not seek help when in distress; in Hyderabad, Deccan a Wahhabi was one who did not drink fermented wine and did not attend the *'urs* ceremonies and fairs; sometimes a Wahhabi had a long beard, clipped moustache and wore short-length trousers. He did not hold the ceremonies of *Mīlād* and the *Fātiḥa* of the 11th of the month of *Rabi'u'l Thānī* in commemoration of the *'urs* of Shaikh Abdul Qadir Jilani; in Bhopal, a Wahhabi did not construct (and take out) *Ta'zia,* did not go to Ajmer or Makanpur, read and teach the *Qu'rān* in translation, and did not partake food distributed in the *nadhar* and *niyāz* ceremonies.[131]

Along with these public discussions the Wahhabis made representations to the higher government authorities too. They defended themselves against the charge of their opponents, particularly of being 'anti-government' as a group. A petition along these lines was submitted to the Lieutenant Governor, Punjab in 1876. The Lieutenant Governor, in reply, expressed satisfaction that the Wahhabis had considered it necessary to explain the position. He added that although the petitioners had expressed oppostion to their being called Wahhabi, he was using the term only because it was widely prevalent, and not at all in a pejorative manner. The Government would not view them with suspicion and hostility as long as their activities were not subversive. As for the opposition to them from other Sunni Muslims on points of rituals, etc. the Government could not do much; it was something they should settle among themselves.

Such effort continued. The lead was taken by Maulana Aby Sayeed Muhammad Husain of Batala who got a petition signed by members of the *Jamā'at-i Ahl-i Ḥadīth* and submitted it to the Governor-General through the Lieutnant Governor, Punjab. The Government of India after due consultations, ordered in 1886 that the term Wahhabi should not be used in official correspondence.[132] Similar instructions were sent to the Governments of Bombay, Madras, Bengal and the North-Western Provinces[133] during 1888-1890. The appellation, however retained popular currency.

3. The Wahhabis on the N.W.Frontier, 1863-1902

After the battle of Ambeyla (1863) the Wahhabis led by Abdullah had moved over to the Chagerzai country, north of the Brandu river, where they settled in the two villages of Tangor and Batora, and stayed there till 1868.[134] This had been arranged through the help of the *Akhund*, whose relations with the Wahhabis, though cordial on the surface, were not without problems. There was a tussle for spheres of influence between the *Akhund* and another spiritually eminent personality of the area, Sayyid Amir, popularly known as *Mullah* of Kotha.[135] The Wahhabis got involved in the tussle for influence between the *Akhund* and the *Mullah* of Kotha because they constituted an armed disciplined body of men whose alliance could be of great advantage to either of the two. The *Mullah* had been one of the early associates of Sayyid Ahmad, and the *Akhund* tried to make use of the Wahhabis against the former's followers. The term Wahhabi had acquired an unsavoury connotation, particularly among the common folk of the area, and the *Akhund* considered it be to be a convenient stick to beat the Kotha *Mullah* with.

The stay of the Wahhabis in the Chagarzai country, though comparatively undistrubed, was not quite free from trouble. They were harassed by the tribesmen, often under the promptings of the *Akhund.*[136] They, therefore, readily accepted an offer of help from Azim Khan of Bajkatta, in Buner, and moved over from Batora to Bajkatta. Their arrival in Buner further increased the *Akhund'* hostility, because he considered it to be his own area of influence, and because Azim Khan was a supporter of the *Mullah.* The *Akhund* called a meeting of the Bonair tribemen, and by 'skilful management' persuaded them to expel 'the Hindustanis'[137] from Buner. For a time, the Wahhabis and Azim Khan repaired to their old centre at Malka and commenced rebuilding their houses and fortifications. A short-lived reconciliation was effected when Abdullah met the *Akhund* and worked out an agreement for the return of the Wahhabis to Bajkatta. But the renewed attempt of Azim Khan and Muqarrab Khan, the dispossessed chief of Panjtar, to forge an alliance with a section of the Bonair and Amzai tribesmen opposed to the *Akhund* finally led to an open conflict. The *Akhund* appeared before Bajkatta, and demanded an expulsion of the Wahhabis who had joined the alliance against him. An evacuation was agreed to, and while the evacuees were passing through a narrow defile between Bajkatta and Batore they were treacherously attacked by the *Akhund* followers. The main body, including Abdullah and Azim Khan, ran the gauntlet and crossed the pass, but the rear-guard was "cut off and after a gallant stand entirely destroyed."[138] After the encounter, the Wahhabis stayed for some time at Gulima Bari in the Chagerzai area, as they received assurance of support by the Amzais and connection of Chagarzais opposed to the *Akhund.* But this proved to be only a temporary relief, and once again the Wahhabis set out in search of a new base. They stayed for some time in Bihar on the right bank of the Indus, and moved to Judbai towards the end of 1868. The chief of Tikari extended some help, and handed over to them his fort and some land in the valley. The chief of Thakot and the Ala'i *jirga* also sought their help in discussing "measures of a resistance against the British.' The latter were watching these moves, and before the allies could move, Major-General Wilde took them by surprise, and the allies quickly dispersed.[139]

Thus, we find that during the years immediately following the battle of Ambeyla the Wahhabis were constantly shifting from one place to another under adverse circumstances. But their military organisation and the resolve to fight against the British government was not shaken.

Some information[140] is available about their surviving leaders, the military units, their relations with the *Akhund*, etc. during the period when they were staying in Bihar across the Indus. Chief among them, besides Abdullah, were Faiyyaz Ali, brother of Ahmadullah, and Amanullah, Matiullah and Abdul Quddus, the sons of Abdullah. Another important person was Ishaq, brother of Maqsud Ali. Their fighting force was divided into eight units, each under a *Jama'dār*. These units were led by Rajab Diyanatullah of Malda, Abdul Ghafur of Hakimpur, Muinuddin and Shariatullah of Rampur Baulesh, Nooruddin of Jessore and Muhammad Akbar of Azimghur. The fighting men of sepoys numbered 362, of whom 57 came from Arrah and Gazipur. There were 70 women and children. They had 27 horses and 27 mules, which were kept in Balooah. They were also reported to have two small guns, some percussion muskets with bayonets.[141] The shortage of funds, however, had led to a state of general distress. This, it was stated, was forcing some of the 'Hindustanis' to desert, but Abdullah had impressed upon them the fact that only 'the prison and the gallows' awaited those who returned.

It was recommended that it would be advantageous if it was proclaimed by the government that all those who returned, except Fayyaz Ali and Abdullah, would be pardoned. That would set in a wave of defection among Abdullah's men and he would be left practically alone and would, probably, retire to Mecca.[142]

The government communication added that the Hasanzais had invited the Hindustanis with offers of land to settle in. The acceptance of invitation had been delayed by the illness of Abdullah. As soon as he recovered there was no doubt "he would be fighting against us." In fact, it seemed strange to Reily, who was then collecting evidence for the trial of Wahhabis in India, that evidence should be required "that these fanatics are waging war with the Queen; *they are in a state of continued hostility against the English. Their professed object is to drive out the English, their attitude is one of perpetual hostility.*"[143]

Another interesting piece of information[144] related to the reported offer of Faiyyaz Ali in March 1869 that if his brothers Ahmadullah and Yahya Ali, who had been transported to the Andaman Islands, and Ibrahim Mandal, then held under detention, were released by the British Government, he and his followers would cease fighting and go over to Malda. The expenses for their journey would have to be borne by the government. It is not known as to how the government reacted to this proposal, but a section of the officers was in favour of letting the waverers return, and isolating the leaders.

The question of the policy to be adopted by the government in permitting some of the Wahhabis on the Frontier to return home, cropped up again in 1873 when the government received certain proposals from Elahi Bakhsh, brother of Maqsud Ali of Surajgarha, and Muhammad Hasan, son of Wilayat Ali. This was not exactly an offer of surrender.[145] Rather, they wanted certain guarantees from the government, including immunity from reprisals after their return. The Magistrate, Patna, felt that although the Wahhabis were no longer "a significant body of men," their presence on the Frontier was a great 'evil," unsettling the minds of the "ignorant and superstitious Mohammadans."[146] He wanted the government to agree to the grant of unconditional pardon to those who wanted to return, but the Commissioner was more conscious of the government's prestige. He was not in favour of an unconditional pardon. He suggested [147] the laying down of two conditions - firstly, that all the Wahhabis, including their leaders, should return and not just those who wanted to do so and, secondly, that those who returned would live within certain specified areas under police surveillance. At the same time, he added that all this discussion was premature since the government had received no formal offer of surrender from the Wahhabis and it was "certainly not the part of the Government to take initiative in such matters."

Ishree Prasad also prepared a comprehensive memorandum for the Commissioner on the subject of the Wahhabis and the grant of pardon to them. He emphasised the important point that "the Mujahedeen were in a country from which they could not derive their subsistence. They must anyhow be supported by the contributions from this country." So long as the centre on the Frontier existed, he pointed out, the leaders there would continue inciting the Wahhabis inside British India to seditious activities. He did not share the common belief that after waiting or some time for the supposed re-appearance of Sayyid Ahmad the Wahhabis on the Frontier would lose heart and return on their own. They might, be argued, also select another 'Prophet'. The *Akhund* of Swat was widely respected in the Frontier, as was Abdullah. He might try to win over the *Akhund*, an old man "on the verge of the grave" (sic) and try to succeed him. He would then command the allegiance of a very large number of Pathans and use them in anti-government activities.[148] Ishree Prasad discounted the possibility of Abdullah being a Wahhabi coming in the way of his succession to the *Akhund*, for "the *Akhund* himself is a Gujar, perhaps a Hindu by caste." It was, therefore, advisable to let all the Wahhabis return to their homes, "loaded with shame and disgrace." Their return itself would remove the halo of glory, and expose the weakness of their cause.

Nothing, however, came out of these premature discussions. Abdullah had already suffered many a hardship and reverse in his long struggle with the government, and he was not likely to falter at the fag end of his career. The government on the other hand, was not willing to take any initiative in the matter which might hurt its prestige. Moreover, it was not willing to permit only some of the rank and file to return and let the leaders remain on the Frontier. That in its opinion, would leave the wounds festering.

After the encounter of 1868-69, the Wahhabis had shifted to Palosi, a village belonging to the trans-Indus Hasanzais. They stayed there for a long time, enjoying a much-needed respite from the constant shifting to which they had been subjected to by the hostility of the *Akhund* and some of the tribesmen under his influence. During this period they had got involved in a sectarian clash of interest between the *Akhund* and the *Mullah*. This had a rather demoralising effect on them. They came to feel that they had got bogged down in tribal conflicts and had moved away from their mission.[149]

The Wahhabis still, had the great advantage of being better armed and trained. That along with their "superior intelligence" gave them a degree of influence.[150] Abdullah once again tried to resume contacts with the anti-British tribes and to continue the struggle with their help and co-operation.[151]

The period of Abdullah's *Imārat* spanned four decades, and his finest hour was the Ambeyla Campaign. The real test of his leadership, however, came during the period following that. He had to face an unbroken chain of adversities, and the hostilities of the tribesmen, but he refused to entertain any idea of surrendering, and had effectively countered the first signs of wavering which, reportedly, had manifested itself momentarily among his followers.

After his death (1901), his brother Abdul Karim was elected *Amīr*, and under him the centre shifted to Asmast (1902), a fertile village situated on the bank of the river Brandu. By now effective and regular contact with the centres in British India had ceased and although the Wahhabi centre on the North-Western Frontier continued to exist,[152] it got merged in the local political surroundings.

Notes

1. Letters from D.I.G., to P.A. to the I.G., Police, L.P., nos. 287 and 319 dated 13th October and 2nd November 1868, respectively.
2. The two towns are situated opposite each other across the Ganges, and the two centres worked in close collaboration. Rajmahal formerly belonged to the Malda district of Bengal but now forms part of the Santhal Pargana district of Bihar.
3. Letter from D.I.G., dated 2nd November 1868 cited above.
4. It was during this time, when he came to conduct an enquiry into the working of the Wahhabi centre, that his interest in the subject was aroused. Later, with the Malda Trial opened he was appointed chief prosecuting officer and was awarded Rs. 3000/- for the able prosecution of the case (Government of Bengal, Judicial Dept., nos. 118 of October, 1870 and no. B. 46 of October, 1871). Soon after, he contributed his long article on the Wahhabis in *The Calcutta Review,* vol. 1, 1870.
5. These were, Nazir Sardar of village, Qazigram, Abdul Wahid of Lakhipur, Ghuran Khan of Muazzapur, Jamuran Shaikh of Lakhopur, Burno Ghazi of Muazzampur, Soorkhun Mallah of Agamilkee, Nawazi Mullah of Muazzampur, and Dhokan Mullah of Agamilkee.
6. *infra,* pp.
7. Letter from Magistrate, Malda, to Officiating Under Secretary, Government of Bengal, Judicial Dept. no. 424, dated 20th October, 1869; also letter from D.I.G., to I.G., Police, L.P., no. 13 Conf., dated 16th April, 1869.
8. Letter from Magistrate, Malda, referred to above.
9. The last, 30th, *juz'* of the *Qur'ān,* beginning with the *Sārah, 'Amma Yatasā'lūn,* and containing the shorter *Sūrahs* with which the boys begin the recitation of the *Qur'ān.* The book was printed in Misriganj in A.H. 1280/1863-64.
10. Letter from Offg. Suptd. and Legal Remembrancer to Secretary, Government of Bengal, no. 1859, dated Fort William, 30th October, 1869.
11. *The Records of the Bengal Government no. XLII* (Papers connected with the trial of Moulvie Ahmedoollah of Patna, and others for Conspiracy and Treason). Calcutta, Alipore Jail Press, 1866.

12. See App. V for extracts from its text.
13. Letter from Offg. Secretary, Government of Bengal to Secretary, Government of India, no. 6051 dated 10 November, 1868.
14. The doctor reported that the room was "damp and badly ventilated. There is no *charpoy* (bed) to sleep on, there is no night privy attached to it; one end of the room is used for that purpose. This latter arrangement could not but render it at times quite disagreeable and hurtful as a bedroom." (Letter from R.C.Chandra, Civil Asst. Surgeon, Santhal Pargana to Commissioner, Rajmahal, no. 240, dated Deoghar, 17 October, 1869.

    It has to be remembered that this was the treatment meted out to a prisoner arrested under Regulation III of 1818, the preamble of which laid down that 'suitable provision' should be made according to the 'rank in life' of the prisoner, and that 'due attention' should be paid to the health of the prisoner. Further, the officers in charge of the jails had been instructed that the prisoners concerned were to be treated as state prisoners, not criminals (Government of Bengal, Judicial Dept. Proceeding no. 184, July 1869; I.G., p. 102).
15. Statement made before C.M.Wilmot, Asstt. Commissioner, Santhal Parganas, on 30th November, 1868. Enclosure to letter from D.I.G., to I.G., Police, L.P., no. 399, dated 28th November, 1868.
16. Letter from D.I.G. referred to above; also see Appendix VI.
17. Letter from Secretary, Government of Bengal, to I.G., Police, L.P., no. 198, dated 11th January, 1869.
18. Government of Bengal, Judicial Dept., Proceedings no. 49 of June, 1869; for an account of the earlier period see *supra*, pp.105-06, 190. Also Government of Bengal, Judicial Proceedings no. 37 of September, 1860.
19. Letter from Major F.G.Stuart, S.P., Raipur, to I.G., Police, L.P., dated Raipur, 28th September, 1869.
20. Ibid.
21. Ibid.
22. He was one of the important leaders of the Movement of 1857-59 in Bihar and had played a stirring role in and outside that state (see my article "Maulvi Ali Kureem: A School-Soldier of Bihar during the Movement of 1857-59," IHRC, vol. XXXIII 1958, pp. 9-15).

    He had later gone over to Bhopal, and the warrant of arrest pending against him was withdrawn at the intercession of the Begum of Bhopal, and he returned to Patna.
23. Letter from Reily, D.I.G., to I.G., Police, L.P. no. 324, dated 1st December, 1869.
24. Government of Bengal, Judicial Dept., Proceedings no. 37, September, 1869. Emphasis added.

25. Letter from J. Jardine, Acting Under Secretary, Government of Bombay, to Secretary, Government of Bengal, Judicial Dept., no. 3999, dated Bombay Castle, 12th November, 1869.
26. Government of Bengal, Judicial Dept. Proceedings no. 314 of January, 1869.
27. Letter from D.I.G., to I.G. Police, L.P., no. 52, dated Delhi, 13th February, 1869.
28. Ibid.
29. Firuz Shah was a cousin of Bahadur Shah II, the last Mughal emperor of India, being the son of a brother of Akbar Shah II. He had gone for *Hajj*, and having returned during the Rising of 1857-58 had taken a leading part in it. After its suppression he had gone to the N.W.Frontier and was there for some time with the Wahhabis.
30. Reily derisively wrote this of Izad Bakhsh: "Anyone in Delhi may buy a yard of calico from one of the Princes of Delhi. So passes the Glory of the World."
31. The following account is based on his biographical study by Fazal Husain, *Al-Hayat Ba'd Al-Mamat*, Agra, 1908.
32. His son, Sharafat Husain (b. 1833) predeceased him at the age of 57 in 1887.
33. The precinct of *Masjid-i-Aurangabadi*, where he had first stayed and taken lessons on his arrival at Delhi, served as his *madrasa* for the next half a century. The mosque was demolished in connection with the extension of railways. Sir Sayyid refers to it and to Nazir Husain's lectures in *Atharu's Sanadid.*
34. In a Supplement to the above-noted work, Fazal Husain gives a list of 500 students of Nazir Husain, arranged province-wise and district-wise for those belonging to India. These belonging to foreign countries came from such places as Kabul, Qandahar, Ghazni, Kashghar, Tibet, Hijaz and Nejd.

    Among the former group, one who became a famous scholar of *Ḥadīth*, was Shamsu'l Haque (A.H. 1273-1329/1856-1911), of village Dianwan, district Patna. After staying at Delhi for some years, he returned to Patna and devoted himself to teaching and writing. He is the author of several books in Arabic, Persian and Urdu, including *'Awnu'l Ma'būd*, a *tadhkirah* of *Ulama* and a collection of his own *fatāva.*
35. Faral Husain, *op. cit.*, p. 81. This perhaps has a reference to the introduction of the post-card, following which the Post Master General had reported that formerly fewer people wrote letters @ 1/2 an anna, but since the introduction of the post-card, more-people wrote letters, and there had been an increase in postal income.

36. Government of Bengal, Judicial Dept. Proceedings no. 219 of April, 1869.
37. He received the title of *Shamsul Ulama* in 1897.
38. Letter from D.I.G., to I.G. Police, L.P., no. 335, dated 10th December 1869.
39. Letter from Secretary, Government of Bengal, to Secretary, Government of Punjab, no. 87, dated 7th January, 1870.
40. *Infra*, pp. 352, 355-56.

    Nazir Husain on to the ripe old age of 97, and died in 1902. His death was widely reported in the local Urdu press, and mourned as a great loss to Islamic learning.

    He was a very prolific writer, and wrote 57 important works. These are in addition to the hundreds of *Fatawa* written or dictated by him in answer to all sorts of queries. His biographer quotes his remark made 27 years before his death that if all his *Fatawa* were to be compiled they would be several times more than the volume of the famous *Fatāwa-i Ālamgari*. He adds, however, that the *Fatāwa* of Nazir Husain given during the last quarter century of his life do not always correctly represent his personal views. Age seemed to have affected his faculties, and his seal was easily available to any one of his students. Where the *Fatāwa* of this period appeared to be contrary to those of an earlier period, the latter were to be preferred. (*op. cit.*, Supplement).
41. Letter from Magistrate Delhi to Deputy Commissioner, Delhi, dated 19th March, 1869.
42. Letter from D.I.G. to I.G., Police, L.P., no. 3 Conf. dated Bankipur, 16th April, 1869; see also pp. 318 above.
43. James Routledge, *English Rule and Native Opinion in India from Notes Taken*, 1870-78, London, 1878, p. 69. For further comments on the writer and the book, see *infra*, p. 344, n.1.
44. Letter from E.E.Lewis, Magistrate, Malda, to Commissioner, Rajshahi, no. 234, dated 12th April, 1869.
45. Letter from Secretary, Government of Bengal, to the Secretary, Government of India, Home Department no. 2813, dated 22nd April, 1869.
46. *I.M.*, p. 100.
47. Statement given by Abdullah, *vide infra*.
48. Letter from D.I.G. to I.G., Police, L.P., no. 185, dated Calcutta 25th June, 1869.
49. Letter from Magistrate, Patna, to Commissioner, Patna, dated 1st June, 1869.
50. Later, he was transferred to the Bhagalpur jail (letter from Secretary, Government of Bengal, to I.G., Police, L.P., no. 4753, dated 28th June, 1869.

51. Letter from S.P. Patna, to D.I.G. Police, L.P., dated Patna 31st November, 1869.
52. Statement of Sheikh Jhagroo, 58, son of Faqir Muhammad of Dinapur, taken under Act V of 1840 before the Cantonment Magistrate, Dinapur, on 21 June 1869; Enclosure to letter from D.I.G. to I.G. Police, L.P., no. 195, dated 25 June, 1869.
53. The statement gives additional proof of the fact that the Indian regiments occupied an important place in the Wahhabi scheme of work. Not only were the men in the units subjected to a careful indoctrination, the movement of the regiments themselves were skilfully utilised to help perform one of the most difficult and dangerous tasks. The Wahhabis believed in bold tactics; who would look for 'traitors' and 'enemy agents' following right in the wake of the army units ?
54. These men were, Haji Din Muhammad, Peer Muhammad, Budhu Khan, Abdul Rahman, Karim, Khuda, Elahi Bakhsh, Budhye Khan, Umelu Khan, Ali Hasan and Sukhu. Some persons from Bengal including Mithu Pramanik, and Jublu of Murshidabad and Ghuran Khan of Malda were also arrested.
55. Letter from D.I.G. to I.G. Police, L.P., no. 279, dated August, 1869.
56. Letter from Secretary Government of India, Home Dept., to Secretary, Government of Bengal, no. 1232, dated Simla, 27th August, 1869.
57. The information against him was given by his nephew, Azizu'l Haque.

    See letters from Officiating I.G. Police, L.P., to Secretary, Government of Bengal, Judicial Dept. no. 7628, dated 9th October, 1869; and letter from Commissioner, Patna to Secretary, Government of Bengal, no. P, dated 10th December, 1869.
58. Government of Bengal, Judicial Dept. Proceedings no. 65 of November, 1869.
59. Ibid.
60. Ibid.
61. *vide infra,* p. 366.
62. Letter from J.H.Reily, D.I.G. Police to I.G. Police, L.P., no. 207 dated 13th October, 1869. Encl.
63. He was the son-in-law of Sayyid Ahmad, also see *infra,* p. 353, n. 1.
64. Letter from Secretary, Government of Bengal, to Secretary, Government of India, Home Dept. no. 4687, dated 26th July, 1869.
65. Government of Bengal, Judicial Dept. Proceedings nos. 7-8 and 11 of January, 1870.
66. Government of Bengal, Judicial Dept. Proceedings no. 52 of August, 1870.

67. *Selections*, p. 155.
68. Government of Bengal, Judicial Dept. Proceedings nos. 46-48 of August, 1870.
69. *Selections*, p. 157.
70. Government of Bengal, Judicial Dept. Proceedings nos. 193-94 of May, 1870.
71. Government of Bengal, Judicial Dept., Proceedings nos. 209-11 of June, 1870.
72. Ibid., Proceedings nos. 27-28 of August, 1870.
73. The information was given by a man belonging to the same village, a disciple of 'a rival Hanfi Moulvi', Muhammad Fasih of Ghazipur.
74. He belonged to village Dehree, P.S. Masaurhi, district Patna, and was the son of Musharraf Ali. He was reporting against his father in the hope of getting a government job.
75. Enclosure to letter from J.H. Reily to I.G. Police, L.P., dated 7th August, 1870.
76. Letter from Magistrate, Patna, dated 23rd July, 1870.
77. *Supra*, p. 202.

    Rahat Ali had three sisters, one of whom was married to Imdad Ali, *Sadar Amin*, Tirhut. Imdad Ali had two sons, Najmuddin and Wahiduddin; the former served for some time as *Sarishtadār* of the Patna Opium Agency and *Diwan* of Raja of Bettiah. He was arrested by Tayler in 1857 for suspected anti-government activities. The sons of the second sister of Rahat Ali were Farzand Ali, Pleader, Chapra Civil Court; Munshi Ismail and Abdul Karim, both of whom were employed in the Judge's Court, Patna, and Abdul Wahab, about whose employment nothing is mentioned. The third sister's son was Muhammad Umar, whose two brothers, Muhammad Yahya and Muhammad Sadiq were *Munsif*, Patna, and Keeper of Records, Judge's Court, Patna, respectively. All of them were suspected to be active sympathisers of the Wahhabis (Letter from Ishree Prasad, Deputy Magistrate, to Commissioner, Patna, dated 27th August, 1870.
78. Letter from Magistrate, Patna, to Commissioner, Patna, dated 23rd August, 1870.
79. A perceptive Englishman, James Routledge, then present in the country, and studying Indian public opinion with reference to some important contemporary events, was present at some of the hearings and took notes. His observations on the Wahhabi trials at Malda (1870) and at Patna (1871) are very valuable from various points of view. The eloquence of his tribute to the fortitude of Amirud Din and his father Rafique Mandal, his empathy for the plight of Amir Khan and Hashmat Dad Khan, and, more importantly, his considered personal opinion on the assassination of

Justice Norman provide useful pieces of contemporary information on the subject. This information has not been noticed at all, and the present writer too had not come across Routledge's book earlier. The various remarks within quotation marks appearing in the account below are all from this book (pp 69-74) unless otherwise specified.

80. Some members of the family still live in *mahalla* Pathan Toli, Alamganj, Patna City.
81. Routledge writes that he was once told by "a highly honourable European merchant in Calcutta," who had met Amir Khan for a business transaction, that he found Amir Khan "seated luxuriously in a sort of state, on a dais.' No one could approach it without taking off his shoes. The European had not done that, but the story showed the manner of Amir Khan's living.

    The same man saw Amir Khan later in jail, "picking jute or oakum in the great gaol of Calcutta...(He) incessantly muttered something to himself and glanced...furtively from under a very contracted forehead" (p.73).
82. Government of Bengal, Judicial Dept. Proceedings nos. 32 and 37 of January and April, 1870, respectively.
83. A leading legal practitioner of Calcutta, he also acted for some time as a Judge of the High Court, and died at Bombay in 1873.
84. He later became a Member of the Governor General's Council from 1877 to 1899.
85. For the details of the legal arguments, see *The Great Wahhabi Case,* an anonymous publication.
86. Routledge, *op. cit.*, p. 72.
87. While the hearings were continuing, a case was filed on behalf of the petitioners against the Governor General Lord Mayo and the Lieutenant Governor Lord Grey in a court in England for 'Oppression and Injury' caused by them to the petitioners. (*The Great Wahhabi Case,* p. 42). The outcome of the case is not known.
88. *The Great Wahhabi Case,* pp. 29, 30.
89. *Infra,* pp. 349 *ff.*
90. Routledge, *op. cit.*, pp. 72-74.
91. Routledge, who was present at the trial and took notes writes; "The Advocate-General wisely confined questions to proving the murder, and abandoned, if he ever had entertained, any hope of discovering the motive of the crime. That a very uneasy feeling prevailed throughout India is certain. People saw in the murder the beginning of a system of warfare in which one man of a body of thugs of a new order would draw a lot which would condemn him to give his life, if need be, to destory that of some distinguished Englishman. Looking at the circumstances of the case, with many

notes before me, I have no doubt that the cause of the murder was the Wahabee trials" (p.70). He also saw some connection between this event and the assassination later, in the Andaman Islands panel colony, of the Governor-General, Lord Mayo, for he went on to add that, "The idea of a new order of thugs passed away, but it was revived a little later by the murder of the Governor-General" (Lord Mayo).

It may be recalled here that William Tayler, the Divisional Commissioner of Patna in 1857, and an officer of some experience of dealing with the Wahhabis, refers to the efforts of some officers not well-inclined towards the Wahhabis trying to establish some connection between Norman's assassination and the Wahhabis (W. Tayler, *Thirty Eight Years in India,* vol. II, pp. 551, 561).

92. *supra,* p. 331.
93. Routledge, op. cit., pp. 70-71. Italics are mine. The prophetic note struck in these lines is remarkable.
94. *T.A.,* p. 82.
95. In the government records, too, relating to the release of the Wahhabi prisoners, there is no mention of Ibrahim.
96. *P.I.T.,* p. 155.
97. The magnificient house of Amir Khan in Colootola Street, Calcutta was sold and all his other valuable assets, worth millions, were seized. See Government of Bengal, Judicial Dept., Proceedings nos. B. 326-29, B. 224, B. 125 and B. 416-19 of April, June, August, July 1874 respectively. Also proceeding Nos. B. 208-09 of August 1875, B. 140-41, 301-02, of November, 1875 and B.1100-1101 of June 1875.

Only a small portion of the valuable property was left to Amir Khan's heir, Zorawar Khan. Later, his grandsons (daughter's sons) Muhammad Yahya Khan and Muhammad Zakariya Khan, were given educational stipends of Rs. 6/- each. It was subsequently increased to Rs. 13.8 per month for studying at Aligarh and Patna, to be enjoyed till the age of 21 years. Finally, Zakariya Khan was given a life pension of Rs. 10/- per month. (*A History of the Freedom Movement,* vol, II, 1831-1905, Part II, Board of Editors, Mahmud Husain, et. al., Pakistan Historical Society Publication, p. 15, Karachi, 1961.

98. *P.I.T.,* p. 158.
99. *T.A.,* p. 82.
100. This confidential enquiry was made by Ishree Prasad in December, 1875.
101. He was the *Nāib-i Awwal* or the *Wazir* of the state and a very influential man; see *Maāthir-i Siddīqi,* vol. III.

102. For a detailed documented biography see, Sayyid Muhammad Hasan Khan, *Maāthir-i-Siddīqī,* vols. I-IV, Lucknow, 1924-25.
103. In keeping with the generous treatment accorded to the widows and other family members of Sayyid Ahmad, as also to the Wahhabis in general, by the rulers of Tonk, a large *jagir* worth Rs. 11000 annually had been given to *Maulawi* Ismail. But the Nawab felt unhappy when he later married a member of the Nawab's own family. He cancelled the *jagir,* and gave him only a subsistence allowance of Rs. 100/- per month (*Mehr,* II, p.456).
104. She ascended the *gaddi* in 1868. Until 1885, when her husband was divested of his titles and powers, she ruled the state with him as a close adviser. She died in .....?
105. *Maāthir-i Siddīqī,* IV, has a supplement listing all his works, arranged alphabetically according to the letters of their titles, and nothing the date and place of their publication, language, subject, etc. The list has 222 entires exclusive of minor tracts written in reply to specific queries. The works are in Arabic, Persian and Urdu, and include a collection of his verses in Persian and Urdu. Most of those were published in the *Maātha-i Siddiqi,* one of the our printing presses in Bhopal, which he looked after. But so treat was the number of his works that it could not cope with it, and some were published in the *Mufid-i Ām* Press Akbarabad.
106. See his *Tarjumān-i Wahhabiyat* and other works.
107. *Supra,* chap.II, p. 60.
108. *Supra,* p. 319, n.1.
109. Abstracts of Secret Intelligence Reports, Calcutta Police; forwarded to Commissioner, Patna, by Lambert, Dy. Commissioner Police, Calcutta, vide memo no. 653, dated 23 February, 1881.
110. Abu Muhammad Ibrahim (A.H. 1264-1322/1847-1905), was the son of Abdul Ali Hakim, *Faujdārī Nāzir* of Arrah Court in 1857. Ibrahim's elder brother, Ali, had taken part in the Rising and had been arrested and sentenced to death. The father, whose duty it would have been to arrange for the hanging of his son, resigned his post. He died later, leaving behind landed property worth an annual income of Rs. 3000/-.

    Like Muhammad Umar, Muhammad Ibrahim was a well-connected man. He was related by marriage to the Sadiqpur family. He was a good organiser and speaker and had travelled extensively. He wrote several books including Fiqh-i *Muḥammadi,* and *al-Qaulu'l Muzid fi Ahkama't Taqlid.*
111. Abstracts of Secrect Intelligence Reports, vide memo no. 1463, dated 5th May, 1881.
112. Letter from P. Nolan, S.P. Police, Patna to the Commissioner, Patna, dated 6th July, 1881. Italics are mine.

113. This, it may be noted, is quite similar to the lines along which the Wahhabis had worked earlier, and this continuity indicates an organisational vitality and a strong sense of discipline.
114. It related to a dispute between the Sunnis and Wahhabis of Arrah for reciting *Āmīn* loudly in the public prayers a practice which often led to disputes and litigatios. In the present case the Sunnis had won in the lower court but the Wahhabis had appealed to the High Court.
115. Letter from G.H.Browne, Dy. Supdt. of Police, Delhi to the S.P., Patna, dated Delhi, 21st July, 1881.
116. Nawab Sayyid Ali Hasan Khan, Director of Education, Bhopal State, had constituted an Advisory Council, *Nazzāratu'l Ma'ārif,* in A.H. 1317 (1899-1900) to suggest inprovements in the educational and administrative set-up of the *madrasas.* Among the *Ulamas* invited from outside Bhopal State, were Shibli Nu'mani (1857-1914) and Ibrahim, and they had prepared a detailed scheme which was published subsequently; see the series of autobiographical articles by Sayyid Ali Hasan Khan in the *Ma'ārif;* see also Sayyid Sulaiman Nadvi, *Ḥayāt-i Shiblī,* Azamgarh, n.d., pp. 325 *ff.*
117. Ibrahim had invited Shibli Nu'mani to the *madrasa* and shown him the boarding arrangements. He was adivsed by the letter to visit Aligarh and see the arrangements there also. For references to the enrolment in the *madrasa,* its sllabi, etc. in the issue of a contemporary Urdu weekly, Al-punch, see J.S.Jha, Aspects of the *History of Modern Bihar,* Patna, 1988, pp. 91 *ff.*
118. The institution is now working under the supervision and guidance of Dr. Abdul Hafeez Sahib, a noted philanthropist and a former Amīr of *Ahl-i Ḥadīth,* Bihar.
119. Letter from J.P.Lal and Bahadur Husain, Inspectors of Police, to Col. R. Skinner, S.P., Shahabad, dated 21st March, 1882.
120. He was a student of Maulawi Nazir Husain of Delhi, and had a large number of *Ahl-i Ḥadith* followers in the districts of northern Bihar and in Bengal. Much later, when the leaders of the Silk Letters Conspiracy were organising an anti-government force, *Junūda'dah,* he was to be included in it.
121. Mehdawan is a village near Maner by the side of the main road from Patna to Dinapur. The ancestors of Elahi Bakhsh of Sadiqpur belonged to this place.
122. The first edition of Hunter's book (1871) was titled *The Indian Musalmans: Are they bound in conscience to rebel against the Queen?* In the second edition (1872) the sub-title was dropped.
123. See pp. 408-09 below.
124. *T.A.* Islamia Steam Press, Lahore, no date, pp. 88, 96-97; see also, *supra,* pp. 266,n.1,309.

125. It is a printed but very scarce work (hereinafter cited as *Māfi'u'l Fasād*). It was published from the *Matba'-i Muhammadi*, Tonk, A.H. 1282 (1865-66), and the references are from this edition.
126. Ibid., pp. 87-90, 93.
127. He wrote much on these points in his numerous works in Arabic and Persian. A summarised version of these points was presented in the *Tarjumān-i Wahhābiya, Matba'-i Mufid-i Āam*, Agra, A.H. 1300 (1882-83) from which these references have been cited.
128. *Tarjumān-i Wahhābiya*, p. 27.
129. *Ibid.*, p. 65; see also pp. 62 *ff.*
130. *Ibid.*, p. 27.
131. *Ibid.*, pp. 76 *ff.*

The writer has overstated his point a bit. The varying impressions about a Wahhabi among different groups of people, which he has enumerated, are indicative of a superficial, not-well-informed, view at the common man's level; they do not have much substance. In fact, a few of the characteristics listed are applicable to Muslims in general.

It may be of interest to note here that in the matter of transliterating the term 'Wahhabi', too, there are wide variations. A modern writer (Norman Daniel, *Islam, Europe and Empire*, Edinburgh, 1966, p.V) commenting on the difficulties of a standardised transliteration of Oriental terms on account of the pronounciations and spellings varying in the original languages, illustrates the point with a reference to this term, and enumerates the following ten variants - Wahabis, Wahhabis, Wahabys, Wahabees, Wayhabees, Wahebis, Vehebis, Wahauby, Vahabees, and Wahabiyin (the term he has himself used).

Hunter drew attention to the point much earlier, in 1871. Pointing out that in Arabic, Wahabi was spelt Wahhabi, he added that it had since become an Anglo-Indian term. In his book he used the term "Wahābi", accenting the middle syllable to show that it was long (*I.M.*, p. 57, n.1).
132. *Maāthir-i Siddiqi*, III, p. 162.
133. In 1901, after the constitution of the North-West Frontier Province, at first under a Chief Commissioner at Peshawar responsible directly to the Government of India, the large area so long called the North-Western Provinces (NWP) was re-named the Agra Province. Subsequently, the whole area including Awadh, came to be called United Provinces of Agra and Oudh (U.P) with headquarters at Allahabad and Nainital. The designation was rather inexact since the headquarters was at Allahabad, not Agra. Awadh was retained to placate local feelings against the merger of the Awadh territories in a larger unit; the government spending some time

each year at Lucknow, capital of the Awadh kingdom. After 1947, with the merger of the territories of some northern hill-states, the area was again re-named Uttar Pradesh (U.P.).

134. Paget & Mason, *op. cit.*, pp. 155-58.
135. Kotha is a place situated in the south-western part of the Yusufzai country. The *Mullah* enjoyed considerable influence in the Swat and Buner areas.
136. Faizullah's statement, *vide infra*.
137. Sayyid Ahmad's followers were commonly called Hindustanis by the tribesmen, and the British officers too often used this term for the Wahhabis on the Frontier during the period after 1850s.
138. Paget & Mason, *op. cit.*, pp. 155-58.
139. Ibid., also *supra*, p. 260.
140. This is based on the reports submitted by Reily when he visited the Frontier area during the investigations of 1868-69.
141. Paget & Mason, *op. cit.*, p. 158.
142. Letter from J.H.Reily, D.I.G.Police, to I.G. Police, L.P., no. 203, dated Abbottabad, 30th September, 1869.
143. Ibid., Italics are mine.
144. This was reported by Faizullah, who was deputed to the Frontier by the Deputy Commissioner, Abbottabad, at the same time when Reily was there. Faizullah maintained a diary, recording his observations during December, 1868-April 1869. The entries indicate continued hostility of the *Akhund*. This particular information regarding Faiyyaz Ali's reported offer is dated 30 March, 1869 (Reily's letter no. 203, cited above; Enclosure).
145. For one thing, the government was not quite sure as to how far they actually represented the views of the Wahhabis on the Frontier.
146. Letter from Magistrate, Patna, to Commissioner, Patna, dated 15 January, 1873.
147. Letter from Commissioner, Patna, to Secretary Government of Bengal, dated 17th January, 1873.
148. Ishree Prasad's speculation was not quite wild, as we know that Abdullah had once met the *Akhund*, and succeeded in removing his misgivings.
149. Faizullah's statement, referred to above.
150. Paget & Mason, *op. cit.*, p. 158.
151. *vide, supra*, pp. 261 *ff*.
152. As late as 1915-16, in connection with the Silk Letters Conspiracy, efforts were made by Mahmudul Hasan, the *Shaikhul Hird*, and Ubaidullah Sindhi to establish contacts with the Wahhabis on the Frontier; see Y.D.Prasad, *The Indian Muslims and World War I, A Phase in the Disillusionment with British Rule* Patna, 1985.

Chapter X

Wahhabi Missionary Literature and Polemical Anti-Wahhabi Writings[1]

1. *The Wahhabi Missionary Literature*

The Wahhabi Movement in India in the course of its operation produced a considerable volume of theological and missionary literature. Prominent among the former group are such works as the *Sirātu'l Mustaqīm* and the *Taqwīyatu'l Imān*.[2] Additionally, we have the large collection of the correspondence of Sayyid Ahmad and the works of some of his chief disciples such as Shah Ismail Shahid, Wilayat Ali and others in which the aims and objectives of the movement have been explained and defended against the criticisms of the *muqallid*, *Ḥanafī*, sections. These writings are mainly theological and are meant for the educated persons well-versed in religious science.

The other group consists of the missionary tracts written by a number of known and unknown Wahhabi preachers during the early and mid-19th century. The two groups are by no means mutually exclusive but the second group is thematically more varied and historically more important. The missionary tracts were written and compiled with the object of propagating the Wahhabi tenets, explaining and inviting the people to join the *Muḥammadī* order, criticising the *Bid'āt* current in the Indo-Muslim society, exposing the 'sinfulness' and socially harmful effects of certain customs and ceremonies, instructing the not-so-well-educated men on how to perform *namāz* (prayers) and *Wuḍū* (ablution before prayers), etc. The writers were careful not to put any 'seditious teaching' in their pamphlets. That was generally left to the itinerant teachers.[3] Some of the tracts, however, such as the *Risāla-Jihādiya*[4] and *Ḥāriqu'l Ishrār*[5] advocated the 'blessings' of fighting for one's religion and freedom.

Others, fewer in number, relate to topics of economic interest, and throw some light on the important question of the social base of the movement. An unnamed *risāla* by Zahurul Haque Azimabadi stresses the merit of earning one's livelihood by some craft or profession. It quotes *Aḥādīth* refuting the misconception that certain professions such as weaving and tailoring, etc., were lowly. All professions, it asserts, were equal before God. This defence of the social status of certain professional groups becomes significant when it is recalled that many adherents of the movement belonged to professional groups, or were agriculturists, and that the movement derived its support largely from people belonging to the middle and lower middle class.

A very large number of such works were published during the period. Wilayat Ali, a prolific writer himself, states that 'thousands' of such *risāi'l* were written,[6] and while this may be an exaggeration the number must have been large. Much of it has, however, been lost. From the mid-1870s, when the movement was largely suppressed and its leaders convicted to long-term imprisonments Wahhabi-baiting became popular,[7] and many people afraid to be found in possession of Wahhabi pamphlets, destroyed their collections. Many of the tracts were proscribed and confiscated by the government.[8]

Copies of many such pamphlets and other Wahhabi papers found their way to London, too, because some of the British officers connected with the investigations and trials of Wahhabi cases took the books and papers home. Act XXV of 1867, which provided for the registration and preservation of books and tracts printed in British India, also helped the building up of collections of periodicals in the Commonwealth Relations Office Library and the British Museum,[9] London. That is how these two public offices came to have a rich collection of Wahhabi pamphlets.[10]

The Wahhabi pamphlets were mostly written in Urdu prose, and a few copies in Hindi too are extant.[11] Such works as were written originally in Arabic or Persian were translated into simple Urdu, and both the original text and Urdu translations were printed side by side on each page. Many of the pamphlets were re-printed several times, and also copied by hand for wider circulation. Some were published anonymously and surreptitiously without mentioning the name of the press or the place of publication.

These tracts complemented the work of the itinerant Wahhabi preachers so graphically described by Hunter. The momentary impact of the roadside preacher was sought to be reinforced and complemented by these pamphlets which the people could read at leisure and ponder upon. The writers seemed to have a clear idea of the kind of readers for whom they were writing. While addressing themselves to specific social groups-the *'Ulama, Sūfia,* the lay gentry, soldiers, artisans, *Shī'as,* etc., they took care to use arguments which were likely to appeal and attract members of that group. Thus, while criticising the commercialisation of the system of *murīdī* by some of the Sufis, they also tried to attract them with prospects of more *murīds* (and hence more income!) if they took to the lines of the *Muḥammadī* order. Similarly, in addressing the *Shī'as,* the fact of Sayyid Ahmad being a Sayyid and a descendant of the *Ahl-i Bait* was emphasised.

All this may well be criticized on grounds of mutual contradiction and a deviation from the Wahhabi tenets, but the tracts were a sort of a popular propaganda literature and their main purpose was to increase the number of adherents. The writers had to take recourse to popular, often even puerile, arguments which were sometimes not in conformity with their own theoretical formulations.

Addressed mainly to the common people the manner of presentation is geared to their mental level. The narrative is simple and conversational. It is in sharp contrast to the ornamental rhymed prose then generally in use. Arguments are backed with quotations from the *Qur'ān* and *Ḥadīth,* translated in Urdu. Didactic stories and similes are used to illustrate the points. The similes used, though homely, indicate an alert and lively imagination. The tenor is often polemical and indicative of a one-track mind. Evidence and arguments adduced in support of their own points of view are regarded as final and irrefutable.

The Wahhabi missionary literature, virtually unnoticed in English, has a linguistic as well as historical significance. The tracts are valuable as early specimens of Urdu prose writing, particularly in eastern India. To realise the significance of the use of Urdu, it is to be noted that Persian was still the chief medium of expression and communication. Urdu prose was sparingly used not only for literary purposes but even personal correspondence by the educated people. The linguistic significance of the Wahhabi pamphlets has been discussed by competent scholars[12] who have compared it with the Puritan literature of 17th century England, and who claim that it prepared the ground for the development of the simple prose style of the Delhi College group and the works of Sir Sayyid.

Historically more significant is the repeated emphasis by the Wahhabis on the translation of the *Qur'ān* and *Ḥadīth* in the vernacular languages so that the people might read them directly. This is a very important point with them. They urged the necessity and utility of people reading the scriptures directly and urged the translation of the *Qur'ān* and *Ḥadīth* in the 'Hindi language'. This did not mean Hindi in Devanagri script : the term was used for Urdu.[13] However, the fact that the Wahhabis also used Hindi in Devanagri script for carrying their ideas to the people is evident from the existence of certain works noted by Faruqi.[14]

A connected point on which the pamphlets provide fresh evidence is the question of adopting new techniques of war. We find no less a person than Wilayat Ali (some of whose family members were uncompromisingly opposed to English education and all that it stood for) advocating the use of guns and cannons in place of catapults used during the time of Prophet Muhammad against the 'cannon-firing infidels' (the British).[15]

The pamphlets constitute a new category of source-materials, giving us fresh insight into the working of the movement and its nature. In these we find vivid glimpses of the socio-religious life[16] of the Muslims in India in the early 19th century, and what is more important they help us correct the one-dimensional view of the Wahhabis as merely a group of anti-government conspirators, as presented to us by the government records.

Reflecting the feelings and thinking of a section of the Indian Muslims in regard to their society, religion and polity, the pamphlets give us a sort of a self-image of the community in the latter half of the 19th century.

In the article of Marc Gaborieau cited above,[17] the contents of a mid-19th century Indian Wahhabi tract, *Al-Balāgh al-Mubīn,* have been closely-scrutinised and some remarks made about the movement of Sayyid Ahmad and the Indian reformist literature. The tract puts forward some arguments for the condemnation of the cult of the saints, and one of these arguments, which Gaborieau finds to be less common but very interesting, and which he takes to form the core of the book, was that the visits to the *dargāh* and the beseeching of aid from the saints made the Muslims resemble 'the Hindu polytheists' among whom they live (p. 22).

It may, however, be pointed out that this line of argument is not a representative, or even a major, theme in the Wahhabi tracts. As against this one tract, whose authorship and exact date of writing is uncertain, there are numerous others in which the wider question of the popular customs and practices have been discussed and the deviations not attributed to the influence of the Hindus. Rather, these have been ascribed to the Muslims themselves moving away from the earlier models of action. Moreover, the Wahhabi missionary literature has many other dimensions, too.[18]

For a more specific assessment of this literature we may examine in detail the contents of two such *risāi'l* entitled *Risāla-i Da'wat* and *Tibyānu's Shirk*,[19] Which are not only representative specimens but have some additional significance of their own. These two are included in the well-known and widely-circulated collection of Wahhabi tracts titled *Risāi'l Tisa'*.[20] As the title indicates, it consists of nine tracts written by different writers. These are as follows:

(i) *Risāla-i Radd-i Shirk*, Persian, pp1.-29; it was written by Wilayat Ali and translated into Urdu by Elahi Bakhsh. Both the texts are written on the same page with a line drawn between the two.It is a concise version of Shah Ismail's *Taqwīyatu'l Imān*, and was published separately under the title, *Hidāyatu't Tauḥīd* from *Matba'-i Dāru'l Saltanat*, Calcutta, A.H. 1314 (1896-97).

(ii) *Risāla-i 'Amal bi'l Ḥadīth*, Persian, pp. 30-45; relating to matters of Islamic jurisprudence, it was written by Wilayat Ali and translated into Urdu by Elahi Bakhsh.

(iii) *Arba'īn fi'l Mahdīīn*,. Arabic, pp. 46-63; compiled by Wilayat Ali, it is a collection of *Aḥādīth* relating to the advent of the *Mahdī* or the Messiah; it was written, probably, in the context of the 'belief' in the 're-appearance' of Sayyid Ahmad.

(iv) *Risāla-i Da'wat*, Urdu, pp. 64-78; to be examined in detail hereafter.

(v) *Risāla-i Taysīru's Salāt*, Urdu, pp. 79-87; written by Wilayat Ali, it relates to the performance of *namāz*.

(vi) *Risāla-i Shajra-i bā-thamar*, Urdu, pp. 88-94; written by Wilayat Ali it criticised some of the practices current in some Sufi *Khānqāhs*.

(vii) *Risāla-i But-Shikan*, Urdu, pp. 94-106; written by Enayat Ali, it strongly condemns the practice of taking out *ta'zias*, as also some other social practices.

(viii) *Risāla-i Manba'u'l Fuyūḍ*; Persian, pp. 106-38; a questionnaire addressed to Faiyyaz Ali relating to religious topics, and the answers thereto. Originally published in Persian as *Faiḍu'l Fuyūḍ*, it was re-published under the above-mentioned title, with the Persian text and its translation into Urdu by Elahi Bakhsh, on the lines of nos. (i) and (ii) above.

(ix) *Tibyānu's Shirk*, Urdu, pp. 142-56; to be examined in detail presently.

Risāla-i Da'wat; Explaining his objective, Wilayat Ali writes that some people would not listen to or accept the oral pleadings of a preacher, so he was writing this tract to enable such persons to read it at leisure and if they found anything worthwhile in it they should accept it and act accordingly.

The *risāla* is divided into several sections addressed specifically to the *'Ulama*, the *Sūfia*, the lay gentry, the professional groups, the *Shi'as*, etc., and invites all of them to join the *Muḥammadī* order.

The section addressed to the *Maulawis* observes[21] that some *Maulawis* acquired religious learning in order to earn their livelihood. They were faced with a dilemma: if they asked people to go to the original sources (*Qur'ān* and *Ḥadīth*) people would ask as to why they did not do so earlier.If, on the other hand, they joined the Wahhabis and took *Bai'at* in the *Muḥammadī* Order they thought they would lose face among the people. It warns them that religion was no more the monopoly of the *Maulawis*, the people could think for themselves on such matters as *Shirk* (Polytheism) and *Bid'at*, *Bai'at* and *Imāmat*, because the *Qur'ān* and *Ḥadīth* had been translated in the 'Hindi' language. If they forbade people to read the *Qur'ān* and *Ḥadīth* then too they would be criticised. Moreover, there were *Maulawis* ('Ālims) among the Wahhabis too who had the *Qur'ān* and *Ḥadīth* on their side, and rationality, too. Wouldn't the people with common sense go to them rather than the *Maulawis*?

Another section is addressed to the *Masha'ikh*, the heads of *khānqāhs* who earned their living by the system of *murīdī* (initiation of disciples). They were of two kinds. Firstly, those whose income did not depend on writing *Shajras*[22] but on grants of lands. Since their income was protected by *jāgīr*, why should they demean themselves by engaging in the usual clap-trap of *khanqahs*? Secondly, there were those whose earnings depended on the preaching of all kinds of

Bid'āt. Such persons made the *murīds* touch their feet, did not initiate people without taking money or sweets, did not write *Shajra* without a fee, did not urge strictly the observance of *namāz* and prohibition of intoxicants, considered musical sessions[23] as a form of prayer, and did not hesitate to accept fees from the ill-gotten money of prostitutes, etc. They could not fool the people all the time because thousands of *risālas* had been written explaining to the people about *shirk* and *bid'at.* Formerly, the people did not have any choice; having no access to the *Qur'an* and *Ḥadīth* they had to go willy-nilly to them (Masha'ikh) whether they were good or bad. Now the curtain of ignorance was being raised, people had developed a taste for acquiring knowledge and they would not take any steps without enquiry. It may come to this that their *murīds* would argue with and them throw the *Shajras* on their face.

The *Muḥammadī* Order was there to tell them of the right path and it was being talked about in streets and lanes. The Wahhabis were gaining adherents and a time would come when the *Mashā'ikh* would be left with only a few *murīds.* The position of such *Mashā'ikh* was like that of a soldier who had obtained service by fraud and keeps a wooden sword in the scabbard but is always apprehensive that he may be caught one day and lose his service. If they could afford a steel sword (right knowledge, as preached by Wahhabis) why carry a wooden one (of pretence and fraud)? They should join the *Muḥammadī* Order, it would add to their knowledge and position and bring in more *murīds.*

The appeal to the *Shī'as* begins by observing that although the *Shīa's* and the Wahhabis differed on the question of *Khilāfat*[24] and *Imāmat* they were united on the question of *Tauḥīd* (Unity of God) and *Rasālat* (prophethood of Muhammad). The Wahhabis and *Shi'as* were united so far as the question of polytheism was concerned; let them concentrate on that for the time being, the other matters could be attended to later on. It appeals to their sentimental attachment to the *Ahl-i-Bait* and points out that Sayyid Ahmad was a Sayyid, and that opposition to the venerable Sayyids and enemity with *Ahl-i-Bait* was the way of Yazīd.[25]

One section is addressed to such persons who were the disciples, pupils or relatives of those opposed to the Wahhabis. Such persons hesitated to join the Wahhabis out of respect for their elders and teachers. It warns them that one should respect the teacher so far as studies were concerned but not in matters of faith. Many Muslims went to the Kayasthas for being taught but they did not become Kayasthas.[26]

Another section is addressed to rich Muslims who thought it below their dignity to accept the guidance of the 'poor' Wahhabis. They should not be proud of their riches; God was the richest and most powerful. Did they not reward a poor man if he brought them news about an approaching enemy? The Wahhabis were giving them similar warning and giving them a chance to improve their lives hereafter.

Similarly, the soldiers were proud of their profession and disdained the appeal of the Wahhabis. They should heed that only God was the most powerful. If one dashed his head against a mountain who would be smashed, the man or the mountain. They should not let false pride stand in the way of accepting the *Muhammadī* Order. If they were true soldiers they should rather exert in the path of God and in suppressing their ego.

Risala-i-Tibyānu's Shirk

This pamphlet deals with the questions of *Shirk* and *Bid'at,* both of which occupy a key position in Wahhabi thinking. They are unsparing critics of *Bid'at.* However, Wilayat Ali points out that *Bid'at* did not mean any and everything new since the time of the Prophet. He points out that there were two sorts of actions.

Firstly, those for which Prophet Muhammad was not divinely commissioned, such as construction of houses, cooking of food, etc. Such works were left to the intellect of the people and a *Bid'at* had got nothing to do with it. The second category concern works for which the Prophet was divinely commissioned. These again were of two kinds. Those for the performance or achievement of which no limits of actions were laid down, such as *jihād.* The object of the follower of the *Shara'* was to achieve victory, whether one fought with swords or guns. Inventing new things which may prove helpful in gaining the objective (victory) cannot be regarded as *Bid'at* (The Prophet is quoted to the effect that he who chalks out a beneficial course of action shall get his rewards and they too who follow it). In the time of Prophet there were catapults, not guns. Now if someone, considering the catapults as useless against the cannon-firing infidels' (the English), used similar guns and cannons it certainly would not be *Bid'at.*

Similarly, the true object of the follower of the *Shara'* is the obtaining of divine knowledge and purity of heart. If he studied some works of grammar and prosody or took to some *shughl*[27] as was done by some *Sūfis*, it is not a *Bid'at*, even though such practices did not exist in the time of the Prophet.

But if one made a fetish of these things, so much so that one who fought with swords and not guns was not regarded as a *mujāhid*, or one who studied the *Qur'ān* without studying grammar and prosody, or one who achieved purity of heart without the guidance of *Sūfis*, was not regarded as a *Walī* then it becomes a *Bid'at*.

There were other works for which the Prophet had laid down the limits of behaviour. To deviate from these is certainly *Bid'at*. For example, if one thought that he could perform his *namaz* lying down, or say that since the burial of the dead body has been ordered without specifying the manner of carrying the body to the cemetery he could get the body dragged there, or argue that since the performance of *Nikāḥ* only is compulsory he could indulge in wasteful expenses on the occasion, he would be in the wrong. One should not transgress the limits laid down in such cases.

It would be evident from the extracts presented above that a closer study of this untapped source-material helps broaden our understanding of the working and the nature of the Wahhabi Movement. The advocacy of the translation of scriptures in the regional languages, and of the use of modern methods of warfare, deserves particular attention. It is in marked contrast to the revivalist nature of the movement in some other respects.

2. The anti-Wahhabi Writings

During the period of the Wahhabi trials and after, there was a general witch-hunting of suspected Wahhabis and their sympathisers. Many took it upon themselves to expose what they considered to be the mistaken ideas and beliefs of the Wahhabis and more particularly their anti-government activities. They brought out books and pamphlets pretending to be sober criticisms but which were very often written in abusive terms and with a view to bringing the Wahhabis into the bad books of the government.

A representative specimen of such writings is Epitome of the History of the Wahhabis by Imdad Ali[28] the Secretary of Bihar Scientific Society[29] and a Judge in the Small Cause Court, in which the author attempts to 'prove' that the Wahhabis were 'excluded from Islam', 'have no connection with Islam', and were 'a faithless, wicked, treacherous and seditious people'. Another such work was *Jawāb-i Dwāzdah Guna*[30] by one Najmuddin. It contained 12 Answers refuting the claims of the Wahhbis'. Forwarding a copy of it to the Commissioner of Patna, the author claimed[31] that he had written it to 'check the wickedness of the Wahhbis,' and added that he did 'not neglect to try to know everything respecting the chief of Wahabees,' and that he and his friend Sayyid Wilayat Ali 'will ever do so.'

Some newspapers and journals were also engaged in scurrilous attacks on the Wahhabis. The *Chashma-i 'Ilm*[32] an Urdu newspaper of Patna in its issue of 16 April, 1875 published an article entitled "New Devices of Wahabees" of which the opening sentence was: "The Wahabees have in these days commenced to bring out their heads like rats from their holes ..."

The motive of such writers was so transparent that often the government officials themselves felt constrained to remark upon it. Commenting on the writing of Imdad Ali, for example, the Commissioner of Patna in a note to the magistrate wrote that "My own view is that Imdad Ali is again humbugging and trying to bring himself into prominence as an exposer of Wahhbis and Wahabism.[33]

It may be noted that, on the other hand, the Wahhabis also received some support, often from unexpected quarters, such as the famous *Sūfi Khānqāh* of Phulwari Sharif near Patna. During the period 1875-1883, the *Sajjādah nashīn* of Phulwari Sharif, for example, came to be suspected of being sympathetic to the Wahhabis.Some of the works, of the "Phulwari Moulvies", which incurred Government's suspicion and displeasure, were *Radd-i Tuḥfa-i Muḥabbat and Mi'yaru'l Mazhab*[34] by Maulana Syed Ali Azam Qadri and *Uswa-i Husna*[35] by Shah Muhammad Ali Habib. The first-named was written in refutation of an earlier publication, *Tuḥfa-i Muḥabbat* by 'some Sunni Hanafi Muslims' levelling 'religious' charges against the Wahhabis. The book was published anonymously and without mentioning the name of the press,[36] but the government suspected "the Moulvi of Phulwari Sharif" to be its author.

The Proclamations issued from Phulwari in support of aid for the Turks further aroused the government's suspicion. In fact, a comprehensive memorandum was prepared on the suspected complicity of the 'Phulwaree Moulvis' with the Wahhabis.[37] It was observed that "the conduct of the Phulwaree people bears a close resemblance with that of the Wahhbis," and that "Phulwaree has begun to walk exactly in the footsteps of Sadiqpur." It was recommended that Phulwaree be made a subdivision, and that a Magistrate "as experienced as Baboo Ishree Prasad"[38] should be posted there.

Criticism of the Wahhabis on the Points of Taqlīd and Jihād

In another, more serious, group of writings the Wahhabis were criticised for being *ghair muqallid* (i.e., not believing in any one of the four recognised *madhāhib* or schools of Islamic jurisprudence) and for preaching *jihād*. It was claimed that the Wahhabis did not believe in any one of the four recognised *madhāhib*, and that they were the followers of Muhammad bin Abdul Wahhab of Nejd, Arabia, and were something like a heterodox sect. Furthermore, it was claimed that the Wahhabis emphasised *jihād* as the bounden duty of all Muslims and regarded British India as *Dāru'l Ḥarb*.

Defending themselves on the former point, the Wahhabis pointed out that there were only four established *madhāhib*: the *Ḥanafi*, *Shāfi'i*, *Māliki* and *Ḥanbalī*, and that there was no school or sect known as Wahhabi. A follower of any one of the four *madhāhib* could not be called a *Bida'tī*. The difference, if any, between the *madhāhib* is often a difference of the direct and derived meaning of a *Ḥadīth*. A *Ḥadīth* is quoted from the *Saḥīḥ Bukhārī* and from Abū Muslim stating that Prophet Muhammad had once sent a group of men to the *Banī Quariza* tribe and directed them to the effect that no one should offer the *'asar* (afternoon) prayer but in the midst of the *Banī Quariza* tribesmen. Some members of the party performed the prayer on the way (at the scheduled time) because they took, the Prophet's instruction to mean that they should reach that tribes territory as soon as possible, not that they should perform the *'asar* prayer only after reaching that territory even if the time of the prayer had passed. Other members of the group, going by the apparent meaning of the words of command, performed the prayer on reaching the *Banī Quariza* territory. Later, on hearing about it Prophet Muḥammad did not reject either of the two actions. So also with the differences between the four *madhāhib*.[39]

Even if it was accepted that a section of the Indian Muslims were influenced by the ideas of Muḥammad bin Abdul Wahhab, and were to be called after him, they should be more aptly called Muhammadis, not Wahhabis. The last mentioned term in fact had no widely accepted meaning, it had acquired different meanings in different parts of the country.[40] As such, it was misleading if not meaningless.

As regard *jihād*, the Wahhabis drew attention to the requirements laid down in the standard works for declaring a country to be a *Dāru 'l Ḥarb*, and for electing an *Amīr* who alone could rightfully lead a *jihād*. It was further pointed out that *jihād* was a *farḍ-i Kifāya*, i.e., if it was performed by the people of one country it was not obligatory upon those of another.[41] The topic of *jihād* was dwelt upon in numerous standard Islamic works but its mere mention, or the teaching of it did not constitute anti-government activity, and could not be taken as the preaching of *jihād*. If such a criterion was to be applied then all Muslims, not just those labelled as Wahhabis, would become suspect.

These anti-Wahhabi writings, it is clear, were aimed at two different groups of audience, the Indian Sunni Muslims in general and the British officials who shared Hunter's misgivings regarding the Muslims generally and Wahhabis in particular. The charge about their being *ghair muqallid* was aimed at arousing the hostility of the Sunnis generally against the Wahhabis, while that about their being *jihādis* was expected to keep alive the government's suspicion and reservations against them.

The Wahhabis defended themselves on both counts but they remained rather on the defensive. They were anxious, under the changed circumstances, to play down the political aspect of the movement. In doing so they were, at times, not only unnecessarily apologetic, but ignored well-established facts and explicit observations of Sayyid Ahmad himself.[42]

Notes

1. A shortened version of this chapter was published earlier as "The Missionary Literature of the Wahhabis: Its Historical Significance," in Christian W.Troll (Ed.) *Islam in India, Studies and Commentaries*, New Delhi, pp. 52-63.
2. Originally planned in two parts, the work presents the Arabic texts from the *Qur'ān Aḥādīth* and their translations into Urdu, bearing on different topics-monotheism, polytheism, *bid'āt*, the efficacy of following the way (*Sunnet*) of Prophet Muhammad, etc. Only the first part was completed when the author died in the battle of Balakote (1831).

The second part, of which only the translations of the Arabic texts remains, was completed by Sultan Muhammad in 1834-35, and published with the title, *Tadhkīral-Ikhwān Baqīyya-i Taqwīyatu'l Imān* many times, and an English translation of it was published by Mir Shahamat Ali in *JRAS*, London, 1852, vol. XIII, pp. 310-72. See also, *Supra*, p. 50, n.1 above.

3. *Cf.* chap. V., pp. 172-74.
4. It was published several times independently, also as part of other writings. O' Kinealy presented an English translation in the *Calcutta Review*, 1870.
5. Published from *Matba'-i Muhammadi*, Delhi. A.H. 1283 (1866-67). It contains 256 *khamsa* (a form of Urdu poetry having five verses in each stanza) printed diagonally in frames with a demarcating line under each. The verses relate to *jihād*, the heroic fighting of Shah Ismail, 'deceitful' *pirs*, etc. It was proscribed by the government.
6. *infra*, p. 383.
7. *infra*, pp. 387 *ff.*
8. I found a group of such confiscated pamphlets in the record room of Patna Divisional Commissioner's office.
9. For a very informative account of the periodical literature in Indian languages available in the Commonwealth Relations Office Library and the British Museum, see N.G. Barrier's article, "South Asia in Vernacular Publications...,' *Journal of Asian Studies*, vol. XXVIII, no. 4 (August, 1969), pp. 803-10.
10. For a list of these see K.A. Faruqi, *Urdu mein Wahhabi Adab*, Delhi University Publication, 1969, pp. 42-51, Urdu.
11. Faruqi, op. cit., pp. 24, 25, 38, 50.
12. Faruqi, *op. cit.*, Kulimuddin Ahmad's (Urdu) article *Apni Telash Mein*, in Urdu monthly *Āhang*, Gaya, November, 1971, pp. 7-28.
13. Shah Abdul Qadir, who first translated the *Qur'ān* into Urdu in 1790-1, calls it in the preface a translation in 'Hindui' language. Ismail *Shahid* in the preface of his *Taqwīyatu'l Imān* writes that he had translated the Quranic verses and *Aḥādith* in 'Hindi' so that people could understand them.
14. K.A. Faruqi, *op. cit.*, pp. 24, 25, 38 and 50.

    Faruqi also refers to the participation of some Hindus in the compiling and circulation of such works. One Beni Narain, poetically surnamed *Jahān*, a *Khatrī* of Delhi, translated into "*zabān-i rekhta Hindi*" the Persian work of Shah Rafiuddin, *Tanbīhu'l Ghāfilīn*, using some of the conventional phraseology of the Wahhabi writers (*ibid.*, p. 23).

    Way back in 1969 I had seen in the Dacca Museum a manuscript in the Bengali language in Arabic script. I do not have its full details at hand but it dealt with some theological matters and was probably written in the late 19th century. I will not be surprised if it turns out to be a Wahhabi tract in *Bengali language in Arabic script.* Examples of such unusual literary attempts can be cited from a slightly earlier period. The versified long romantic tale, *Qissa-i Amīr Hamza,* of which there are several recensions, was translated into *Bengali verse in Arabic script* by Shah Gharibullah and Sayyid Hamza of Hugli district between the years 1783 and 1794 (see Abdul Wali Khan's article "A Bengali Book Written in Persian Script," *Journal of the Asiatic Society,* New Series, 1925-21 : 191-203).

15. *Vide infra.*
16. The observations of the Wahhabi writers often get striking confirmation from other independent sources of quite a different type; see chap. I p. 9, n.2.
17. *Supra,* p. 44, n. 1.
18. *Supra,* pp. 377-78, *infra,* pp. 385-87.
19. These were probably written during 1830s or early 1840s.
20. Several manuscript and printed editions of the work are available. Many of these are available singly too, both in print and manuscript. The present references are from an undated edition printed in *Maktaba'-i Faruqi,* Delhi, pp. 1-156.
21. Only a summarised English version of the relevant portions is given below.
22. A document recording the name of the *murīd* and enumerating the chain of spiritual preceptors with whom he was linked by the process of *Bai'at.*
23. Some Sufis believed in the efficacy of musical sessions (*sama'*) in bringing about a trance during which one had a feeling of nearness to God. Other Sufis, and much more so the Wahhabis, regarded such sessions as sinful.
24. The arrangement devised by the Muslims after the death of Prophet Muhammad (632) to select a successor to guide their affairs brought into existence the institution of *Khilāfat.* The *Sunnis* regard the *Khilāfat* as a temporal, non-dynastic institution. On the other hand, the *Shī'as'* concept of the office of the successor of Muhammad, the *Imamat,* is spiritual and dynastic. They regard the *Imām* as their spiritual and temporal head (the kings are theoretically regarded as the deputies of the Twelfth and last *Imām* who 'disappeared' and who is expected to reappear). The *Shī'as* believe that the office should belong only to the successors of Prophet Muhammad and Ali. This controversy created the first division in the ranks of Muslims.

25. The Umayyad *Khalīfa* (680-83) who ordered the fight against *Imām* Husain at Karbala.
26. This is a very interesting piece of information. The proficiency of Kayasthas in Persian and Urdu is well-known. It appears that many Muslims had Kayastha tutors.
27. Certain practices performed by *Sūfis* such as meditation, concentration, counting of beads, etc.
28. The work was translated into English by Musa Ali, Translator, Calcutta High Court. I found a hand-written copy of the work in a government record room at Patna.
29. First established in 1868 as the British India Association in 1868, it was re-constituted as the Bihar Scientific Society in 1872 at Muzaffarpur, and its character was changed from a political to an educational, pro-government institution. Among its objectives was the translation of European scientific works into Urdu, the establishment of a printing press, a newspaper and *madrasas*. Its founder was Imdad Ali Khan, then a sub-judge at Muzaffarpur. It worked in collaboration with the Aligarh Scientific Society, and brought out an Urdu newspaper, *Akhbāru'l Akhiyār,* edited by Munshi Qurban Ali. A branch of the Society was opened at Patna in 1873 under S. Wazir Ali, and another at Gaya under M.A., Gregory.

    For further details, see my chapter, "Islam", K.K. Datta, *Comprehensive History of Bihar,* vol. III, pt. II. pp.100 *ff.*, and J.S. Jha, "Origin and Development of Cultural Institutions in Bihar," *Journal of Historical Research,* Ranchi, vol. VIII, no. 1, 1965, pp. 1-13.
30. Published from the Muhammadan Press, Patna, in 1878.
31. Letter from Najmuddin to E.W. Maloney, Commissioner., Patna.
32. It was published by Suraj Mul, Deputy Inspector, Patna.
33. Commissioner's (Patna) note on a letter from the Magistrate, Muzaffarpur, dated 28 Feb. 1871.
34. First published in A.H. 1228 (1813-14), second edition from *Matba'-i Nizami* Kanpur, A.H. 1292 (1875-76). It was written in Persian, and covered 162 pages.
35. Published from *Matba'-i Muhammadi,* A.H. 1292 (1875-76). It was written in Persian.
36. This was in contravention of Act XXV of 1867, and the government issued a notification announcing that anyone giving information about the author and publisher of the book would receive half the amount of fine (Rs. 1000/-) levied on the parties concerned under the Act.
37. The suspicion appears often to be based on flimsy grounds. Objection was taken, for example, to the use by Maulana Ali Azam Qadri and Muhammad Ali Habib of certain epithets for the "chief

of the Wahhabis", such as 'Sun of Spiritualism' 'Prop of the Pious', and 'Moon of the Godly.'

38. For his role in the trial and prosecution of the Wahhabis, see chap. VIII, p. 283, notes 3 & 4.
39. *Dāfi'u'l Fasād*, pp. 93-94.
40. *Supra* p. 361.
41. Siddiq Hasan Khan, *Tarjumān-i Wahhābiya*, pp. 22-24.
42. One of them even made modifications and alterations in the texts of some of Sayyid Ahmad's letters published by him. On this point, see *infra*, chapter XI.

    It may also be noted here that such shifts in attitudes are not uncommon among the followers of a movement encompassing a long period of time, witnessing major political, social and economic changes.

Chapter XI

An Appraisal of the Wahhabi Movement

1. Source-Material and Historiography

The source-material for a study of the history of the Wahhabi Movement comprise several distinct groups, different in terms of language, volume and the type of information contained. The material covering the early part, upto the battle of Balakote, is mostly in Persian and Urdu, and much of it is still unpublished. Among the more important works, mention may be made of the *Sirātul Mustaqīm,*[1] the Letters of Sayyid Ahmad,[2] the *risā'il* (tracts) of Shah Ismail,[3] the *Makhzan-i Ahmadī,*[4] the *Manzūra,*[5] and the *Waqāi.*[6] The *Sirātu'l Mustaqīm,* carrying as it does the considered views of Sayyid Ahmad on contemporary social and religious conditions in the country and his programme of work, may be regarded as a manifesto of the movement. The letters of Sayyid Ahmad are addressed to a large number of persons ranging from ruling chiefs to common followers of the movement, and they shed light on the aims and objectives of Sayyid Ahmad and the changing day-to-day situation, mainly after 1826. Shah Ismail was an ideologue of the movement, and his tracts and letters are useful for an understanding of the ideological aspect. The *Makhzan* and the *Manzūra* are the two earliest biographies of Sayyid Ahmad. The former was written in Sayyid Ahmad's lifetime by his nephew Ahmad Ali, and covers the period upto the journey for *Hajj.* The latter was written by Jafar Ali Naqvi, the chief *Munshi* of Sayyid Ahmad, and covers the period after the migration from British India (1826); it is particularly useful for an account of the wars on the N.W. Frontier. The *Waqāi* is a large corpus of reminiscences of Sayyid Ahmad's close associates about his life and activities, put together at the instance of Nawab Wazirud Dawlah of Tonk (1834-64).

Assignable to this category but a distinct work by itself, is Mahtab Singh's *Tawārikh-i Hazāra,*[7] which gives a graphic objective account of the battle of Balakote. Surprisingly, it has escaped the attention of all the writers on the subject.

It will be noticed that much of this group of source-materials relates to the earlier phase. It is invaluable for an understanding of the origins of the movement, of Sayyid Ahmad's view of the contemporary Indo-Muslim society and his policies and actions. It has been drawn upon extensively by several writers in Urdu, most eminent among them being Abul Hasan Ali Nadwi[8] and Ghulam Rasul Mehr[9]. It has also been utilised well by Hafeez Malik, writing in English[10].

There is also a neglected category of source-materials, the theological and missionary literature[11] produced by the Wahhabis during the course of their activities. It helps us correct the one-sided view of the Wahhabis as only anti-government conspirators, as it appears from the government records, and adds depth to our understanding of the working of the movement, and its nature.

A smaller group is that of the private papers of some members of the Sadiqpore family. It includes some valuable documents and books belonging to the members of the family who had taken an active part in the movement, and contain, in some cases, notes by these persons, and their successors, who possessed some inside information.[12]

The Government records in English constitute another very large and valuable group of source-materials. It consists mainly of the correspondence between district officials and the Commissioners, on the one hand, and the Secretary to the Government of Bengal and the Government of India, on the other. It sometimes includes, as enclosures to the letters, translated extracts in English from Persian or Urdu books and documents bearing on the subject, ranging from small marginal notes in pencil on the rough drafts and formal letters to long, well-researched memoranda[13] on Wahhabism and the Wahhabis.

The records of the trials[14] of the Wahhabi leaders, the books and official publications on the wars[15] fought against the Wahhabis and the private papers of some Englishmen, from the Governors-General[16] to the district magistrates and presiding officers of lower courts constitute other sub-groups of source-materials in English.

In a miscellaneous group of some printed works in English, containing valuable bits of information, mention may be made of the *Memoirs of Alexander H. Gardner* [17] giving us a unique, eye-witness, acount of the last moments of the battle of Balakote and of Sayyid Ahmad falling dead while fighting. The *Distirct Gazetteer, Bareilly,*[18] refers to Nawab Amir Khan's men carrying their raids into the newly acquired British territory of Rohilkhand, to an uprising in Bareilly in 1816, and to its leaders, Mufti Muhammad Iwad Khan moving out to Tonk after the suppression of the rising, thus showing linkages between the people of this area and the Court of Nawab Amir Khan at a time shortly before Sayyid Ahmad's joining the services of Nawab Amir Khan.

Even more important is the book, *British Rule and Native Opinion.*[19] Apparently unconnected with the subject of the Wahhabis, it nevertheless contains very useful information. The author had come to India in early 1870s to study public opinion with reference to some important contemporary events. The Wahhabis were much in the news then and the author was present at the Malda (1870) and Patna (1871) trials and had taken notes. The eloquence of his tribute to the integrity and fortitude of Amiruddin and his father Rafiq Mandal is striking. More noticeable is his remark, which now seems to be prophetic, that he took it "to be among the certainties of life" that the history of these trials would "some day be read with just pride in India."[20]

The source-material in English, both archival and published, are different in nature and content from the former group in Persian and Urdu. They represent the government officials' view of the Wahhabis, and the focus is on their anti-government activities. Though some awareness is shown of the religious backround, the Wahhabis are presented mainly as conspirators, rebels and 'Fanatics'. Nonetheles, this category of source-material is invaluable for a detailed reconstruction of the Wahhabis' activities in all its phases.

This vast material has been utilised, though not always wisely, by writers in English, from James O'Kinealy and William Hunter onwards. Hunter[21] maintained that the Indian Muslims suffered from political and economic deprivations under British Rule and nursed a deep and abiding resentment against it. This contention of Hunter has been questioned by some modern writers, notably by Anil Seal[22] and Peter Hardy[23]. It was pointed out that Hunter's book was a sort of 'command performance,' and that it was virtually a 'demi-official publication.' More importantly, it was pointed out that the position of the Indian Muslims ouside Bengal was comparatively better.

The view that Hunter's book was a 'demi-official publication' has been denied by Hunter himself.[24] He also noted that his observations only applied to "Lower Bengal, the Province with which I am best acquainted, and in which, so far as I can learn, the Muhammadans have suffered most severely under British Rule.'[25]

As for the point about the position of the Indian Muslims outside Bengal being better, it has been shown elsewhere[26] that this criticism of Hunter ignores the demographic aspect of the situation and also the question as to what the Indian Muslims themselves thought about their position.

Hunter's finding was also questioned by some in the official circles. It was a time when the perceived danger of a Russian forward policy in Central Asia loomed large in the official thinking, and it was felt that Hunter's thesis about a large, restive Indian Muslim population might encourage Russia. It was urged that there was a need to correct the view presented by Hunter.

Leaving aside considerations of imperial policy, and looking at it in the context of the historiography of the Wahhabi Movement, it is clear that Hunter's book is in many ways a perceptive and well-rounded account of the Wahhabis' activities. In regard to the origins of the movement, however, Hunter completely ignores the impact of the ideas of Shah Waliullah, in his preoccupation with linking of the movement in India to that in Arabia led by Muhammad bin Abdul Wahhab.

One finds that among the books on the Wahhabi Movement, there are those which deal with the earlier phase only,[27] or are well-documented on this phase,[28] those which refer to it in the context of the movement of 1857-58,[29] or the history of the freedom movement in the sub-continent[30]. Then there are those which examine it in the larger frame of Muslims in India from the late 18th century onwards.[31] One misses a rounded view[32] of the rise and growth of the Wahhabi Movement, its operation over the whole period and area, its nature and its impact.

2. *The Nature of the Wahhabi Movement*

The Wahhabi Movement started under a socio-religious impulse but it soon acquired a political character also. The socio-religious aspect related to the advocacy of reforms in the Indo-Muslim society while the political aspect involved the struggle against the 'alien' rulers. Both these factors, as also some additional ones, influenced the movement during the course of its progress. Their relative importance varied from time to time but there is a perceptible trend that the political aspect was gaining ascendancy, more clearly since 1840. Of course, stress continued to be laid on the observance of prayers *(Namāz)*, fasting *(Roza)* alms-giving *(Zakāt)* and other obligatory religious duties, but the main work of the Wahhabi missionaries came to be the collection of funds and the 'tampering' with the loyalty of the Indian units of the Company's army stationed in the different parts of the country.[33] The burden of their preaching was the great 'merit' of fighting against the 'alien' rulers. One of the early writers on the history of the movement remarks, "These tidings of rebellion gradually so encroached themselves upon the original tenets of the Wahhabis, such as morality, purity of life, abolition of idolatrous usages, which were at first ardently insisted upon, that they threw them completely in the background."[34]

Instances where the missionary discoursed only on the religious, and abstained from the political topics, became fewer, and had, moreover, the effect of thanking the audience.[35]

The movement was active for well over half-a-century and covered the greater part of northern India. It need hardly be stressed that the conditions in the large area stretching from the mountainous North-Western Frontier to the marshy plains of Bengal varied vastly. The agrarian character of the movement in eastern and northern Bengal is not to be seen in the North-Western Frontier. Any generalisation about the nature of the movement, based on the position in a particular area during a particular period, is, therefore apt to be misleading.

One of the misconceptions about the movement which appeared in many of the early writings in English, and to a lesser extent in Urdu too, was that it was directed against the Sikhs. Sayyid Ahmad had selected the North-Western Frontier tribal area as the base of his operation due to ideological, tactical and strategic considerations. It led, among other things, to a clash with the forces of the Sikh *darbār* whose territories lay between Sayyid Ahmad's base and British India. But that constitutes only a short period in the early phase of the movement. Even during that short period, if one were to judge by the yardstick of battles fought, there was more fighting between Sayyid Ahmad and the tribal Muslim chiefs than between him and the forces of the Sikh *darbār*.

Sayyid Ahmad stated his main objectives explicitly in a number of his letters addressed to different persons, including a few non-Muslims too.[36] There are several unpublished collections of his letters, but in one of the earliest published versions[37] of some of them, small but vital changes were made in the text which completely changed or distorted the contents. Thus, for example, the word *"Nasrāniān"* (Christians) was substituted by the word *"Drāz Mu'iyān"* (the long-haired ones, i.e., the Sikhs), and similar other changes and deletions made in many letters.[38] In a letter addessed by Sayyid Ahmad to the Shah of Bukhara, the text in the published version reads "the ill-natured Christians... had gained control over the western parts of India from the banks of the river Indus to the capital city of Delhi," whereas the text in the manuscript copy reads "the ill-natured Christians... had gained control over the various parts of India stretching from the banks of river Indus to the shores of the ocean *(Dariyā-i Shōr),*" which covers a distance of six months' journey.[39]

The distortions created by such substitutions hardly need to be commented upon, but what needs to be pointed out is that although attention was drawn to these distortions more than forty years ago,[40] no recent work published on the subject has taken note of it. It must be remembered that it was precisely after the end of the Sikh rule in the Punjab that the major battles between the Wahhabis and the British forces took place. The clash between Sayyid Ahmad and the forces of the Sikh *darbār,* which occurred during a short period in the beginning, should not be taken as a characteristic feature of the movement.

The point was not lost upon some of the early British writers who are so forthright in emphasising the anti-British character of the movement. J.D. Cunningham, the well-known historian of the Sikhs, who was in personal contact with a brother-in-law and close follower of Sayyid Ahmad, writes, "After an absence of four years he (Sayyid Ahmad) returned to Delhi and called upon the faithful to follow him in a war against the infidels. *He acted as if he meant by unbelievers the Sikhs alone, but his precise objects* are imperfectly understood.'[41] Another writer draws attention to the continuing activities of the Wahhabis during the earlier and later period by remarking that "He (Bayazid, the leader of the 16th century Raushaniya Movement on the North-Western Frontier) and his followers became to 'Akbar what the

Wahabis were to the Sikhs and the Hindustani Fanatics to the British Government."[42]

R.C. Majumdar comments briefly on the nature of the movement in the context of the history of the freedom movement in the country. He gives to the Wahhabis the credit for the "First organised attempt on a large scale to drive out the English after they had established their paramountcy in India," but adds that the movement had "certainly no claim to be called national in the sense in which we understand the term today. For it was a struggle for freedom, *of the Muslims and by the Muslims.*"[43]

The remark shows that Majumdar has not examined the origins of the movement in depth and has overlooked the changing em phasis from the religious to the political aspect over a period of time[44], and the resultant wider appeal of the movement to a larger section of the people. There is also some overlapping, and contradictions, in his account, of the Faraidi Movement in Bengal and the larger Wahhabi Movement. After giving an account of the Baraset Rising (1831), which he characterises as 'Communal'[45] he writes, "Thus ended a stirring episode which may not be unfittingly described as the first fight for freedom in Bengal against British rule. It has justly been described by a writer[46] as an early instance of 'passive noncooperation among the masses by refusing service under the English and by refusing to go to British Courts'".

The increased stress on the political aspect led to a broadening of the support for the movement. The area of its activity and the extent of its influence expanded. The network of the Wahhabis' centres, which had "enveloped the whole of Bengal in their meshes"[47] during 1850s, had extended during 1860s from Peshawar to Bijapur and from Dacca to Poona, as revealed by the police inquiries conducted by Reily[48]. The activities encompassing such a large area could not have been sustained without the active support of wider, non-Muslim masses. The anti-government activities of the Wahhabis, as distinct from the socio-religious preachings, was something they could attune themselves to and were willing to follow.

The role of Hindu bankers in the secret transmission of money from British India to the Wahhabis on the North-Western Frontier during the time of Sayyid Ahmad, as also the presence of Hindu gunner in the latter's forces, has already been referred to.[49] The participation of the Hindu bankers increased during the later period. Some of the bankers must have had an inkling of the fact that these were not normal commercial transactions but had some secret, perhaps subversive, purpose. Merely the desire to earn some extra profit cannot adequately explain the ready participation of so many banking firms.

There is also the somewhat remarkable and inexplicable instance of one Nundlall, a resident of Fatuha, district Patna, going all the way to Amabala as a defence witness to depose in favour of the Wahhabis, accused of treason.[50]

More revealing is the testimony provided by the letters written by Sayyid Ahmad to two Hindu chiefs. The first letter, addressed to Lala Sukh Ram, opens with the benedictory phrase "May God the Most High protect him." It appears that Lala Sukh Ram was a man of some consequence in the North-Western Frontier area and was in correspondence with Sayyid Ahmad on the eve of some engagement against Painda Khan. Sayyid Ahmad writes to him that he got acquainted with the state of affairs through his letter. He (Sayyid Ahmad) was a servant of God, and if someone offered him terms of peace he would not act against him. But a war was a war, and if Painda Khan acted according to his promise, well and good, but if he went against his understanding he would be wiped out swiftly. The letter assures Sukh Ram that there was no need for him to worry in either eventuality; he should act according to his promise.[51]

The other more important letter[52] is addressed to Raja Hindu Rao, a brother-in-law of Maharaja Daulat Rao Sindhia of Gwalior. The addressee is assured that "In the event of the land of Hindustan being cleared of the alien enemies and these (weak) people (Sayyid Ahmad's followers) succeeding in their efforts, the rank and offices of the State and Government would be entrusted to the seekers (of these), and the roots of their power and authority would be strengthened."[53] Hindu Rao was further requested to render assistance[54] to the family members of the bearer of the letter, *Haji* Bahadur Shah, who had migrated from British India along with Sayyid Ahmad.

That Sayyid Ahmad was not only giving an assurance of restoration of power to Raja Hindu Rao but also seeking more positive help from him is very significant. We may also recall here that after the battle of Mayar (1830), when Peshawar came under the control of the Wahhabis, a cross-section of the local people including *seths* and *Sahukars* (Hindu businessmen and bankers) made their submission, and were consoled and assured of protection. Further, in the attempt to win the support of the Indian units of the army the Wahhabis made use of the system of having a Pandit and a Maulawi deputed with the units and approached both of them.[55] Sayyid Ahmad and the other leaders of the movement conceived of and implemented their programme of work entirely with reference to the existing situation in the country, and their ideas and actions do not show any extra-territorial dimension.

All this does not suggest a lesser emphasis upon the religious character of the movement. Its mainspring was religious, but the religious aspect related to certain reforms for strengthening and revitalising the society. Sayyid Ahmad was relentless in his denunciation of the 'polytheistic' and 'hypocritical' Muslims. The reforms he advocated were to have a cleansing effect on society to enable it to fight the alien rulers. The religious character of the movement, stressed by many writers, was there, of course, but these writers have ignored the other side, which gained increasing ascendancy.

Some writers have tried to explain that the movement was not anti-British. Sir Syed in his Review, [56] of Hunter's book wrote at length to counter Hunter's contention that the Muslims *per se* were hostile to the British government on account of the political and economic deprivations they had suffered. Sir Syed's views on the political aspect of the movement are, however, not sustainable.[57] We can explain these only with reference to the fact that Sir Syed represented a new school of thought which postulated that the future of the Indian Muslims lay not in keeping aloof from Western ideas and education but in adapting themselves to those very ideas. The continuance of a movement directed against the British Government and Western ideas ran counter to his views. At the same time, an evident feeling of sympathy and admiration for the socio-religious reforms preached by the Wahhabis is evident in parts of his Review and some other writings too.[58]

The case of Muhammad Jafar Thanesari, who also wrote specifically to couner Hunter's contention, has already been examined earlier.

It would be instructive to note, along with the views of such writers, the remarks of some English writers who are more forthright in emphasising the anti-British character of the movement since the beginning. Cunningham's remark has already been referred to.[59] Similarly Hunter, while commenting on the situation at the end of the Ambeyla Campaign (1863) writes, "Our prison gates have closed upon batch after batch of unhappy misguided traitors, the Courts have sent one set of ring-leaders after another to lonely islands across the sea; yet the whole country continues to furnish money and men to the forlorn hope of Islam on our Frontier and persists in its bloodstained protest against Christian rule."[60] Another writer remarks, "Nevertheless the colonies re-established by Syed Ahmad's lieutenants... were left as a legacy to the British Government, perhaps one of the most troublesome legacies we took with the Punjab."[61]

To a high ranking police official, inquiring into the Wahhabis' activities during 1860s; it seemed strange that evidence should be required to prove, "that these fanatics are waging war with the Queen; they are in a state of continued hostility against the English. Their professed object is to drive out the English, their attitude is one of perpetual hostility."[62]

The disintegration of the Mughal imperial authority and the increasing dominance of the British, on the one hand, and the impact of the Waliullahi tradition, on the other, were the twin sets of circumstances which led to the beginnings of the movement. The initial resistance against the British was led by the Mughal ruling class. An incisive case-study of the course and nature of this initial resistance in eastern India by Rajat K. Ray[63] characterises it as "a Mughal patriotic war." Accepting a discontinuity between the "initial resistance to the English and the later Indian nationalism,"Ray stresses the need, nonetheless, "to try and clarify the changing forms of discontent, disaffection and patriotism in the first century of British rule in India." He characterises the Mughal patriotic wars as "a sort of proto-nationalism, albeit one that had no connection with the modern nationalism of the nineteenth century." Further, raising the point as to whether the "old-world Mughal patriotism of the later eighteenth century was informed by a sense of Indian nationality, or whether membership of the political nation was understood to be confined to Muslim noblemen alone," he maintains that the "the latter was by no means the case."

Two points deserve attention in this context. Firstly, the long tradition of hostility of the Muslim ruling class to the encroachments of the British did not die down; it continued.[64] The Wahhabi Movement represented, among other things, a continuation of this anti-*firangi* tradition, and it left behind a legacy to which people looked back in later times, as during the movement of 1857, or even much later.[65] Secondly, the concept of patriotism has to be understood in a wider sense. Its working can be seen in events quite separated in place and time, as in Joan of Arc's wars against the English, and the uprising in Delhi against the Soldiery of Nadir Shah. If we can talk of an 'old world patriotism' and of 'proto-nationalism, albeit one that had no connection with modern nationalism of the nineteenth century,'[66] these characteristics, in the late 18th century, can as well be applied in the case of the Wahhabi Movement, despite some differences.

The evolution of the Wahhabi Movement and its nature, as also the question as to where to place it in the history of the struggle against foreign rule, has to be viewed against this background. The Wahhabi Movement does not fit neatly into any one of the categories into which the study of the history of early resistance to foreign rule has been divided chronologically or thematically.[67] It cuts across them, both in time and content. While sharing something of the character of the Mughal 'partriotic wars' and of 'a sort of proto-nationalism,' the Wahhabi Movement also marks the beginnings of new tendency which gained prominence during the subsequent period, reaching out to a wider circle of people and advocating new modes of action, such as winning the support of the Indian units of the army, the preaching of passive non-cooperation with the established authority and promoting the formation of self-governing institutions at the local levels.

3. The Suppression of the Movement and its Legacy.

The small state founded by Sayyid Ahmad on the North-Western Frontier and the organisational centre which were established in British India subsequently were the two pivots around which the activities of the Wahhabis revolved. The Frontier tribal area was elected in the hope of moral, material and armed support from the Pathan chiefs and small rulers in the area. The expected support, however, did not materialise; on the contrary, Sayyid Ahmad had to spend much of his time and resources in meeting the machinations and opposition of some leaders of the tribesmen. It has been stated by a number of early British writers, and following them by many recent writers too, that it was the puritanical zeal of the Wahhabis which alienated the tribesmen. But there is no evidence to indicate that the attitude of the tribesmen would have been any different if these 'puritanical' measures had not been followed. Right from the beginning, when the small band of Sayyid Ahmad's followers were in no position to enforce their ideas, the tribesmen were being unpredictable. Sayyid Ahmad could not succeed in obtaining the same kind of response there as he had in the plains. It was this failure which rendered the Wahhabis, during the post-Balakote period, increasingly dependent on the support from the centres inside the country, the other pivot.

The securing of a safe and short line of supply, easily defensible, is an elementary military precaution, and the Wahhabis must surely have realised the great risks involved in a supply line not only hundreds of miles long but passing right through the enemy's territory. Secrecy and fidelity alone could not have kept it going for long. The Wahhabis realised it but there was no way out, at least for some time.

While the Wahhabis' preachings and pamphlets laid great stress upon the 'obligation' to migrate to the *Daru'l Islam*, they gave option to those who for some reason could not migrate to extend financial help to the movement, for the time being. Thus, there developed numerous centres all over the country which supplied men and money to the state on the Frontier. The Wahhabis perhaps hoped that after they had consolidated their position on the Frontier they would be less dependent upon this aid from British Indian centres, but that stage never came.

In essence, it was the failure of the Wahhabis to develop material resources even remotely matching those of their adversaries which decided the issue finally. Sheer enthusiasm devotion and spiritedness could not be a substitute for material resources. In this the Wahhabis, as the whole of the Orient, during the 18th and the 19th centuries, were victims of circumstances not quite within their control. The Industrial Revolution and the subsequent technological advances had made available to the West resources, particularly means of war, far superior to anything that the Orient could hope for. The crude manufactory of the Wahhabis at Malka and their cruder hand-made guns could never be a match for the Enfield Rifles which were put to use in the N.W. Frontier for the first time during Cotton's expedition of 1858. It was this superior military capability of the West which turned out to be the decisive factor. It had proved to be deciding factor in many larger clashes between the West and the East, ranging from the opening of Japan and the defeat of the Safavid and Mughal empires to the suppression of the Rising of 1857.

This crucial point about the military superiority of the West was obvious to some contemporary observers too. One of them was al-Bahbahani, an observant scholar-traveller from Persia who travelled through northern India and has made very significant observations on the political, social and cultural state of affairs in his work *Miratu'l Aḥwāl-i Jahān Numa*[68] written at Patna around 1809. Writing about Lake's campaign against Holkar (1805), Bahbahani attributes Holkar's failure to the superiority of guns over swords[69] (no doubt, there were guns on the Maratha side too but Bahbahani is referring to the overwhelming superiority of the British in this respect).

Some of the Wahhabi pamphlets do show an awareness of this factor[70] but not much was done in practice to meet the problem. When the significance of a factor is not adequately realised the question of taking remedial measures, naturally, does not arise.

It would be wrong, however, to think of the movement as a total failure. Militarily, of course, it was suppressed but the social reform activities continued, and its impact was many-sided.

The Wahhabis with their compact organisation covering the whole of northern India, their secret cells in the army and contacts in various princely states such as Tonk and Hyderabad, provided a base and a model which was used directly or indirectly by many during the movement of 1857-58 and subsequently. Of the former, one of the most intrepid fighters, Ahmadullah Shah—who is referred to as the 'Maulavi of Fyzabad' in the contemporary English records but who actually belonged to Chinpattan (Madras)—shows the influence of the Wahhabis' ideas.[71]

The Wahhabis were the earliest to realise the importance of the Indian Units of the Company's army, and made several attempts at different cantonments to win them over, or to 'tamper' with their allegiance', as the official records put it.[72] The secret organisation built up by them for the relay of vital information and the supply of men and money across the whole length of the British Indian territory to the Wahhabi state on the North-Western Frontier was so effective that it elicited the admiration of some police officers and magistrates connected with the investigation and trial of the cases.

The unobtrusive and effective method of the Wahhabis for collecting money and foodgrains by the *muthia* system was specifically cited as a model by the early leaders of the Indian National Congress. At a meeting held in Calcutta in July 1883, Surendranath Bannerjee while moving a resolution for raising a National Fund for carrying on the struggle for constitutional rights, said, "How do the Wahhabis raise their funds? I speak of the Wahhabi reformers, not the Wahhabi rebels, so you need not be afraid. They do it in this way. Every householders puts by a handful of rice before he takes his meal, and these handfuls are all collected in course of a week and then they are taken to a mosque for the Wahhabi missionary to come round and take them up. In this way a Fund is raised for the maintenance of the Wahhabi Mission."[73]

The method of social boycott of 'loyalist' elements, which Reily noticed during his investigations, and described as *hukka pani bund* (not sharing a puff of the *hukka,* or a glass of water), the promotion of a spirit of passive non-cooperation by the *Faraidis*- all these were developed into powerful methods of political agitation subsequently. It should be remembered that these had their beginnings during the course of the Wahhabi Movement.

Turning to the impact in the socio-religious field, it may be recalled that Sayyid Ahmad represented a happy blend of spiritual enlightenment and practical efficiency. It was this which distinguished him from the Sufis in general, and enabled him to give a practical form to the ideas of Shah Waliullah.[74] Sayyid Ahmad gave much attention to the problem of popular reform of customs and practices. Some of these were spiritually harmful, as making people susceptible to committing sinful acts, and, more seriously, towards a compromise with the doctrine of *tauḥīd,* the bedrock of Islam. These were also materially harmful, leading people to wasteful expenditure and indebtedness.[75] The baneful effects of customs and practices associated with birth, circumcision, marriage, death, visitations to tombs and celebrations of *a'rās* (death anniversaries of saints) have been spelt out in detail and strongly criticised in the *Sirātu 'l Mustaqīm,* and many other tracts written subsequently. The Wahhabis also stressed the efficacy of direct reading and understanding, as far as possible, of the religious texts. They advocated a strong affirmation of *tauḥīd,* and rejection of *bid'āt* in the day-to-day life, and, at the intellectual level, the validity of the doctrine of *ijtihād.* The overall effect of all these was a lessening of the stranglehold of the worldly-minded *'ulamā* and the *Sūfiā* on the life of the common people, and a simpler and cleaner way of life.

Widow-remarriage, enjoined by Islam, had come to be frowned upon, particulary by the people belonging to the well-to-do groups, forcing a large number of women to a life of isolation, drudgery and humiliation. The Wahhabis denounced this attitude, and many of them, beginning with Sayyid Ahmad himself, set an example by marrying widows. Wilayat Ali and other members of his family followed the example, setting the earliest precedents for such marriages among the gentries of Patna.[76] On some other points, too,—undertaking the journey for *Hajj* in spite of the dangers on the way to the life of the pilgrims they set precedents for action.

The Wahhabis made good use of the methods of oral preachings by a host of itinerant preachers and missionaries, to whose education and training much attention was paid.[77] The two roles of the preachers and the writers were not mutually exclusive. In the case of many a person we find the two roles combined.[78]

The medium of the lithographic press was effectively utilised, particularly from 1850s onwards. Tracts were written on doctrinal and theological topics but more so on simple matters of day-to-day needs—how to perform *namāz* and *wudū*, explaining the meaning of texts of some *Aḥādīth,* criticising the harmful effects of certain customs and ceremonies, etc. In addition to circulation by copying, a large number of such tracts were printed and re-printed. Badiuzzaman of Burdwan, a disciple of Wilayat Ali, played a major role in this work by purchasing a printing press for the purpose. Many books printed from this press are still available. We do not have even a rough idea of the number of such works, but judging on the basis of the copies still available the output must have been quite high. It inculcated the habit of reading among the common people, helped enlarge the circle of the reading public and promoted education in general.

The Wahhabis made increasing use of the Urdu language for the popular-level tracts. Persian was still the chief medium of expression, not only for serious works but also, to some extent for correspondence among the educated people. The Wahhabis wrote most of their missionary tracts in Urdu prose, and translated into Urdu such works as were written originally in Persian; in some cases the Persian text and its Urdu translation were printed side by side in opposite columns of a page. The contribution of the Wahhabis to the growth of Urdu prose-writing in the second half of the 19th century is a separate subject by itself, and although it has received some attention recently a definitive study is yet to be made.

Finally, it is to be noted that the suppression of the Wahhabi Movement turned the attention of the people to alternative courses of action, including that of the assimilation of English education and Western sciences, advocated by Sayyid Ahmad's namesake - Sir Syed Ahmad Khan (1808-98). Sir Syed's work, marking the beginning of all modern social and educational reforms in Indo-Muslim society, was started in a way as a reaction to the Wahhabi Movement, and to that extent owed its origins to it.

NOTES

1. See Bibliography.
2. See Bibliography.
3. See Bibliography.
4. See Bibliography.
5. See Bibliography.
6. See Bibliography.
7. See Bibliography.
8. *Sirat-i Sayyid Ahmad Shaid*, vols. 1 and 11, Karachi, 1975 and 1974
9. *Sayyid Ahmad Shahid*, vols. I-IV, Lahore, 1954-55.
10. *Moslem Nationalism in India and Pakistan*, Washington, 1963.
11. See chapter X; also my article, The Missionary Literature of the Wahhabis: Its Historical Significance, Christian W. Troll *(ed) Islam in India; Studies and Commentaries*, vol. I, New Delhi, 1982 pp. 52-63.
12. See Bibliography for Shah Munammad Husain's personal *ms.* copy of the *Sirātu'l Mustaqīn* containing a copy of the *Sanad* of *Khilafat* given by Sayyid Ahmad to Shah Muhammad Husain (App.1) and for a copy of the *Tadhkira-i Sādga* belonging to Abdul Ghaffar Sahib; also, chap V, p. 168 no.1.
13. T.E. Ravenshaw's Memorandum on the Wahhabis, Mayo Papers, Cambridge University Library,*ms*, 7490, Box 13.
14. *Selections from the Records of the Bengal Government*,vol. XL11, (Trial of Moulvi Ahmedoollah, of Patna, and Others for Conspiracy and Treason), Calcutta, 1866. See also chapter VIII.
15. W.H. Paget, *Records, of the Expeditions Undertaken Against the North-West Frontier Tribes*, Calcutta, 1874 (it was revised and brought up to date by A.H. Mason, London, 1884), Colonel John Adye *Sitana: A Mountain Campaign on the Borders of Afghanistan in 1963*, London, 1867; *Gazettee Extraordinary, Government of India*, 30 January, 1864. see also chapter VII, p. 240 n.3.
16. Mayo papers, mentioned above. Also, the papers of Ripon, President of Board of Control and James O' Kinealy.
17. Pearse, Hugh, *ed., Memoirs of Alexander H. Gardner, London,* 1911.
18. Nevill, H.R., *District Gazetteer Bareilly*, vol. XIII, Allahabad, 1911.

Surprisingly, both these books have somehow escaped the attention of the writers on the subject, including the present writer who had not used them in the first edition of this book.

19. James Routledge, *English Rule and Native Opinion in India,* London, 1878.
20. *Vide Supra,* pp. 344, 348.
21. *The Indian Musalmans, Are they bound in conscience to rebel against the Queen ?* London, 1871. The sub-title was dropped in the second edition of the book.
22. *The Emergence of Indian Nationalism,* Cambridge, 1968.
23. *The Muslims in British India,*Cambridge, 1972.
24. Hunter, op. cit, Preface, 2nd edition.

    See also article by Muhammad Delawar Husain, Life and Works of Sir William Wilson Hunter (1840-1900)," *Journal of the Asiatic Society of Bangladesh,* 1976, 21(2), pp. 76-97.
25. *I.M.* p. 142
26. *Vide supra,* pp. 27-29.
27. Jafar Thanesari, *Sawāniḥ Aḥmadī,* which ends with the battle of Balakote. Abul Hasan Ali Nadwi, *Sirat-i Sayyid Ahmad Shahid,* 1949 edition, which covered the portion upto the journey for *Hajj* only. In the subsequent editions of 1975 and 1974, the coverage was extended to the whole movement.
28. Mehr, op. cit.
29. Malleson, G.B., *History of the Indian Mutiny,* vol. 1; Majunmdar, R.C., *The Sepoy Mutiny and the Revolt of 1857.*
30. Mahmud Husain et al. *(eds.) A History of the Freedom Movement in Pakistan,* Karachi,; Tarachand, *A History of the Freedom Movement in India.* vol. 11, Majumdar, R.C. *History of the Freedom Movement in India,* vol.1.
31. Hafeez Malik, op. cit. Seal. op. cit. ; and Hardy, op.cit.
32. Hunter's book, the first independent study of the movement, does cover the period from the time of Sayyid Ahmad to the Ambela campaign but its use of the early, non-English sources is rather limited. On the other hand, its strong point is the awareness shown of the crucial role of the internal organisation, and an account of its working.
33. See chapter V, pp. 188 *ff.*
34. J. Rehatsek's article in *J.R.A.S.* (Bombay Branch), 1880, vol. XIV, p. 362.
35. Rehatsek's article cited above.
36. *Vide infra,* 406-07
37. These letters were published in the *Sawāniḥ Aḥmadī,* one of the earliest biographical account of Sayyid Ahmad written by Jafar Thanesari, an active follower of the movement.

38. See Appendix VII.
39. *Sawanih Ahmadi,* pp. 189-90, P.U. Lirary *ms.*, f 36.
40. S.H. Askari, Political Significance of the Movement of Syed Ahmed Brailvi, *Proceeding, vol.* I.C.H.R., 1955 31 Pt. 11: 174-81.

    See also, *Mehr,* 111, pp. 11-15 where extracts from such letters are given. The point about the distortions made in the published text has been mentioned elsewhere; *ibid.,* p.22.
41. Cunningham, op.cit., Calcutta, 1904, p. 265. Italics are mine.
42. Oliver, *Across the Border,* London, 1890, p. 288.
43. R.C. Majumdar, *History of the Freedom Movement in India* vol. 1, Calcutta, 1971, p. 252; see also, pp. 219-20
44. The book under reference is arranged in two parts, titled, respectively, *Sporadic Outbursts Against British Rule* and *The Indian Nation in the Making.* The former examines the establishment of British rule and the early resistance to it, first in Bengal and then in other parts of the country. Majumdar characterises the resitance as originating from political and economic causes, religious frenzy and primitive tribal instincts, putting the *Faraidi* Movement in the category of religious frenzy. He then gives a detailed account of the Rising of 1857, and in the concluding chapter of part.1, titled *Anti-British Outbreaks After 1857,* he gives a brief account of the Wahhabis' activities. Thus, the origins of the movement as also the continuing Wahhabis' activities and its different phases have not received due attention.
45. Majumdar, op. cit., p. 118.
46. Ibid., p.121. The name of the writer has not been mentioned, but the portion of quotation within single inverted commas is from the first edition of the present book, Calcutta, 1966, p. 95.
47. *Vide supra,* p. 174.
48. *Vide supra,* pp. 323 *ff.*
49. *Supra,* pp. 183, 66.
50. Mayo Papers, University Library, Cambridge, U.K.: *Ms.* 7490 Box 13, Memorandum by T.E. Ravenshaw.
51. P.U. Library *ms.* of Sayyid Ahmad's Letters, p. 146.
52. For the full text of the letter, see Appendix 11.
53. Ibid.
54. In a letter addessed to Nawab Sikandar Jah, Nizam of Hyderabad (1805-28), (Patna University Library *ms.* of Sayyid Ahmad's letter, p. 129) a similar request for financial assistance was made.
55. See pp. 195 *ff.*
56. Titled *Hunter par Hantar* (with a pun on the word 'Hunter' which means a lash in Urdu), it was published separately, and extensive extracts from it, translated into English, are reproduced in G.P.I. Graham, *The Life and Works of Sir Syed Ahmad,* London, 1885, pp.

205-44; see also, K.M. Ashraf's article "Muslim Revivalists and the Revolt of 1857" in P.C. Joshi, (ed.), *Rebellion 1857: A symposium*, p. 78 and note 27.

57. See also, K.A. Nizami, *Sayyid Ahmad Khan*, New Delhi, 1966, pp. 131-32.

58. For the use of terms of high respect which Sir Syed prefixed with the names of Sayyid Ahmad and Shah Ismail, see *Athāru's Sanādīd, 1st ed.* (1846). The chapter was deleted from subsequent editions and have been republished as *Tadhkira-i Ahl-i Dehlī* by Anjuman-i Taraqqi-i Urdu (Pakistan), Karachi, 1955.

    Attention may be drawn here to Abul Kalam Azad's view of the Wahhabi Movement as expressed in his 'Review', or rather Foreword, to the first edition of the *Tadhkira-i Sādiqa* (1901). of the text of the Review and the chronogrammatic verses appended to it. See appendix VIII.

59. *Supra*, p. 403.
60. *Supra*, p. 259.
61. Oliver, op.cit., p. 290
62. Letter from J.H. Reily, D.I.G. Police, to I.G. Police, L.P., no. 203, dated Abbotabad, 30th Sept., 1869.
63. Rajat Kanta Ray, "Colonial Penetration and the Initial Resistance: The Mughal Ruling Class, The English East India Company and the struggle for Bengal, 1757-1800," *I.H.R.*, 1985-86, XII (1-2): 1-105.
64. K.M. Ashraf in his article providing useful insights into the nature of the Wahhabi Movement, observes." the Wahhabi outlook on politics and religious life embodied the century-old hostility of the Muslim ruling classes to the growing encroachments of the British as also the urgings of the working masses for better and happier conditions of life. It is not, therefore, surprising if the Wahhabi leaders of the day (i.e. during (1857-58) displayed both the vigour and tenacity of the working people, and the confusions of a decadent ruling class." (P.C. Joshi, ed., *Rebellion 1857: A Symposium*, PPH, 1957. pp. 71-72.
65. *Vide infra*, p. 418
66. Rajat K. Ray's article, cited above, p. 103.
67. The arrangement of the matter in R.C. Majumdar, *History of the Freedom Movement in India*, vol. 1, has already been referred to (*Supra*, p.404, n.3)

    Tarachand, *History of the Freedom Movement in India*, vol. 11, has a somewhat similar arrangement. Chapter 1 (pp. 1-37) titled "Resistance and Insurrections." has twelve sections of which one, titled the Waliullahi Movement" (pp. 23-30), is about the Wahhabis. Chronogically put together at one place before the events of 1857.

(The Revolt of 1857 constitutes the second chapter), the account itself shows that the Wahhabi Movement continued till long afterwards.

68. On the significance of this work as a useful source-material for the study among other things of the rise of British power in India see my article 'Calcutta, 1806. Observations of an Iranian Scholar-traveller', R.N. Chakrabarti (ed.), *J.N. Sarakar Felicitation Volume*, Calcutta.

    An English translation of somc portions of this work relating to India is being prepared by Mr F. Haider, Professor of Persian, Patna College, with the financial assistance of Indian Council of Historical Research, New Delhi.

69. Madrasa Sulaimaniya (Patna City) *ms.* Copy, f. 330.

    It may be added here that Holkar was later made to recognise the independent status of his former commander Amir Khan as Nawab of Tonk. When Amir Khan too was brought into treaty-relationship with the British and virtually disarmed, Sayyid Ahmad, who was then serving in his army advised the Nawab against the alliance, and on his advice being ignored left the Nawab's army (*Supra*, pp. 10,49).

70. *Supra*, pp. 378, 386.
71. For an account of Ahmadullah Shah, making use of a scarely noticed versified biography of the Shah and some other non-English source materials, see. S.Z.H. Jafri, "Ahmadullah Shah in the 1857 Rebellion", presented in the seminar on Rebellion of 1857 at AMU, Aligarh, 1988, (proceedings to be published soon).
72. *Supra*, pp. 188 *ff*.
73. Printed Report of the Proceedings of National Fund Meeting held on the 17th July, 19883, Sen Press, Calcutta, 1883. I owe this reference to my friend Dr. Jatashamkar Jha, former Director, K.P. Jayaswal Research Institute, Patna.

    The distinction drawn by Surendranath Sen between the efforts of the Wahhabi preachers and the Wahhabi 'rebels' was for obvious reasons; otherwise the authorities would have objected to the advocacy of a method used by 'rebels'.

74. *Supra*, p. 91.
75. *Supra*, p. 21.
76. For references to such cases in the Sadiqpur family of Patna, see *T.S.*
77. *Supra*, p. 107.
78. See chapter X.

Appendix I

English translation of the text of the *Sanad*[1] of *Khilāfat* given by Sayyid Ahmad to Shah Muhammad Hussain at the time of his visit to Patna (vide, p. 47).

In the name of the merciful God

Be it known to those who seek the way of God in general, and to those in particular, present and absent, who are the friends of Syed Ahmad, that the object of those who become the disciples of holy men by the ceremony of joining hands is to secure the way of pleasing God and depends on the observance of the laws of his prophet. He who believes that the way of pleasing God can be found without observing the laws of prophet is a false and deluded man his pretensions are false and untenable. The law of the prophet is founded on two things, *viz.*;

1st : The not attributing to any creature the attributes of God.

2nd: Not inventing forms and practices which were not observed in the days of the prophet or his successors or Khalifs.

The former consists in disbelieving that angels, spiritual guides, disciples, teachers, students, prophets or saints remove one's difficulties; in abstaining from having recourse to any of the above creatures for the attainment of any wish or desire; in denying that any of them has the power of granting favours or of removing evils; in considering them as helpless and ignorant as oneself in respect to the power of God; in never making any offering to any prophet, saint, holy man or angel for the obtaining of any object, but merely to consider them as friends of God, to follow them with the view of being made similarly acceptable to God; to consider them as guides to the way of pleasing God; to believe that they have power to rule accidents in life, and that they are acquainted with the secret knowledge of God is downright (*kufr*) infidelity. No true faithful follower ought to be implicated in any of the above dogmas.

With regard to the second point, viz., non-introduction of novelties in religion, (it) consists in strongly adhering to all the devotions and practices in the affairs of life, which were observed in the time of the prophet, in avoiding all such innovations in the marriage ceremonies; the mourning ceremonies; the adorning of tombs; the erection of large edifices over tombs; the lavish expenditures on the anniversaries of the dead; the construction of "Tajeeahs"[2] and the like, and in endeavouring, as far as may be practicable, to put a stay to these practices. A man must first leave off such practices, and next invite the attention of all Mussulmans to the fact that it is as much obligatory on them in following the law of the prophet as to obey the commandment of God in doing what he commands to be done and in refraining from what he forbids, since the above is well impressed on my mind, it behoves all who seek God to place the matter before their eyes and now by joining each others hands to abide by it, and to do so particularly with Shaik Mahomed Hossein, who has pledged to do the same by joining his hands with mine and to whom I have fully explained all the above matters, and authorised him to take such vows from you and to teach you holy practices in the room of myself, so it behoves the said Shaik Mahomed Hossein to adopt the law as above explained, to direct his body and soul to God; to follow the law in spirit and acts; to shake off any dirt of "*Shirk*" and of innovations ("*Biddat*") that may be on him to strive and incite people to make their vows by joining their hands with his. Those who will take vows by joining their hands with those of any of my friends will derive benefit therefrom, and will be purified from the ceremonies of "*Shirk*" and the superiority of law will take hold in their hearts. I will also pray for them and their vows will bring them money and great benefit. Sincere and hearty exertions should be used in the instruction of the faithful. Their vows taken and instruction given them for holy employments. May God grant that I and all my friends may be brought into the company of those who believe in the oneness of God and are the followers of the law.

Seal
Ismahoo Ahmad
1235.[3]

Notes

1. The original *Sanad* was found in the house of Yahya Ali at the time of its search by the police (1863) and was included as an exhibit

(no. 218) in the trial of Ahmadullah, *Selections*, pp. 32-34. The present translated English texts has been reproduced from it, and the old spellings have been retained.

A copy of the original, Persian text is attached to the copy of the *Sirātu'l Mustaqīm* prepared for the personal use of Shah Muhammad Husian, and another copy was available with the late Zaid Sahib, son of Abdul Ghaffar Sahib. of Sadipore.

Although Sayyid Ahmad appointed numerous *Khalifas* all over the country this is perhaps the only available copy of such *Sanads*. The document is important as reflecting Sayyid Ahmad's religious thinking.

2. Paper-made replicas of the mausoleum of Imam Husain at Karbala, taken out in the *Muḥarram* processions.
3. The date A.H. 1235, corresponds to 1819-1820, a little earlier than the date of Sayyid Ahmad's arrival in Patna. This discrepancy in the date on the seal can be explained by recalling that such personal seals had the legend and/or the date engraved on them. The seals often continued to be used after the year had changed, and hence there used to be discrepancy between the actual year and the date on the seal. The present writer has seen many such impressions of seals.

Appendix II

English translation of the text of Sayyid Ahmad's letter[1] addressed to Raja Hindu Rao[2] (vide, p. 48).

"From the Chief of the Faithful, Sayyid Ahmad, for the perusal of Raja Hindu Rao, high-stationed and exalted in rank, the mine of generosity and kindness, the asylum of men of the sword and the pen, master of treasures and establishments, commander of troops and levies and formulator of the policies of the stately dominion, may he enjoy prosperity and success and may he be imbued with pleasure and happiness in life;

Let it be known after expressing the due compliments of cordiality that this humble self with a band of servants of the Almighty Cherisher of the World is engaged in the vicinity of Peshawar in furthering the cause of the religion of Islam and strengthening the cause of the Community and the chief of Mankind (Prophet Muhammad), and is expecting the fruits of their good labour from the Threshold of the Bestower of Bounties. It is manifest to your exalted self *that alien people from distant lands have become the rulers of territories and Time, and traders and vendors of goods have attained the rank of sovereignty*. They have destroyed the dominions of the big grandees and the estates of the nobles of illustrious ranks, and have eroded their honour and authority. Since the rulers and administrators of justice have retired into the nook of obscurity, inevitably the penniless and powerless have risen up to the occasion. This group of weak people have girded up their loins with a view of serving the cause of the Faith of the Cherisher of the Two Worlds and are on no account motivated by worldly things and its glory ad grandeur. It is only to serve the cause of the Glorious God and not because of a covetousness for wealth and property that they have risen to the occasion. *In the event of the land of Hindustan being cleared of the alien enemies and these (weak) people succeeding in their efforts, the rank and offices of the State and Government would be entrusted to the seekers (of these), and the roots of their power and authority would be strengthened.* These weak ones have only this much to seek from the nobles and grandees of high station, that they should heartily help and support the cause of Islam and be firmly seated as the occupants of throne.

Although this group of Derveshes is, apparently, utterly destitute of resources yet they are happy and contented with the fostering care and protection of the Lord and Master which they enjoy. They detest the desire and yearnings for rank and dignity, and are free from cupidity and avarice of wealth and property. They do not aim at the satiation of personal or carnal desires either at present or in future. They would strengthen the basis of the government of all those ancient chiefs who would strive to help and support them.

As the bearer of this, Haji Bahadur Shah, acceptable to the Court of God, is one of the elder companions of the weak one, therefore, the task of furnishing the details and explaining these points has been entrusted to his truthful tongue. What else remains to be written except a repeated emphasis on your getting at the essence of this letter and realising the importance of the situation.

I would like to add that the Haji Sahib has since long been engaged in serving the cause of the Almighty and as such is unable to look after to the interests and comforts of his family. As he is determined to accompany the Islamic Army in future too, he is not expected to come to the rescue of his family even in future. Accordingly it is being written to your exalted self that his brother and son be provided with jobs in your state so that the Haji Sahib may be engaged wholeheartedly in serving the cause of God.

Salutation

Notes

1. P.U. library *ms.* of Sayyid Ahmad's Letters, ff. 102-03. Italics are mine. On the significance of this letter, see Chapter XI, p. 10.
2. As stated above, Raja Hindu Rao was the brother-in-law of Maharaja Daulat Rao Sindhia, and Sayyid Ahmad had met him at Gwalior, on his way to Peshawar. Hindu Rao's influence at the *darbār* must have increased when his sister ascended the *gaddi* after the death of Daulat Rao Sindhia (1827). She was later deposed and with her brother sought the help of the British. Hindu Rao had bought a house at Delhi, called Bara Hindu Rao in which William Fraser the famous British Resident at Delhi had resided for some time. (Hearn, *Seven Cites of Delhi*, London, 1906).

Appendix III

List[1] of some terms used in the Wahhabis' correspondence and the aliases by which the chief 'conspirators' were known (p. 141):

Jehad—Holy War for Mahomedan faith against all *Kafirs* or infidels.

Zakat—A contribution from profits of trade, paid by members of the Wahabi sect, the proceeds being in the custody of the Patna Moulvies; and expended for the purpose of *Jehad*.

Recruits for the war are called, *Jehadis*, *Khidmutgars* (servants), *Beoparies* (merchants), *Mosafirs* (travellers), *Nargow* (bullocks).

Bands of recruits are called Kalifa. Mulka Sittana is spoken of as *Burrah* Godown, Patna as the *Chota* Godown.

A battle is called the *mokurddama* (suit or case in court).

God is spoken of as the Mooktar or agent.

Gold mohurs are called large red rubies, large Delhi gold embroidered shoes and large birds.

Malf mohurs are called small red beads and small embroidered shoes.

Remittances in mohurs are spoken of as rosaries of red beads.

Draft or *hoondies* are called white stones, and the amount, intimated by the number of white beads as on a rosary.

Remittances of money are spoken of as the price of books and merchandise.

The *Kafila* is used to designate the premises belonging to the Moulvis at Sadikpore in Patna City, and more particularly that part formerly occupied by Moulvie Wilayat Ali and by Abdool Ruheem.

Wahhabi Aliases

Moulvie Ahmedoolah, alias Ahmad Ali, Mahomed Ali or Ahmad Khan.

Abdoollah, alias Baboo Sahib, Baboo Jaun Khan Sahib, and Babu Meea Jaun Khan Sahib.

Fiaz Ali, Alias Busseeroodeen of Fiaz Alum.
Esau, alias Ruhullah, a paraphrase of Essau Messy of God.
Hafiz Abdool Majeed, alias Hafiz Sahib.
Abdul Kareem, alias Kareem Buksh.
Yahiya Ali, alias Mohioodeen.
Abdul Ruheem, alias Mirza Ruheeem Beg.
Mahomed Shuffee, alias Shifayat Ali.
Kazee Meea Jaun, alias Mahomed Shakur or Abdul Ruhaman.
Abdul Ruheem, alias Mirza Ruheem Beg.
Mahomed Shuffee, alias Shifayat Ali.
Kazee Meea Jaun, alias Mahomed Shakeer or Abdul Rahman.

Christians or British troops are called the heirs of Hazrat Ruhullah (Jesus Christ), deceased.'

Notes

1. The list forms one of the enclosures to the notes, memoranda, etc. prepared by T.E. Ravenshaw at the time of Ahmadullah's Trial, and is given in the trial papers; see *Selections*, pp. 161-62.

   The old Spellings have been retained. So also the meaning/definition of the terms *Jihād* and *Zakāt* which do not correspond to the correct position.

Appendix IV

English translation of a joint letter[1] addressed by Abdullah and Sayyid Imran to a Frontier Tribal Chief on the eve of the Ambeyla Campaign, (p. 185).

"After compliments; a large force of the infidels has arrived at Selim Khan, Yar Husain and Shaikh Jana with the object of plundering this country. It is therefore incumbent on you immediately on the receipt of this letter to gird up your waist and proceed to Chumla and after issuing notices to the other allies of the pass (Ambeyla) to occupy Sirpati and Landai, that is the Chinglai Valley, and maintain a firm hold of your position. You should not allow a moment's delay in carrying out the above instructions. Should however any delay occur, the evil-doing infidels will plunder and devastate the whole of the hilly tract-especially the provinces of Chumla, Bonair, Swat, etc., and annex these countries to their dominions, and then our religion and worldly possessions would entirely be subverted. Consequently, keeping in consideration a regard for Islam, the dictates of faith and worldly affairs, you ought by no means to neglect the opportunity. The infidels are extremely deceitful and treacherous, and will, by whatever means they can, come into these hills, and declare to the people of the valley that they have no concern with them, that their quarrel is with the Hindoostanees, that they will not molest the people, even as much as touch a hair of their head but will return immediately after extirpating the Hindoostanees, and that they will not interefere with the country. They will also tempt the people with wealth. It is therefore proper for you not to give in to their deceit, or else, when they should get an opportunity, they will entirely ruin, torment, and put you to so many indignities, appropriate to themselves your entire wealth and possessions, and injure your faith. You will then obtain nothing but regret. We impress this matter on your attention.

Seal of	Seal of
Sayyid Imran	Abdullah

Notes

1. Paget and Mason. op. cit.

Appendix V

Extracts from "A Regulation (Regulation III of 1818) for the Confinement of State Prisoners Passed by the Vice-President in the Council on the 7th April, 1818" (p. 238).

"Preamble : I. Whereas reasons of State, embracing the due maintenance of the alliance formed by the British Government with foreign powers, the preservation of tranquillity in the territories of native princes entitled to its protection, and the security of the British dominions from foreign hostility and from internal commotion, occasionally render it necessary to place under personal restraint individuals against whom there may be sufficient ground to institute any judicial proceedings, or when such proceedings may not be adapted to the nature of the case, or may for other reasons be unavoidable or improper;

and whereas it is fit that, in every case of the nature herein referred to, the determination to be taken should proceed immediately from the authority of the Governor-General in Council;

and whereas the ends of justice require that, when it may be determined that any person shall be placed under personal restraint, otherwise than in persuance of some judicial proceedings, the grounds of such determination should from time to time come under revision and the person affected thereby should at all times be allowed freely to bring to the notice of the Governor-General in Council all circumstances relating to the supposed grounds of such determination, or to the manner in which it may be executed;

and whereas the ends of justice also require that due attention be paid to be health of every State Prisoner confined under this Regulation, and that suitable provision be made for his support according to his rank in life, and to his own wants and his family.

and whereas the reasons above declared sometime render it necessary that the estates and lands of *zamindars, tallokdars,* and others situated within the territories dependent on the Presidency of Fort William, would be attached and placed under the temporary management of the revenue authorities without having recourse to any judicial proceedings;

and whereas it is desirable to make such legal provisions as may secure from injury the just rights and interests of individuals whose estates may be so attached under the direct authority of the Government;

the Vice-President in Council has enacted the following rules which are to take effect throughout the provinces immediately subject to the Presidency of Fort William, from the date on which they may be promulgated.

II. First When the reasons stated in the preamble of this Regulation may seem to the Governor-General in Council to require that an individual should be placed under personal restraint, without any immediate view to ulterior proceedings of a judicial nature, a warrant of commitment under the authority of the Governor-General in Council and under the hand of the Chief Secretary of one of the Secretaries to the Government, shall be issued to the officer in whose custody such person is to be placed...

III. Every officer in whose custody any State Prisoner may be placed shall, on the 1st of January and 1st of July of each year, submit a report to the Governor-General in Council through the Secretary to Government in the Political Department, on the conduct, the health, and the comfort of such State Prisoner in order that the Governor-General in Council may determine whether the orders for his detention shall continue in force or shall be modified...

V. The officer in whose custody any State Prisoner may be placed is to forward, with such observations as may appear necessary, every representation which such State Prisoners may from time to time be desirous of submitting to the Governor-General in Council.

VI. Every officer in whose custody any State Prisoner may be placed shall, as soon after taking such prisoner into his custody as may be practicable, report to the Governor-General in Council whether the degree of confinement to which he may be subjected appears liable to injure his health, and whether the allowance fixed for his support be adequate to the supply of his own wants and those of his family, according to their rank in life.

VII. Every officer in whose custody any State Prisoner may be placed shall take care that the allowance fixed for the support of such State Prisoner is duly appropriate to that object..."

Appendix VI

A Case-Record of some of the high-handed and arbitrary methods of J.H. Reily and N. Ghose, D.I.G. and S.I., Police, Special Department, Lower Provinces (p. 239).

In August, 1867, a complaint was filed against Nobokisto Ghose, S.I., Police, for having wrongly and maliciously instituted criminal proceedings against one, Tiloke Singh, for the theft of some *thalees* (brass plates) with a view to harassing and injuring the complainant. The complaint was heard in the court of E. Drummond, Magistrate Patna, who committed the accused Ghose to Session Trial on 19 August.

The trial[1] was held in the court of W. Ainslie, the Session Judge, who was assisted by a jury. The accused was charged with having wrongfully instituted proceedings against the complainant with an intention to injure him.

The jury held him guilty and sentenced him to rigorous imprisonment for one year and a fine of Rs. 100/-. The judge concurred with the findings of the jury.[2]

The judgement of Ainsile on the case is in the best tradition of an independent and fearless judiciary keen to uphold the equality before law of all men, high and low. Some extracts from the judgement are given below as they indicate the high-handed and arbitrary methods of Reily and his subordinates.

"The order even of a Government, if such an order could be imagined, in this case is no authority for an act opposed to the written law of the land much less the order of an inferior authority. If Mr. Reily has pledged himself to hold the prisoner let him redeem his pledge with that I have no concern. That with which I am concerned is that law should have its course, that the charge against the prisoner brought before this court being within the jurisdiction of this court should be tried to conclusion... It is nothing to me whether the prisoner is convicted or acquitted on the merits of the case, but it is my duty to dispose of the plea under which it is sought to stop the action of this court. I cannot believe, and no sane man can believe, that the Government ever directed or authorised Mr. Reily and his subordinate to apprehend every man accused of an offence by such a man as Lakah Dusadh, without first satisfying themselves by independent testimony that his accusation was probably true... and then, not before, to take steps involving risks to the liberty, even perhaps to the life of their fellow-subjects, their equals before the law...

I must proceed to go on to notice the plea that the Special Police are not bound by those parts of the law relating to the General Police which refer to officers in the charge of a police station ... Mr. Reily says he can give no idea of the authority vested in his Department, he cannot even refer to the Government order constituting it. Now, I cannot believe he could not enlighten me a little if he would, or that his memory is so defective as it appears in this trial his position as the Head of such a Department forbids my believing this..."

The case was not related to the Wahhabis. But it occurred just on the eve of the commencement of the Wahhabi investigations in 1868. The two chief actors in this drama were the same as in the Wahhabi inquiries. Their arbitrary and vindictive methods in this case, so bluntly castigated by the Session Judge, are typical of their subsequent proceedings. The case gives us an idea of the arrogant attitude of Reily who considered that his Special Department was something above the law of the country and that it conferred upon him unfettered powers of arresting and prosecuting all and sundry.

The case also explains the unusual excitement and anger of the Divisional Commissioner, Patna, over the deputation by Reily of a man with such a tarnished reputation to Patna (the very place where he had been convicted) to carry on investigations against the Wahhabis.

Notes

1. Record room of the District Judges Court, Patna Bundle No. 1 (1867), session cases 1-56.
2. The present record relates to the session trial in which Ghose was convicted. But he was, probably, acquitted later, otherwise he could not have continued to be in government service in 1868 and afterwards. The acquittal is, however, not referred to in these papers.

Appendix VII

Texts of some letters of Sayyid Ahmad and his chief disciple, Shah Isma'il, and the interpolations made in them (pp. 66-67 and 301).

Presented below in opposite columns are the English translations of some relevant extracts from the letters of Sayyid Ahmad and his chief disciple, Shah Ismail, as published in Muhammad Jafar's *Sawāniḥ Aḥmadī* and as given in the unpublished manuscript collection of Sayyid Ahmad's Letters.

Sawanih Ahmadi	*Patna University ms.*
1. The ill-natured Sikhs and the ill-fated polytheists have gained control over the western parts of India from the banks of Indus to the capital city of Delhi. (Letter of Sayyid Ahmad Sahib to the Shah of Bukhara, pp. 189-93; the extract occurs on pp. 189-90).	The ill-natured Christians and the ill-fated polytheists have gained control over the *various parts of India* stretching from the banks of Indus *to the shore of the Ocean, which covers a distance of six* month's journey.[1] (f. 36).
2. The long-haired infidels (Sikhs) who have suzerainty over Punjab are very experienced, clever and deceitful. (same letter, p. 192).	The *Christian infidels* who have gained possession over *India* are very artful and deceptive (f. 39).
3. My real object is the establishment of *jihād* against the Sikhs of the Punjab and not to stay in the countries of Afghanistan and Yaghistan.[2] (Letter of Sayyid Ahmad to Shahzada Kamran, pp. 182-83;	My real object is the establishment of *jihād* and carrying *of war into Hindustan* and not to stay on in the country of lands of Khurasan. (f. 81).

the extract occurs on p. 183).	
We may not have power and resources like Ranjit Singh but who has told you that the Imam intends to proceed with his little force to Lahore? (Letter from Shah Ismail to Mir Shah Ali, pp. 210-13; the extract occurs on p. 211).	We may not have power and resources like those of Ranjit Singh *and the Company*, but who has told you that the Imam intends to proceed to *Lahore and Calcutta* with this little force? (f. 99).

Notes

1. Attention is drawn to the dropping of the qualifying sentence, about the distance being of Six month's journey, in the published version otherwise, the sentence would have been self-contradictory.
2. *i.e.*, independent territories.

Appendix VIII

Ab'ul Kalam Azad's 'Review'[1] of the *Tadhkira-i Sūdqa* (1901), (p. 304).

"Review of the Excellent Book, *Tadhkira-i Sādqa,* By the embodiment of grace and kindness, the gifted poet, matchless master of the language, *Maulāna* Abu'l Kalam Muhyu'd Din *Sāhib* (poetically surnamed) *Azād,* of Delhi, residing at Calcutta; (in Arabic) May God Save him from the evil designs of the jealous (persons), All praise is to Allah who has made his *Kalām* (the *Qur'ān*) a source of guidance for the people with insight, and (has made) (the hearts of) men of piety the repository of (Divine) secrets. We offer our salutations to (Prophet Muhammad) who came with the Manifest Book, and to all his descendants and Companions.

Verse (in Persian)

The way of the world is not worth having a second look.
For none who left this caravan (of Life) ever turned his face back.

'(Writing) the account of the preceding generations is a commentary upon (the activities of) the succeeding generations" is a good Arabic proverb, of which a confirmation is provided by this "Tadhkira-i Ahl-i Sādiqpurs". Its compiler is a scion of that family, *Janāb* Abdu'r Rahim *Sāhib Sadipūri,* who has given an account of his 'life'[2] on pages 130-58 of the book.

The learned compiler has given a full account of the family and biographical sketches of all members of the family. At a time when the affairs of the family have fallen into disarray, there are very few sources of information left, this book is very useful; it is one of the sources on the basis of which the family has come to earn everlasting fame.

If you look at it closely, there are very few accounts like this, which recalls to our minds the vicissitudes (of time) so effectively, and very few events, affecting the human feelings, like those which this family has gone through.

Firstly, the outline of the 'Rise and Fall' which this account presents can hardly be bettered by (an account of) any other set of events. For a family to rise to such heights that there be no parallel to such an accumulation of the wealth of learning as also of material possessions; that there were thousands of persons who were acquainted with it, and were willing to render all sacrifices for it; that the entire family should come to settle at one place, and this accidental congregation should acquire the name of 'Sadiqpur' (abode of the truthful), that although the name might be that of a ward of a town but its fame should rise from a local to a higher level because of the attainments of its residents; that if you were to look (at the family's history) from the point of view of eminence in learning you would find eminent authors and preachers in it, if you were to look at it from the point of wealth, you would find it placed high among the wealthy ones : and then, for that family to fall into the whirlpool of decline as a result of which all its achievements were to be set to nought, or, in a way, the whole lot were to get drowned; no one was to be left to remember it, or to offer any sacrifice for it; the rulers of the times themselves were, like an ill-fortune, to turn their face away from it; everything was to disappear in the twinkling of an eye; and when a person having shut his eyes for a moment were, on re-opening them, to find a desolate desert instead of a lofty palace, and nothing was to be seen of the towering structures, and of the Sadiqpuri walls[3]; only a revolutionarily transformed situation makes the viewer feel astounded. Oh, where is that Sadiqpore, and where are the residents of that Sadiqpore? Neither the houses have their residents, nor the residents their (former) grandeur. O' my God, what is all this?

Why did all this happen, come about? Oh, we do not know: (We can only say that) this is one of the revolution-creating powers of that Omnipotent Wisdom, the Creator of the Two Worlds. To transfer a rise into a fall. Its apparent cause cannot be considered as anything other than disunity.

Now look at it, this account teaches mankind the (ever-lasting) truth of His all-powerfulness, and of the evils of disunity. How deeply it (the account) affects the listeners. If only you were to put your hands on your heart you would feel how fast it is beating, what a terrifying effect it is creating. What impact would be greater and more powerful than this?

Then, in what a way did this ill-revolving, Heaven treat those (of the family) who were left? What misfortune did not befall them? What hardships did they not undergo? At the same time, their matchless fortitude and patience and their thankfulness to God, even under such trying circumstances, teaches us such a fine lesson of being ever-thankful and obedient to God, that no better way of imparting such a lesson is possible.

And after all this, for unity and perseverance to yield fruit again, due to the efforts of one effort-maker, for the fortunes of the family to rise again, and for the school[4] to be established, and help promote education: The happening of all this by *ittifāq* (by chance) : Does it not teach us the blessings of *ittifāq* (unity)?[5]

Truly, this book from the beginning to the end presents before the eyes (of the readers) a 'photo'[6] of certain special kinds of feelings and events. May God recompense the compiler who prepared this account by striving hard to gather information from different quarters. (He has) like the ants gathered bits of sugar and prepared *laddū* (a sweetmeat) for us to partake of it, and has given to us an opportunity to be benefitted by it.

At the instance of my kind friend, *Janāb Maulāna* Muhammad Yusuf[7] *Sāhib* Jafri, Chief Maulawi, Board of Examiners, Calcutta, I had composed a *mathnawī* (long poem) as a *taqrīz* (to this book) but due to difficulty of space it could not be printed here; (instead), I am presenting below three chronogrammatic *qiṭa'*.

A qita' recording the date of the writing of *Tadhkira-i Sādqa* :

"Glad tidings : O, admires of 'Sadiqpure.

Glad tidings : O, ardent lovers of (the beautiful) face of the Motherland.

Ḥaḍrat-i Maulawi 'Abd-i Rahim'.

the learned, and the master of every arts

He has written this (historical) account,

in the praise of which the tongue stammers;

Each dot (on the pages) of which is like a mole on the face of the beloved,

Each page of which is glistening like the walk of a garden.

The events have been recorded truly, exactly.

There is no gainsaying the facts in it.

An (historical) account of the country has been written,

The lovers of the country are very fond of it.
In it is written an account of 'Sadiqpore'.
Which, once, was a garden of learning.
Which once, was the refuge of the revered ones,
Which, once, was the abode of the revered ones.
The scholars, the learned, the litterateurs, the philosophers;
in short, (which was) a mine of the accomplished ones.
They were like candles in the gathering of the select,
who illuminated the house of learning.
This (gathering) may be reckoned as the purest gold,
(And) that (house) as the repository of learning.
Oh, look at the turns of (the wheel of) Time,
Oh, look at the ways of the world,
The autumn ('s wind) has carried away every thing,
Now, there are neither the flowers nor the garden.
Only some of the progeny are now left,
who add lustre to their (the ancestor's) names.
My revered one, *Ḥaḍrat-i* Ranjūr.[8]
To praise whom (adequately) is impossible.
He desired that should compose the chronogram (of the book)
He urged that I do so quickly.
I was lost in this thought,
when, suddenly, immediately.
Azad's heart echoed its chronogram,
'Remembering (the achievements) of the countrymen adds lustre (to history)'
A.H. 1319 (20 May, 1901-9 April, 1902)."
Another chronogram from the same person:
"Who can (adequately) praise this book,
Truly, it is a beneficial work.
Each account in it is authoritative,
Each reference in it is dependable.
O: Azad, write afresh the *Hijrī* year (of its compilation),
'This book is a bliss for the whole world'.
A.H. 1319."

A *qiṭa'* recording the year of the publication of the book, a chronogram from the same person :

This fine book has been printed,
a hundred praises for those who thought of it,

The lips of the (Invisible) Crier called out,
'May (the book) serve as collyrium for the eyes of the readers'.
A.H. 1320 (10 April, 1902-30 March, 1903)."

Outwardly, the review does not say anything specific about the movement as such. A tone of caution, in the cryptic reference to the 'rulers of the times' turning their face away from the members of the family is discernible. The focus is on the members of the family, their status, academic attainments and on the patriotism which motivated them. Underneath all this, however, a note of sympathy with, and appreciation for, all that the movement stood for can easily be seen, particularly in the verses of the chronograms. The idiom of Urdu poetry gives greater scope for the expression of Azad's true feelings. Here, he talks of the 'the motherland', and of 'the lovers of the country' being 'fond' of the book. He adds, significantly, that 'Remembering (the achievements) of the countrymen adds lustre (to history)'. All this cannot be explained away as literary flourishes and poetical effusion. The verses give an indication of the way in which Azad looks at, and places, the Wahhabi Movement in the larger framework of the history of the struggle against foreign rule.

Notes

1. This is the actual English word, written in Arabic script, used by the reviewer, and printed in the first edition. In the second edition (1924) it was substituted by a Persian word, *taqrīz*, which means commendatory. Comments usually are put at the end of a book. In the third edition (1964), the same position was maintained.

   Azad got the review reprinted with some modifications in his Urdu newspaper *isāmer's Sidqui*. See my article Abu'l Kalam Azad on the. Wahhabi Movement, Azad's Review of *Tadhkira-i Sādqa* (1901)', in the forthcoming volume to be brought out by the K.P. Jayaswal Research Institute to mark the birth centenary celebrations of Azad.
2. Another English word, written in the Arabic script.
3. The reference here is obviously to the demonlition of the members of the Sadiqpore family by the orders of the government.
4. This refers to the Mohammadan Anglo-Arabic School, Patna City, (established 1884), of which the founding-Secretary was Muhammad Hasan (1847-89) another distinguished member of the

Sadiqpore family. For biographical details, see *Tadhkira-i Sādqa*, 1964, pp. 214-17.

On the school's history, see Q. Ahmad, *ed. Mohammadan Education Committee and Mohammadan Anglo-Arabic School, Patna City, Centenary Celebrations Souvenir Volume*, 1986.

5. There is a pun on the Urdu word *Ittifāq*, which means both 'by chance' and 'unity'.
6. Once again, an English word written in Arabic script. The use of English words in such an early writing of Azad deserves notice.
7. Muhammad Yusuf Jafri (1863-1923); poetically surnamed Ranjur (grief-sticken), was a son of Yahya Ali the chief accused in the Ambala Trial. Azad had very close relations with Ranjur, and held him in high regard as is evident from the verses. Azad must have heard from him and other members of the family who during the period, were often visiting Calcutta, on their way to the Andaman Islands, about the movement in which their ancestors had taken a leading part. Azad's sense of patriotism, evident even at this young age, must have been stirred by these accounts.
8. See note above.

Bibliography

A. *Manuscripts*: Persian and Urdu (arranged alphabetically according to the titles of the works).*

1. *Amīr Nāmah*, by Basawan Lal, Calcutta University Library *ms.* copy. (Life of Nawab Amir Khan of Tonk).
2. *Durr-i Maqāl*, by Abdul Haq (of Arrah), Patna College Library *ms.* section. (A printed edition, entitled *Ḥālāt-i Jung-i Malka wa Asthāna* by Abdul Haq, pen-name *Hādhiq*, has been referred to; Storey, C.A., *Persian Literature*, Section 11, London, 1939, p. 674, but it is very scarce.
3. *Khutūt wa Fatāwa*, A collection of Sayyid Ahmad's letters by an unknown compiler, Patna University Library, *ms.* section, dated A.H. 1297 (1879-80). It contains some 90 letters and other writings of Sayyid Ahmad and some of his close associates, covering the period A.H. 1242-45 (1826-30).
   There are several other collections of Sayyid Ahmad's letters, both published and unpublished, including the India Office Library *ms.* copy. A photographic reproduction of a *ms.* copy dated A.H. 1301 (1883-84) in the hand of Ubaidullah Ghulam Husain was published by Maktaba-i Rashidiya Limited, Lahore, 1975.
4. *Makhzan-i Aḥmadī*, by Muhammad Ali, Khuda Bakhsh, Oriental Public Library, Patna, *ms.* copy dated A.H. 1262 (1845-46). It is the earliest *ms.* copy of the work which was originally written in A.H. 1262 (1846). The Arabic and Persian Research Institute, Tonk, Rajasthan has another copy of the work, and also a printed edition, dated A.H. 1283 (1864-65). The author was a nephew of Sayyid Ahmad and accompanied him on the journey for *Ḥajj*, and his account is upto the return from Arabia. The earliest biographical account of Sayyid Ahmad's life, it is useful for the pre-migration (1826) phase.
5. *Manzuratu's Su'adā' fi Aḥwāl-i Ghuzāt wa's Shuhadā'*, also referred to as *Tārīkh-i Aḥmadia*, by Munshi Jafar Ali Naqwi, Punjab University

Library *ms.* copy. It was written in A.H. 1272 (1855-56), and it is very useful for the post-migration phase, the author having first-hand information about many of the events described. The Punjab University *ms.* has a Supplement giving an account of the Baraset Rising (1831), which is the only available source material in Persian on that topic.

6. *Sirātu'l Mustaqīm,* compiled by Shah Ismail and Abdul Hayy in A.H. 1233 (1817-18). A large number of published and *ms.* copies exist, including a very rare tri-lingual manuscript copy (Persian text with translations in Arabic and Urdu) which was prepared at the instance of Nawāb Muhammad Ali Khan of Tonk (1864-67) at Benares in A.H. 1295 (1878) when he was exiled there by the British. This and some early printed editions are available at Tonk. The work has also been translated into Urdu and printed. I have also consulted a *ms.* copy belonging to Shah Muhammad Husain whom Sayyid Ahmad appointed as his *Khalīfa* at Patna. A copy of the Persian text of the *Sanad* was appended to it; the original was produced as an exhibit in the Ahmadullah trial, *Selections,* pp 32-34. The Persian text and its translation into English agree.
7. *Tārīkh-i Hazāra* by Mahtab Singh, India Office Library *ms.* copy. The writer was a Kayastha of Kanpur district who had gone to the North-West Frontier area in search of employment, and after working under Kunwar Kharak Singh and some others had served in the *daftar* of *Sarkār* Hazara for thirty years (1824-54). It was written at the instance of James Abbott, the first British administrator in the area, and gives an account of the establishment of Sikh rule in the Hazara and adjacent areas of Jammu & Kashmir upto the accession of Gulab Singh.
   It gives a very graphic account of the battle of Balakote, whose value is enhanced by the fact that the writer could well afford to describe dispassionately a struggle between the two erstwhile enemies of his masters.
8. *Waqāi 'Aḥmadī,* also referred to as *Tārīkh-i Kabīr,* Arabic and Persian Research Institute, Tonk, *ms.* copies, of which a transcirpt is available in the Raza State Library, Rampur, too. It is an anonymous, voluminous compilation containing reminiscences of Sayyid Ahmad's activities by several of his associates, put together by the efforts of *Nawāb* Waziru'd Dawla. Its strength lies

in the richness of detail provided, though there are some credulous stories, too.

9. *Muzaffar Nāmah* by Karam 'Ali, Khuda Bakhsh, Oriental Public Library, Patna, *ms.* copy. A detailed account of the history of Bengal from the time of *Nawāb Alivardi Khan Mahābat Jung* to that of the deposition of *Nawāb* Muzaffar Jung by the English (A.H 1186/1772). The author, who was in the service of *Nawāb* Muzaffar Jung, states that a general discontent prevailed in Bengal after the *Nawab's* arrest, and that he engaged himself in writing this work "to alleviate his grief." The account gives interesting glimpses of the impact of early British rule in the *Sūbah*.

B. Records Series:

National Archives of India, New Delhi.
Foreign Political and Foreign Secret Departments' series, relevant volumes from 1831.
Central Records Office, Calcutta.
Judicial Department series, 1831-59.
Central Records Office, Patna.
Judicial Department Series, from 1840s (printed from 1859) onwards.
Record Room, Divisional Commissioner's Office, Patna.
(i) From and to Magistrate series, 1821 onwards.
(ii) Mutiny and important judicial papers (in red, cloth bound bundles, each containing a number of dockets).
(iii) Some unattached papers kept separately in an almirah. All these papers are in a file entitled Wahhabi Confidential Papers. Some of the proscribed Wahhabi pamphlets (Chapter X) were also in it when I saw these papers in the mid-1950s.
Record Room, District Judge's Court, Patna.
Sessions Cases (records arranged year-wise) in cloth bundles.
Bundle no. 1 (1867), Session cases 1-56.

Mayo Papers, Cambridge University Library, U.K. *ms.* 7490.

C. Books, English.

Adye, Col. J., *Sitana: A Mountain Campaign on the Borders of Afghanistan in 1863,* London, 1867.

Ahmad, Aziz, *Studies in Islamic Culture in the Indian Environment,* London, 1964.

Ahmad, Mohiuddin, *Saiyid Ahmad Shahid: His Life and Mission*, Lucknow, 1975.

Ahmad, Rafiuddin, *The Bengal Muslims 1871-1906: A Quest* for Identity, OUP.

Aitchison, C.H. *Collection of Treaties, Engagements and Sunnuds*, Calcutta, 1862.

Beams, J., *Memoirs of a Bengali Civilian*, London, 1961.

Broome, A., *History of the Rise and Progress of the Bengal Army*, London.

Bellew, H.W., *A General Report on the Yusufzais*, London, 1864.

Blunt, Lady Anne, *A Pilgrimage to Nejd*, 1881.

Bosworth-Smith, R., *Life of Lord Lawrence*, London, 1863.

Bourne, W.F.G., *Hindustani Musulmans*, Calcutta, 1914.

Buckland, C.E., *Bengal under the Lieutenant-Governors*, Calcutta, 1901.

Burckhardt. J.L., *Notes on the Bedouins and Wahhabys*, 1831.

Chaudhuri, S.B., *Civil Disturbances during the British Rule in India*, Calcutta, 1955.

Caroe, Sir Oliver, *The Pathans : 550 BC—AD. 1957*, London, 1964.

Cotton, S., *Nine years in North-West Frontier of India*, London, 1868.

Cunningham, J.D., *History of the Sikhs*, Calcutta, 1904.

Datta, K.K., *Biography of Kunwar Singh and Amar Singh*, Patna, 1957.

__, *Shah Alam II and the East India Company*, Calcutta, 1965.

Doughty, C.E., *Travels in Arabia Desertā*, Cambridge, 1881.

Dutta, Abhijit, *Muslim Society in Transition, Titu Mirs' Revolt (1831)*, Calcutta, 1987.

__, *Christian Missionaries on the Indigo Question in Bengal*, Calcutta, 1989.

Edwardes, H.B., *A Year on the Punjab Frontier, 1848-49*, London, 1851.

Edwardes, Lady Emma, *Memorials of Life and Letters of Sir H.B. Edwardes*, London, 1886.

Edwardes, H.B., Merivale and Herman, *Life of Sir Henry Lawrence*, London, 1873.

Faruqi, B.A., *The Mujaddid's Conception of Tawhid*, Lahore, 1940.

Forest, G.W., *A History of the Indian Mutiny*, London, 1904-12.

__, *Life of Sir Neville Chamberlain*, London, 1909.

Fraser, *Our Faithful Ally, the Nizam*, London, 1865.

Germanus, J., *Modern Movements in Islam*, Calcutta, 1932.

Gibbon, F.P., *Lawrences in the Punjab*, London, 1908.

Graham, G.P.I., *The Life and Work of Sir Syed Ahmad*, London, 1885.

Griffin, L., *Ranjit Singh*, Oxford, 1892.

Hardy, Peter, *The Muslims in British India*, Cambridge, 1972.

Holmes, T.R.E., *A History of the Indian Mutiny*, London, 1898.

Hunter, Sir William W., *The Indian Musulmans : Are they bound in conscience to rebel against the Queen?* London, 1871.

__, *A Statistical Account of Bengal*, Vol. XI, (Reprint.)

__, *The Imperial Gazetteer*, Vol XII (Tonk), Reprint.

Husain, Mahmud et. al., eds., *A History of the Freedom Movement*, Vol. 11, 1831-1905, Karachi, 1961.

Irvine, William, *The Later Mughals*, Vol. 11, Calcutta, 1922.

Jha, J.S., *Aspects of History of Modern Bihar* (K.P. Jayaswal Memorial Lectures), Patna, 1988.

Joshi, P.C., *Rebellion 1857, A symposium*, PPH, 1957.

Kaye, J.W., *History of the Sepoy War in India*, London, 1872.

Khan, M.A., ed. *Selections from Bengal Government Records on the Wahhabi Trials*, (1863-1870), Dacca, 1961.

__, *History of the Fara'iḍi Movement in Bengal*, (1818-1906), Karachi, 1965.

Khera, P.N., *British Policy Towards Sind upto its Annexation, 1843*, Lahore, 1941.

Latif, M., *History of the Punjab*, Calcutta, 1870.

Macrae, C.C., *Report on the Proceedings in the Case of Amir Khan*, Calcutta, 1870.

Majumdar, R.C., *The Sepoy Mutiny and the Revolt of 1857*, Calcutta, 1957.

__, *History of the Freedom Movement in India*, vol. 1, Calcutta, 1962.

Malik Hafeez, *Moslem Nationalism in India and Pakistan*, Washington, 1963.

Malleson, G.B., *History of the Indian Mutiny*, London, 1878.

Mallick, A.R., *British Policy and the Muslims in Bengal, 1757-1856*, Dacca, 1961.

M'Gregor, W.L., *History of the Sikhs*, London, 1846.

Mason, A.H., *Report on the Hindustani Fanatics*, London, 1878.

Mason, A.H. and Paget, W.H., *Record of the Expedition Against. The North-West Frontier Tribes Since the Annexation of Punjab*, London, 1884. (see also under Paget, Lt. Col., W.H.).

Mendes, L.A., *Report on the Proceedings in the matter of Amir Khan and Hashmatdad Khan*, Calcutta, 1870.

Metcalf, Barbara D., *Islamic Revival in British India : Deoband 1860-1900*, New Jersey, 1982.

Mujeeb, Muhammad, *The Indian Muslims*, London, 1957.

Murray, Titus, *Indian Islam.*

Nevill, H.L., *Campaigns on the North-West Frontier,* 1848, London, 1912.

Nizami, K.A., *Sayyid Ahmad Khan,* Pub. Divn., 1966.

Oliver, E.E., *Across the Border,* London, 1890.

Paget, Lt. Col., W.H., *Record of the Expeditions Undertaken Against the North-West Frontier Tribes,* Calcutta, 1874.

(Subsequently updated by Mason, A.H., and published with a modified title as listed above).

Philby, J.B., *Arabia,* London, 1884.

Prasad, Bisheshwar, ed. *Ideas in History,* New Delhi, 1968.

Prasad, Y.D., *Indian Muslims and World War I, A phase in the Disillusionment with British Rule, Patna.*

Prinsep, H.T.T., *Memorie of a Pathan Soldier of Fortune, Nawab Amir Khan of Tonk,* Calcutta, 1832.

Raymond, F. (Eng. tr.) Ghulam Husain Khan's *Siyaru 'l Mutakhkhirin,* Calcutta, 1902.

Rizvi, S.A.A., *Muslim Revivalist Movements in Northern India in the Sixteenth and Seventeenth Centuries,* Allahabad, 1966.

__, *Shah Wali Allaḥ and His Times, A study of Eighteenth Century Islam, Politics and Society in India,* Canberra, 1980.

__, *Shah 'Abd al-'Aziz. Puritanism, Secterianism, Polemics and Jihad,* Canberra, 1982.

Routledge, James, *English Rule and Native Opinion in India, from notes taken in 1870-74,* London, 1878.

Sarkar, Jadunath, *Fall of the Mughal Empire,* Vol. V, Calcutta.

Sen, S.N., *1857, Delhi,* 1957.

Sinha, N.K., *Ranjit Singh,* Calcutta, 1933.

Singh, Ganda, ed. *The Punjab in 1839-40,* Patiala, 1952.

Skrine, F.H., *Life of Sir William Wilson Hunter,* London, 1901.

Sleeman, W.H., *Journey Through the Kingdom of Oude, 1849-50,* London, 1858.

Spear, P., *Twilight of the Mughals,* Cambridge, 1951.

Tayler, William, *Our Crisis,* Calcutta, 1858.

__, *Thirty Eight Years in India,* London, 1882.

Tarachand, *Influence of Islam on the Indian Culture,* Allahabad, 1967.

__, *History of the Freedom Movement in India,* Vol. 11, New Delhi, 1967.

Thornton, E., *History of India,* Vol. V, London, 1843.

Trotter, L.J., *Lord Auckland,* Oxford, 1893.

Wade, C.M., *Our Relations with the Punjab,* London, 1823.

—, *A Narrative of Services, Military and Political*, 1804-44, London, 1847.
Yasin, M., *A Social History of Islamic India*, Lucknow, 1958.
Younghusband, G.J., *The Story of the Guides*, London, 1908.

D : Books, Urdu and Persian.

(*Ḥakīm*) 'Abdul Hamid, *Mathnawī Shahar Ashōb*, Unani Dawakhana Press, Allahabad, n.d.

'Abdur Rahim, *Ad-Duraru'l Manthūr fi Tarājim Ahl-i Sādiqpūr*, commonly called *Tadhkira-i Ṣādiqa*, first published 1901, 2nd ed. Allahabad, 1924.

I have used a copy of this 2nd edition of the book belonging to Abdul Ghaffar Sahib. He was related to the author and one of the best informed men in the family about the history of the movement. His copy had extensive marginal notes in his hand providing additional information about members of the family and the working of the organisation.

(3rd ed. Patna, 1964, reproduces the text of the 2nd ed. with supplementary notes on some points by Hakim Abdul Khabir, a son of a daughter of the original writer.)

Abu Muhammad Ibrahim, *Fiqh-i Muḥammadī*.

—, *Al-Qaulu'l Mazīd fi Aḥkāmu't Taqlīd*.

Abu Yahya Imam Khan Naushahrawi, *Tarājim 'Ulamā'-i Ahl-i Ḥadīth Hind*, Delhi, 1937.

Abul Hasan Ali Nadwi, *Sirat-i Sayyid Aḥmad Shahīd*, Vols. I and II, Karachi, 1975, 1974.

Abul Wafa Thanaullah Amritsari, *Fatūḥāt-i Ahl-i Ḥadīth*, Amritsar, 1912.

Akhtar Ahmad Orainwi, *Bihār Mēn Urdū Zabān wa Adab Kā Irtiqā'*, Patna, 1957.

Fazal Husain, *Al-Ḥayāt Ba'd Almamāt*, Agra, 1908.

Ghulam Rasul Mehr, *Sayyid Ahmad Shadhīd*, Vols I and II.

Jamā'at-i Mujāhidīn, Vol. III *Sargudhasht-i Mujāhidīn*, Vol. IV; Lahore, 1952-55.

Kalimuddin Ahmad, *Apnī Talāsh Mēn*, Patna.

Khwaja Ahmad Faruqi, *Urdū Mēn Wahhābī Adab*, Delhi University Publication, 1969.

Manazir Ahsan Gilani, *Hindustān Mēn Musalmānōn Kā Nizām-i Ta'līm wa Tarbiyat*, Delhi, 1944.

Masud Alam Nadwi, *Hindustān kī Pahlī Islāmī Taḥrīk*, Rawalpindi, 2nd ed., Rawalpindi, 1958.

Muhammad Daud Raza, *Hayāt-i Thanā'ī*, Delhi, A.H. 1396 (1976-77).
Muhammad Ismail, Panipati *Maqālāt-i Sir Sayyid*, Lahore, 1962.
(A multi-volumed collection of Sir Syed's talks and writings arranged topic-wise; Vol IX containing the review of Hunter's book, *Dāktar Hunter Kī Ghalat Fahmiyōn Kā Izālā*)
Muhammad Hairat, *Ḥayāt-i Taiyyaba*, 3rd ed. Lahore, 1958.
Muhammad Jaffar Thanessari, *Tārīkh-i 'Ajīb* (History of Port Blair) 1880, 2nd ed. Nawalkishore press, 1892.
(An unnoticed valuable account of the penal colony of the Andaman Islands and its aboriginees, containing 33 short conversational sentences in 'Asian' languages.)
__, *Kālā Pānī or Tawārīkh-i 'Ajīb*, Islamia Steam Press, Lahore, n.d.
__, *Sawāniḥ Ahmadi* or *Tawārīkh-i Ajība*, Delhi, A.H. 1309.
(The slight variations in the titles, *Tārīkh-i 'Ajīb, Tawārīkh-i 'Ajīb, Tawārīkh-i 'Ajība*, are to be noted; they are chronogrammatic titles yielding the dates of the writings of the respective books.)
(*Hakīm*) Muhammad Shoaib, *A'yān-i Watan*, Phulwari Sharif (Patna).
__, *Diwān-i Shāh Abu'l Hasan Fard*, Kanpur, A.H. 1332 (1913-14).
Murtaza Khan Rampuri, *Dāfi'u'l Fasād Nāfi'u'l 'Ibād Qāti'u'l Shirk Wa'l Bida'āt*, Matba-i Muhammadi, Daru'l Islam Muhammadabad, *'urf* Tonk, A.H. 1284 (1867-68).
(Nawab) Siddiq Hasan Khan (of Bhopal), *Tiqsār Jiyūdu'l Aḥrār Min Tadhikara Junūdu'l Abrār*, Bhopal, A.H. 1295 (1878).
__, __, *Tarjumān-i Wahhābiyat*, Mufid-i 'Am Press Agra, A.H. 1300 (1882-83).
(He was a prolific writer, and an alphabetically arranged list of his works in Persian, Urdu and Arabic has 222 entries. Most of these were published in the Matba-i, Siddiq, Bhopal, in one of his four presses. Many of his tracts are apologetic in nature, trying to show that the Wahhabis were not hostile to the British Government.)
(*Nawāb*) Wazirud Dawlah (of Tonk), *Wasāya al-Wazīr* 'Alā *Tarīqatu'l Bashīr wa'l Nadhīr*, Matba-i Muhammadi, Tonk, A.H. 1284 (1866-67).
(Shah) Muhammad Ismail, *Mansab-i Imāmat*, Matba-i Faruqi, n.d. (an Urdu tr. by Muhammad Husain Alawi, Lahore, 1949).
__, *Taqwīyatu'l Imān*, Barqi Urdu Press, Bangalore, A.H. 1371 (1951-52).
(English trans. by Mir Shahamat Ali, *J.R.A.S.*, 1852, Section 'D'

below. A concise edition of it is Wilayat 'Ali's *Risāla-i Radd-i Shirk*, listed below.

(Shāh) Waliullah, *Wasiyyat Nāmah*, Lucknow, 1894.

__, *'Iqdu'l Jid fi Bayān Aḥkāmu'l Ijtihād wa'l Taqlīd*, Matba-i Faruqi, Delhi, A.H. 1290 (1873-74). Arabic text with interlinear translation into Urdu.

__, *Al-Qaul'l Jamīl fi Sawā'u's Sabīl*, Delhi, n.d. (Urdu tr. *Shifā'u'l 'Alīl* by Khurram Ali, Matba'-i Yusufi, Delhi.

Shaikh Muhammad Ikram, *Āb-i Kauthar*, Lahore, 1975.

__, *Rūd-i Kauthar*, Lahore, 1975.

__, *Mauj-i Kauthar*, Lahore, 1975.

Shamsu'l Haq, Dianwi, *'Awnu'l Ma'būd.*

Sita Ram Kohli, ed., *Zafar Nāmah-i Ranjit Singh* by Diwan Amar Nath, Punjab University, Lahore, 1978.

(Bala) Sohan Lal Suri, *'Umdatu't Tawārīkh*, Lahore, 1880. (English translation of the Persian text by V.S. Suri, published by Punjab Itihas Prakashan, Chandigarh, 1972.

Syed Muhammad Hasan *Maāthir-i Siddīqī*, Lucknow, 1924-25.

(Sir) Syed Ahmad Khan, *Athāru's Sanādīd*, Matba'-i Sultani, Qala'-i Delhi, A.H. 1270 (1853-54).

__, Review of Hunter's book, cited above.

Ubaidullah Sindhi, *Shāh Walīullāh aur Unkī Siyāsī Tahrīk*, Wilayat 'Ali, *Risā'il-i Tisa'*, Maktaba'i Faruqi, Delhi, n.d. (A collection of nine *risā'il*, of which seven are by Wilayat Ali. These provide useful insights into the history of the Movement.)

E. Articles.

Abbot, Freeland, "Jihad of Sayyid Ahmad Shahid," *The Muslim World*, Conn. (USA), 1962.

Askari, S.H., "Political Significance of the Movement of Syed Ahmad Brailvi," *Procs. Vol. I.H.R.C.*, 1955, 31 : 174-81.

Bal, S.S., "British Interest in Creating the Dogra State of Jammu and Kashmir," *Procs. Vol. I.H.C.*, 1967, 29 : 40-50.

Bari, Abdul, "A Nineteenth Century Muslim Reform Movement." in Makdisi, G., *ed., Arabs and Islam, Studies in Honour of H.A.R. Gibb.*

Barrier, G., "South Asia in Vernacular Publications, "*J. of Asian Studies*, 1969, 28 (4): 803-10.

Ali, Mir Shahamat, "Translation of the *Takwiyat-ul-Iman*," preceded by a Notice of the Author, Maulavi Isma'il Hajji, *J. of the Royal Asiatic Society*, 1852, XIII, 310-72.

Chaudhuri, N.C., "The Wahhabi Conspiracy in Hyderabad State, 1839-40," *Procs. Vol. I.H.C.*, 1956.

Gaborieau, Marc, "A Nineteenth Century Indian 'Wahhabi' Tract Against the Cult of Muslim Saints : Al-Balagh al-Mubin," in Troll, Christian W., *ed.*, *Muslim Shrines in India : Their Character and Significance*, Delhi, 1989, pp. 198-239.

Hunter, WW., "An Indian Conspiracy of 1864," *C.R.*, *1*860, 40:

Husain, M., "Origins of Indian Wahhabism," *Procs. Vol. I.H.C.*, 1939.

Husain, M., "The Mystery of Sayyid Ahmad Shahid's Death," *J. of Pakistan Historical Society*, Karachi, 1955, 167-73.

Hussain, Muhammad Delawar, "Life and Works of Sir William Wilson Hunter (1840-1900)," *J. of the Asiatic Society of Bangladesh*, 1976, 21 (2) : 76-97.

J.R.C., "Notice of the Peculiar Tenets Held by the Followers of Syed Ahmad, Taken Chiefly from the 'Sirat-ul-Mustaqim', a Principal Treatise of that sect, written by Moulvi Mahommed Ismail," tr., *The J. of the Asiatic Society of Bengal*, 1832, I, 479-98.

Jha, J.S., The Patna Conspiracy of 1857, *Procs. Vol. I.H.R.C.*, 1956, 32:

—, "Origin and Development of Cultural Institutions in Bihar, "*J. of Historical Research, Ranchi*, 1965, 1-13.

Nizami, K.A., "Shah Waliullah Dahlavi and Indian Politics in the Eighteenth Century," *I.C.*, 1951, 25 (:)

—, "Shah Waliullah of Delhi : His Thought and Contributions," *I.C.*, 1980, 54 (3) : 141-52.

O'Kinealy, James, "A Sketch of the Wahhabis in India, up to the Death of Syed Ahmad in 1831," C.R., 1870, 50 : 73-104;
ibid, The Wahhabis in India, 1870, 51, 177-92;
ibid., The Wahhabis in India : 381-99.

Rahman, Jamalara, "The Sitana Campaign of 1863-1864 and the problem of Central Control," *J. of the Asiatic Society of Bangladesh*, 1984, 29 (1) : 64-69.

Ray, Rajat K., "Colonial Penetration and the Initial Resistance: The Mughal Ruling Class, The East India Company and the struggle for Bengal, 1756-1800," *I.H.R.*, 1985-86, 12 (1-2): 1-105.

Rehatsek, E., "History of the Wahhabys in Arabia and in India, "*J.R.A.S.* (Bombay branch), XIV, 1880.*

Sethi, R.R., "The Revolt in Kashmir," *BPP*, 1946:112-21.

Siddiqui, Aslam, "Sayyid Ahmad Shahid's End," *I.C.*, 1948.

Wahaba, Sir Hafiz, "What Actually is Wahabism?" *I.C.*, 1949.

J.I.H., August, 1933: 251-68.

F. Gazettes, Gazetteers, Selections from Bengal Government Records series, Bengal Administration Reports, Special Publications for Restricted Circulation, some Proscribed Wahhabi pamphlets and some old Urdu newspapers & periodicals, etc.

District Gazetteer series :

H.R. Nevill, *Lucknow : A Gazetteer,* Vol. XXXVII of the District Gazetteers of the United provinces of Agra and Oudh, Allahabad, 1904.

__, *Rae Bareli, A Gazetteer,* Vol. XXXIX, of the District Gazetteers of the United Provinces of Agra and Oudh, Allahabad, 1905.

Bareilly : A Gazetteer, Vol. XIII of the District Gazetteers of the United Provinces of Agra and Oudh, Allahabad, 1911.

L.S.S. O'Malley, *Patna,* Bihar and Orissa District Gazetteers, Patna, 1907.

Watson, H.D., *ed., Gazetteer of the Hazara District,* 1907, London.

Gazette Extraordinary, Government of India, 30 January, 1964.

Selections from the Records of the Bengal Government (Published by Authority), *Vol. XLII,* papers connected with the Trial of Moulvie Ahmedoollah of Patna, Calcutta, 1866.

Bengal Administration Report, 1871-72, Calcutta, 1872. *Lahore Political Diaries,* Vol. III and IV.

Hartshorne, A.G., *Diary of the Sitana Campaign,* (Publication for private circulation), 1864.

Copy of papers relating to the late Disturabances in the North-West Frontier of India, ordered by the House of Commons, London, to be printed in 1864.

Hughes, *Dictionary of Islam.*

Gibb, H.A.R., Krammers, J.N., *ed., The Shorter Encyclopaedia of Islam,* Leiden, 1961.

Encyclopaedia of Islam.

Some Proscribed Wahhabi Pamphlets :

Hāriqu'l Ashrār, author's name not given, Matba'-i Muhammadi, Delhi, A.H. 1283 (1866-67).

(Contains 256 *Khamsas* (five verses in a stanza), printed diagonally in frames with a demarcating line under each, relating to *Jihād,* the valiant fighting of Shah Ismail, the 'deceitful' *pīrs,* etc.

It was found in the Patna Divisional Commissioner's Record Room, *vide* section B above).

Radd-i Tuḥfa-i Muḥabbat, author's name not given, in refutation of an earlier work, *Tuḥfa-i Muḥabbat,* by 'some Sunni Hanafi Muslims levelling religious charges against the Wahhabis.
(Printed in violation of Act XXV of 1867 under which the name of the author and printer should be printed. A Government notification was published to the effect that half the amount of Rs. 1000/- to be levied upon the offending party would be given to the person giving information about the author and the printers). For further references to such literature, see chapter X).

Old Newspaers, periodicals :

Ishā'at-i Sunnat-i Nabawīyya, Printed from Riyadh-i Hind Press., Amritsar.
(Volume IV, No. 11, November, 1881, contains 3 articles by an anonymous writer, the first two presenting arguments against the followers of Sayyid Ahmad being regarded as Wahhabis, and the third presenting a general account of the Wahhabis in India, which may be compared with O'Kinealy's articles in the *Calcutta Review, vide* section E above).

Ahl-i Ḥadīth, Urdu Weekly (Estd. 1903).

Ma'ārif, Monthly Urdu Magazine, Azamgarh.

* Nos. 2, 4 and 6 were also printed, but these are very scarce, excepting no. 6.

* Rizvi, S.A.A., "Ideological Background of the Wahhabi Movement in India in the XVIII and XIX Centuries", Prasad, B., *Ideas in History,* Delhi, 1968, 93-109.

Index